2/14/74

DOWN
THE
LINE

DOWN THE LINE

The Collected Writings of
BAYARD RUSTIN

Introduction by
C. VANN WOODWARD

QUADRANGLE BOOKS
Chicago
1971

Library of Congress Catalog Card Number: 70–143569
SBN 8129–0185–1

To A. Philip Randolph and the thousands of people,
young and old, who have marched, gone to jail, and
struggled with us to build a just and free society.

ACKNOWLEDGMENTS

I am the product of movements for democratic social change. Those people who stood with me in demonstrations, or who discussed and planned strategy with me, or whom I consulted in writing these essays, cannot be separated into neat categories. They are part of my life and work—just as, I hope, I am part of theirs. I am forever indebted to Jervis Anderson, Charles Bloomstein, Paul Feldman, Carl Gershman, Robert and Joyce Gilmore, Ernest Green, Michael Harrington, Norman and Velma Hill, Rachelle Horowitz, Tom Kahn, Arthur and Marion Logan, Bessie LeBon, Ernest Rice McKinney, John Morsell, Norman Podhoretz, Max Shachtman, Albert Shanker, Don Slaiman, and Emma Thomas. And finally, without the personal encouragement and professional skill of Midge Decter and Joseph Epstein this book would not have been possible.

INTRODUCTION

Beginning the eighth decade of the century with the weight of six decades on one's shoulders has advantages as well as disadvantages. Bayard Rustin bears the weight of the years lightly. His appearance, as Robert Penn Warren has noted, is "a strange mixture of strength and sensitivity." The accumulating frost on top sits incongruously on his tall, athletic frame, and the accumulated experience of a varied past informs his judgments of the young and inexperienced without alienating him from them. Rather, it deepens his sympathy with them and his understanding of their problems. Like the majority of them now, and unlike the majority of their elders, his background is urban and Northern rather than rural and Southern. His career embraces all the experiences they are likely to have had, plus a range and variety they are unlikely ever to equal.

A native of West Chester, Pennsylvania, Rustin grew up in a fatherless home where the burdens of rearing and breadwinning were borne mainly by hard-pressed grandparents. It was, he remembers, "a town where Negroes had few rights, where they could not safely walk through certain streets." At school he distinguished himself in football and track, and at the City College of New York in the 1930's he supported himself by singing with Josh White and Leadbelly. At the time of the Scottsboro Case, in his early twenties, he was attracted to Marxism and joined the Young Communist League, but broke with the Communists over the war crisis of 1941. Returning to the Quakerism of his early years, he became race relations secretary for the Fellowship of Reconciliation. At about the same time, he became a socialist and served as a youth organizer in A. Philip Randolph's March on Washington. In 1942 he was elected the first field secretary of the newly founded Congress of Racial Equality, an offshoot of the pacifist Fellowship of Reconciliation.

Whether because of his Quakerism, his socialism, or his identification with organized labor, Bayard Rustin has all along aimed at broader social objectives than have other major figures in the movement for Negro rights. "I reject the idea of working for the Negro," he said in 1965, "as being impractical as well as immoral, if one does that alone." Negro rights, he has constantly maintained, can be secured only as a part and consequence of wider and deeper social reform. His active concern for races and oppressed minorities other than Negro Americans is one aspect of this world view. During World War II he worked in California for a time in behalf of the interned Nisei. After serving three years in Lewisburg Penitentiary as a conscientious objector, he made several trips to India, one of six months' duration, working as chairman of the Free India Committee and guest of the Congress party. In the 1950's he worked for a while in West Africa with Azikewe and Nkrumah, took a leading role in the Aldermason Peace March in England, and later took part in the All African Peoples' Conference in Addis Ababa.

During those years Rustin was also an activist in the front ranks of the civil rights movement. Long before the period of Freedom Rides, he took a police beating in 1942 rather than comply with Jim Crow law on a Tennessee bus, and as the consequence of the first Freedom Ride of CORE in 1947 he did twenty-two days on a North Carolina chain gang. This was only one of the twenty-four times he has been arrested in the struggle for civil rights. In all this he has adhered to the principle of nonviolence. Common adherence to this principle, among many other views they shared, drew Rustin to Martin Luther King. He helped King organize the Montgomery bus boycott in 1955. At King's request he prepared the original plan for the Southern Christian Leadership Conference and worked as special assistant to Dr. King for seven years. The most widely known of his achievements for the civil rights movement was his organization of the great March on Washington in 1963. The following year he directed the school boycott in New York City. Since 1964 he has been executive director of the A. Philip Randolph Institute.

Year in and year out for more than four decades, always near the center of action, Bayard Rustin has kept close watch on the ebb and flow of the movement for Negro rights—from violence to nonviolence, from hope to despair, from integration to separatism and back again. He can recall a time in the Harlem renaissance when "they thought the race problem had at last been solved by art" and, later, times when "they" thought the problem had been, or would soon be, solved by Moscow, or Mecca, or Delhi, or Havana, or Peking. He has been a close observer of the endless fashion parade in styles of Negro leadership—Southern, Northern, West Indian, African, Marxian, Gandhian, Islamic, Fanonesque—the ninety-day wonders, the ego-trippers as well as the durable, gray institutionalized symbols. Fashions in slogans and objectives—freedom, equality, preferential treatment, reparations, black capitalism, utopian communism, community autonomy, national sovereignty, and all the varieties of nationalism—have been as varied and often as irreconcilable as the styles of leadership and the dynamics of foreign inspiration.

To keep any sense of balance, any consistency of policy and principle, any reasonable perspective while operating daily at the center of such a whirligig required an extraordinary amount of "cool"—a quality with which Rustin seems natively endowed. For those of his contemporaries who choose to live in a world of fantasy and preach a gospel of escape or utopianism he has understanding, even a generous amount of sympathy and patience, but no support or agreement. In his newspaper columns, magazine articles, speeches, pamphlets, and in the heat of rallies and policy meetings he has always hammered away at the hard realities of American demography, American capitalism, and American politics. This is not a black Caribbean island surrounded by blue water, he keeps telling them, but a black ghetto surrounded by white people. Nor are Afro-Americans living in an African republic, in a Muslim society, in a Third World commune, or in nineteenth-century America.

As often as he can make himself heard, Rustin has been reminding his people that the way out of their plight lies not through hair styles and bizarre costume. Soul courses and soul food are no real answer. It may provide emotional release "to think black, dress black, eat black, and buy black," but it places one on a reactionary course. The real problems, from which all this is escape, are those of employment, wages, housing, health, education, and they are not to be solved by withdrawal and fantasy. They can only be solved in alliance with elements from the majority of the electorate, and the cement for such a coalition is not love but mutual interest. The way lies through nonviolence, integration, and coalition politics.

Contrary moods of violence, withdrawal, separatism, and nationalism conform to a theory of black history that Rustin has developed, a theory that makes a great deal of sense to anyone familiar with the story of the black man in white America, especially the post-slavery part of the story. It is a cyclical theory. The model of the cycle begins with an upsurge of hopes and expectations inspired by bold promises and commitments. This is followed by a phase of disappointed hopes and betrayed promises, which is followed in turn by frustration, despair, withdrawal, and separatism of one variety or another. Each phase produces leaders and doctrines that accommodate the accompanying mood. The third phase takes many forms, but some of them invariably attract support from reactionary elements of white society.

Sometimes Rustin extends his theory to the early years of the Republic and pictures the shattered promises of the Revolution and the aborted movement toward emancipation as stimulating black impulses favoring the Colonization Society and a return to Africa. Mainly, however, he confines the thory to post-slavery history and sees the cycle repeated in three classical instances. The first came in the aftermath of the Civil War and Reconstruction, a period of splendid promises and soaring expectations terminated by the despair prompted by terror and repression and the reactionary Compromise of 1876, and followed by accommodation to segregation and disfranchisement led by Booker T. Washington in the name of self-help and black capitalism. The second frustration-separatist cycle came in the aftermath of Woodrow Wilson's crusade to save the world for democracy and the hopes it inspired in black Americans. When these were shattered by lynchings, Ku Klux terror, and mass unemployment, millions of despairing blacks found outlet for impulses of withdrawal and separation in supporting the Back-to-Africa movement of the Jamaican Marcus Garvey.

The third repetition of the classical cycle is familiar to all who have followed the fortunes and reverses of the movement of Negro rights during the period since 1954. For some the buildup of hopes and expectations reached its crest at the March on Washington in 1963. For others it crested in the Civil Rights Acts of 1964 and 1965. But by that time the despair of frustration had set in, with the realization that more Negro children were in segregated classrooms than in 1954, that the black ghettos were more crowded and explosive than ever, that unemployment among black youth was still growing, and that the rate among black family men was twice that of whites. The burning of Watts in the summer of 1965 and scores of flaming cities in the summers that followed registered the ensuing black frustration, despair, and rage. Accompanying these outbursts of violence, there appeared the expected apostles of withdrawal and separatism to complete the classical cycle.

Rustin holds that "in all three periods, the turn to separation has been a frustration reaction to objective political, social, and economic circumstances." He finds it thoroughly understandable and inevitable that people subjected to deep frustration should act in a frustrated manner. However justifiable and understandable, these impulses when turned into dreams of separate sovereignty in America, political secessionist movements, returning to Africa, or economic separatism through black capitalism are unrealistic and, he believes, dangerous delusions. Racial pride, ethnic unity, and contact with black people abroad are all desirable and not to be belittled, but these objectives must be gained in ways that are healthy and not ways doomed to frustration and more bitterness.

The critical acumen and insight that Rustin brings to bear upon proliferating separatist and nationalist dogmas derive from a life experience with mass movements and political maneuvers. His unerring ability to identify class interests and reactionary impulses hiding behind masks of racial unity or progressive coloration probably owes much to his socialist training. Those who single out race as the dominant principle of organization for any economic, social, political, or educational enterprise have his formidable realism to reckon with. He knows perfectly well that whites who stereotype Negroes and discriminate against them especially because of color impose a certain degree of unity upon the race. But this indiscriminate blindness of white prejudice and ignorance, he observes, "should hardly serve as a model of belief for those blacks who wish to abolish racism in America." Nor should it prevent Negroes from seeing through the "myth of black unity" and its reactionary consequences.

Not only is black unity obstructed by generational conflict as great as that among whites, but it is also divided by Northern and Southern traditions, rural and urban backgrounds, native and West Indian origins. Philosophical cleavages are indicated by the differences that separate NAACP, CORE, Muslims, and Black Panthers. But more profound, and of special significance to Rustin's analysis, are differences of class. "It is utterly unrealistic," he writes, "to expect the Negro middle class to behave on the basis of color alone. They will behave, first of all, as middle-class people." They may do this unconsciously and in perfect good faith, but this does not make their interests identical with those of the mass of working-class blacks. "A good deal of the talk about separatism," he observes, "reflects a class problem within the Negro community." He does not stress the nature of the awkward problem, but he is quite aware that historically the Negro middle class of entrepreneurs, teachers, and professional people, the educated and privileged class, was rooted in a segregated society that guaranteed a monopoly. The sociologist E. Franklin Frazier called it "a privileged status within the isolated Negro community." With the removal of the legal foundations of that system, the ironically "deprived" class sought compensation in benefits derived from racial unity, separatism, and black nationalism.

"The irony of the revolutionary rhetoric uttered on behalf of the Negroes," says Rustin, "is that it has helped in fact to promote conservatism." Black capitalism is endorsed not only by Roy Innis of CORE but by President Nixon and various corporate interests. It does not cost much, and it leaves ghettos intact. The vast majority of black people, of course, are not capitalists and never will be, and they stand to lose from "buying black." For black workers to define their problem primarily in terms of race is to ally themselves with white capitalists against white workers. It is the old strategy of Booker Washington in new guise. As Marcus Garvey put it, "The only convenient friend the Negro worker or laborer has in America at the present time is the white capitalist."

Virtually all the components and programs of black nationalism, many of them contradictory, have in common the ironic element of class interest and reactionary social implications. "Black power" is by now an old slogan that has served many uses and interests without as yet producing any program addressed to the needs of the mass of black people. "The advocates of 'black power,'" in the opinion of Rustin, "have no such program in mind; what they are in fact arguing for (perhaps unconsciously) is the creation of a *new black establishment*." Once Roy Innis' "black colonies" have been "liberated," all conflicts with the outside world can be resolved by negotiations between the black ruling class and its white counterpart, while internal difficulties would become the responsibility of the new black elite.

Advocates of "black community control" are not black workers but educated Negroes with an eye on administrative posts in public offices, schools, and social service. The movement is "an adjustment to inequality rather than a protest against it," in Rustin's opinion. Its success would leave the ghetto "faced with the same poverty, deteriorated housing, unemployment, terrible health services, and inferior schools," but leave it also something of an asset to those in control. As Booker Washington put it, "Cast down your buckets where you are." James Foreman cast down his bucket in the white churches for "black reparations." He drew in a few pails of silver, but in doing so he deflected pressure away from the federal government, the only source capable of the aid required, further isolated blacks from political allies, and built on the shifting sands of moral suasion and white guilt. The effect was as politically reactionary as that of black power and community control. Eldridge Cleaver and Bobby Seale could ride the wave of black rage to fame and notoriety, but could propose no solution to the injustices that produced the rage. Pseudo-revolutionaries of the New Left romanticized the black violence Cleaver and Seale preached, but only enhanced the repression the blacks had to bear and the rage it inspired.

As a former teacher with a special interest in youth, Rustin has been deeply concerned over the direction black studies have taken in many colleges, particularly those that have given rein to militant demand for black autonomy, separatism, and politicalization of academic life. He finds black studies guilty of choosing faculty on "the basis of race, ideological purity, and political commitment—not academic competence." They have "mythologized history" to facilitate "political mobilization" and unwittingly fostered the white-racist line that "black history is irrelevant to American history."

They have permitted or encouraged black students to avoid competition and hard technical training and to seek refuge in "soul courses" that provide "a soothing comfortable experience, somewhat like watching television." Like so many aspects of black separatism, this kind of black studies furnishes "another example of symbolic victory where a real victory seems too difficult to achieve."

Throughout the years of tumult and shouting, pseudo-revolutionaries, miraculously appearing and disappearing "black leaders," and overnight reversals of strategy and goals, Bayard Rustin has hewed to the line he has pursued all along. This is the line of civil rights, equality, and integration, and the strategy of the ballot, the union card, and coalition politics. While the demand for equality itself is not revolutionary, he insists that "the response that must be made in order to satisfy the demand very much is. By this I mean that justice cannot be done to blacks in the absence of a total restructuring of the political, economic, and social institutions of this country." Never willing to settle for a "symbolic victory" or a pseudo-revolution, he holds out for "nothing less than the radical refashioning of our political economy."

Too ripe a political philosopher to hope for instant solutions, he is able to hold to his belief in revolution and accept the inevitable frustrations and setbacks. Too experienced in the ways of the world to expect reason and logic always to prevail, he is ready to take account of the irrational and the illogical as means to an end as well as obstacles to be overcome. Even in the myths he has exploded he sees signs of hope—as protest against injustice and refusal to accept inequality. As much an opponent of separatism as he is, he is willing to stake out "a kind of in-between position—stay here and try to separate, and yet not separate." By this seeming illogic and inconsistency, he is only describing what the Jewish people have accomplished in America in holding on to what is Jewish and yet integrating where it matters.

In the body of Bayard Rustin's writings is much that is worth preserving and cherishing. Written on the run as much of it was, phrased sometimes to hail a new prophet, at other times to expose a charlatan, now to quiet some raging hysteria, and again to arouse people to a mighty demonstration and stir them to the roots, the fugitive pieces as well as the studied essays and policy papers maintain a tone of reason and humane concern that is rare in times of rebellion. His words will bear comparison with those of other spokesmen of revolt in our history, and it is not the rebels alone who stand to profit from their wisdom.

C. VANN WOODWARD

CONTENTS

Acknowledgments   vii
Introduction by C. Vann Woodward   ix

1. THE FORTIES

Nonviolence vs. Jim Crow   5
The Negro and Nonviolence   8
We Challenged Jim Crow   13
Twenty-two Days on a Chain Gang   26
Civil Disobedience, Jim Crow, and the Armed Forces   50

2. THE FIFTIES

Montgomery Diary   55
Fear in the Delta   62
Getting On with the White Folks   88
New South . . . Old Politics   92
"Even in the Face of Death"   99

3. THE SIXTIES

The Meaning of Birmingham   107
In Answer to Senator Thurmond   109
From Protest to Politics: The Future of the Civil Rights
    Movement   111
The Influence of the Right and Left in the Civil Rights
    Movement   123
Making His Mark: The Autobiography of Malcolm X   132
The Watts "Manifesto" and the McCone Report   140
"Black Power" and Coalition Politics   154
Guns, Bread, and Butter   166
Dr. King's Painful Dilemma   169
The Premise of the Stereotype   171
On Langston Hughes   174

In Defense of Muhammad Ali 176
A Way Out of the Exploding Ghetto 178
The Lessons of the Long Hot Summer 187
Minorities: The War Amidst Poverty 200
Memo on the Spring Protest in Washington, D.C. 202
The Mind of the Black Militant 206
Integration Within Decentralization 213
Reflections on the Death of Martin Luther King, Jr. 222
The Anatomy of Frustration 230
Soul Searching vs. Social Change 238
Now Kennedy: The Bill Mounts Higher 240
The Choice Is Clear 242
Negroes and the 1968 Elections 244
Separate Is Not Equal 253
How Black Americans See Black Africans—And Vice Versa 255
What About Black Capitalism? 259
The Total Vision of A. Philip Randolph 261
No More Guns 267
Fear, Demagogues, and Reaction 269
The Role of the Negro Middle Class 271
Nature, Nurture, or Nonsense? 277
An Exchange with Daniel Moynihan and Thomas A. Billings 280

4. 1970-71

The Failure of Black Separatism 291
Benign Neglect: A Reply to Daniel Moynihan 309
Violence and the Southern Strategy 316
Death in Black and White 318
A West Side Story 320
The Story of a Black Youth 323
Feminism and Equality 325
A Word to Black Students 327
The Blacks and the Unions 335

Index 351

DOWN
THE
LINE

1
THE FORTIES

NONVIOLENCE VS. JIM CROW

Recently I was planning to go from Louisville to Nashville by bus. I bought my ticket, boarded the bus, and, instead of going to the back, sat down in the second seat. The driver saw me, got up, and came toward me.

"Hey, you. You're supposed to sit in the back seat."

"Why?"

"Because that's the law. Niggers ride in back."

I said, "My friend, I believe that is an unjust law. If I were to sit in back I would be condoning injustice."

Angry, but not knowing what to do, he got out and went into the station. He soon came out again, got into his seat, and started off.

This routine was gone through at each stop, but each time nothing came of it. Finally the driver, in desperation, must have phoned ahead, for about thirteen miles north of Nashville I heard sirens approaching. The bus came to an abrupt stop, and a police car and two motorcycles drew up beside us with a flourish. Four policemen got into the bus, consulted shortly with the driver, and came to my seat.

"Get up, you ——— nigger!"

"Why?" I asked.

"Get up, you black ———!"

"I believe that I have a right to sit here," I said quietly. "If I sit in the back of the bus I am depriving that child—" I pointed to a little white child of five or six— "of the knowledge that there is injustice here, which I believe it is his right to know. It is my sincere conviction that the power of love in the world is the greatest power existing. If you have a greater power, my friend, you may move me."

How much they understood of what I was trying to tell them I do not know. By this time they were impatient and angry. As I would not move, they began to beat me about the head and shoulders, and I shortly found myself knocked to the floor. Then they dragged me out of the bus and continued to kick and beat me.

Knowing that if I tried to get up or protect myself in the first heat of

From *Fellowship: The Journal of the Fellowship of Reconciliation*, July 1942.

their anger they would construe it as an attempt to resist and beat me down again, I forced myself to be still and wait for their kicks, one after another. Then I stood up, spreading out my arms parallel to the ground, and said, "There is no need to beat me. I am not resisting you."

At this three white men, obviously Southerners by their speech, got out of the bus and remonstrated with the police. Indeed, as one of the policemen raised his club to strike me, one of them, a little fellow, caught hold of it and said, "Don't you do that!" A second policeman raised his club to strike the little man, and I stepped between them, facing the man, and said, "Thank you, but there is no need to do that. I do not wish to fight. I am protected well."

An elderly gentleman, well dressed and also a Southerner, asked the police where they were taking me.

They said, "Nashville."

"Don't worry, son," he said to me. "I'll be there to see that you get justice."

I was put into the back seat of the police car, between two policemen. Two others sat in front. During the thirteen-mile ride to town they called me every conceivable name and said anything they could think of to incite me to violence. I found that I was shaking with nervous strain, and to give myself something to do, I took out a piece of paper and a pencil, and began to write from memory a chapter from one of Paul's letters.

When I had written a few sentences, the man on my right said, "What're you writing?" and snatched the paper from my hand. He read it, then crumpled it into a ball and pushed it in my face. The man on the other side gave me a kick.

A moment later I happened to catch the eye of the young policeman in the front seat. He looked away quickly, and I took renewed courage from the realization that he could not meet my eyes because he was aware of the injustice being done. I began to write again, and after a moment I leaned forward and touched him on the shoulder. "My friend," I said, "how do you spell 'difference'?"

He spelled it for me—incorrectly—and I wrote it correctly and went on.

When we reached Nashville, a number of policemen were lined up on both sides of the hallway down which I had to pass on my way to the captain's office. They tossed me from one to another like a volleyball. By the time I reached the office, the lining of my best coat was torn, and I was considerably rumpled. I straightened myself as best I could and went in. They had my bag, and went through it and my papers, finding much of interest, especially in the *Christian Century* and *Fellowship*.

6

Finally the captain said, "Come here, nigger."

I walked directly to him. "What can I do for you?" I asked.

"Nigger," he said menacingly, "you're supposed to be scared when you come in here!"

"I am fortified by truth, justice, and Christ," I said. "There's no need for me to fear."

He was flabbergasted and, for a time, completely at a loss for words. Finally he said to another officer, "I believe the nigger's crazy!"

They sent me into another room and went into consultation. The wait was long, but after an hour and a half they came for me and I was taken for another ride, across town. At the courthouse, I was taken down the hall to the office of the assistant district attorney, Mr. Ben West. As I got to the door I heard a voice, "Say, you colored fellow, hey!" I looked around and saw the elderly gentleman who had been on the bus.

"I'm here to see that you get justice," he said.

The assistant district attorney questioned me about my life, the *Christian Century*, pacifism, and the war for half an hour. Then he asked the police to tell their side of what had happened. They did, stretching the truth a good deal in spots and including several lies for seasoning. Mr. West then asked me to tell my side.

"Gladly," I said, "and I want *you*," turning to the young policeman who had sat in the front seat, "to follow what I say and stop me if I deviate from the truth in the least."

Holding his eyes with mine, I told the story exactly as it had happened, stopping often to say "Is that right?" or "Isn't that what happened?" to the young policeman. During the whole time he never once interrupted me, and when I was through I said, "Did I tell the truth just as it happened?" and he said, "Well . . ."

Then Mr. West dismissed me, and I was sent to wait alone in a dark room. After an hour, Mr. West came in and said, very kindly, "You may go, *Mister* Rustin."

I left the courthouse, believing all the more strongly in the nonviolent approach. I am certain that I was addressed as "Mister" (as no Negro is ever addressed in the South), that I was assisted by those three men, and that the elderly gentleman interested himself in my predicament because I had, without fear, faced the four policemen and said, "There is no need to beat me. I offer you no resistance."

THE NEGRO AND NONVIOLENCE

Since the United States entered the war, white-Negro tension has increased steadily. Even in normal times, changes in social and economic patterns cause fear and frustration, which in turn lead to aggression. In time of war, the general social condition is fertile soil for the development of hate and fear, and transference of these to minority groups is quite simple.

Organized violence is growing in the North and South. The Ku Klux Klan is riding again, employing more subtle methods.

Negroes and whites in Southern iron ore mines, as well as in Mobile, Alabama, shipyards, are going armed to work.

Negro soldiers often are forced to wait at Jim Crow ticket windows while whites are being served, frequently missing their buses and trains. Often bus drivers refuse to pick up any Negroes until all whites are seated, sometimes causing them hours' delay. Scores of Negroes have been beaten and arrested in Memphis, Tennessee; Beaumont, Texas; Columbus, Georgia; and Jackson, Mississippi, for insisting on transportation on buses overcrowded because of war conditions. Beaumont has threatened severe punishment for violation of Jim Crow bus laws.

There have been numerous wildcat strikes, in both North and South, where white employees refuse to work with Negroes. Several white and Negro CIO officials have been attacked. One was twice assaulted by white workers for trying to get jobs for Negroes.

Negro soldiers and civilians have been killed by whites. On June 27, Walter Gunn of Macon County, Alabama, wanted on a charge of drunkenness, was shot in the leg, stripped of his clothes, and beaten to death by a deputy sheriff in the presence of Gunn's wife and children. A similar police brutality occurred on the streets of New York City when a liquor-dazed young Negro was killed for refusing to remove his hand from his pocket.

A soldier was shot in the streets of Little Rock, Arkansas, because he refused to tip his hat to a local policeman and address him as "sir."

The world-famous singer Roland Hayes was beaten and jailed because

---

From *Fellowship: The Journal of the Fellowship of Reconciliation*, October 1942.

his wife, who had taken a seat a "few yards forward" in a Georgia shoe store, insisted upon being served "where she was" or trading elsewhere.

On July 28, two Texas policemen, Clyde and Billy Brown, forced Charles Reco, a Negro soldier, into the back seat of a police car and drove him to the police station because in a Beaumont bus he took a vacant seat reserved for a white. During the ride they shot him once in the shoulder and once in the arm.

Racial feeling has increased since June 1942, when the Fair Employment Practices Committee began hearings on anti-Negro discrimination in Birmingham, Alabama. It has been fed by the anti-Negro propaganda stirred up by Governor Dixon of Alabama, Governor Talmadge of Georgia, and Representative John Rankin of Mississippi. This propaganda has encouraged such minor politicians as Horace C. Wilkinson, who has suggested developing a "League of White Supremacy" to make sure "that this menace to our national security and our local way of life will disappear rapidly."

Governor Dixon, in refusing to sign a government war contract because it contained a nondiscrimination clause, said, "I will not permit the citizens of Alabama to be subject to the whims of any federal committee, and I will not permit the employees of the state to be placed in the position where they must abandon the principles of segregation or lose their jobs." Following this statement, Alabama's Senator John Bankhead wrote General Marshall, army chief of staff, demanding that no Negro soldiers be brought South for military training.

These and other humiliations have had a very marked effect on great masses of Negroes, who are being told by the press that "equality of opportunity and social and political recognition will come *now or never*, violently or nonviolently." The Pittsburgh *Courier* and the *People's Voice*, typical of the general Negro press, constantly remind the masses that greater economic and political democracy was supposed to have followed World War I. Instead, they pointed out, the Negro found himself the scapegoat, "last hired and first fired," in a period of economic and social maladjustment that has lasted until the present time. Thus the average Negro is told, "There can be no delay. What achievement there will be must come now."

An increasingly militant group has it in mind to demand *now*, with violence if necessary, the rights it has long been denied. "If we must die abroad for democracy we can't have," I heard a friend of mine say, "then we might as well die right here, fighting for our rights."

This is a tragic statement. It is tragic also how isolated the average Negro feels in his struggle. The average Negro has largely lost faith in middle-class whites. In his hour of need he seeks not "talk" but dynamic action. He looks upon the middle-class idea of long-term educational and cultural changes with fear and mistrust. He is interested only in what can be achieved immediately by political pressure to get jobs, decent housing, and education for his children. He describes with disgust the efforts in his behalf by most middle-class Negro and white intellectuals as "pink tea methods—sometimes well-meanin' but gettin' us nowhere." It is for this reason, in part, that the March on Washington movement, aiming to become a mass movement, has tended toward "black nationalism." Its leadership, originally well motivated, now rejects the idea of including whites in its constituency or leadership. One local official said, "These are Negroes' problems and Negroes will have to work them out."

The March on Washington movement is growing but at best is only a partial answer to the present need. While the movement already exerts some real political pressure (President Roosevelt set up the FEPC at its request), it has no program, educational or otherwise, for meeting immediate conflict. To demand rights but not to see the potential danger in such a course, or the responsibility to develop a means of meeting that danger, seems tragic.

Many Negroes see mass violence coming. Having lived in a society in which church, school, and home problems have been handled in a violent way, the majority at this point are unable to conceive of a solution by reconciliation and nonviolence. I have seen schoolboys in Arkansas laying away rusty guns for the "time when." I have heard many young men in the armed forces hope for a machine-gun assignment "so I can turn it on the white folks." I have seen a white sailor beaten in Harlem because three Negroes had been "wantin' to get just one white" before they died. I have heard hundreds of Negroes hope for a Japanese military victory, since "it don't matter who you're a slave for."

These statements come not only from bitterness but from frustration and fear as well. In many parts of America the Negro, in his despair, is willing to follow any leadership seemingly sincerely identified with his struggle if he is convinced that such leadership offers a workable method. In this crisis those of us who believe in the nonviolent solution of conflict have a duty and an opportunity. In all those places where we have a voice, it is our high responsibility to indicate that the Negro can attain progress only if he uses, in his struggle, nonviolent direct action—a technique consistent with the ends he desires. Especially in this time of tension we must point out the practical necessity of such a course.

Nonviolence as a method has within it the demand for terrible sacrifice and long suffering, but, as Gandhi has said, "freedom does not drop from the sky." One has to struggle and be willing to die for it. J. Holmes Smith has indicated that he looks to the American Negro to assist in developing, along with the people of India, a new dynamic force for the solution of conflict that will not merely free these oppressed people but will set an example that may be the first step in freeing the world.

Certainly the Negro possesses qualities essential for nonviolent direct action. He has long since learned to endure suffering. He can admit his own share of guilt and has to be pushed hard to become bitter. He has produced, and still sings, such songs as "It's Me, Oh Lord, Standin' in the Need of Prayer" and "Nobody Knows the Trouble I've Seen." He follows this last tragic phrase by a salute to God—"Oh! Glory, Hallelujah." He is creative and has learned to adjust himself to conditions easily. But above all he possesses a rich religious heritage and today finds the church the center of his life.

Yet there are those who question the use of nonviolent direct action by Negroes in protesting discrimination, on the grounds that this method will kindle hitherto dormant racial feeling. But we must remember that too often conflict is already at hand and that there is hence a greater danger: the inevitable use of force by persons embittered by injustice and unprepared for nonviolence. It is a cause for shame that millions of people continue to live under conditions of injustice while we make no effective effort to remedy the situation.

Those who argue for an extended educational plan are not wrong, but there must also be a plan for facing *immediate* conflicts. Those of us who believe in nonviolent resistance can do the greatest possible good for the Negro, for those who exploit him, for America, and for the world by becoming a real part of the Negro community, thus being in a position to suggest methods and to offer leadership when troubles come.

Identification with the Negro community demands considerable sacrifice. The Negro is not to be won by words alone, but by an obvious consistency in words and deeds. The *identified* person is the one who fights side by side with him for justice. This demands being so integral a part of the Negro community in its day-to-day struggle, so close to it in similarity of work, so near its standard of living that when problems arise he who stands forth to judge, to plan, to suggest, or to lead is really at one with the Negro masses.

Our war resistance is justified only if we see that an adequate alternative to violence is developed. Today, as the Gandhian forces in India face their critical test, we can add to world justice by placing in the hands of thirteen million black Americans a workable and Christian technique for the righting of injustice and the solution of conflict.

WE CHALLENGED JIM CROW

On June 3, 1946, the Supreme Court of the United States announced its decision in the case of Irene Morgan versus the Commonwealth of Virginia. State laws demanding segregation of interstate passengers on motor carriers are now unconstitutional, for segregation of passengers crossing state lines was declared an "undue burden on interstate commerce." Thus it was decided that state Jim Crow laws do not affect interstate travelers. In a later decision in the Court of Appeals for the District of Columbia, the Morgan decision was interpreted to apply to interstate train travel as well as bus travel.

The executive committee of the Congress of Racial Equality and the racial-industrial committee of the Fellowship of Reconciliation decided that they should jointly sponsor a "Journey of Reconciliation" through the upper South, in order to determine to how great an extent bus and train companies were recognizing the Morgan decision. They also wished to learn the reaction of bus drivers, passengers, and police to those who nonviolently and persistently challenge Jim Crow in interstate travel.

During the two-week period from April 9 to April 23, 1947, an interracial group of men, traveling as a deputation team, visited fifteen cities in Virginia, North Carolina, Tennessee, and Kentucky. More than thirty speaking engagements were met before church, NAACP, and college groups. The Morgan decision was explained and reports made on what was happening on buses and trains in the light of this decision. The response was most enthusiastic.

To clarify the incidents described below, it will be necessary to list the sixteen participants by race.

Negro. Bayard Rustin, of the Fellowship of Reconciliation and part-time worker with the American Friends Service Committee; Wallace Nelson, freelance lecturer; Conrad Lynn, New York attorney; Andrew Johnson, Cincinnati student; Dennis Banks, Chicago musician; William Worthy, of the

---

A report prepared in 1947 by Bayard Rustin and George Houser for the Congress of Racial Equality and the Fellowship of Reconciliation; published in *Fellowship*, April 1947.

New York Council for a Permanent FEPC; Eugene Stanley, of A. and T. College, Greensboro, North Carolina; Nathan Wright, church social worker from Cincinnati.

White. George Houser, of the FOR and executive secretary of the Congress of Racial Equality; Ernest Bromley, Methodist minister from North Carolina; James Peck, editor of the Workers Defense League *News Bulletin;* Igal Roodenko, New York horticulturist; Worth Randle, Cincinnati biologist; Joseph Felmet, of the Southern Workers Defense League; Homer Jack, executive secretary of the Chicago Council Against Racial and Religious Discrimination; Louis Adams, Methodist minister from North Carolina.

During the two weeks of the trip, twenty-six tests of company policies were made. Arrests occurred on six occasions, with a total of twelve men arrested.

THE TEST TRIPS

The report of what happened on the test trips should be much more complete than is here possible. For purposes of brevity, many important comments and psychological reactions have had to be omitted.

Between eight and ten men participated in simultaneous tests. This made it possible to split the group into two parts—either for two separate tests on the same bus line or for testing both Greyhound and Trailways buses when both companies ran buses to the next point on the itinerary.

WASHINGTON, D.C., TO RICHMOND, VIRGINIA, APRIL 9

No difficulties were encountered. On both the Trailways and Greyhound buses the Negroes in the group sat up front and the whites in the rear. Other passengers tended to cross the color line too. A white couple sat on the back seat of the Greyhound with two Negroes. A Negro woman sat beside a young white man in the center of the bus when she could have taken a vacant seat by a Negro man. Rustin gave his seat, third from the front, to an elderly Negro woman, then sat by a white lad directly behind the driver. Nothing was said.

RICHMOND TO PETERSBURG, VIRGINIA, APRIL 10

Because there have been so many cases in the Richmond courts testing segregation in interstate travel, no more arrests were being made there. Both the Greyhound and Trailways groups reached Petersburg without incident. The Trailways bus was local, running only between the two cities. The tickets used were interstate, of course. The Greyhound bus was a crowded through-bus, but no attempt was made to force Rustin and Johnson to move from the front. Nelson and Lynn rode in front on the Trailways bus. A Negro man in the rear spoke to Houser and Roodenko, saying a Negro might be able to get away with riding up front here, but some bus drivers are crazy, "and the farther South you go, the crazier they get." Two Negro women talking about Peck, sitting in the rear of the Greyhound reading his *New York Times*, said, "He wouldn't know what it was all about if he was asked to move." Then they laughed.

PETERSBURG TO RALEIGH, NORTH CAROLINA, APRIL 11

Before the Trailways bus left the station Lynn was arrested for sitting in the second seat from the front. The bus driver was courteous but insistent. Lynn explained the Morgan decision quietly. The driver countered that he was in the employ of the bus company, not the Supreme Court, and that he followed company rules about segregation. He said aloud, so all passengers could hear: "Personally, I don't care where you sit, but I have my orders. Are you going to move?" Lynn said that he could not. The driver got the police. There were no threats nor abusive language. It took about an hour and a half to get a warrant for Lynn's arrest. The magistrate in Petersburg would not sign the warrant until the bus company attorney in Richmond had been called, and dictated the statement of the warrant over the telephone. The warrant read that Lynn was guilty of disorderly conduct for not obeying the reasonable request of the bus driver to move to the rear, in compliance with the company rules. The bus operator apologized for having to arrest Lynn. A policeman, referring to equality for Negroes, said, "I'm just not Christian enough." Passengers on the bus were patient, and relatively neutral, while they waited almost two hours. A Negro porter made the only fuss when he boarded the bus. Looking at Lynn, he said, "What's the matter with him? He's crazy. Where does he think he is? We know how to deal with him. We ought to drag him off." Lynn was released on $25 bond.

PETERSBURG TO DURHAM, NORTH CAROLINA, APRIL 11

On the Greyhound to Durham there were no arrests. Peck and Rustin sat up front. About ten miles out of Petersburg the driver told Rustin to move. When Rustin refused, the driver said he would "attend to that at Blackstone." However, after consultation with other drivers at the bus station in Blackstone, he went on to Clarksville. There the group changed buses. At Oxford, North Carolina, the driver sent for the police, who refused to make an arrest. Persons waiting to get on at Oxford were delayed for forty-five minutes. A middle-aged Negro schoolteacher was permitted to board and to plead with Rustin to move: "Please move. Don't do this. You'll reach your destination either in front or in back. What difference does it make?" Rustin explained his reason for not moving. Other Negro passengers were strong in their support of Rustin, one of them threatening to sue the bus company for the delay. When Durham was reached without arrest, the Negro schoolteacher begged Peck not to use the teacher's name in connection with the incident at Oxford: "It will hurt me in the community. I'll never do that again."

RALEIGH TO CHAPEL HILL, NORTH CAROLINA, APRIL 12

Lynn and Nelson rode together on the double seat next to the very rear of the Trailways bus, and Houser and Roodenko in front of them. The bus was very crowded. The one other Negro passenger, a woman seated across from Nelson, moved to the very rear voluntarily when a white woman got on the bus and there were no seats in front. When two white college men got on, the driver told Nelson and Lynn to move to the rear seat. When they refused on the basis of their interstate passage, he said the matter would be handled in Durham. A white passenger asked the driver if he wanted any help. The driver replied, "No, we don't want to handle it that way." By the time the group reached Durham, the seating arrangement had changed and the driver did not press the matter.

DURHAM TO CHAPEL HILL, APRIL 12

Johnson and Rustin were in the second seat from the front on a Trailways bus. The driver, as soon as he saw them, asked them to move to the rear. A station superintendent was called to repeat the order. Five minutes later the police arrived and Johnson and Rustin were arrested for refusing to move when ordered to do so. Peck, who was seated in about the middle of the bus, got up after the arrest, saying to the police, "If you arrest them, you'll have to arrest me, too, for I'm going to sit in the rear." The three men were held at the police station for half an hour. They were released without charge when an attorney arrived on their behalf. A suit will be pressed against the company and the police for false arrest. The conversation with the Trailways official indicated that the company knew there was an interracial group making a test. The official said to the police: "We know all about this. Greyhound is letting them ride. But we're not."

CHAPEL HILL TO GREENSBORO, NORTH CAROLINA, APRIL 13

Johnson and Felmet were seated in front. The driver asked them to move as soon as he boarded. They were arrested quickly, for the police station was just across the street from the bus station. Felmet did not get up to accompany the police until the officer specifically told him he was under arrest. Because he delayed rising from his seat, he was pulled up bodily and shoved out of the bus. The bus driver distributed witness cards to occupants of the bus. One white girl said: "You don't want me to sign one of those. I'm a damn Yankee, and I think this is an outrage." Rustin and Roodenko, sensing the favorable reaction on the bus, decided they would move to the seat in the front vacated by Johnson and Felmet. Their moving forward caused much discussion by passengers. The driver returned soon, and when Rustin and Roodenko refused to move, they were arrested also. A white woman at the front of the bus, a Southerner, gave her name and address to Rustin as he walked by her. The men were arrested on charges of disorderly conduct, for refusing to obey the bus driver and, in the case of the whites, for interfering with arrest. The men were released on $50 bonds.

The bus was delayed nearly two hours. Taxi drivers standing around the bus station were becoming aroused by the events. One hit Peck a hard blow on the head, saying, "Coming down here to stir up the niggers." Peck stood quietly looking at them for several moments, but said nothing. Two persons standing by, one Negro and one white, reprimanded the cab driver for his violence. The Negro was told, "You keep out of this." In the police station, some of the men standing around could be heard saying, "They'll never get a bus out of here tonight." After the bond was placed, Reverend Charles Jones, a local white Presbyterian minister, speedily drove the men to his home. They were pursued by two cabs filled with taxi men. As the interracial group reached the front porch of the Jones home, the two cabs pulled up at the curb. Men jumped out, two of them with sticks for weapons; others picked up sizable rocks. They started toward the house, but were called back by one of their number. In a few moments the phone rang, and an anonymous voice said to Jones, "Get those damn niggers out of town or we'll burn your house down. We'll be around to see that they go." The police were notified and arrived in about twenty minutes. The interracial group felt it wise to leave town before nightfall. Two cars were obtained and the group was driven to Greensboro, by way of Durham, for an evening engagement.

GREENSBORO TO WINSTON-SALEM, NORTH CAROLINA, APRIL 14

Two tests were made on Greyhound buses. In the first test Lynn sat in front; in the second, Nelson. A South Carolinian seated by Bromley on the first bus said, "In my state he would either move or be killed." He was calm as Bromley talked with him about the Morgan decision.

WINSTON-SALEM TO ASHEVILLE, NORTH CAROLINA, APRIL 15

From Winston-Salem to Statesville the group traveled by Greyhound. Nelson was seated with Bromley in the second seat from the front. Nothing was said. At Statesville, the group transferred to the Trailways, with Nelson still in front. In a small town about ten miles from Statesville, the driver approached Nelson and told him he would have to move to the rear. When Nelson said that he was an interstate passenger, the driver said that the bus was not interstate. When Nelson explained that his ticket was interstate, the driver returned to his seat and drove on. The rest of the trip to Asheville was through mountainous country, and the bus stopped at many small towns. A soldier asked the driver why Nelson was not forced to move. The driver explained that there was a Supreme Court decision and that he could do nothing about it. He said, "If you want to do something about this, don't blame this man [Nelson]; kill those bastards up in Washington." The soldier explained to a rather large, vociferous man why Nelson was allowed to sit up front. The large man commented, "I wish I was the bus driver." Near Asheville the bus became very crowded, and there were women standing up. Two women spoke to the bus driver, asking him why Nelson was not moved. In each case the driver explained that the Supreme Court decision was responsible. Several white women took seats in the Jim Crow section in the rear.

ASHEVILLE TO KNOXVILLE, TENNESSEE, APRIL 17

Banks and Peck were in the second seat on the Trailways. While the bus was still in the station, a white passenger asked the bus driver to tell Banks to move. Banks replied, "I'm sorry, I can't," and explained that he was an interstate passenger. The police were called and the order repeated. A twenty-minute consultation took place before the arrest was made. When Peck was not arrested, he said, "We're traveling together, and you will have to arrest me too." He was arrested for sitting in the rear. The two men were released from the city jail on $400 bond each.

KNOXVILLE TO NASHVILLE, TENNESSEE, APRIL 17

Wright and Jack sat at the front of a Greyhound bus. Before the driver boarded, a redheaded soldier asked him if he was going to move Wright. The driver approached Wright and asked him politely, "Would you like to move?" Wright said he would not. The driver disappeared for fifteen minutes. Two Negroes in the rear of the bus discussed the situation audibly, saying, "They are going to get the police, and they'll probably hit him." The other said, "When in Rome, I believe in doing as the Romans do." When the bus driver returned, he drove off without raising any more questions. This bus trip was at night.

KNOXVILLE TO LOUISVILLE, KENTUCKY, APRIL 18

Worthy and Roodenko sat in the front of a Greyhound bus. The bus reached Corbin, Tennessee, some hundred miles from Knoxville, before Worthy was asked to move. The driver hinted that there would be violence from the crowd if Worthy did not move. A white woman from Tennessee talked with the officials in the bus station and to the bus driver, protesting threatened arrests. The bus driver received orders to drive on.

NASHVILLE TO LOUISVILLE, KENTUCKY, APRIL 19

Wright and Jack had reserved seats on an all-coach reserved train of the Louisville and Nashville railroad. There was no difficulty in getting on the train. Two conductors approached to collect the tickets. One asked Jack if Wright were his prisoner. Learning they were friends, he told Wright that company rules meant he would have to move to the Jim Crow car. "This is the way it is done down here," he concluded. When Wright refused to move, he said he would be back later. When he came back he said, "If we were in Alabama, we would throw you out of the window." He threatened to have Wright arrested in Bowling Green, Kentucky, but no arrest took place. A woman sitting in the second seat behind the men approached them after the conductor left, giving them her name and address and saying that they could call on her for help.

WEAVERSVILLE, NORTH CAROLINA, TO BRISTOL, VIRGINIA, APRIL 19

No test was made. Banks was the only Negro on the bus, and he was on the rear seat. The bus was extremely crowded. The driver asked Banks to move from the rear seat to the double seat in front of the rear seat so that only one white person, and not four, would have to sit beside him. Banks complied. He had a friendly conversation with a young white farmer who sat beside him.

BRISTOL TO ROANOKE, VIRGINIA, APRIL 19

Banks and Peck rode together on a Greyhound. The driver approached them twice, but on neither occasion insisted that they move.

CINCINNATI, OHIO, TO ROANOKE, APRIL 19

Worthy and Houser had coach reservations on the Norfolk and Western. The railroad man at the gate expressed consternation that Worthy had a seat in a white coach, but no attempt was made to keep him from taking it.

ROANOKE TO WASHINGTON, D.C., APRIL 20

Worthy and Bromley sat together in a white coach on the Norfolk and Western. No questions of any kind were raised. Bromley got off at Charlottesville, Virginia. For the last part of the trip to Washington, a white girl sat beside Worthy rather than sit on her suitcase in the aisle.

ROANOKE TO LYNCHBURG, VIRGINIA, APRIL 21

Banks and Houser sat together in the front of a Greyhound bus. No incident occurred.

LYNCHBURG TO WASHINGTON, D.C., APRIL 22

Nelson and Houser were seated at the front of the Trailways bus. The driver did not see Nelson until the bus was about five miles out of the station. When he stopped at a service station, he asked Nelson to move to the rear. Nelson refused on the ground that he was an interstate passenger. Houser explained that they were traveling together. The driver said they could ride in the rear. Houser asked whether that too would not be breaking the Jim Crow rules of the company, by which the driver said he was guided. The driver then said that Houser would have to sit one seat in front of Nelson in the rear. It took more than an hour to get a warrant for Nelson's arrest. State police took Nelson to the small town of Amherst, where he was held for $50 bail. The bus driver apologized profusely for his action when Houser got off at Amherst to put up the bond for Nelson. The passengers were very patient, rather neutral in attitude.

AMHERST, VIRGINIA, TO WASHINGTON, D.C., APRIL 22

Nelson and Houser took a train on the Southern Railway at Amherst. They asked the conductor where they could ride together. He asked if Nelson were Houser's prisoner. Upon learning that they were friends, he said it was against the rules for them to ride together on that train. He said, "I'll turn you over to the officials at Charlottesville if you sit together." They sat together in the Jim Crow car, where the conductor asked Houser if he refused to move. Again he threatened arrest in Charlottesville, but no arrest was made.

CHARLOTTESVILLE, VIRGINIA, TO WASHINGTON, D.C., APRIL 23

Banks rode alone in the front of the Trailways bus. Peck and Randle were riding on the rear seat. For two hours out of Charlottesville there was no incident. In the small town of Culpeper, Virginia, the driver told Banks to move to the rear. It took about an hour and a half to get a warrant issued for Banks's arrest. A Negro woman who had a concession selling bus tickets in town came on board the bus and offered to help Banks in any way she could. The warrant read that Banks was guilty of not obeying the order of the driver. Nothing was said to Peck or Randle, in spite of the fact that the rules of the company state that white persons shall not sit in the rear. Banks was released on $25 bond.

THE TRIALS

By July 6, 1947, four trials had been held. In Petersburg, Virginia, Conrad Lynn received a $10 fine. In Chapel Hill, North Carolina, Bayard Rustin and Igal Roodenko were found guilty of violating the state Jim Crow law. Rustin was sentenced to thirty days on the road gang, while Roodenko was given sixty days. The judge said he purposely discriminated against the white person involved. Likewise, when Andrew Johnson and Joe Felmet were tried on June 24, Felmet was given the maximum sentence of thirty days on the road gang, while Johnson received a $25 fine. The judge tried to give Felmet six months, only to discover this was beyond the maximum permitted. The indictment for the four arrested in Chapel Hill was changed from disorderly conduct and interfering with arrest to a violation of the state Jim Crow law, on the ground that since the men were planning stopovers in three cities within the state, they were not interstate passengers.

The Asheville case against Peck and Banks came up for trial in the police court before Judge Sam Cathay. Curtis Todd of Winston-Salem was their attorney. (There were no Negro attorneys in Asheville, and this was the first time a Negro attorney had appeared in the court.) The indictment was that the men had violated the Jim Crow law. The two witnesses for the state—the bus driver and the policeman—testified so accurately that it was not necessary to call defense witnesses. They both said there was no disorder on the part of the arrested men. Neither the judge nor the state's attorney knew about the Morgan decision, and they had to borrow Attorney Todd's copy of it. When the judge learned the maximum sentence was thirty days, he gave thirty-day sentences, to be served under the supervision of the highway commissioner. Pending appeal, the men were released on $250 bonds.

The cases in Amherst and Culpeper were scheduled for trial pending the outcome of another case involving the same legal principles.

All convictions were appealed.

GENERAL OBSERVATIONS

The one word which most universally describes the attitude of police, of passengers, and of the Negro and white bus riders is "confusion." Persons taking part in the psychological struggle in the buses and trains either did not know of the Morgan decision or, if they did, possessed no clear understanding of it. Thus when police officers and bus drivers in authority took a stand, they tended to act on the basis of what they knew—the state Jim Crow law. In the South, where the caste system is rigidly defined, this confusion is extremely dangerous; it leads to frustration, usually followed by aggression in some form.

The great majority of the passengers were apathetic and did not register their feelings, even when their faces clearly revealed how they felt about the action the group was taking.

It was generally apparent that the bus companies were attempting to circumvent the intentions of the Supreme Court in the Irene Morgan decision by reliance on state Jim Crow laws, by company regulations, and by subtle pressures. Negro passengers tended to follow the dominant reaction of the other riders. There were exceptions to this, of course, but generally they showed fear first, then caution. When cautious Negroes saw resistant Negroes sitting in the front of the bus unmolested, many moved forward too.

There were no acts of violence on the buses. The most extreme negative reactions were verbal, but without profanity. Typical was the young marine who said, "The KKK is coming up again, and I guess I'll join up." The one act of violence against a member of the group was on the part of a taxi driver outside the bus station at Chapel Hill. This act—a single but hard blow to the head—was directed against a white man.

On three occasions when Negro members of the group protested discrimination by sitting in the front, other Negroes—a porter, a schoolteacher, and a day laborer—urged the resisters in very emotional terms to comply with the law. Their request was either the result of fear or, as in the case of the Negro porter, an attempt to ingratiate themselves with white authorities. Such reactions are to be expected in a caste system and represent the kind of personal degradation which ought to spur us on to eliminate caste.

Policemen and bus drivers have a great responsibility in social change of this kind. Success or failure, violence or peaceful change is in large part determined by the position they take. White persons generally ignored Negroes riding in the front of buses or in the non–Jim Crow cars on trains until the bus drivers or train conductors raised the issue. We are of the opinion that in most cases if the bus drivers had not taken action, the passengers would have continued to ignore the Negroes sitting in the front of a bus or in coaches for whites. Between Statesville and Asheville, North Carolina, a clear statement from the driver explaining the Morgan decision quieted protesting white passengers. It is our belief that when those in authority take a clear stand, passengers who might otherwise resent a Negro's presence in a nontraditional position will accept the situation with a typical shrug of the shoulder: "Well, this is the law. What can you do?"

In no case of arrest was there a single example of police inconsideration. The police were polite and calm, and if any of them were anti-Negro there was no indication of it. In fact, one officer, when pressed for a reason for his unwillingness to sit beside a Negro, said, "I'm just not Christian enough, I guess." This would not necessarily be true in the lower South.

Without exception those arrested behaved in a nonviolent fashion. They acted without fear, spoke quietly and firmly, showing great consideration for the police and bus drivers, and repeatedly pointed to the fact that they expected the police to do their duty as they saw it. We cannot overemphasize the necessity for this courteous and intelligent conduct while breaking with the caste system. We believe that the reason the police behaved politely was that there was not the slightest provocation in the attitude of the resisters. On the contrary, we tried at all times to understand *their* attitude and position first.

Another reason for the lack of tension was the interracial character of the group. We did not allow a single situation to develop in which the struggle seemed to be between white and Negro persons; rather it appeared that progressives and democrats, white and black, were working by peaceful means to overcome a system which they felt to be wrong.

Much was gained when someone in our group took the lead in discussion with bus drivers or train conductors and when police appeared. Those who seemed certain of their facts, and who spoke clearly and assuredly, set the tone. Attitudes were greatly accelerated in the proper direction whenever a person of liberal sentiments spoke up first.

As the trip progressed it became evident that the police and bus drivers were learning about the Irene Morgan decision as word of the "test cases" was passed from city to city and from driver to driver. We see here again the need for incidents as "teaching techniques." The following paragraph from a letter written by a student at Chapel Hill supports this contention: "I don't know whether all the stir has been in vain or not. Everyone on this campus now knows about the Fellowship of Reconciliation, the Congress of Racial Equality, and the Supreme Court decision. What is more important, many people, including my two very conservative roommates, are thinking seriously about the whole nonviolent approach to social problems."

The incident at Chapel Hill indicates that one of the chief dangers of violence arises when crowds gather outside buses. Such persons are unable to hear the discussion or to know and debate the facts given inside the bus. They merely pick up bits of hearsay and false rumors. It is also true that taxi drivers, pool-room fellows, and idlers are likely to be in the groups which hang around bus terminals. Many of them depend on Jim Crow for personal status. No matter how poor they are, they can "feel better than the niggers."

It is our belief that without direct action on the part of groups and individuals, the Jim Crow pattern in the South cannot be broken. We are equally certain that such direct action must be nonviolent.

It appeared that women are more intelligently inquisitive, open for discussion, and liberal in their sentiments than men. On several occasions women not only defended those who broke with Jim Crow, but gave their names and addresses, offering to act as witnesses. In appealing for aid in the psychological struggle within the bus one might do well to concentrate on winning over women.

All the arrests occurred on Trailways buses. It is difficult to account for the difference between the two bus lines. One possible reason might be the fact that Trailways largely serves Southern states, and is not used so universally in interstate travel as the Greyhound lines.

If the attitude of those Southerners who did speak up could be put in a nutshell, it was expressed by one Southerner, who said, "The South is the South and will always be this way. We don't care about the Supreme Court decision." This is not so much an attitude of resistance to change as one of despair and cynicism.

We believe that the great majority of the people in the upper South are prepared to accept the Irene Morgan decision and to ride on buses and trains with Negroes. One white woman, reluctantly taking a seat beside a Negro man, said to her sister, who was about to protest, "I'm tired. Anything for a seat."

Persons who did not wish to see change, particularly the bus drivers, became more angry with the white participants than with the Negroes. This is an important observation, since, except in extreme cases, white resisters may have to bear the brunt of hostility.

The situation in the upper South is in a great state of flux. Where numerous cases have been before the courts recently, as in northern Virginia, the barriers are already down, and Negroes can, in general, ride without fear of arrest. Repeated arrests have occurred in other parts of Virginia as well as North Carolina, eastern Tennessee, and Kentucky.

TWENTY-TWO DAYS ON A CHAIN GANG

Late in the afternoon of Monday, March 21, 1949, I surrendered to the Orange County court at Hillsboro, North Carolina, to begin serving a thirty-day sentence imposed two years before for sitting in a bus seat out of the Jim Crow section. As afternoon waned into evening, I waited alone in a small cell of the county jail across the street. I had not eaten since morning, but no supper was forthcoming, and eventually I lay down on the mattress-less iron bed and tried to sleep. Next morning I learned that only two meals were served daily—breakfast at seven A.M. and lunch at noon.

That morning I spent reading one of the books I had brought with me and wondering where I would be sent to do my time. At about two P.M. I was ordered to prepare to leave for a prison camp. Along with two other men I got into the "dog car"—a small, brown enclosed truck with a locked screen in the rear—and began to travel through the rain. An hour later we stopped at the state prison camp at Roxboro, and through the screen I could see the long, low building, circled by barbed wire, where I was to spend the next twenty-two days.

The camp was very unattractive, to put it mildly. There were no trees, grass only near the entrance and to one side. There was not one picture on the walls and no drawer, box, or container supplied for storing the few items one owned. While an effort was made to keep the place clean, there was always mud caked on the floor as soon as the men got in from work, since there was no change of shoes. Roaches were everywhere, though I never saw a bedbug. Once a week the mattresses were aired.

In the receiving room, under close supervision, I went through the routine

---

Bayard Rustin introduces this personal account as follows: "In 1947, after repeated reports that the various states were ignoring the Morgan decision, the Fellowship of Reconciliation set out to discover the degree to which such illegal separation patterns were enforced. In what has since become known as the Journey of Reconciliation, sixteen white and Negro young men, in groups ranging from two to four, traveled through North Carolina, Virginia, Kentucky, and Tennessee making test cases. It was on one of these cases that I was arrested. Finally, after the North Carolina supreme court upheld my thirty-day sentence, I surrendered and spent twenty-two days at Roxboro. I was released eight days early for good behavior." An edited version of this account appeared in the *New York Post* and the *Baltimore Afro-American*.

of the new inmate: receiving a book of rules and a change of clothing, finger-printing, and—"You'll have to have all your hair cut off."

An inmate barber gleefully shaved my head and, with an expression of mock sadness, surveyed me from various angles. Finally he brought a small mirror and ceremoniously held it up for me. The final touch was his solemn pretense of brushing some hairs from my shirt. Then he told me to go out to the corridor, where an officer would show me to my bed. As I left, the three inmates who were in the room doubled up with laughter. Apparently they had discovered the reason for my schoolboy nickname, "Pinhead"!

Wordlessly the officer outside unlocked the dormitory door and motioned for me to go through.

Inside I found myself in one of two rooms into which a hundred men were crowded. Double-decker beds stood so close together that one had to turn sidewise to pass between them. Lights bright enough to read by remained on all night. The rule book states: "No inmate may get out of bed after lights are dimmed without asking permission of the guard," and so all night long men were crying out to a guard many yards away:. "Gettin' up, Cap'n," "Closing the window, Cap'n," "Goin' to the toilet, Cap'n." I did not sleep soundly one night during my whole stay at Roxboro, though I went to bed tireder than I had ever been before.

The camp schedule at Roxboro began with the rising bell at five-thirty. By seven beds had been made, faces washed, breakfast served, and lines formed for leaving the camp for the ten-hour-day's work. We worked from seven until noon, had a half-hour for lunch, resumed work at twelve-thirty, and worked until five-thirty. Then we were counted in and left immediately for supper, without so much as a chance to wash hands and face. From six o'clock we were locked in the dormitory until lights were dimmed at eight-thirty. From then until five-thirty A.M. we were expected to sleep.

On the morning of March 23, my second day at camp, I shaved hurriedly. When I had finished, Easy Life, an inmate who had a nearby bed, apologetically asked if he might borrow my razor. He had a week's growth of hair on his face.

"Most of us ain't got no razors and can't buy none," he said.

"But don't they give you a razor if you can't afford one?" I asked.

He looked at me and smiled. "We don't get nothing but the clothes we got on and a towel and soap—no comb, no brush, no toothbrush, no razor, no blades, no stamps, no writing paper, no pencils, nothing." Then he looked up and said thoughtfully, "They say, 'Another day, another dollar,' but all we gets for our week's work is one bag of stud."

I suppose my deep concern must have been reflected in my face, for he added, "Don't look so sad. T'ain't nothin! The boys say 'So round, so firm, so fully packed,' when you roll your own."

The guard swung open the doors for breakfast, and as Easy Life rushed to the front of the line he yelled back, "But the damn stuff sure does burn your tongue—that's why I like my tailor-mades," meaning factory-made cigarettes. He winked, laughed heartily, and was gone. I picked up my toothbrush and razor, and slowly walked to my bed to put them away.

A week later I was to remember the conversation. The one towel I had been given was already turning a reddish gray (like the earth of Persons County) despite the fact that I washed it every day. That towel was never changed as long as I stayed at Roxboro. Some of the men washed their towels but once a week, just after they bathed on Saturday.

Each week we were given one suit of underclothing, one pair of pants, a shirt, and a pair of socks. Even though we worked in the mud and rain, this was the only clothing we would get until the next week. By Tuesday, the stench in the dormitory from sweating feet and encrusted underclothing was thick enough to cut. As one fellow said, "Don't do no good to wash and put this sweat-soaked stuff on again."

Two weeks later I saw Easy Life borrowing my toothbrush. "My old lady's coming to visit today and I gotta shine my pearls somehow," he apologized.

I offered him thirty-five cents for a toothbrush. He accepted the money, thanked me, and said, "But if you don't mind I'll buy stamps with it. I can write my old lady ten letters with this. I can borrow Snake's toothbrush if I wanna, but he ain't never got no stamps, and I ain't never got no money."

I started from the camp for my first day's work on the road with anything but an easy mind. Our crew of fifteen men was met at the back gate by the walking boss, who directed the day's work, and by a guard who carried both a revolver and a shotgun. We were herded into the rear of a truck where we were under constant scrutiny by the armed guard, who rode behind in a small, glass-enclosed trailer. In that way we rode each day to whatever part of Persons County we were to work in. We would leave the truck when we were ordered to. At all times we had to be within sight of the guard, but at no time closer than thirty feet to him.

On this first day I got down from the truck with the rest of the crew. After several moments of complete silence, which seemed to leave everyone uneasy, the walking boss, whom I shall call Captain Jones, looked directly at me.

"Hey, you, tall boy! How much time you got?"

"Thirty days," I said politely.

"Thirty days, *Sir.*"

"Thirty days, Sir," I said.

He took a newsclipping from his pocket and waved it up and down.

"You're the one who thinks he's smart. Ain't got no respect. Tries to be uppity. Well, we'll learn you. You'll learn you got to respect us down here. You ain't in Yankeeland now. We don't like no Yankee ways." He was getting angrier by the moment, his face flushed and his breath short.

"I would as lief step on the head of a damyankee as I would on the head of a rattlesnake," he barked. "Now you git this here thing straight," and he walked closer to me, his face quivering. "You do what you're told. You respect us, or. . . ." He raised his hand threateningly but, instead of striking me, brought the back of his hand down across the mouth of the man on my left. Then he thrust a pick at me and ordered me to get to work.

I had never handled a pick in my life, but I tried. Captain Jones watched me sardonically for a few minutes. Then he grabbed the pick from me, raised it over his head, and sank it deep into the earth several times.

"There, now," he shouted. "Let's see you do it."

I took the pick and for about ten minutes succeeded in breaking the ground. Then my arms and back began to give out. Just as I was beginning to feel faint, a chain-ganger called Purple walked over and said quietly, "O.K. Let me use dat pick for a while. You take the shovel and, no matter what they say or do, keep workin', keep trying, and keep yo' mouth shut."

I took the shovel and began to throw the loose dirt into the truck. My arms pained so badly that I thought each shovelful would be the last. Then gradually my strength seemed to return.

As Purple began to pick again, he whispered to me, "Now you'se learnin'. Sometimes you'll give out, but you can't never give up—dat's chain-gangin'!"

An hour later we moved to another job. As I sat in the truck I racked my mind for some way to convince Captain Jones that I was not "uppity," and at the same time to maintain self-respect. I hit upon two ideas. I would try to work more willingly and harder than anyone in the crew, and I would be as polite and considerate as possible.

When the truck stopped and we were ordered out, I made an effort to carry through my resolution by beginning work immediately. In my haste I came within twenty feet of the guard.

"Stop, you bastard!" he screamed, and pointed his revolver at my head. "Git back, git back. Don't rush me or I'll shoot the goddamned life out of you."

With heart pounding I moved across the road. Purple walked up to me, put a shovel in my hand, and said, "Follow me and do what I do."

We worked together spading heavy clay mud and throwing it into the truck. An hour later, when the walking boss went down the road for a Coca Cola, I complained to Purple about my aching arms. Purple smiled, patted me on the back, and said as he continued to work, "Man born of black woman is born to see black days."

But my first black day was not yet over. Just after lunch we had begun to do what the chain-gangers call "jumpin' shoulders," which means cutting the top from the shoulders of the road when they have grown too high. Usually the crew works with two trucks. There is scarcely a moment of delay and the work is extremely hard. Captain Jones was displeased with the rate of our work, and violently urged us to greater effort. In an attempt to obey, one of the chain-gangers struck another with his shovel. The victim complained, instantly and profanely. The words were hardly out of his mouth before the Captain strode across the road and struck the cursing chain-ganger in the face with his fist again and again. Then Captain Jones informed the crew, using the most violent profanity, that cursing would not be tolerated.

"Not for one goddamned moment," he repeated over and over.

No one spoke; every man tried to work harder yet remain inconspicuous. The silence seemed to infuriate the Captain. He glared angrily at the toiling men, then yelled to the armed guard.

"Shoot hell out of the next one you find cursin'. Shoot straight for his feet. Cripple 'em up. That will learn 'em."

The guard lifted his rifle and aimed it at the chest of the man nearest him.

"Hell, no!" he drawled. "I ain't aimin' fer no feet. I like hearts and livers. That's what really learns 'em."

Everyone spaded faster.

On the ride back to camp that evening, I wondered aloud if this were average behavior for Captain Jones.

"Well," said Easy Life, "that depends on how many headache powders and Coca Colas he takes. Must of had a heap today."

Back in camp Easy Life continued the conversation.

"Dat was nothin', really," he said. "Cap'n might have done them up like the Durham police did that old man over there."

He pointed to a small, thin man in his middle fifties, dragging himself slowly toward the washroom. His head was covered with bandages and one eye was discolored and bruised.

"Dad," as the men already were calling him, had come up from the country to Durham a few days before for a holiday. He had got drunk, and when the police tried to arrest him he had resisted, and they had beaten him with blackjacks. After three days in jail he was sentenced to Roxboro. When he got to the prison camp he complained that he was ill, but nonetheless was ordered to go out on the job. After working an hour, Dad told the walking boss that he was too sick to continue and asked if he could be brought in. He was brought in and the doctor summoned, but he had no temperature and the doctor pronounced him able to work. When he refused to go back to his pick and shovel he was ordered "hung on the bars" for seventy-two hours.

When a man is hung on the bars he is stood up facing his cell, with his arms chained to the vertical bars, until he is released (except for being unchained periodically to go to the toilet). After a few hours, his feet and often the glands in his groin begin to swell. If he attempts to sleep, his head falls back with a snap, or falls forward into the bars, cutting and bruising his face. (Easy Life told me how Purple had been chained up once and gone mad, so that he began to bang his head vigorously against the bars. Finally the night guard, fearing he would kill himself, unchained him.)

The old man didn't bang his head. He simply got weaker and weaker, and his feet swelled larger and larger, until the guard became alarmed, cut the old man down, and carried him back to bed.

The next day the old man was ordered out to work again, but after he had worked a few minutes he collapsed and was brought back. This time the doctor permitted him to be excused from work for a week. At the end of the week, when Dad came back to work, he was still very weak and tired but was expected to keep up the same rate of work as the other members of the crew.

A few days later, I told several of the boys that I had decided to talk to the Captain to try to improve relations on the job, since I was sure the guards were taking it out on the men because of me. They urged me to keep still. "Quiet does it," they said. "No need to make things worse," they admonished. "He'll kick you square in the ass," Purple warned.

Nevertheless I stopped the Captain that morning and asked to speak with him. He seemed startled. I told him that I knew there were great differences in our attitudes on many questions but that I felt we could be friends. I said that on the first morning, when I had failed to address him as "Sir," I had meant no disrespect to him and if he felt I had been disrespectful I was willing to apologize. I suggested that perhaps I was really the one who deserved to be beaten in the face, if anyone did. I was willing to work as hard as I could, and if I failed again at my work I hoped he would speak to me about it and I would try to improve. Finally I said I could not help trying to act on the basis of my own Christian ideals about people but that I did try to respect and understand those who differed with me.

He stared at me without a word. Then after several moments he turned to the gun guard and said in an embarrassed tone, "Well, I'll be goddamned." Then he shouted, "Okay, if you can work, get to it! Talk ain't gonna git that there dirt on the truck. Fill her up." (Later I learned that the Captain had said to one of the chain-gangers that he would rather I call him a "dirty-son-of-a-bitch" than to look him in the face "and say nothin'.")

That evening he called us together.

"This Yankee boy ain't so bad," he said. "They just ruined him up there 'cause they don't know how to train you-all. But I think he'll be all right and if you-all will help him I think we can learn him. He's got a strong back and seems to be willing."

The chain-gangers glanced at one another. As we piled into the truck one of them turned to me and said, "When he says he'll learn you, this is what he means:

"When you're white you're right,
When you're yellow you're mellow,
When you're brown you're down,
When you're black, my God, stay back!"

The chain-gangers laughed. We pulled the canvas over our heads to protect us from the rain that had begun to pour down, and headed back to camp to eat supper.

The book of regulations said: "No talking will be permitted in the dining hall during meals." Not until I experienced it did I realize what a meal is like when a hundred men are eating in one room without a word spoken. The guards stood with clubs under their arms and watched us. I had the feeling they too were unhappy in the uneasy silence.

At one evening meal, I was trying by signs to make the man next to me understand that I wanted the salt. I pointed toward the salt and he passed the water, which was close by. I pointed again, and he passed the syrup. When I pointed again, he picked up the salt and banged it down angrily against my plate. Forgetting the rule, I said quietly, "I'm sorry." One of the guards rushed across the room to our table and, with his stick raised, glared at me and said, "If I catch you talking, I'll bust your head in." The spoons and forks were no longer heard against the aluminum plates. The dining room was perfectly quiet. The guard swung his club through space a couple of times, then retired to a corner to resume his frustrating vigil. The tin spoons and forks rattled again on the aluminum plates.

The morning after my conversation with Captain Jones we were instructed to go to the cement mixer, where we were to make cement pipe used in draining the roads and building bridges. We had been working twenty minutes when the Captain came to me carrying a new cap. He played with the cap on the end of his finger for a while and stared at my shaved head.

"You're gonna catch your death of cold," he said, "so I brought you a cap. You tip it like all the other boys whenever you speak to the Captain and the guards, or whenever they speak to you."

I had noticed the way the men bowed obsequiously and lifted their hats off their heads and held them in the air whenever they spoke to the guard. I had decided I would rather be cold than behave in this servile way. I thanked the Captain, put the cap on my head, and wore it until lunchtime. After lunch I put it in my pocket, never to wear it again in the presence of the Captain or the guards.

Some of the men left their caps in the camp rather than wear them on the job, and for good reason. There was a rule that when leaving for work in the morning a man was not permitted to wear his hat until he was beyond the barbed-wire fence that surrounded the camp. On several occasions, men going to or coming from work would rush thoughtlessly through the gates with their caps on, and be struck severely on the head with a club. As Softshoe, a chain-ganger distinguished for his corns and bunions, said, "No use courting trouble. If you don't wear no hat, you ain't got to doff it."

One day the chain-gangers were on fire with the news that an old prisoner had returned. Bill was slender, tall, good-looking and sang very well. Some three years before he had raped his own three-year-old daughter and been put in jail for a year. This time he was "up" for having raped his eight-year-old niece.

It was difficult to believe all the tales the men told about Bill. One evening he came to me and asked me if I had time to talk with him. We talked for almost two hours. He was quite different from the description I had heard. He had provided well for his family, he had gone to church, but, as he pathetically admitted, he had "made some terrible mistakes." It was apparent that he wanted to wipe the slate clean, but in Roxboro jail he could never discover the reason for his unhappiness and troubles

As I lay awake that night I wondered how ten hours a day of arduous physical labor could help this young man to become a constructive citizen. The tragedy of his being in the prison camp was highlighted by the extraordinary success that good psychiatrists and doctors are having today with men far more mixed up than Bill. I thought of the honesty with which he had discussed himself, of the light in his eyes when he had heard for the first time of the miracles modern doctors perform—and I knew that Bill deserved the best that society could offer him: a real chance to be cured, to return to his wife and children with the "devils cast out."

Then there was a young boy who had been arrested for stealing. It was obvious from his behavior that he was a kleptomaniac. I would see him spend half an hour going from one section of the dormitory to another, waiting, plotting, planning, and conniving to steal many small and useless items. Although he did not smoke, I saw him spend twenty minutes getting into a position to steal a box of matches, which he later threw away.

One day, after I had written a long letter for him, he began to tell me that he had stolen even as a child but that now he wanted to stop. As tears came to his eyes, he explained that he had been able to stop stealing valuable things but that he could not stop stealing entirely. I asked him if he really wanted to change. He said he thought so. But he added: "It's such a thrill. Just before I get my hands on what I'm gonna take, I feel so excited."

After that, as I watched him evening after evening, I wondered how many men throughout the world were languishing in jails—burdens to society— who might be cured if only they were in hospitals where they belonged. One thing was clear. Neither this boy, who reluctantly stole by compulsion, nor Bill could be helped by life on the chain gang. Nor could society be protected, for in a short time these men and thousands like them return to society not only uncured but with heightened resentment and a desire for revenge.

Early one morning Easy Life was talking with one of his friends, who had done time for stealing and was to be released that day. To the despair of those trying to get a few last winks, Easy Life was singing:

> Boys, git up, grab your pone,
> Some to the right-a-ways, some to the road—
> This fool's made it and he's headin' home.

Easy Life's companion smiled and said for all to hear:

> Boys, you stole while I took,
> Now you roll [work hard] while I look.

"I can work," Easy Life said, "and I can work plenty, for work don't bother me none. No sir! Boys, it's the food that gits me down." And he went to rhyming one of his spontaneous verses:

> Kick me, shout me, pull ma teet',
> But lemme go home where I can eat.

As I lay in bed for a few last minutes' rest, I began to think about the food. We had beans—boiled beans, red beans, or lima beans—every day for lunch. Every day, after five long hours of hard physical labor, we had beans, fatback (a kind of bacon without lean meat), molasses, and corn pone. Many of the men who had spent years on the road were no longer able to eat the beans at all, and I saw several men, working for ten hours day after day, with nothing to eat after breakfast for the entire day but molasses and corn pone. One of the most frequently quoted bits of folk poetry described the lunch:

> Beans and cornbread
> Every single day.
> If they don't change
> I'll make my getaway.
> How long, Oh Lord,
> How long?

For breakfast we usually had oatmeal without sugar or milk, a slice of fried baloney, stewed apples, and coffee. In the evening the two typical meals were cabbage and boiled white potatoes, and macaroni and stewed tomatoes. On Sundays the meal consisted of two vegetables, Argentinian corned beef, and apple cobbler. Except for being struck with clubs, the thing that the men complained most about was the food. They often recited another bit of folk poetry:

> The work is hard,
> The boss is mean,
> The food ain't done,
> And the cook ain't clean.

Actually both the cooks and the dining room were relatively clean; the protest was against the monotony of the food.

The hour was getting near for Easy Life's companion to depart. They brought in the pillowcase in which his clothes had been stored three months earlier. As he dumped his clothes onto the bed, they made one shapeless lump. He opened out his pants and began to get into them. They had a thousand creases. Then he put on the dirty shirt he had worn when he came in, and dressed in this way he left to begin a new life. He had no comb or toothbrush or razor, nor a penny in his pocket. The "dog cart" would come to pick him up and drop him somewhere near the railroad station in Durham.

I looked at him, his face aglow, happy that he would once again be "free," and wondered how he could be so happy without a cent, with no job, and with no prospects. I wondered what he would go through to get his first meal, since he had no home. I wondered where he would sleep. He said he knew a prostitute who might put him up. Prostitutes and fairies, he had said, "will always give a guy a break." I wondered where he would find a decent shirt or a pair of pants. Would he beg or borrow or steal?

I wondered if he would return. One day on the job the Captain had offered to bet ten to one that the man would be back before the week was up. As I saw him start forth, so ill prepared to face life in the city, I too felt that he would return. I asked Easy Life what he thought his friend would do when he got to town. Easy Life said, "He'll steal for sure if they don't get him first." I asked him what he meant. He said, "If the bulls don't get him for vagrancy 'fore sundown, he'll probably snatch something for to eat and some clothes to cover his ass with for the night."

"For vagrancy?" I asked.

"For vagrancy! Sure enough for vagrancy," Easy underlined. He then told me the story of a friend from South Carolina who had been on the chain gang. He, like all the others, was released without a penny in his pocket. While thumbing his way home, he was arrested for vagrancy soon after he crossed into South Carolina, and was back in jail for ninety days, less than two days after being released.

Between supper and "lights out" was our time for recreation. But for most of the men it was not a creative period. The rules permitted "harmless games," but there was not one set of checkers or chess or dominoes available, no material for the development of hobbies, and no books, only an occasional comic book. One newspaper came into the place, and few men had access to it. There were no organized sports, no library, no entertainment other than one motion picture a month.

Under these circumstances, recreation was limited to six forms, five of them definitely destructive. The first of these was *dirty dozens,* a game played by one or two persons before an audience. Its object was to outdo one's opponent in grossly offensive descriptions of the opponent's female relatives—mother, sister, wife, or aunt. If a "player" succeeded in making a clever combination of obscene and profane words, the audience burst into laughter, and then quieted down to await the retaliation of the opponent.

He in turn tried to paint a still more degrading picture of the relatives of his partner. No recreation attracted larger crowds or created more antagonism, for often men would be sucked into the game who actually did not want to play and became angered in the course of it.

Another form of recreation was the *telling of exaggerated stories about one's sex life.* These included tales of sexual relations with members of the same sex, with animals, with children and close relatives, and with each other. It was generally recognized that 70 per cent of these tales were untrue, but the practice led to lying, to experimentation in abnormal sex relations, and to a general lowering of the moral standards of younger inmates, who continually were forced into the position of advocating strange practices as a means of maintaining status with the group.

Stealing "for the thrill of it" was yet another way in which numbers of men entertained themselves. One of the best friends I had in the camp had stolen stamps from me, returned them, and then described to me how he had done it. He had sent a friend to talk with me and had given the man who slept in the bed next to mine an old comic book to reduce the possibility of being detected. I asked him why he went to all that trouble, only to return my stamps. He explained that he had stamps, but, having nothing else to do, he wanted to "keep my hands warm."

Gambling was perhaps the chief form of recreation for those who had anything to gamble with. Men gambled for an extra sock stolen on the day of clothing exchange, or a sandwich smuggled from the kitchen, or a box of matches. The three games most widely used for gambling were Tonk and Skin, games played with an ordinary deck of cards, and throwing dice. Cheating was simple and common and led to constant arguments.

There was little or no effort to control the gambling, though it was against the rules. When a new night guard came on duty and complained to an old hand that the boys were playing dice in the rear of the dormitory, the older guard was overheard to say, "What da hell do I care! They gotta do sumpin, and dice keep 'em quiet."

Gossip and talking about one's sentence also consumed a great deal of time. Over and over again men related the story of their trial and told one another how they were "framed on bum raps." The gossip session was the stool pigeon's chief means of getting information to carry "up front." Even though men feared talking about one another, they did so because they felt that the gossip-mongers had to have something to tell the superintendent. As one of the chain-gangers expressed it, "That stool pigeon has got to sing sumpin, so it's better for me to give him sumpin good [i.e., helpful information for the authorities] to carry about somebody else, before somebody gives him sumpin bad to carry about me." This created an atmosphere of universal mistrust.

The most creative form of recreation was *rhyming and singing.* There were several quartets and trios and much informal singing, both on the job and in the dormitory. The poetry was almost always a description of life in the camp or of the desire for women or of the "fear of time." Occasionally it was the bragging of a tough guy:

> I was born in a barrel of butcher knives,
> Sprayed all over with a forty-five.
> Bull constrictor bit me.
> He crawled off and died.
> I hoboed with lightnin'
> And rode the black thunder,
> Rode through the graveyards
> And caused the dead folks to wonder.
> Sixty-two inches across my chest,
> Don't fear nothin' but the devil and death.
> I'll kick a bear in the rear
> And dare a lion to roar.

Much of the best poetry was directed against those who complained. The following is an excellent example:

> Quit cryin'!
> Quit dyin'!
> Give dat white man
> Sumpin on your time.
>
> I would-a told you,
> But I thought you knowed,
> Ain't no heaven
> On the county road.
>
> Six months ain't no sentence,
> Twelve months ain't no time,
> Done been to penitentiary
> Doing ninety-nine.
>
> Quit cryin'!
> Quit dyin'!
> Give dat white man
> Sumpin on your time.

The following verses are some of the more imaginative statements about the relationship between the chain-gangers and the walking bosses and guards.

Cap'n got a pistol and he thinks he's bad;
I'll take it tomorrow if he makes me mad.

What I want for dinner they don't serve here.
Thirty-two thirty and some cold, cold beer.

Cap'n says hurry. Walker say run.
Got bad feet—can't do more 'n one.

One of the most stifling elements of life on the road gang is the authoritarianism. The prisoner's life is completely regulated. He is informed that obedience will be rewarded and disobedience punished. Section 1 of the rules and regulations makes this clear.

> Every prisoner upon arrival at any prison after being sentenced by the court shall be informed of the rules and regulations of the camp and advised what the consequences will be if he violates these rules. He shall also be informed as to what privileges he will receive if he obeys the rules and conducts himself properly.

Such unquestioning obedience may appear to be good and logical in theory, but in experience authoritarianism destroys the inner resourcefulness, creativity, and responsibility of the prisoner and creates, in wardens and prisoners alike, an attitude that life is cheap. The following illustrations indicate the degree to which respect for personality is violated.

—One day when we were digging ditches for draining Highway 501, we were working in water about a foot deep. A chain-ganger who had very large feet could not be fitted to boots. After attempting to do as much as he could from the dry banks of the ditch, he finally tried to explain to the Captain that he could not work in water over his shoe tops. "Get the hell in that water—I don't give a good goddamn if it is up to your ass," the Captain yelled at him. "You should have thought about that before you came here. The judge said ninety days, and he didn't say nuthin' about your havin' good ones."

—The walking boss was heard commenting on one of his ace workers who had come back for the third time. "Now ain't that a shame—and he only got a year. I sure wish he had ten or more."

—Every day after lunch the walking bosses and armed guards would send the food remaining in their lunch kits to the chain-gangers. After the kits had been emptied, I noticed that the water boy always filled one of them with the corn pone from the prisoners' meal. One day I asked the water boy why he did this. He explained that the Captain fed that "stinkin' pone to his pigs." For a moment no one spoke. Then Softshoe said, "Pigs and convicts."

—Visiting days were the first and third Sundays of the month; visiting hours, from one to four. The visiting took place in the prison yard. There were two wire fences about five feet apart. The convicts stood in front of one, the visitors behind another. There in the yard, in summer, winter, rain, snow, sleet, they talked—if they could be heard. Visiting day was an event both longed for and dreaded because, as one of the chain-gangers so aptly put it, "We gotta meet the home folks like animals in the zoo."

—The supreme authority in a state prison camp is the superintendent. The superintendent at Roxboro was a silent man who appeared chiefly at mealtimes. His major contacts with the men came when he observed them as they ate and when he directed them to their work in the morning. One of the few times I heard him speak to the men was when a newly arrived inmate violated one of the many petty rules of the dining hall and came down the wrong aisle. The superintendent raised his club and said, "Get around there before I knock the shit out of you."

We must bear in mind that one result of the authoritarian system is to develop in the prisoners many of the same attitudes they themselves decry in the officials. The majority of the prisoners accept the idea that punishment can be just. In fact they share this basic premise with most of the judges whom they eternally criticize. Many prisoners would be more severe than judges in making the punishment fit the crime. In discussing a young man who had raped two children I heard Easy Life say, "The no-good bastard should have got ninety-nine years and one dark day." When a young man came into the camp who reportedly had stolen eight hundred dollars, his mother's life savings, a prisoner suggested, "They should have built a jail on top of him." To which another replied, "That's too damn good for the bastard. They should have gassed him, but quick."

The prisoners, like the judges, hold the superstition that two wrongs can make a right. A chain-ganger claims that his incarceration clears him; hence the deprivations of prison life are equal to his crime. He feels he is doubly absolved when he gets the worst of the bargain. But any punishment that affects his body or causes him to fear while in prison, he looks upon as unjustified. Consequently he feels, often while in prison and certainly upon release, that he is entitled to avenge this injustice by becoming an enemy of society. Thus the theory that two wrongs make a right becomes a vicious circle, destructive to wardens, prisoners, and society.

Let us see what the punishments are on the chain-gang. Section 5 of the rules book states:

> For Minor Offenses—[The superintendent will be permitted to] handcuff [the prisoner] and require [him] to remain in standing or sitting position for a reasonable period of time.

This form of punishment produces swollen feet and wrists, muscular cramps, and physical fatigue. During the period, if the prisoner is standing up, he does not eat but is taken down for fifteen or twenty minutes every few hours to urinate, defecate, and relax.

> For Major Offenses—Corporal punishment, with the approval of the Chairman of the State Highway and Public Works Commission, administered with a leather strap of *the approved type* and by some prison officer other than the person in immediate charge of said prisoner and only after physical examination by a competent physician, and such punishment must be administered either in the presence of a prison physician or a prison chaplain.

Another section of the rules book dealing with punishment and discipline states that the superintendent may place a prisoner on "restricted diet and solitary confinement, the period of punishment to be approved by the disciplinarian."

One chain-ganger whom I got to know very well had recently finished a period of such confinement in "the hole." For fourteen days James had been without any food except three soda crackers a day. "The bastards gave me all the water I could drink, and I'll be damned if I wasn't fool enough to drink a lot of it. Soon I began to get thinner, but my gut got bigger and bigger till I got scared and drank less and less till I ended by drinking only three glasses a day."

Although he was very weak, he was forced to go to work immediately. He was expected to work as hard as the others and be respectful to the same captain he felt was responsible for his hardship.

James had been sentenced to sixty days for larceny, which good behavior would have reduced to forty-four days. Because of one surly remark he not only had to spend fourteen days in that unlighted hole, on crackers and water, but also lost the sixteen days of good time. Actually James had begun to hate himself as much as he hated the Captain. "A man," he said, "who tips his hat to a son-of-a-bitch he hates the way I hate him ain't no man at all. If I'd-a been a man, I'd-a split his head wide open the minute I got half a chance."

Some punishments were administered that were not listed in the rules book, as when officers kicked, punched, or clubbed the inmates.

One day when we were working at the cement mixer I heard the Captain yelling to an elderly man that he had better increase his rate and do more work. The old man attempted to work faster. "Cap'n says I'm lazy, but I'm plumb wore out," he complained. Then I noticed the Captain rushing toward him. "You goddamn lazy bastard," the Captain shouted. "I told you to get to work. When I work a man, I expect a man's work." As the old fellow turned to the Captain and began to explain that he was tired, the Captain kicked him heavily and said, "Don't talk, work." When the Captain had gone away, the old man said over and over, in mixed fear and resignation, "The Captain says I'm lazy, but I'm plumb wore out."

One chain-ganger, a man named Joe, aged about fifty-two, was at the camp for thirty days—his fifth or sixth time to receive that same sentence for drunkenness. He said he was tired all the time, that he had pains in his back. Some of the chain-gangers said he was "damn lazy." For two days the Captain urged him to work harder. "Get some earth on that spade. I'm getting tired of you, Joe. You'd better give me some work." All the second day the Captain kept his eye on Joe. In mid-afternoon he walked over to Joe and said, "You're not going to do no work till I knock hell out you." He calmly struck Joe several times vigorously in the face. "Now maybe that will learn you," the Captain said as he walked away. Joe took off his cap, bowed obsequiously, and said, "Yessa, yessa, that sure will learn me." When the Captain had walked away Joe spat on the ground and said, "He's a dirty son-of-a-bitch and I hope he rots in hell."

The first thing a man did when he awoke in the morning was to look out the window. "How's the weather?" was always the first question. A heavy rain meant a day without work, and the fellows prayed for "sweet rain." It was not just because the work was hard but also for four other reasons, all having to do with working conditions:
1. The work was never done.
2. Thought and creativity in any form were not permitted.
3. Staying "under the gun" made for crowded, tense conditions.
4. The men felt like "things" rather than people on the job.

I believe they most disliked the feeling that no matter how hard they toiled, "the work on the highway ain't never done." When one job was finished there was always another. "Let's ride," the Captain would say, and off we would go. One fellow complained, "If we only knew that we had so much

to do in a day, then I wouldn't mind the aches so much 'cause I could look
to some rest at the end."

I had never before realized the importance, even to men doing the most
monotonous manual labor, of knowing clearly the reasons for doing a job,
and the dejection of spirit that subconsciously creeps in when men cannot
see a job completed. One day when we dug out patches in the road which
another crew would fill in, Purple expressed this feeling: "I reckon these
holes will be filled by some fool 'rrested in Durham tonight, and he'll wonder where the hell they come from."

On the job the men were not permitted to use the kind of imagination
that they put into their rhymes. Over and over again the walking boss would
say, "Don't try to think. Do what I *tell* ya to do." Once when a resourceful
chain-ganger offered a suggestion that might have improved or simplified the
task, the walking boss said, "*I'm* paid to think; *you're* here to work." Softshoe
used to say,

> When you're wrong, you're wrong,
> But when you're right, you're wrong anyhow.

On two or three occasions when the Captain was away, the assistant walking boss was in charge of the crew. He was quite inexperienced as compared
with one of the chain-gangers, James, who knew almost as much about the
job as the Captain. One day in the Captain's absence James suggested to the
assistant that a ditch should be cut a certain way. The assistant captain ordered otherwise. So fifteen men spent three and a half hours in water and
mud digging a ditch forty feet long, four feet wide, and in places five feet
deep. The next day the Captain told us that the work would have to be re-
done. The men looked knowingly at one another and started digging.

There was a regulation that each prisoner, except the trusties, must at all
times be within eyeshot and gun range of the armed guard. The prisoners
called this "under the gun." Another regulation was that at no time could
a chain-ganger be seen to rest during his ten-hour day except during the
two fifteen-minute smoking periods. These regulations made for continuous
tension.

When digging or clearing ditches, our crew of fourteen to sixteen men
was usually divided, half of them assigned to each side of the road. Since the
amount of work on each side was seldom equal, the logical thing would have
been for the crew that finished first to move on down the road. They could
not do so because then they would not have been "under the gun." Or the
crew that finished first could have rested for a few minutes and then moved

on with the group. But the regulation that "all must be busy at all times" precluded such a step. The solution accepted was to put all fourteen men on one side, where we were jammed in so tightly on one another that work was dangerous, slow, and inefficient. We got on one another's nerves and often struck each other with tools.

Certain men in the crew, to avoid hardship and to give the impression they were working harder than the others, indulged in hiding other men's tools, pushing, or criticizing one another's work in loud voices in order to place themselves in more favored working positions or to get in a good light with the Captain for informing. Whenever we worked on ditches, tension in the evenings in the dormitory often ran high.

To me the most degrading condition of the job was the feeling that "I am not a person; I am a thing to be used." The men who worked us had the same attitude toward us as toward the tools we used. At times the walking bosses would stand around for hours while we worked, seeming to do nothing —just watching, often moving from foot to foot or walking from one side of the road to the other. It was under these conditions that they would select a "plaything." One boy, Oscar, was often "it." Once the bored gun guard ordered Oscar to take off his cap and dance. With a broad smile on his face, he warned Oscar, "I'll shoot your heart out if you don't." As the guard trained his rifle on Oscar's chest, Oscar took off his cap, grinned, and danced vigorously. The guard and the walking boss screamed with laughter. Later most of the crew told Oscar that they hated him for pretending he had enjoyed the experience. But almost any of them would have reacted the same way.

To return to the story of my relations with Captain Jones. He had learned of my case and knew I was from the North. Several chain-gangers agreed that the newsclipping he waved about on the day he first lectured me was the Durham *Sun's* article on my surrender. At any rate I am sure he felt that I was going to shirk and be difficult—that I would try to show off and challenge his authority.

My aims were really far different. I wanted to work hard so I would not be a burden to other chain-gangers. I wanted to accept the imprisonment in a quiet, unobtrusive manner. Only in this way, I believed, could the officials and guards be led to consider sympathetically the principle on which I was convicted. I did not expect them to agree with me, but I did want them to believe I cared enough about the ideals I was supposed to stand for so I could accept my punishment with a sense of humor, fairness, and constructive good will.

It would have been easy to be either servile or recalcitrant. The difficulty was to be constructive, to remove tension, and yet to maintain my balance and self-respect, at the same time giving ample evidence of respect for the Captain's personality.

I found him to be a very fine craftsman, who knew well the skills of his trade. I noted, too, that when it began to rain hard he was much more careful to leave immediately for the dormitory than were most of the other captains. Soon after our first unfortunate encounter, I mentioned these facts to him.

One morning when he came toward me with what I considered a hostile expression on his face (I was unskillfully making cement pipe), I decided to take the initiative. Before he could reach me I called over to him, "Captain Jones, I seem to need help. Would you have the time to show . . . ?" I could not finish my sentence.

"Damn well you need help," he said, but already I could notice a difference in his expression. He showed me how to scrape the steel forms and how to oil them. Thanking him politely, I told him that if he saw me doing poorly I hoped he would speak to me because I wanted to use the rest of my sentence to pick up as much knowledge as possible. He said, "Well, I can learn you," and walked away.

An hour later he returned, looked over my work, found it satisfactory, and said, "Well, Rusty, you're learnin'." That was the first time he had not called me "tall boy" or "hey-you-there."

For three days our relations improved, but on the fourth day when I reported for work he seemed very agitated. It turned out that an informer among the prisoners had told him I was urging the men not to wear caps so as not to have to tip them. Actually I did look upon the tipping of caps as degrading, for most of the men did it as a gesture of respect while inwardly they not only cursed the captains but also lost self-respect. When asked, I had told the men about my attitude but also had made it clear that my first concern was what the tipping did to them inside.

That same day I had another talk with the Captain. He seemed very impatient, but he did listen as I explained my position on wearing caps. Although he said nothing more to me, I later heard that he informed several men who had recently begun to go bareheaded that they should wear caps the year round or not at all. One of the prisoners said, "There is goin' to be some coldheaded spooks 'round here next January!" After that there was no further discussion of the caps and no effort to get men to wear them.

The next morning the Captain offered us cigarettes during smoking period. Since I did not smoke, I felt I should not take any and attempted to return

and have begun to utilize the terrific healing and therapeutic power of forgiveness and nonviolence.

On the final Saturday of my stay, the Captain was away and his assistant directed the work. While the assistant was not so skillful as the Captain, he was more gentle, more considerate, and willing on occasion to consult the crew on procedure. Before we began work he explained clearly what was to be done. For five hours that morning, in the presence of a director who was not tense, who did not curse, and who permitted the men to help plan the work, many constructive things occurred. The men were cooperative, they worked cheerfully, tension was reduced, and the time passed more quickly than usual. When we returned to the dormitory, Purple, who had a way with turning phrases, referred to the morning's work as a "halfday of heaven."

Stealing was the chief problem in the dormitory. The night I arrived, my fountain pen, stamps, razor, and twenty blades were stolen. The next morning my writing paper disappeared. All these things had been locked away in a box, so I decided to follow the policy of not locking up my belongings. I announced that in the future all my stamps, money, food, writing paper, etc., were for the use of the community, but that in order to divide things according to need, I hoped that before anyone took anything he would consult me. As small boxes of food and other things were sent to me, they were added to the community kit. Gradually the following things occurred:

1. After a week, except for four candy bars, there was no stealing from the community kit.

2. Other men made contributions to the community kit.

3. Inmates began to unlock their unsafe strongboxes and bring things to the open community kit for safekeeping. As one of the fellows said, "If anyone is caught snatching from *that* box, the boys won't think much of him."

4. Two packages of cigarettes were stolen from a chain-ganger. Then it was announced that unless they turned up, money would be taken from the community kit to pay for them. The cigarettes were found on the floor the next morning.

Finally there is the example of our party. Near the end of my second week in camp several boxes of candy, cookies, cakes, dates, peanuts, and fruit juice were sent in to be added to the community kit. It was suggested that we have a party, but practically all the inmates were against it. They said, "The fellows will behave like pigs." It would be impossible to keep order, they added, and a few husky people would get all the food.

The decision was that I should select the committee to put on the party. I purposely chose the three men known to be the biggest thieves in the camp, and they accepted. The others were disheartened. "Now we know the party is wrecked. Those guys will eat half the stuff themselves before it even starts!" they groaned.

Nevertheless the boxes were turned over to them to be kept for two days until the party. Except for the disappearance of the four candy bars already mentioned, all the food was kept intact, and six candy bars were donated to replace the four stolen ones. The party itself was well organized and orderly, and the left-over food was returned to the community kit. Perhaps more significant was the fact that one man, noted for stealing, became known as one of the most capable men in the camp. He was so thorough that he appointed a sergeant-at-arms for the party, whose business was to patrol the floor to watch for stealing or disorder. Fortunately the sergeant-at-arms had no business at all and gave up his job before the party was half over.

I certainly do not want to imply that we had in any real sense dealt with the problem of stealing in the camp. However, the stimuli of expectancy, trust, and responsibility had, for the moment at least, brought about positive responses—faithfulness to duty, imagination, and sharing. Would more such gentle stimuli over longer periods of time, accompanied by proper diet, medical care, music education, good quarters, and respectful treatment, be more effective finally than retribution and punishment? If the law of cause and effect still operates in human relations, the answer seems clear.

CIVIL DISOBEDIENCE, JIM CROW,
AND THE ARMED FORCES

It is a real opportunity to speak with American citizens who seriously seek to remove racial and religious intolerance from our national life, for recent history amply reveals that America cannot gain moral leadership in the world until intolerance of minority groups has been eliminated at home. The Journey of Reconciliation was organized not only to devise techniques for eliminating Jim Crow in travel, but also as a training ground for similar peaceful projects against discrimination in such major areas as employment and in the armed services.

The use of these methods against Jim Crow military service is a regrettable necessity. Today no single injustice more bitterly stands out in the hearts and minds of colored people the world over, or continues more successfully to frustrate the United States' efforts abroad, than the continuation of discrimination and segregation in our military forces.

As a follower of the principles of Mahatma Gandhi, I am an opponent of war and of war preparations and an opponent of universal military training and conscription; but entirely apart from that issue, I hold that segregation in any part of the body politic is an act of slavery and an act of war. Democrats will agree that such acts are to be resisted, and more and more leaders of the oppressed are responsibly proposing nonviolent civil disobedience and noncooperation as the means.

On March 22, 1948, A. Philip Randolph and Grant Reynolds, trusted Negro leaders, told President Truman that Negroes "do not propose to shoulder another gun for democracy abroad while they are denied democracy here at home." A few days later, when Mr. Randolph testified before the Senate Armed Services Committee, he declared that he openly would advise and urge Negro and white youth not to submit to Jim Crow military institutions. At this statement, Senator Wayne Morse interrupted and warned Mr. Randolph that "the Government would apply the legal doctrine of treason to such conduct."

A talk delivered by Bayard Rustin on April 11, 1948, accepting a Thomas Jefferson Award "for the advancement of democracy" given by the Council Against Intolerance in America.

This is a highly regrettable statement for a United States Senator to make. Certainly throughout Asia and Africa millions must have agreed with the lovers of freedom here who reasoned that if treason is involved, it is the treason practiced by reactionaries in the North and South who struggle to maintain segregation and discrimination and who thus murder the American creed. The organizers and perpetuators of segregation are as much the enemy of America as any foreign invader. The time has come when they are not merely to be protested. They must be resisted.

The world and the United States should know that there are many younger leaders, both black and white, in positions of responsibility who, not wishing to see democracy destroyed from within, will support Mr. Randolph and Mr. Reynolds.

We know that men should not and will not fight to perpetuate for themselves caste and second-class citizenship. We know that men cannot struggle for someone else's freedom in the same battle in which they fasten semi-slavery more securely upon themselves. While there is a very real question whether any army can bring freedom, certainly a Jim Crow army cannot. On the contrary, to those it attempts to liberate, it will bring discrimination and segregation such as we are now exporting to Europe and to South America. To subject young men at their most impressionable age to a forced caste system, as now outlined in the Universal Military Training and Selective Service bills, is not only undemocratic but will prove to be suicidal.

Segregation in the military must be resisted if democracy and peace are to survive. Thus civil disobedience against caste is not merely a right but a profound duty. If carried out in the spirit of good will and nonviolence, it will prick the conscience of America as Gandhi's campaigns stirred the hearts of men the world over.

Therefore, in the future I shall join with others to advise and urge Negroes and white people not to betray the American ideal by accepting Jim Crow in any of our institutions, including the armed services. Further, I serve notice on the government that, to the extent of my resources, I shall assist in the organization of disciplined cells across the nation to advise resistance and to provide spiritual, financial, and legal aid to resisters.

If Senator Morse and the government believe that intimidation, repression, prison, or even death can stop such a movement, let them examine past struggles for freedom. If the government continues to consider such action treason, let it recall the advice that Justice Jackson gave the German people at the opening of the Nuremberg trials: "Men," he said, "are individually responsible for their acts, and are not to be excused for following unjust demands made upon them by governments." Failure of the German citizens to resist antisocial laws from the beginning of the Hitler regime logically ended in their placing Jews in gas furnaces and lye pits. Justice Jackson indicated in conclusion that individual resistance to undemocratic laws would have been a large factor in destroying the unjust Nazi state.

I believe that American citizens would do well to ponder Mr. Jackson's remarks. Civil disobedience is urged not to destroy the United States but because the government is now poorly organized to achieve democracy. The aim of such a movement always will be to improve the nature of the government, to urge and counsel resistance to military Jim Crow in the interest of a higher law—the principle of equality and justice upon which real community and security depend.

I sincerely hope that millions of Negroes and white people who cherish freedom will pledge themselves now to resist Jim Crow everywhere, including the military establishments. Thereby the United States may, in part, achieve the moral leadership in world affairs for which we so vigorously strive. I urge you to register this intention now with your Senators and Congressmen.

It is my supreme desire that those who resist will do so in that spirit which is without hatred, bitterness, or contention. I trust that all resisters will hold firm to the true faith that only good-will resistance, in the end, is capable of overcoming injustice.

2
THE FIFTIES

MONTGOMERY DIARY

February 21, 1956

I arrived in Montgomery this morning and had an interview with Reverend Abernathy, one of the leaders of the nonviolent protest. The situation is so tense that men watch his home in shifts while he and his family sleep. I was warned that I will be watched while in town and that it is important that I have the bolts tightly drawn on the windows in my hotel. As one person put it, "This is like war. You can't trust anyone, black or white, unless you know him."

This afternoon I talked with E. D. Nixon, whose home was bombed on February 1. For years he has been a fearless fighter for Negro rights. He suspects that his home will be bombed again but says, "They can bomb us out and they can kill us, but we are not going to give in."

Later I sat in on a conference with a committee of the Montgomery Improvement Association, which coordinates the protest activities. Three recommendations were accepted:

1. The movement will always be called a *nonviolent protest* rather than a boycott in order to keep its fundamental character uppermost.

2. A pin should be designed for all those who do not ride the buses, to wear as a symbol of unity, encouragement, and mutual support.

3. The slogan for the movement will be "Victory Without Violence."

Tonight I walked past Reverend King's house. Lights are strung all around the house, and it is being carefully guarded by Negro volunteers. White police patrol the Negro section of town, two by two. A hotel employee advised me not to go into the streets alone after dark. "If you find it necessary to do so, by all means leave in the hotel everything that identifies you as an outsider. They are trying to make out that Communist agitators and New Yorkers are running our protest."

From *Liberation*, April 1956. The magazine's editors asked Bayard Rustin to spend two weeks in Montgomery, Alabama, investigating the bus boycott there. This article is Rustin's report.

February 22

One hundred leaders of the protest received word that they had been indicted. Many of them did not wait for the police to come but walked to the police station and surrendered. E. D. Nixon was the first. He walked into the station and said, "You are looking for me? Here I am." This procedure had a startling effect on both the Negro and the white communities. White community leaders, politicians, and police were flabbergasted. Negroes were thrilled to see their leaders surrender without being hunted down. Soon hundreds of Negroes gathered outside the police station and applauded the leaders as they entered, one by one. Later those who had been arrested were released on $300 bail. They gathered at the Dexter Avenue Baptist Church for a prayer meeting and sang for the first time a song which had been adopted that morning as the theme song for the movement. The four stanzas proclaim the essential elements of a passive struggle—protest, unity, nonviolence, and equality. Sung to the tune of the spiritual, "Give Me That Old-time Religion," the text is:

> We are moving on to vict'ry
> With hope and dignity.
>
> We shall all stand together
> Till every one is free.
>
> We know love is the watchword
> For peace and liberty.
>
> Black and white, all are brothers
> To live in harmony.
>
> We are moving on to vict'ry
> With hope and dignity.

After the prayer meeting I went to the home of Mrs. Jeanette Reece, a Negro woman who had informed the police that she had not known what she was doing when she signed legal papers to challenge bus discrimination in the courts. A few days earlier her attorney, one of the two Negro lawyers in Montgomery, had been arrested for fraud because of Mrs. Reece's retraction. Although the police had provided no protection for King and Nixon after their houses had been bombed, I found two squad cars parked before Mrs. Reece's home. In addition, a policeman was patrolling the area with a machine gun. After ten minutes of negotiation, the police finally permitted me to see Mrs. Reece. Her only comment was, "I had to do what I did or I wouldn't be alive today." I felt sorry for her.

February 23

This morning Reverend King invited me to attend a meeting of the protest committee. The committee decided not to hold any more mass meetings but only prayer meetings. This was to emphasize the moral nature of the struggle. The meetings will center around five prayers:

A prayer for the success of the meeting.

A prayer for strength of spirit to carry on nonviolently.

A prayer for strength of body to walk for freedom.

A prayer for those who oppose us.

A prayer that all men may become brothers to live in justice and equality.

This afternoon at three-thirty the Negroes began to fill the church for the seven o'clock prayer meeting. From four o'clock on, without leadership, they sang and prayed. Exactly at seven the one hundred who had been arrested worked their way to the pulpit through five thousand cheering men, women, and children. Overnight these leaders had become symbols of courage. Women held their babies to touch them. The people stood in ovation. Television cameras ground away, as King was finally able to open the meeting. He began: "We are not struggling merely for the rights of Negroes but for all the people of Montgomery, black and white. We are determined to make America a better place for all people. Ours is a nonviolent protest. We pray God that no man shall use arms."

February 24

Forty-two thousand Negroes have not ridden the buses since December 5. On December 6, the police began to harass, intimidate, and arrest Negro taxi drivers who were helping to get these people to work. It thus became necessary for the Negro leaders to find an alternative—the car pool. They set up twenty-three dispatch centers where people gather to wait for free transportation.

This morning Rufus Lewis, director of the pool, invited me to attend the meeting of the drivers. On the way, he explained that there are three methods, in addition to the car pool, for moving the Negro population: hitchhiking, the transportation of servants by white housewives, and walking.

Later he introduced me to two men, one of whom has walked seven miles and the other fourteen miles every day since December 5.

"The success of the car pool is at the heart of the movement," Lewis said at the meeting. "It must not be stopped."

I wondered what the response of the drivers would be, since twenty-eight of them had just been arrested on charges of conspiring to destroy the bus company. One by one they pledged that, if necessary, they would be arrested again and again.

This afternoon the coordinating committee rejected a proposal that people be asked to stop work for one hour on March 28. I was impressed with the leaders' response, which adhered to the Gandhian principle of consideration for one's opponents. As King put it, "We do not want to place too much of a burden upon white housewives nor to give them the impression that we are pushing them against the wall."

This evening a few of the leaders got together to consider a constructive program for inculcating the philosophy of nonviolence in the community. After hours of serious discussion, several proposals were accepted. The following impressed me as being particularly significant:

An essay contest for high school students on the subject "Why We Should Use Nonviolence in Our Struggle."

The distribution of a pamphlet on nonviolence.

The importance of preaching nonviolence in the churches.

The possibility of a workshop on the theory and practice of nonviolence.

This meeting concluded with agreement that the committee should do everything possible to negotiate the issues. The Montgomery Improvement Association is asking for these assurances:

Greater courtesy on the part of drivers.

Accepting first-come, first-served seating within the pattern of segregation while the question of intrastate segregation is being decided in the courts.

The employment of some Negro drivers on predominantly Negro routes.

February 25
This morning I had a long talk with Reverend Hughes, a white Southerner who is executive secretary of the Alabama Interracial Council, with offices in Montgomery. Hughes indicated that his association with an interracial group has always tied his hands in dealing with the conservative whites, who distrust anything interracial. Now the liberals, to whom his group normally appeals, are also alienated because of the psychological confusion in the changed situation.

For generations the status quo has been based on violence, with the Negro as victim. A few whites have managed to be liberal without feeling a direct threat to their social position. Now, as the Negroes reach the stage where they make specific, if minimum, demands, a new and revolutionary situation has developed. There is little middle ground on which to maneuver and few compromises that are possible. For the first time, the white liberals are forced to stand for racial justice or to repudiate the liberal principles which they have always wanted to believe in.

The one definite principle they can cling to is to condemn overt violence. Even the nonviolence of the Negroes has not counterbalanced their horror of the violence which they fear will break out sooner or later. The result is that they are immobilized by confusion and fear.

This afternoon I was finally able to get an original copy of a handbill I had been hearing about since I reached Montgomery. It was distributed by unidentified individuals at a meeting sponsored by the White Citizens Council at Montgomery's State Coliseum on February 10. Twelve thousand people attended and Senator Eastland spoke. There's no proof that the leaflet was in any way a part of the official proceedings, but it is reliably reported that thousands of copies were distributed in the meeting hall and that none of the speakers denounced its distribution.

I cannot believe that this leaflet reflects the thinking of all white people in Montgomery. Thousands of them no doubt would be nauseated by it. Yet I report its distribution because such hate literature, against both Negroes and Jews, is being circulated in Alabama and unfortunately is an aspect of the emotional climate in which grave problems must be solved.

The leaflet called for the annihilation of Negroes in these terms:

> When in the course of human events it becomes necessary to abolish the Negro race, proper methods should be used. Among these are guns, bow and arrows, slingshots and knives.
>
> We hold these truths to be self-evident: that all whites are created equal with certain rights; among these are life, liberty and the pursuit of dead niggers.
>
> In every stage of the bus boycott we have been oppressed and degraded because of black, slimy, juicy, unbearably stinking niggers. The conduct should not be dwelt upon because behind them they have an ancestral background of Pygmies, Head hunters and snot suckers.
>
> My friends it is time we wised up to these black devils. I tell you they are a group of two legged agitators who persists in walking up and down our streets protruding their black lips. If we don't stop helping these African flesh eaters, we will soon wake up and find Reverend King in the white house.
>
> LET'S GET ON THE BALL WHITE CITIZENS

This evening I met with several women of the community who were setting up an artistic wing of the movement to carry the philosophy of nonviolence to the community. They designed a pin with a cross (to show that the movement is Christian) and a heart (for nonviolence). Two feet are superimposed as a symbol of walking for freedom. On the branches of the cross will appear the words RESISTANCE, NONVIOLENCE, BROTHERHOOD, and LOVE.

February 26 (Sunday)
Together with a number of Negro and white reporters, I attended King's packed church. He spoke simply, emphasizing the nonviolent nature of the struggle, and told his congregation: "We are concerned not merely to win justice in the buses but rather to behave in a new and different way—to be nonviolent so that we may remove injustice itself, both from society and from ourselves. This is a struggle which we cannot lose, no matter what the apparent outcome, if we ourselves succeed in becoming better and more loving people."

This afternoon I received word that the white community has learned that I am in Montgomery, that I am being watched, and that efforts will be made to get me out of town. I was warned under no circumstances to go into the white areas of the city.

Tonight I spent discussing the protest campaign with Reverend and Mrs. King over coffee in their kitchen. I asked King if he felt that the activities of the White Citizens Council would lead to further bombings and other violence and whether he felt some elements in the Negro community would return violence with violence. He said that he felt the behavior of the White Citizens Council could very easily lead to serious violence and that the results might be catastrophic. "But," he added, "give us six weeks. The spirit of nonviolence may so have permeated our community by that time that the whole Negro community will react nonviolently."

February 27
I learned this morning from reliable sources that there is some indication that the bombing of the King and Nixon homes was not the work of irresponsible youth or cranks, but had the support of powerful vested interests in the community. There is some evidence that even the dynamite used passed through the hands of some people in the community who should be responsible for the maintenance of order.

This afternoon I attended another meeting of the working committee, which has been up against great problems because the protest, originally planned for one day, is now running into the twelfth week. I am impressed with the seriousness and determination of these people. They are handling their money very carefully and anyone who contributes can be certain that the funds will be spent carefully.

Reverend Abernathy concluded the meeting with a statement which was unanimously adopted:

1. We have all worked hard to make our protest known around the world.

2. We have kept our struggle Christian and nonviolent and intend to keep it so.

3. Although many have been arrested, we continue our protest, for none of our actions has been illegal.

4. The car pool continues.

5. All who were arrested are out on bail, thanks to our community's fine spirit.

6. We have received moral support and encouragement from all over the United States.

7. The NAACP will help us carry on the legal aspects of the struggle.

8. We shall have occasional days of prayer and pilgrimage.

9. We pray God for strength to carry on nonviolently.

As I watched the people walk away, I had a feeling that no force on earth can stop this movement. It has all the elements to touch the hearts of men.

FEAR IN THE DELTA

The 1950 United States Census records that there are about two million people in Mississippi. Almost half of these are Negroes, living predominantly in the northwestern corner of the state. This section, the cotton-producing Delta, is the backbone of the state. There the real economic and political power is concentrated. Much of the remainder of Mississippi is poor and the people depressed.

It was with these facts in mind that Senator Eastland recently said at a meeting of the White Citizens Council: "Whoever controls the Delta controls Mississippi." The Senator made this remark in discussing the potential registration and voting power of Negroes in the state. Before him stood a large map of the twenty counties in and around the Delta where the Negro population is two and three times larger than the white.

After carefully impressing these "frightful figures" upon his audience he concluded, "We must not be overrun; our way of life must not be taken away by usurping courts or by the subversive NAACP." What he really meant was this: Under no circumstances must the Negro in the Delta vote. While numerically white men can control him forever in the remainder of the state, they could not in the Delta. If the Negro votes there, he will outvote the whites, integration will come, white economic privileges resting on segregation will be destroyed and, according to Eastland, the whites therefore enslaved.

The Senator has spent this summer building fences and making similar talks in crowded halls throughout the Delta. One must see through the political demagoguery and understand the Senator's aims, tactics, and appeal if one is to understand the elements of reaction in the South today, to feel the pressure upon confused white workers, to sense the businessmen's fear of the NAACP, and to appreciate the position of white liberals. In a profound sense the Senator speaks for the Delta. It is the voice of fear: first, the white men's fear of losing their favored position; then, their fear that if ever the Negro wins equality, he will use his overwhelming political power to give

This record of Bayard Rustin's journey into the Emmett Till country of Mississippi appeared in part in the magazine *Liberation*, October 8, 1956.

the white man the same kind of treatment he has given the Negro—and which the white man feels he himself deserves.

Fear in the Delta is Kenya's fear; reaction to fear in the Delta is South Africa's reaction. If one is fully to understand the forces at work in the Southern mind and heart today, one must know what fear has wrought upon the Delta:

—Emmett Till was kidnaped and brutalized there, and his confessed kidnapers and proved murderers released as "innocent."

—The NAACP is feared by many black men and hated by almost all white people.

—The legislature has provided for a private school system at state expense.

—Economic pressure is brought against the eight thousand Negroes who have dared to register and attempted to vote.

—Negro leaders are systematically driven from the state or murdered in cold blood.

—Negro farmers are driven from their land by intimidation and by economic double-dealing.

—Police brutality is widespread.

—The state has recently passed an amendment raising voter qualifications in an effort to disfranchise the Negro further.

—Federal agencies such as the Farm Home Administration are locally misused as a means of controlling and harassing Negro workers and farmers.

All this has begun in the Delta. It was, moreover, at Indianola, in the heart of the Delta, that the White Citizens Council was founded in 1954. Today this organization dedicated to white supremacy holds the state in its grip and dares pulpit, labor, press, or citizens openly to defy it. No one does. Fear has settled over the Delta.

KU KLUX KLAN IN BUSINESS SUITS

On May 17, 1954, the United States Supreme Court outlawed segregation in public education. By October 12, 1954, the White Citizens Council of Indianola, Mississippi, had become a state-wide organization. Today its first major report of accomplishments boasts:

> In less than two years of activity, 65 of our 82 counties in Mississippi have been organized with a membership of 80,000. . . . The state office has published over two million pieces of literature in the 48 states . . . which give concrete, convincing reasons for the absolute necessity of maintaining segregation in the South.
>
> REPORT TO EXECUTIVE COMMITTEE," AUGUST 1956

The report then calls the committee's attention to the declaration of March 12, 1956, by 101 Southern Congressmen attacking the Supreme Court decision, and concludes:

> The Citizens Council is proud of the part it played in the expression of this sentiment against the tyrannical actions of the Supreme Court.

Section two of the report deals with the NAACP:

> We have proven to our Negro citizens that the NAACP is a left-wing, power-mad organ of destruction that cares nothing about the Negro. We have the support of the thinking, conservative Negro people who believe in segregation. We want to help them develop social pride in a segregated society.

There is no shame expressed in the report as to how this "support of the thinking, conservative Negro people" was in part obtained. It was done by the use of paid Negro agents who have carried tales, some true and many false, creating confusion and discord until no one knows whom he can trust. Many are thus afraid to act at all. The report puts it this way:

> Information is received by the Council concerning all activities of the NAACP. Sources of this information cannot be divulged. It is important that the NAACP leaders in all vicinities be known. A list of the NAACP membership is being compiled.

This compilation of the NAACP list has numerous ramifications. Professional Negroes in the Delta are afraid of economic reprisals and do not now join the NAACP. Teachers, doctors, pharmacists, and businessmen are kept under terrific pressure.

A teacher in Cleveland, Mississippi, would receive me only after dark if I walked to her home. "That NAACP man's car you ride in will cause a commotion. Anyhow, you're a stranger, and somebody may think you are from the NAACP. Come late and walk." At the close of our conversation, she said: "Well, I really don't know what to think, but I know Mr. Smith [a white businessman and member of the WCC] is correct. He said that integration can't happen in Mississippi and if I lose my job the NAACP can't give me one. You can't give me one either, so please don't come here any more and don't speak to me if you see me on the street."

A businessman in Charleston, Mississippi, who is not an NAACP member, told a story too long to repeat in detail. It classically illustrates the forces faced by someone who is even *reported* to be an NAACP member.

Family pressure. His wife finally divorced him and left the South for Chicago.

Harassment. At night his telephone rings constantly. Often no one speaks when he answers it. Occasionally all he hears is "Nigger, nigger" and then silence.

Ostracism. Most of the middle-class Negroes in the town and many of the more prosperous farmers in the county do not speak to him on the street. No one calls at his home any more.

Economic pressure. He cannot buy at wholesale prices in the area.

Fear. A "liberal" white man who had lent him money over the years recently refused to do so again. He said, "Amos, you're a good boy, but I don't know why you won't get out of that NAACP. Don't you have no pride in your race? Anyhow, I can't lend you money. I don't want to be called a nigger-lover."

This pressure is applied to white people also. Some months ago Dr. Alan Knight Chalmers, a white minister long associated with the NAACP, visited Cleveland, Mississippi. He was not on NAACP business. He came out of Christian concern to see if an interracial ministers' committee could be set up to discuss integration. His mission failed, but while in Cleveland he called upon Reverend Duncan Gray, white Episcopal rector. After Dr. Chalmers left town, the rector was threatened, members of his church are reported to have resigned, and he was told, "Leave the state or behave yourself."

The Council not only threatens the progressive Negroes and white people in the community, but, as its report makes clear, it

> has given backing to the conservative class of Negro in the area
> and has given them courage to speak out in opposition to the
> radical NAACP element.

In the Delta the Negro church is bought and paid for by the Council, with very few exceptions. Many ministers are in debt to members of the Citizens Council. These clergymen denounce the NAACP as radical and misguided. They call for "a new Booker T. Washington—someone to lead who is not interested in racial equality."

On September 30, I was invited to speak at a county-wide song contest at Mt. Moria Baptist Church near Bobo, Mississippi. At the end of the meeting I told the story of the Montgomery protest and related the walking of Negroes there to Moses walking with the Hebrew children out of slavery in Egypt. The talk was received by the rural population with enthusiasm. But no sooner had I sat down than Reverend J. A. Butler was on his feet urging the people to remember that God alone, in his own good time, could lead the Negro to freedom. The congregation sat in absolute silence as he spoke.

When the service was over, some of the country people got in their old cars and drove away while the rest walked. Reverend Butler kissed a few children, climbed into his Cadillac, warned me not to stir things up lest I get his flock into trouble, and drove away.

As he picked up speed well down the road, a young sharecropper turned to me and said: "I liked your sermon, Brother Rustin. Now don't you pay Reverend Butler no mind. The white folks pays for his car and he's satisfied. But you better be careful. He's headin' toward Mr. Smith's now to tell him what you been preachin'."

Where the bought clergy and frightened middle class don't pay off, stronger methods are used. A good example is the careful plan carried out by the WCC in Charleston, Mississippi.

Three years ago Charleston had a small but thriving NAACP group; today it has only four members. They operate as the underground did in Nazi Germany. On the surface all is well, and recently nobody has tried to vote or to discuss integration. What caused this group, so active a short time ago, to become so quiet now?

The militant leader in Charleston, Robert Smith, had urged the Negroes to vote, had said integration was inevitable, so why not now? He was a good farmer and collected burial insurance. He was prosperous.

Then one day he was seen talking to a white man downtown. The woman who saw him said he looked mighty scared. That night he left town. Nobody yet knows why. All anyone will say is, "Don't know how they got him out. It must have been something terrible, 'cause he was a good man and he always stood up and fought for his people." But Robert Smith is gone. Behind him he left a business, a house, a truck, and his farm. No one, not even his sister, knows for sure where he is. "Some folks," she says, "tell me he's in Chicago. God knows. He might be dead."

A few weeks after Robert Smith disappeared, John Wesley Logan was sitting in a dingy Negro cafe talking with his wife. The waitress called him to the phone. When he returned to the table he told his wife that he had to "see some white man about a job." The next day they pulled him out of Tilletopa Creek. All his wife could say was, "He sure beat up a poor white man who insulted him a while back. I guess the white folks done got him." Everyone in town knew John Wesley Logan was the only day laborer who would not say "Sir," and who bragged that "I hits white folks if they hits me."

"John Wesley Logan weren't cold in the ground yet," an old man said, "before Professor J. R. Gray lost his job at Sherman Creek, down the road a piece." For "his great learnin'," Professor Gray was greatly beloved by Negroes all over the county, but, they say, "He sure made two bad mistakes." He gave the impression that he was against segregation and he bought a car outside the county because he could get it cheaper. But nobody knows for sure, because Professor Gray has never said. He left school after many years and started to farm. "Folks say he doin' fairly well. Got two bales of cotton this year. "But," said the old man, "he done lost his purpose and his self-respect. You can see dat in his face. Poor man, he don't look like the same person."

Five miles down the road from Professor Gray's farm, the Reverend L. Terry used to have his rural church and a neat cabin alongside it. Every morning during the Emmett Till trial, Reverend Terry put on his best clothes and drove over to Sumner. He sat erect in the court. One day he paused and shook hands with Representative Diggs of Michigan, who was at the trial, and the following Sunday he told his congregation that Diggs was one of the "smartest and most politest men" God had given him the pleasure to gaze upon. The following Wednesday Reverend Terry called a meeting of his board and told them that for the good of the community he was leaving town. Six carloads of white men with shotguns had told him to get out or innocent people would suffer with him. He sold his cabin and his car. He left the next day for Arkansas. "Some weeks later," the old man said, "one of those same crackers who run him off bought his plantation for half what it was worth. It's a sin, son. It's a sin."

Now Charleston is quiet. Robert Smith, symbol of integration, is gone. John Wesley Logan, symbol of dignity, is dead. Reverend Terry is gone, and whatever militancy the Negro church has went with him. Yes, Charleston on the surface is quiet. And some fearful Negro businessmen have been given courage to speak out in opposition to the radical NAACP element. The WCC further reports that "inroads of NAACP upon local Negro sentiment have been severely crushed." This is true. But outside this sentiment and beneath the quiet are four Negroes who love their race, who respect the NAACP, and who are quietly carrying on in Charleston—underground.

Another and similar method of keeping Negroes from pressing for equality in the Delta was made clear by Edward Pemberton, Bolivar County chairman of the White Citizens Council. After he had ruthlessly driven a family of "uppity niggers" from his land, he told them: "Now you'll go to the NAACP and see if they can take care of you. You niggers can't live unless we let you. Your food, your work, and your very lives depend on good-hearted white

67

people. When the likes of you learn your place, race relations can be cordial. Trouble is, you don't respect your race." In other words, if you want to eat, to work, and to live, denounce integration for all to hear.

The most servile Negroes are suspect, and every means is used to impress upon them the power of the White Citizens Councils. Even police brutality can be put to good use. An incident in Ruleville, Sunflower County, birthplace of the Council, will illustrate the point. Preston Johns, Negro renter on Senator Eastland's plantation near Blane, is a "good nigger who knows his place." One day in May 1955, Preston's wife got into a fight with another Negro woman in the Jim Crow section of the Ruleville theater. The manager threw the women out and notified the police. While the police were questioning the women, Preston's daughter came up to see what was happening to her mother. Without warning, a policeman struck her over the head with the butt of his gun. She fell to the pavement bleeding badly. The police left her there. Someone went for her father. When he came up, the police threatened to kill him. Preston left and called Mr. Scruggs, one of Eastland's cronies. After half an hour, Scruggs came and permitted the girl to be lifted from the street and taken to the hospital.

When Scruggs left, he yelled to the Negroes across the street: "You'll see who your friend is. If it wasn't for us Citizens Council members, she'd have near about died." One old Negro answered back, "I been tellin' these niggers Mr. Scruggs and Mr. Eastland is de best friends dey got." A few days later, Senator Eastland came to Ruleville to look the situation over. Many Negroes lined the streets and beamed at their "protector."

MR. PATTERSON'S MASTER PLAN

Among the group of fourteen men who formed the first White Citizens Council in the living room of Dave Hawkins of Indianola, Mississippi, was one Robert Patterson. Patterson later became secretary of the Citizens Councils of Mississippi, and, in January 1956, he became executive secretary of the Citizens Councils of America upon its formation in New Orleans. The national headquarters is at Patterson's office in Greenwood, Mississippi.

According to its stated purpose, the national movement is "dedicated to the maintenance of peace, good order and domestic tranquillity in our communities and our state and to the preservation of states' rights."

According to documents smuggled from Patterson's headquarters, read by this reporter, and hurriedly returned, it appears that his idea of the "maintenance of peace, good order and domestic tranquillity" begins with what he calls the master plan. The plan has what a wise old Negro woman described as a "smart but ignorant" introduction in which Patterson finally concludes that tens of thousands of Negroes will vote in Mississippi within ten years "as the result of congressional, judicial and executive action which the South cannot stop short of widespread violence." He has no illusions that cloture can be maintained in the United States Senate.

These are not surprising admissions, since on Thursday, August 30, Senator Eastland, speaking before the Cleveland, Mississippi, Rotary Club, had said:

> The South has absolutely no influence with the Judiciary of the United States and is losing ground on cloture in the Senate. We have nineteen sure votes and we need thirty-four to block civil rights legislation. The control of the legislative machinery enjoyed by the South, due to seniority, is our only source of power.

What is surprising, however, is Patterson's bold solution to this problem. His plan calls for at least 500,000 Negroes to leave Mississippi by 1966. About 200,000 will leave voluntarily, having been forced out by the tractor, the mechanical cotton picker, the desire of the younger generation to head for the cities, and the decline of the small independent farmer. Another 100,000 will leave "if industries coming into the state are made to understand that Negroes are not to be hired." The remaining 200,000 may need to be "assisted to leave through economic pressure."

For those who are concerned lest the absence of Negro labor create problems, the Patterson plan is reassuring. Plantations will grow in size. Skeletal groups of "Negroes who have pride in their race"—that is, who believe in segregation—will be kept on "under the supervision of strict and carefully trained white supervisors." They will live in "modern but strictly segregated compounds." They will have good housing, hot water, bathrooms, and be permitted to establish their own churches. Just as Southern industry now has chaplains paid by management, so large farmers will be encouraged to hire "good spiritual leadership" for the segregated compounds. In other words, of the 70 per cent of the Negro population who are tenants and sharecroppers, over half, according to the Patterson plan, are to leave the state.

Already thousands of Negroes are leaving the Delta. Last year 240 Negro families were tenants on the R. M. Dakin plantation, one of the largest in the Delta. This fall all but forty families have been told to leave. Machinery and the Patterson plan are replacing them.

The plan also calls for driving the radical NAACP element out of the state immediately. It is argued that the masses of Negroes "will do what is for the common good" if only the dangerous leaders are curbed or driven out first. To understand how completely in earnest Mr. Patterson undoubtedly is requires only the most cursory recital of the fate of Negroes who have stood up for their rights in the Delta:

—On May 7, 1954, the Reverend George Lee of the Belzoni, Mississippi, NAACP was shot and killed on the street after refusing to stop distributing literature urging Negroes to vote.

—In November 1955, Gus Courts, chairman of the Belzoni NAACP, was shot for carrying on the fight in which Reverend Lee was killed. After a month in the hospital and a short stay in Jackson, Mississippi, he left the state for Texas.

—In Columbus, Mississippi, a cafe thought to belong to Dr. Emmett Stringer was forced to close. His wife was threatened night after night.

—Shots were fired into the home of Dr. McCoy, the president of the state NAACP conference, in Jackson.

—Professor Hennington, principal of the Negro school at Merigold, Mississippi, was found dead in Long Lake, near Whitney, Mississippi. Although spies accused him of NAACP membership, he did not actually belong to the organization.

In other words, to accept leadership in the NAACP means signing one's own death warrant. There was nothing specific in the master plan about killing and shooting men, and Patterson claims that he is opposed to both force and violence. However, the plan does call for driving out the radical elements. With respect to methods of accomplishing this aim, the plan states: "The organization in each city and town is independent and autonomous." Patterson has provided only the outline: 500,000 Negroes out of Mississippi by 1966.

One point in Patterson's careful plan has already been achieved—the establishment of the Mississippi Sovereignty Committee. Set up by the legislature in the summer of 1956, it aims to sell segregation to the public. The committee has $250,000 appropriated for its use. Some small part of this has gone to pay Negroes and white people who spy on the NAACP. The committee, composed completely of WCC legislators, has power to seize records, sends speakers over the state and into the North, publishes anti-Negro literature, holds hearings, attacks the NAACP and the Urban League, and works with the press. On October 2, 1956, at the committee's expense, ten journalists were invited from the New England states to tour Mississippi and to see for themselves how peaceful race relations are in the state.

How the committee operates in the Negro community is revealed by the case of Aaron Henry. Henry has been one of the few militant Negro leaders.

Vice-president of the local NAACP, owner of a thriving pharmacy, a leader in the struggle of Negroes for the vote, he had the respect of the Negro day laborers and farmers in his area. However, when the Myrtle Hall Parent-Teacher Association at Clarksville, Mississippi, began to discuss school facilities, Henry appeared to be a totally different man than the one the community had known. He had drawn up a document calling for "separate but equal" schools in the entire Cohoma County school district and urged the parents to support it.

A few days later, R. L. Drew of Clarksdale reported to Amzie Moore of the Cleveland NAACP that Henry was a very troubled man. He had been visited by a representative of the Sovereignty Committee. Henry told Drew that of course he felt as he always had, but the economic position of the Negro made it impossible to put up a fight in the Delta. Furthermore, he argued, "We can't really depend on any help from the outside. We can't fight against impossible odds. We had better forget integration for the present and try to get equalization of teachers' salaries, decent libraries, gyms, tennis courts, and the like. I know Eastland will agree to do all these things."

Drew felt that Henry had been told by the committee to cooperate or give up his drugstore and leave the state. Henry, however, was only one of the six men who had worked on the "separate but equal" statement. Drew, president of the United Order of Friendship, admitted that the following persons, in addition to himself and Henry, had agreed to the statement:

—H. H. Humes, president of the General Baptist Convention.

—J. H. White, president of Mississippi Vocational College, one of the state's three institutions of higher learning for Negroes.

—James Gillian, grand master of the Free and Accepted Masons.

—John Melcher, executive vice-president of the Regional Council of Negro Leadership.

Drew was ashamed of himself and kept repeating, "What can a man do, up against such pressure?"

Amzie Moore's reply was, "A man can try to be a man."

ECONOMIC PRESSURE

THE KEENAN CASE

Theodore Keenan is a tall, well-built brown man forty-eight years old. He was reared in the Delta and is a good farmer. He is proud that he has never been arrested, has four children, and goes every Sunday "to hear the word of God." He has believed in integration, has taught his children "to. look white folks in the face," and has tried to help his neighbor when the need arises.

Everyone will tell you that Ted Keenan is a brave man—for in 1955 he did a brave thing. He walked to town, signed an affidavit that a number of Negroes' voting ballots had been destroyed, and sent it to the FBI. This was the first time a Negro in the Delta had done such a thing. He even gave the names of the poll-keepers who destroyed the ballots: C. K. Fisackerly and Claud Fisackerly. And for the first time the FBI came into the county to investigate. "Nothing was done, but Theodore Keenan did a brave thing by calling them," the people in the county will tell you.

Whenever Keenan prayed aloud at church, he asked God to "remove all segregation and discrimination from the land." The minister warned him long ago to hold his tongue. But instead of listening to his pastor, he "kept moving," joined the NAACP, and worked to get others to join it whenever his work was done on the farm. Keenan's farm is a great responsibility. He owns 240 acres and has three tenants and their families helping to run it. There are four houses, a car, two trucks, three tractors, one combine, a hay baler, twenty-five head of cattle, and all the little things to take care of. But Keenan is used to hard work and he has prospered. Only two other Negroes in the county own anything comparable—J. W. Lee and George Hall, both of Indianola. Neither will have any dealings with the NAACP, and they used to warn Theodore Keenan that he was "headin' for trouble, sure."

In 1954, Keenan had a "short crop" and borrowed $10,000 from a bank. In 1955 he had a "fair crop" and paid $6,000 on the previous year's debt. He then went to another bank in the county to borrow $4,000 on a second mortgage, but they turned him down. "Niggers that work with the NAACP ain't welcome here," they said. Keenan tried several other banks and was refused everywhere. Finally, early in August, Keenan went to the Farm Home Administration and requested a disaster loan of $4,000 in order to repay the balance on the 1954 bank loan. The agency promised to grant the loan, but when he returned a few days later, the FHA local representative said the county had used up all its disaster funds. Keenan was desperate.

When he got home he received a call from Eugene Fisackerly, local leader of the White Citizens Council. Fisackerly said he had called him on advice of Keenan's friend and offered to lend him the $4,000 at 6 per cent interest *if* Keenan would not vote in the August 23, 1956, second primary. Keenan was noncommittal.

The next day W. P. Scruggs, Eastland crony and spokesman for the Citizens Council, sent for Keenan. He was rude and blunt and made three things clear:

1. Since June 1956 the WCC had been working to see that Keenan would get no credit or loans anywhere in Mississippi.

2. Keenan must resign from the NAACP.

3. He must sign a statement that he would immediately resign from the NAACP; if not, he had better "leave Mississippi before the sun comes up."

Keenan admits that he was terrified and confused. He wanted to stand and fight, but he thought about his wife, his children, and his tenants. Reluctantly he signed to renounce the NAACP. When he left, Mr. Scruggs smiled and said, "You'll see, you'll get on without trouble if you keep your promise. And if you don't . . . well, I know you will."

The next day Keenan asked that his request for the FHA disaster loan be reopened. He waited and waited but got no reply. Then he went to see Mr. Scruggs and reminded him that he needed the money badly. Scruggs picked up the telephone and told the superintendant of the FHA, Malcolm French, that he was sure Keenan was now OK, so "Let him have the money."

Scruggs hung up the phone and told Keenan, "Mr. French says he will be glad to let you have the money." Keenan said, "I went there yesterday and he wouldn't even see me." Scruggs replied, "You get on over there. You'll get it. You're truthful. We like that. We had to take time to check on you. We checked on whether you were at the big meeting [the state NAACP meeting in Jackson]. I'm going to see you over the hump. You'll have no worries as long as you're a good boy."

Following this talk, Keenan was also able to borrow $475 on open notes from the Bank of Ruleville, whereas earlier he could not get a $100 loan for seed even though he had security.

Shortly after Scruggs had sent for Keenan, the White Citizens Council sent J. H. White, Negro president of the Mississippi Vocational College at Itta Bena, to see Keenan. President White came quickly to the point: "Mr. Keenan, I want you to line up with the aims and purposes of the Council. Vocational College has a great role to play and I need your help." Keenan refused.

Later Scruggs told Keenan that White was working with the Council, and "he is doing all right for himself and for your people." Scruggs wanted Keenan to function for the Council as a spy on the NAACP and the activities and plans of other Negro leaders in the radical element. Keenan said he had left the NAACP and that was all he could do. Scruggs suggested that he "think the matter over . . . carefully . . . very carefully."

A short while afterward, President White visited Keenan again and literally begged him to give him a list of all the local Negro leaders associated with the NAACP. Keenan told him, "The only man I know in Mississippi associated with the NAACP is Amzie Moore of Cleveland." (Moore was so well known that Keenan knew he was not divulging any secret.) White asked Keenan to try to get Moore to sign a pledge that he would cease his NAACP activities. Keenan replied, "I can't do nothing with Moore. Why don't you see him?" White replied, "I guess it's no use. Mr. Scruggs says that Moore got a big loan from the NAACP. I can't reach him yet."

About a week later, Malcolm French, the FHA superintendant who earlier had refused Keenan the disaster loan, called Keenan and offered to buy him 40 acres of land. He further offered Keenan a loan to build a house on a separate eighty acres Keenan already owned. Keenan thanked him but refused the offer on the pretext that he was already overburdened with property.

I asked Ted Keenan what he had learned from the experience. Here are his answers:

1. Negroes in the South cannot stand up to economic pressure without help from outside.

2. The WCC wants to create a situation in which only those who give up NAACP membership and go along with the Council can live, be protected, and prosper.

3. The federal government's agencies, including farm relief, are being used at the county level to break the Negroes' will and to build the WCC.

4. He had jumped from the frying pan into the fire, and any day he could end up in the river.

What Keenan meant by the last point was this: After signing the statement that he would leave the NAACP in order to save his land and his family, he had continued to contribute to the NAACP, to collect memberships from "safe people," and to work quietly with Amzie Moore and the NAACP regional secretary. He knew his every move was watched, but he says, "Amzie Moore is right. A man may be forced part of the way but he has to do the best he can—a man is still a man. But if they find out what I'm doin', I'm a dead duck. Pray for me!"

THE MOORE ENTERPRISES

In the winter of 1953, Ruth and Amzie Moore were deeply troubled. They had been watching the steady flow of young Negroes out of the Delta. "There is nothing to keep them here," Ruth told Amzie. "We

74

need more Negro businesses, more people for them to see owning something." Amzie got to thinking. He talked some more with Ruth and they came up with an idea: the Moore Enterprises. The plan called for a service station, restaurant, and a beauty shop on a good piece of land on the main highway running through town.

In January 1954 Ruth and Amzie, with little more than their hands and a good idea, started working. They bought a lot 130 by 65 feet on Highway 61 South, Cleveland, Mississippi, for $1,500. Then they leveled it off with 200 loads of dirt costing $800. The $2,300 to do this was borrowed from J. O. Alexander, a Negro minister. On February 1, they borrowed $6,600 at 6 per cent interest and a 10 per cent brokerage fee from J. T. Smith, a white attorney in Cleveland. A few days later, construction was started, but within two weeks their funds had been exhausted on steel, brick, labor, etc. For six weeks they waited for another loan and finally in April J. T. Smith lent them another $1,500.

Meanwhile Amzie Moore, on the basis of his credit rating and home, negotiated a loan of $17,000 from the Standard Life Insurance Company of Jackson, on completion of the Moore Enterprises building on July 17, 1954. This money was immediately paid out for back bills and toward air-conditioning, which cost $10,000.

Now there were no funds for operational equipment for the gas station, the restaurant, or the beauty parlor. So Amzie tried to arrange for a loan of $7,500 from the Tri-State Bank in Memphis, Tennessee. The bank offered to lend him $1,600, but the Moores could find no one in Mississippi with such a balance in the Tri-State Bank to endorse the loan. So Moore wangled the most basic materials on credit.

At this point, Dr. Howard, president of the Regional Council of Negro Leadership, publicly announced in October 1955 that Moore was so deep in debt that foreclosure was inevitable. He then appealed for Negroes all over the country to deposit funds in the Tri-State Bank to help save Negro business in Mississippi. Although more than $200,000 was deposited with the bank, Moore could not use any of it for failure to obtain endorsers. He was in even deeper trouble because Howard's appeals in Northern papers angered Southerners who had lent Moore money.

In December 1955, following Dr. Howard's dramatic appeal in Moore's name, Cleveland City Alderman Hutchinson, County Tax Assessor Chriss, and Local Policeman Noel came to Moore and demanded that he put a "For Colored Only" sign on the building housing the three enterprises. Moore refused. Thereupon the local banks which had given him small loans on a short-term credit basis—for operational needs such as gas, oil, light, and water bills—were instructed by the White Citizens Council not only to refuse further loans but also to cut off his credit.

With the receipts from the restaurant, gas station, and beauty shop, and funds raised by the Moores themselves, doing side jobs, they were able on November 1 to pay J. T. Smith all the $8,100, plus interest and fees, except $900. But on December 1, 1955, the WCC sent word that Moore could get no more day labor in the county. A few days later, J. T. Smith posted a notice at the courthouse that Moore's house, on which he had a second mortgage for $900 and on which the Veterans Administration had a mortgage of $6,000, was to be sold at auction. An appeal was made to the NAACP, which lent Moore $1,200 to pay J. T. Smith in full.

As the result of the pressure of the WCC, the agencies which had given Moore time to get money for equipment delivered on credit threatened to remove it. Moore applied to the National Sharecroppers Fund for help. Although the NSF cannot make such loans itself, it did get certain individuals to place $4,000 in escrow with the Tri-State Bank in Memphis, to help liquidate Moore's indebtedness on real estate and personal property.

In the summer of 1956 a special fund of the American Friends Service Committee sent Moore $900. He planned to spend this to stock his business, but instead had to use it to bring his building loans up to date, or else lose everything.

Of the $30,400 borrowed to build the Moore Enterprises, Moore has repaid all but $15,000. In addition to this sum still owed on the building, he owes the Tri-State Bank $4,000 and equipment firms (for the three enterprises) $2,000, making a total of $21,000 owed on the enterprises.

Since 1954 no funds have been available from local banks or private citizens for stocking the business. At the end of the 1955 business year Moore took the Enterprises' books to a white certified public accountant, who turned them over to the state tax examiner rather than post the books and file the proper income and sales tax returns for the last quarter of 1955. The tax examiner multiplied the gross income by 3½ per cent and told Moore that this sum, $586, represented the balance due the state sales tax commission. This was too high, and, after checking with the American Friends Service Committee and the NAACP, Moore decided nothing could be done. He wanted to instigate a legal suit, but the Negro business community urged him not to, lest the action be used as a pretext for economic reprisals against all Negro business and Moore, on whom they depended, be driven out. Moore agreed to try to raise the funds elsewhere.

J. A. Faduccia, a white attorney, appealed in Moore's behalf to the National Sharecroppers Fund, which referred the matter to an organization and saw that Moore received a check for $586, the total delinquent sales tax for 1955.

Moore could not pay the sales tax for the first quarter of 1956. He had used the money to buy gas and oil after the WCC had made it impossible for him to obtain these commodities on a credit basis.

In order to try to hold on to the Enterprises, Moore is at present working at the U.S. post office as a mail handler. The remainder of his time he gives to the Enterprises and to NAACP work all over the Delta. At present his financial situation is this:

1. There are no funds to employ qualified labor for the Enterprises.

2. There are no funds for stock such as batteries, seal-beam headlights, fan belts, tires, tubes, and parts—all items on which substantial profit is made.

3. The cost of gas and oil is too high. Moore must pay $29.90 and sell at $34.50. Dealers fix wholesale prices and do not wish to sell to Moore so he can make a profit.

4. Both Negro and white businessmen have advised him to sell out.

The WCC is stepping up pressure. Moore feels it is imperative not to sell for the following reasons:

1. Some Negro leaders must stand firm in the face of WCC economic pressure and harassment.

2. As one of the four militant Negroes in the Delta, he owes it to the people to try to stay on against all odds.

3. If Moore sells, other businessmen who look to his leadership will also sell and run.

4. A Negro businessman who defies the WCC is a necessity in the situation.

5. Moore cannot remain militant, or chairman of the NAACP, unless he can finally build up a business and remain independent of WCC pressure.

6. The experience he gains in attempting to do this will be invaluable for others who, if a new course is not found, must either run away or submit.

DRUGGIST WITHOUT DRUGS

Claude Bariol was a poor boy who worked his way through Xavier College in New Orleans as a paint sprayer. After college he came back to Cleveland, Mississippi, married, and worked as a poorly paid pharmacist for M. D. Ragsdale. Ragsdale is anti-Negro, but certainly not hypocritical. He frankly told Claude that he hired him because he could get him cheap and "anyhow there ain't nobody else around." Yet Ragsdale was always polite and never called Claude "boy."

But Claude had been talking with Amzie Moore and had decided he should do something, on his own, with his education. Furthermore, he did not like the idea of working for a man who belonged to the White Citizens Council. So when a Negro businessman suggested putting up the capital for a drugstore, Claude jumped at the chance even though he would have to support his wife and family on $25 a week for a year or so. Claude felt good, for the contract stated that if after a year business flourished, his salary would gradually rise to $100 a week and, if he desired it, he could buy up to 50 per cent of the business.

In May 1955 the store opened. There was very limited operating capital, so Claude did all the advertising posters by hand and carried them around the neighborhood. Arrangements had been made with Ellis-Bagwell Drug Company of Memphis, Tennessee, to stock the store with drugs. Members of the firm had come to see Claude, looked over the plans, and told him, "Of course we will handle your supply. Get in touch with us a couple of weeks before you open." They left a good supply of order blanks and showed Claude how to fill them out. Two weeks before the announced opening, Claude sent in his order. By return mail he got a short note saying, "We cannot fill your order, and there is no further need for you to contact us." Claude later learned that the very day they came to look at the store, they had gone uptown and been told by the WCC: "We don't want that nigger drugstore in this town."

Next Claude tried McKesson and Robbins in Memphis. They refused to open a regular account but said they would ship what he needed from time to time COD. This would not be easy, for he had used every penny in fixing up the store.

Finally, he wrote Standard Drug at Meridian, Mississippi. They replied, "You are too far outside our regular territory." So Claude started ordering COD from McKesson and Robbins.

At first pharmaceutical firms would not send their salesmen to the store; then finally Upjohn, Sharp and Dohme, Massengill, and Tilden did agree to sell Claude prepared medicines. But getting drugs for prescriptions was a real problem. Druggists in a town are usually cooperative. If one is out of a drug, the others are happy to fill a prescription at cost. There were three white druggists in Cleveland. At first, Simmons Drug Company was helpful, but after a week they said there was an agreement not to sell him anything and they did not feel they could break it. Claude then telephoned Owens Drug

Store and asked the owner's assistant for two ounces of sulfose suspension. But he hung up when he heard the owner yell to his helper, "Tell the nigger we ain't got none."

So he gathered his courage and called Mr. Ragsdale, his former boss. Ragsdale refused, saying he did not like the NAACP crowd Claude was hanging out with. But a few days later he called back and asked Claude to come to his home that night. He told Claude how the Citizens Council had laid down the law, how they planned to freeze him out, and how the Negro schoolteachers had been warned to stay out of his store. . . . But he added, "We can work together on the quiet. I don't have anybody to fill my prescriptions and you sure need drugs."

At this point Claude and his partner began trying to negotiate a loan through the local banks. But although the building and land are worth $10,000, they have not been successful.

So Claude is limping along with the makeshift arrangement which depends on Ragsdale's whims.

As I left the store, Claude looked at a bottle Ragsdale had sent to his house the night before, and said: "Worst thing is, in a way I am still working for Mr. Ragsdale of the White Citizens Council."

THE WRINKLED UNIFORM

In 1949 the lily-white Cleveland City Hospital turned over an $1,800 contract for laundering nurses' uniforms to Watson's Laundry. To this day there has been no complaint about the work done for the hospital. Later Charles Watson got all the laundry for the Friendship Clinic at Mound Bayou, an all-Negro town. When the Cleveland Motel, for whites only, was set up in 1953, it too gave Watson its laundry. Encouraged, Watson expanded when he won a $21,721 contract for the laundry at Greenville Army Air Base for the fiscal year 1955–1956. He took on four new workers and bought $3,000 worth of new machinery to handle the job.

There were regular inspections of the work, and all seemed to be in order until July. Just after Independence Day, July 4, someone reported that Watson was an active member of the NAACP. Everywhere he went, white people mentioned the NAACP and pressed him for his views of it and its activities. Then his telephone began to ring late at night. Finally, Watson said he was not a member and did not know who was. The white folks frankly did not believe him.

In August he began to hear reports from the air base that his work was not neat. He was upbraided because a sheet from the Negro hospital got mixed in with the air base laundry. Then he received a registered letter from Major William P. Johnson, air force contracting officer, saying in part:

> An official complaint has been registered by Chief Nurse 3505th USAF Hospital to the effect that the type of service being rendered on nurses' uniforms is thoroughly unsatisfactory. . . . We must insist that finished work be of first-class quality. . . . Complaints . . . certainly indicate that such is not the case. This letter is your notification that failure to correct discrepancies that now exist in the quality of your work, and failure to maintain acceptable standards of work, will be cause for termination of part or all of your contract consistent with provisions of Clause 7 of your contract entitled "Default." Request that receipt of this letter be acknowledged in the space provided therefor, and a copy be returned.

The next day the owner of the Cleveland Motel called Watson in. After some embarrassment, he said he had no choice but to turn his work over to the Cleveland Laundry, a firm owned by a member of the WCC. He promised Watson that he would return to him, if he could, "after all this fuss about you and the NAACP dies down, if it ever does."

Watson was sure the letter from the air base would lead to his losing the contract. It was a well-known fact that officers from the base attended Citizens Council meetings. It was also known that the base was doing everything possible to keep on the friendliest terms with the leading citizens of Cleveland.

Were Watson to lose the contract, he would be over $8,000 in debt. Already he had been told that no bank in the state would lend him money. In addition, he would have to lay off six workers. All his labor, operations, equipment, and maintenance budget had been geared to the air base contract.

When I suggested he try the Tri-State Bank in Memphis, he said, "But $8,000! Who will sign for that much money?" I told him I did not know but to keep up his spirit, for the contract was not broken yet.

The next day I stopped in to pick up two shirts. I asked Watson if I could see some of the nurses' uniforms. He smiled and took me into a clean room where they hung in long, neat lines. I looked at them carefully—there was not a wrinkle to be seen. "I'm watching them carefully," he said. "God knows we can't have a single wrinkle." Then he paused, took my hand, and said, "Son, please pray for me. I need that contract."

A JOURNEY INTO THE TILL COUNTRY

On the last Saturday of September 1956, Amzie Moore, president of the Cleveland, Mississippi, NAACP, drove me through the three counties that Negroes call the "Till Country": Le Flore County, where Emmett Till was abducted; Sun Flower County, where he was killed; and Tallahatchie County, where Milam and Bryant dumped his scarred body into the river.

Amzie knows that country well. As an adventurous boy he had roamed through the area, swum in the Tallahatchie River, and visited churches, singing with a quartet. He had sadly investigated the Till murder, got the first facts on the case, and telephoned them to the NAACP in New York.

"First," he said, "I want you to see the barn where they murdered that boy. It's just the other side of Ruleville—on a farm where Milam's brother used to live. He ain't there no more; white folks drove him out. A man named Wyman lives there now. He's a mean cuss—don't let nobody go near that barn. But I think we can see it from the road." "You mean," I asked, "that we have to go close to a white man's farm to see it?" "Well," he said, "I'm not sure. I think, if I remember right, there's a public road that goes by it."

At that moment the barn came in sight. "Yes," Amzie said, "this is the road." We turned into it, only to discover we were going up the driveway to Mr. Wyman's house. There was no public road past the barn. "Perhaps we had better get out of here quick," I said. We were almost at the house and could see the barn some fifty feet away. In front of it stood Mr. Wyman, shotgun in hand.

"This is no time to turn back," Amzie said quietly, and slowly stopped the car at the rear of the house. He opened the car door, got out, walked deliberately over to a white woman near the garage, tipped his hat, and politely asked for directions to Ruleville. At this point Mr. Wyman, who had been moving toward us, stopped about twenty feet away and stood, legs apart, shotgun in hand. The woman looked at us uneasily, then at him, and paused in bewilderment. A tall, well-built young Negro man ran from behind the house and stood next to her. Then she relaxed and pointed out the road to Ruleville. Amzie thanked her politely and came back to the car. We turned and drove ever so slowly down the dirt road. "Man!" Amzie said, "If we had turned back or looked nervous, we'd sure have got shot. He's a mean one." I looked back and saw Mr. Wyman still standing in front of the barn with his gun.

"Did you get a good look at that Negro?" Amzie asked. Before I could answer he continued, "Well, he was actually milkin' in the barn and heard Till being murdered. He ran down the road to a Negro woman to get help, but they was all scared. He told us about it. We tried to get him to testify, but he wouldn't or, I guess, couldn't. Scared to death. They was all scared."

"But how could he go on working there after that?" I asked. Amzie thought for a moment and replied: "Some of these folks don't know nothing but this farm. They'd be afraid to leave. Been working here all their lives. They don't know no better. They're conditioned." He paused. "But do you see all these empty cabins along this road?" I looked; practically every cabin was empty. "Well," Amzie continued, "those folks left after the murder. They were conditioned too, for a long time, but that boy's death sure unconditioned them. They're gone. I don't say they did the best thing—running—but at least they did something."

We drove on for a while in silence. Then Amzie said, "Just down the road we will be able to see the Tallahatchie River, where they threw him." In a few minutes we were on the banks of the river. The water was dirty, and the spot a lonely one. I told Amzie that the trees leaning toward the river would make a beautiful picture and suggested that he take one. "Yeah," he said bitterly as he reached for the camera, "these trees are beautiful, but they bear some strange fruit." In a moment he was smiling. "You know," he said, "I've heard of this river all my life. There's an old man down the way claims to be over a hundred. Says more than 1,100 Negroes been thrown in here since 1900. Could you believe it?" "I don't know," I said. "I don't either," he replied as he shook his head, "but sometimes you can believe almost anything."

We climbed back in the car and headed for Money, where the Till drama had begun. I asked Amzie if he had read the *Look* article and if there was any truth to the report that Till had made advances to Mrs. Milam (Bryant?). "I wouldn't say advances," he said. "I'd say what the kids who was with him reported was true. Some of them dared him to go in and ask her for a date. You know kids, especially him being from the North and needing to show off. He walked right in and acted like he was in Chicago—speaking fresh and friendly-like. He was kinda big for his age and he scared that woman plenty. She ran out and got a gun from her car. When the other kids saw the gun, they knew they was in for trouble. They called Till and all of them beat it fast."

"Pity they did not get him out of town," I said. "They should have known that, scared as you say she was, she would certainly start trouble."

"Wait," said Amzie. "You have to give credit where it's due. That woman never told her husband. Seems like she didn't want him to know. It was the colored boy who worked there that told him. I don't suppose the boy wanted to get anybody hurt. He was just trying to prove he was a 'good nigger'—or maybe just trying to protect himself."

By now we were in Money—a small town with one main street. On one side of the street runs the railway. The other side looks like a Hollywood set for a western—a small town with its flat-topped, square buildings poorly painted. We parked the car by the railway tracks and passed through small knots of Negro shoppers, who turned to look at us strangers as we passed. We walked into the small store where Till had agreed to take that dare and thereby signed his death warrant.

A white man and woman with sour, tight faces sat in rocking chairs before a dirty spittoon. When we entered, they looked at us and kept their eyes on us until we left. I bought a candy bar from the tall, red-faced man behind the counter, and we walked out. He came to the window and watched us until we got in the car. As we walked back to the car, I noticed a large sign before a drygoods store. It read, "Do unto others what you would have them do unto you." I called it to Amzie's attention. He smiled and said, "That ain't up there for them. It's for us."

As we drove out of Money, I asked Amzie if the man who waited on us was Milam. "No," he said, "the white folks ran him out of town shortly after the trial." "Ran him out?" I asked. "Yes, sir," Amzie replied. "Seems like the city fathers told him he was a disgrace and to get out right away. 'We don't want you here.' That's what they said. And he left, too. He left real quick." "How do you explain that?" I asked. "Well," Amzie said, "white folks is hard to explain. For one thing, they are all tied up inside. Seems as if they considered what he'd done a bad thing—but at the same time, mind you, they were defending him for all they was worth. I guess their running him out just shows how mixed up they are about this whole question." It was dark now and we decided to go back to Cleveland.

Two days later we went to Sumner, where the trial had taken place. We parked in the square in front of the courthouse. Amzie had been there throughout the trial. Before we got out of the car he pointed out the main rear door. "That's where they searched us," he said. "Yes, sir, every Negro who came to town was searched just by that door. They searched the cars, too. Far as I know they never found a Negro with a gun on him. But some had them hid, 'cause all the white males from thirteen on had guns and carried them where you could see them. They meant business, too."

"What is that statue?" I asked. "A Civil War general—probably Lee's," Amzie said. "What else on the courthouse lawn?" The statue stood on one side of the entrance and a beautiful tree on the other. "What kind of tree

is that?" I asked. "I don't know for sure," Amzie replied, "but I think it's
an oak. Big, ain't it? Strong, too. Been there a long time."

For a moment he sat still and full of thoughts. "Let's look around town,"
I said. "Wait," he replied. "You just gave me a thought. *There's* a picture
of the South if I ever saw one. That Southern general and that tree. One is
the dead past and the other the living present. This South is sure caught in
between—between life and death."

We got out of the car and Amzie took me to see the restaurant where
Negro leaders and Representative Diggs of Michigan ate during the days
of the trial. On an unpaved street behind the courthouse, Jessie Griffin's
Cafe was still trying to stand up. Plaster was falling off the walls, roaches
walked about with freedom, flies were plentiful, and a loud jukebox blared
wild music. The floor was strewn with beer cans and bottles. At three tables
men were gambling. A woman came running in, hysterical with anger, and
dared a man sitting alone to slap her. He looked at her with compassion and
said, "Git home, Mary, you's done and got drunk again. You ought to be
'shamed yo'self." As Mary continued to rant at him, he got up and walked
out, muttering, "My people, my people."

Amzie pointed to a corner of the room and said, "There, at that table, with
the jukebox going, with people running in and out, the lawyers planned their
strategy during the trial. Diggs and I ate lunch here with them every day."
I asked him if this was the only place where Negroes could eat in town. "No,"
he said, "this ain't the only place, but it's the best."

We left the restaurant and walked around the square. In every store there
were ten to fifteen Negro shoppers. Amzie pointed out that the shopkeepers
there depend upon Negroes for about 85 per cent of their business. "But,"
he said, "you know one thing. These sales people treat Negroes like dogs.
Trouble is, these Negroes don't own nothing. Think what changes would
be made if a few Negroes owned some business here, and had sense enough
to buy where they are treated like human beings. But they're mostly sharecroppers and they're afraid."

We ambled back to the car and Amzie drove around the town. He pointed
out a house in which a white man was living with a Negro woman. "They
got three little bastards, but nobody says anything about that. The Negroes
keep quiet about her, and the white people dismiss him as crazy."

Just then I saw a strange-looking factory on the left and asked Amzie what
it was. He explained that it was a cotton oil mill. "They employ mostly Negroes. It's hard work and poor pay," Amzie said. "After the Till murder so
many Negroes left this county that they were short sixty hands. I hear they
ain't running full yet."

We turned up a small dirt road and onto the highway. Amzie was suddenly very quiet. "What's on your mind?" I asked. "I was thinking about Twotype and Logan," he said. "They used to hang out around here." It developed that they were the two Negro witnesses who disappeared and could not be found until after the Till trial was over. Amzie explained that the sheriff had picked them up and held them in the county jail at Charleston, Mississippi, so they could not testify for the state. This seemed hard to believe. But a few days later in Charleston, an old Negro man said: "Yes, they were here, all right. At night they slept in the jail and by day they worked nearby. I was as close to them once or twice as I am to you. But we knew it was best not to get mixed up in that mess. So we kept quiet. God will take care of them and those white folks too. He sure will and in his own good time. We all pays for what we do in this world."

As we drove down the highway and out of the Till country, we passed a large, well-kept graveyard. At one end of it there was a section in very bad condition, separated from the rest by a high iron fence. "That's the Negro section," Amzie remarked, "but I don't get excited about that. The graveyard is the only place where things can be separate . . . *and* equal."

NELLIE PUTS HER TRUST IN GOD

Just east of Ruleville, Mississippi, south of Herman Lucas' small farm, lie sixty-four acres of rich soil worth $300 an acre. They belong to Nellie Lenor, a Negro woman just past sixty. Nellie's father was a hard-working man and managed to pull through the depression by doing day labor as well as farming. When Nellie's mother died last year, her last words were, "Don't let them take this land away from you."

After her mother's death, J. T. Smith, white banker and attorney, called Nellie into his office. He explained to her that he had always taken care of the family and would do the same for her. He showed Nellie a pile of papers, old bills, and the like—but Nellie "didn't pay no 'tention to them," for she didn't read much and couldn't understand what he said. Furthermore, she said, "Mr. Smith had always done business and kept things straight for my mother. I trusted him. I didn't have to remember."

But there were some things Nellie did remember. She knew that her family and two neighboring families together borrowed $780 annually from Mr. Smith. She knew that Mr. Smith asked 60 per cent interest and 10 per cent "broking" fee, for many was the time her mother mentioned that it seemed "a bit steep." But before her father died, he told her mother that Mr. Smith was as good a white man as any in the county and to let him take care of her. So each time Nellie asked her mother why she didn't try someone else, her mother would say, "Your father knowed these men. We better do as he say." Nellie knew that they always turned over the cotton to Mr. Smith to sell, and she remembered how many bales they got each year. For example, Nellie remembered that the first year Mr. Smith was paid in full, but "'course there wasn't no receipt 'cause we trusted Mr. Smith."

Year after year, Nellie had paid Mr. Smith what she could. Mostly it had been according to the price of cotton—but she was not sure. Things went along all right, and Mr. Smith's loan money, $130 a month for the three families, came between November and April when life was difficult on the farm.

This year Nellie had a fairly good crop and assumed everything was all right. But on September 24, Mr. Smith called her into his office and told her that she owed him $4,290.22. He went over the record. Nellie did not understand it, but she knew something was wrong. "He just didn't look right," she said over and over. "There was somethin' funny about his lips. He just didn't look right."

With no records available we tried to help Nellie reconstruct what had and had not been paid. It was a hopeless and impossible task. But figuring cotton at the low price of $150 a bale, and counting in the exorbitant tax and broker's fee, it was clear that Nellie had twice repaid the loan—except for two factors.

First, two years ago Mr. Smith had sent out an old John Deere "B" tractor, equipped with secondhand plow, middle buster, cultivator, planter, and a broken harrow. Although the most modern model cost only $1,800 new and no more than $1,000 secondhand, Mr. Smith told Nellie on September 24, 1956, that he had charged her $2,500 when he had brought it to her two years before. "But," he added, "that of course included price of delivery."

Second, he had arranged all matters when Nellie's mother died. He told Nellie, "As your lawyer I get a fee for all that work." But Nellie did not know she was supposed to pay for such help from Mr. Smith. To her he was a trusted friend and adviser.

Finally, Mr. Smith told Nellie he was sorry she had let the debt get so large. He said he would hate to turn her out, but he had to pay *his* debts, too. So if she couldn't pay in full by November 25, he would have to foreclose. Nellie was stunned. But she didn't think Mr. Smith really would turn her out. She went home and prayed.

Two days later she went back and talked with Mr. Smith again. This time she knew he was in earnest. Then she got to thinking. Nellie said, "I says to myself, that land's worth $300 an acre. If I sell some of it, I can pay him off.

But I been lookin' and nobody wants to buy it." What Nellie did not know was that Mr. Smith had already made a deal with other white men in the county. If and when Nellie's land were sold, Mr. Smith himself would buy it at a fraction of its worth.

I asked Nellie what she planned to do if she could not keep the farm. She pulled herself up straight and said, "I'll kill that white man." Then she settled back and said, "I've lived here all my life." Tears came to her eyes and she continued, "I guess I'd beg him for an acre to die on. My preacher told me you can't trust man. He's a weak vessel. Now I know I can't put my trust in nobody but God. He'll take care of me!"

GETTING ON WITH THE WHITE FOLKS

The pernicious physical effects of the overcrowded and inadequate housing which results from racial segregation are widely known. But the psychological effects of segregation, which are just as far-reaching and vicious, are much less understood. Efforts to survive in a prejudiced society lead many Negroes at a very early age to adopt stratagems which continue into adulthood, even if they escape from squalor and Jim Crow laws.

These stratagems of Negro children are like camouflage. In a city not very far south a young Negro boy, taking the only work he could find, joined an older friend at shining shoes. Each day he witnessed a disturbing ritual. One of the regular customers, when his shoes had been polished, would take a quarter and a five-dollar gold piece from his pocket, put them behind his back, and then, with a wink to the other white folks, would present his two closed fists to the older Negro in such a way that an intelligent person could tell which one held the more valuable coin. The Negro would look puzzled, scratch his head, and invariably choose the hand holding the quarter, to the amused satisfaction of the white patrons.

When the infuriated young boy upbraided him, the older man replied: "Look, kid, I ain't so dumb. If I took that gold piece, it would be the last I'd get. If I plays along and lets him think I'm dumb, I'll get a lot more than five bucks out of him in the long run." Within a few days the boy was dancing, flashing his teeth, making mistakes in grammar, and obsequiously flattering his customers. He too had learned how to get a quarter instead of a dime from the "mighty white folks."

Even more serious are the unconscious rationalizations with which discrimination provides the Negro child. In his all too human effort to avoid facing his own shortcomings and weaknesses, he often blames them on segregation. This lamentable dodge is then buttressed by the conscience-stricken white liberal who, heartily ashamed of the prejudices of his race, leans over backward to applaud the performance of any Negro, however mediocre.

From *Liberation*, September 1956.

The first Negro to attend a leading prep school was lionized and feted by students and faculty alike. He was accorded every honor, including the presidency of his class, not because of his personal qualities but because the white students wanted to prove to him and to themselves that they were unprejudiced. The constant extracurricular activities interfered with his studies, and at the end of the year he was about to fail several subjects. Knowing this, the boy spread among his friends the rumor that such and such professors were going to flunk him because he was a Negro. Greatly perplexed, one of the professors, after consultation with an expert in race relations, had the courage and good judgment to fail the boy, with the result that the next year he studied hard and overcame the oppressive effects of his white friends' guilty good will.

The white liberals who cannot believe that Emmett Till, in a normal adolescent search for status among his new Southern friends, may indeed have made some trifling improper advances to a white woman exhibit the same unfortunate frame of mind as those teen-age white girls who have sexual relations with Negroes not because they love them but because they fear that a normal rejection would appear as prejudice. This white liberal syndrome reinforces the illusion of many Negro children that their personal deficiencies are attributable to segregation. In this way they feel absolved at a critical age from efforts toward self-improvement.

Negro children tend to develop early a basic lack of self-respect. They may show this, for example, by their shameful rejection of such aspects of their cultural heritage as Negro spirituals. A prominent Negro singer has been met several times just before high school concerts by committees of Negro children asking him not to sing spirituals. "They remind white folks of our past slavery, and we don't like it," one teen-ager explained.

It is almost impossible to mention Africa to Negro boys and girls in school without provoking embarrassed laughter. Even African students studying in America are sometimes affected in the same way. One such student, looking at African sculpture in a New York apartment, laughed wryly at its "crudity" and said, "My people have a long way to come," oblivious to the rare beauty of the work.

It is a familiar social pattern for oppressed people to imitate their oppressors. Negro children are encouraged (often by their parents) to straighten their hair and lighten their skins with Nadinol. While this behavior is understandable as unconscious identification with the majority, it cripples self-esteem. When these same children grow up, they will try to marry wives or

89

husbands of much lighter complexion in order to increase their status. The lighter the skin, the higher the status. Such preferences betray a very deep sense of inferiority.

Dr. Kenneth Clark, of City College, New York, who was coordinator of the sociological, psychological, and historical research for the NAACP Supreme Court case on school segregation, demonstrated this lack of self-respect through a dramatic experiment. He asked Harlem children to evaluate a group of dolls. Provided with a white doll, a Japanese doll, and a Negro doll, the children overwhelmingly liked the black doll *least*.

Along with the lack of self-respect, Negro children learn very early to hate white people. Many of their earliest experiences with the white folk are negative and destructive: "Don't sit here; Negroes belong over there." "I'm sorry. My mother won't let me bring you to the party." "This medical line is for little white boys, Sam." In the past half-century of international war many Negroes have inwardly applauded the battles in which "the white folks are killing each other off." Negro servants, even in the North, sometimes secretly spit in the food before bowing and scraping to serve it to white masters.

Accustomed to the Southern system of putting Negroes in the first dirty car behind the engine, a Negro child, upon hearing about a train wreck in which many people were killed in the last coaches, exclaimed: "Good! They were all white." Even the most highly educated may feel this way. The Negro novelist J. Saunders Redding, who teaches at Atlanta University and lives near the Atlanta slums, has described how, on a very cold night in Georgia, he saw a drunk white woman in rags stagger down an alley, empty her bottle, and fall unconscious in the gutter. His initial reaction was, "Good! She's white." Only after a considerable inner struggle was he able to add, "But, my God! She's also human," and go to her aid.

Negro children often turn their hatred upon members of their own race. One Negro boy, beaten by a white gang, stormed into a community center and began to pound a smaller Negro girl. When the director intervened, he screamed, "That white trash beat me. I'll kill all you niggers." The psychologist John Dollard in his classic study, *Frustration and Aggression*, describes this pattern in detail. If frustration is great enough, aggression follows. If one dare not take on the strong, one takes on the weak—if not the weak outside the group, then the weak within it.

Negro children early acquire the habit of identifying with the social prejudices of white people. The subconscious thought runs like this: "I can't eat, live, or mix with the white folks. I can't belong. But at least I can think what the white folks think." By hating other minority groups, the Negro child attempts, first, to deflect the hostility of the white people to the others and away from himself; and, second, to avoid any appearance of being out of step as a troublemaker as well as a Negro. A Negro boy running a Puerto Rican boy out of his block was overheard yelling, "You may look whiter than us, but we've been here longer than you." Leaders at high school conferences report that even the most enlightened Negroes tend to defend vigorously the economic and political status quo. Negro boys and girls are anti-Semitic to a surprising degree.

The Negro child early learns that we are living in a historical period of white domination. Sooner or later the colored people of the world will, he believes, rise up to throw off the white rule. Then they will dominate the whites. This philosophy of history, often held subconsciously, persists in the child's mind throughout life. It is supported by the biblical statement often repeated in Negro homes, "Ethiopia will stretch forth her hands."

While the physical effects of racial prejudice are bad enough, they are in reality superficial compared to the deepest scars of all—the scars left by intolerance and injustice upon the hearts and minds of little children.

NEW SOUTH . . . OLD POLITICS

Few areas in the world are witnessing such a drastic and far-reaching transformation as is under way in the South today. American industry, in its flight from outmoded methods, uneconomical plants, and stultifying industrial traditions in the North and East, is migrating to the South on a large scale. The transition of the South from a culture and economy basically agrarian to urban industrialization has acquired the dimension of a revolution.

Between 1940 and 1950, two million white workers were added to Southern industry. During the same period, over three million Negro workers quit the South, thus turning the problem of race relations from a sectional to a national one. In ten years, the number of Negroes outside the South rose 60 per cent.

The really significant development, however, is that over one third of poor white and Negro labor has moved from farms to cities. Cotton, oil, chemicals, and textiles have created a new economy and a new urban middle class. Yet despite this economic transformation, the South has clung to its old agrarian and feudal attitudes and sought to incorporate them in the new emerging industrial society.

The confusing and frustrating major party setup in this country, marked by the "solid" Democratic South, stems largely from this Southern "backwardness." Not only Negro leaders but Southern politicians of every complexion are well aware that the South cannot play a part that makes sense in national political life so long as a one-party pattern exists. Genuine national unity of either major party will come only as the Southern vote is divided between them, or, what would be more significant, between one of the old parties and a new political entity. This would, however, entail a thorough political regrouping in the entire country.

The questions which now arise in every presidential election as to whether certain Southern states may go Republican, whether Southerners are well advised to support the Democratic party nationally or might more advan-

---

From *Liberation*, October 1956.

tageously put up Dixiecrat candidates, and so on, reflect the South's transitional situation.

The growing influence of the Republican party in the South stems from the fact that in the struggle between Northern industry and Northern labor to extend their power in the South, industry has so far triumphed and hence has determined the nature of the rising white urban middle class. Composed of new plant managers, technicians, doctors, tradesmen, lawyers, newspaper publishers, and realtors, this middle class has assumed the role of rebel in Southern politics. Its Republican sympathies have engendered real pressure for two-party politics. Locally cornered and nationally homeless, this group's revolt against the old agrarianism may draw still other Southerners into the Republican fold.

At the moment it appears that Eisenhower may get fewer Southern votes this year than in 1952. It is unlikely, however, that the Republican party in the country as a whole will move to the left. It seems, therefore, that Southern industrial and financial elements will eventually find a home in the GOP —despite memories of "the War Between the States."

The Democratic party, on the other hand, cannot in the long run accommodate sufficiently to the increasing conservatism of considerable sectors of its Southern wing without alienating its Northern following. The leaders of organized labor cannot repeatedly make the shabby compromises which they made in Chicago this year and keep their following. The Democratic party has to remake itself radically or fall apart.

The behavior of the Negro will be the determining factor in the political revamping of the South because the economic and social position of the Negro has been the foundation of the reactionary one-party system in the South. In his rise to a new status the Negro can exert sufficient pressure to determine the nature of the new alignments. The Negro masses can break— and have an immense stake in breaking—the existing political pattern, which obviously is detrimental to the nation as a whole through the hold of Southern Democrats over key Congressional committees and in other ways.

The significance of the nonviolent protests in Montgomery and Tallahassee is thus national. The refusal of Negroes to tolerate further segregation will, if it continues to grow, decisively influence all our lives. The Negro may force the South to choose between true democratic support for social revolution and the suppression of it by a movement to the extreme right. In either case, the South will be transformed. Nationally, unless one of the major parties genuinely supports the Negro, a strong impetus will be given for a new party composed of farmers, white industrial workers, and Negroes to emerge in the South. These will be the decisive element in any new national party.

In his political thinking about strategy today the Negro must take cognizance of two dangers. The first is that the industrial revolution of the South may make him less important economically. It is significant that before the Second World War, Southern white businessmen sought to discourage the northward migration of Negroes, but after the war they encouraged it. In 1940 one-fourth of the labor force was Negro. Ten years later it had fallen off to one-fifth. Industrialization, the effect of mechanized cotton pickers and harvesters, the ease with which part-time white farmers have moved into the factories, the difficulties surrounding Negro membership in unions, and the failure to pass the Fair Employment Practices Act have tended to weaken the position of the Negroes in relation to whites.

The second danger is that when the present economic boom slackens, the Negro will be the hardest hit by unemployment and will be further displaced from the land. The full effects of agricultural mechanization are yet to be seen, and it is doubtful that Southern industry will be able to absorb the rapid growth of the population even with the northward Negro migration.

Under the shadow of these two dangers the Negro people must move carefully but swiftly while the initiative is theirs, or they may discover that they and the democratic impulses for which they stand are on the defensive or even forced to retreat. Whether consciously or unconsciously, the response of Negro leaders in Montgomery and Tallahassee indicates their realization that to go slow is to go backward.

Considering his political course and deciding, for example, how to vote, the Negro should not lose sight of the basic weapon of nonviolent noncooperation and protest. It is difficult to assess the importance of a one-shot performance at the polls in November. But the tremendous effects of day-to-day nonviolent protest go on through the year. There can be no doubts about the profoundly positive response of the entire nation to the nonviolent direct action in Montgomery and elsewhere. Such action exerts immediate social and economic pressure to which the South has no choice but to accommodate itself. The more widespread it becomes, the greater will be its effectiveness as real political action.

It is true that direct action has profoundly disturbing effects within a locality. To a large extent, however, the fears roused are modified and ultimately dispelled if the action is nonviolent. In any case, the fact that resistance to injustice is bound to have a disturbing effect cannot be the basis for inaction and submission. We therefore urge the Negro people to extend their nonviolent protest against segregation now. Action patterned after Montgomery and Tallahassee is a truly total vote of infinitely greater importance than any ballot cast in November.

Insofar as the Negro retains the nonviolent approach he will be able to win white sympathy and frustrate the aims of the White Citizens Council. Nothing is so terrifying to white supremacists as the fear that if Negroes gain power they will visit upon their former masters violence and oppression similar to that employed by whites against Negroes in the past. Nothing can so thoroughly disarm their terror as the determined adherence of Negroes to nonviolence. The initial reaction of the whites will be one of distrust, since deceit and violence form the larger part of their experience of intergroup relations. But in time the fact that Negroes have eschewed retaliation of this nature will be borne in upon them.

This will not be easy. The Councils dimly recognize this coercive psychological power of nonviolence and will be bent on inciting violence from Negroes. Should they succeed, the Negroes will lose their moral initiative, liberals will become even more frightened and inactive, and a deeper wedge will be driven between white and black workers. If, on the other hand, despite this provocation, the Negro holds fast to the spirit of Montgomery he will be able to work with white workers and farmers to create a new political force for social progress.

All this does not mean that the Negro can or should struggle alone to achieve freedom for himself. The mass of Negroes are farmers or workers, and their interests are fundamentally allied to those of other farmers and workers. The role of the Negro is unique only in that his especially demeaned position and, consequently, unprecedented new drive for dignity and self-respect lend him a momentum and initiative lacked by Southern white workers. The Negro is, therefore, now pivotal to the resolution of the major problems confronting all classes in the South.

The historical facts of segregation shed a flood of light upon the basic nature of the relationship of black and white labor in the South. During the period of Reconstruction following the Civil War, Negro and white workers, many of them illiterate, worked together effectively in Southern legislatures for progressive legislation of all sorts, such as the present laws providing for free universal education in North Carolina. Not until 1876 did Northern and Southern capital realize the threat such a progressive union of black and white workers offered to its own interests. At that time it conspired to destroy this unity by the resurrection of the doctrine of white supremacy. From 1880 to 1890 such efforts met with small success, although from this period dates the transformation of the remnants of the Confederate underground into the Ku Klux Klan. In 1890 prejudice was legislated in the form of segregation laws. Jim Crow laws date primarily from the period between 1890 and the First World War. This stratagem on the part of Northern and Southern capital has continued till today.

When the industrial revolution began to accelerate in 1940, the American labor movement, primarily concerned with wages and hours, faced a dilemma. On the one hand, it could attempt to oppose the powerful capitalist-inspired program of segregation by organizing white and Negro labor into integrated unions. On the other, it could more expediently organize separate white and Negro locals, and sacrifice the strength of true solidarity. Where Negroes were brought into the factories, labor chose the latter course and for a number of years this system seemed to work.

Today, however, organized labor faces a quite different situation. The White Citizens Councils—the KKK in gray flannel suits—are well aware that organized labor is part and parcel of the racial and economic progressive forces they loathe. The Councils' prejudice against Negroes, Catholics, and Jews is superficial in comparison with their main objective—to castrate the labor movement by preventing a coalition of Negro and white workers. The forces behind the Councils have thrived by keeping white workers poor and Negro workers poorer, and, as in the past, their prime device against any strong union of laborers is to fan the flames of religious and racial intolerance.

This situation is as critical for all American labor as it is for the Negro. For labor now to sidestep the Southern racial issue means suicide. Already in Mississippi, Alabama, and Georgia, local labor leaders, influenced by the White Citizens Councils, are urging unions to withdraw from the AFL-CIO. They want to create a Southern Labor Organization of lily-white, strictly segregated company unions. As the South becomes more and more an industrial center, it takes little imagination to see how an unorganized, company-unionized South would undermine the unions throughout the whole nation.

American labor is as yet oblivious to this danger or is unwilling to face it. But enlightened American workers must bring their unions to understand that the time for equivocation is past. Sooner or later labor will have to accept the Negro as a first-class citizen. To attempt now to organize white workers in a position of superiority or privilege is to play into the hands of the White Citizens Councils by pushing Negroes, one-fifth of the labor force, into the position of potential scabs.

But when the unions finally embrace the Negro they can no longer expect to limit their attention to wages and hours. The effort to organize Negro and white workers on a basis of equality in the face of political splintering and racial upheaval will make it imperative for labor, as it deals with these issues, to evolve a political philosophy. The combination of Southern white farmers, workers, and Negroes in a political alliance which will also draw in labor and progressive elements from the rest of the country will create a new labor movement. Labor then will no longer be obliged to seek favors from existing political groups and, in exchange for them or in fear of losing them, support an adventurist and warlike foreign policy.

Negro and white workers face essentially the same dilemmas and inevitably, if they are intelligent, experience the same frustration in trying to find a party worth voting for. The Negro is nevertheless in one respect in a unique position. For him, disfranchised as he now is for the most part, the mere act of casting his ballot constitutes in a sense a revolutionary achievement. It is imperative for him to register as widely as possible, pay his poll tax where necessary, and *vote*. The fight for the ballot is integral to the revolt against oppression.

Yet the bitter resentment of the Negroes at the handling of the civil rights issue, both at Chicago and at San Francisco, and their marking time in deciding for whom to vote, clearly indicate that no real and satisfactory choice is open to them. There is something fantastically unreal and at the same time tragic about fighting desperately at the risk of one's livelihood, or even life itself, to gain admission to a polling booth in a typical Southern state, and then having to use this hard-won achievement to indicate a choice between the present Democratic and the present Republican party.

It would be presumptuous for us to attempt to make specific suggestions, much less to lay down directions, for Negro voters. The situation will inevitably remain profoundly unsatisfactory until basic attitudes on the race question are altered and labor is effectively organized. What is clear in the meantime is that the paramount object when making up one's mind how to vote must be to make the vote instrumental in the disruption of the "solid South." In some areas Negroes will probably decide that the reconstitution of Southern politics will be best served by voting Republican, in others by voting Democratic. In areas where there is a sizable Negro population, it has been suggested that a write-in vote might be cast for a Negro candidate, such as Martin Luther King, Jr. In all cases, the Negro vote should be designed as effectively as possible to confuse the old guard and to diminish and rapidly destroy its power.

When the Negro comes back from the polls he must face problems that cannot be solved by voting. Northern Negroes have had the right to vote for years without gaining economic or social equality. The same is true of most workingmen, regardless of their color. More often than not, reliance on voting in periodic elections has sidetracked them from using the more powerful weapons of direct action.

Labor, both white and Negro, must address itself to the real economic issues by organizing fully integrated locals; aiding the struggle for racial equality in Montgomery, Tallahassee, and elsewhere; supporting the victims of economic boycott in Mississippi and South Carolina; fighting the Smith Act and similar repressive measures; and opposing restrictive immigration laws. By engaging in the continuous struggle for justice and human welfare, workers will gain a realistic political education and will cast the only ballot worth casting—the daily ballot for freedom for all.

"EVEN IN THE FACE OF DEATH"

"Not one hair of one head of one white person shall be harmed in the campaign for integration."

At first this sounds like the defensive slogan of a Southern White Citizens Council. Instead it is the motto adopted unanimously by sixty Negro leaders to serve as a rallying point for a South-wide campaign for nonviolent integration.

At the close of the meeting in Atlanta, on January 11, 1957, at which this slogan was adopted, a press conference was held. The *New York Times* correspondent asked, "Do you mean that all of you accept this motto?"

"We do," came the answer.

Turning to Martin Luther King, Jr., chairman of the conference, the correspondent continued, "Do you mean it, *even if others start the violence?*"

"Individuals had better speak for themselves on that," said King. "But *I* mean it."

The correspondent queried the others. One by one, all sixty said "Yes," or nodded their heads in assent.

Last November, when the Supreme Court confirmed its earlier ruling that segregation in bus transportation is illegal, the Negro people of Montgomery, Alabama, were jubilant. After several prayer meetings, much planning, and a week of rededication to nonviolence, they returned to the buses on December 24 for the first time in over a year. For the first time in Montgomery history they "rode like men."

Within a few days, protests similar to the one in Montgomery swept the South. In Atlanta, Birmingham, Baton Rouge, New Orleans, Norfolk, Tallahassee, and many other cities, Negroes "moved up front." Most Southern white persons accepted integration; there were only a few acts of violence on the part of a tiny minority. But by the beginning of January, the occasional beating or shooting had grown into organized terror. The terror was supported by legal subterfuge. It became clear that the opposition was plan-

From *Liberation*, February 1957.

ning to frustrate the court decision by organized violence and "a century of hopeless litigation."

At this point, Reverend Martin Luther King, Jr., of Montgomery, Reverend F. L. Shuttlesworth of Birmingham, and Reverend C. K. Steele of Tallahassee, leaders of the three major protests, began consultations. They came to several conclusions:

> None of the other protests were apt to succeed if the one at Montgomery was defeated. For whites and Negroes alike, Montgomery had become a symbol.
> Integration might not win at Montgomery unless the protests continued to spread throughout other areas of the South.
> The increasing violence was being carefully planned and organized on the theory that the Negroes would back down when faced with such incidents. *Therefore* Negroes had no alternative but to extend and intensify this struggle.
> The majority of white persons were "teetering" between a desire to cling to the pattern they had always known and a feeling that integration must take place. Any hesitation or temporary retreat on the part of Negroes would confuse white persons and drive them back to the old pattern.
> The time had come for Negro leaders to gather from all over the South to "share thinking, discuss common problems, plan common strategy, and explore mutual economic assistance."

King, Steele, and Shuttlesworth issued a call on January 5 for a two-day conference to be held in Atlanta, beginning five days later.

Despite the daily emergencies that each of the leaders had to face, the conference was well planned. It was not to be a matter of coming together simply to exchange details about the bombings and shootings most of them had undergone. Papers were prepared in advance, not only on the practical problems of coordination and planning but on such underlying questions as the relationship of the major economic groups to the struggle for integration; how to encourage and maintain a nonviolent attitude among all Negroes; and the relationship between state power and a nonviolent movement. As violence has mounted, the leaders have been under pressure to call for FBI investigations, for the use of the National Guard or other army units to maintain order. Is this compatible with the spirit of a nonviolent movement?

King and Abernathy arrived at Atlanta the night before the conference was scheduled to open. But neither was present when the first session began. At 5:30 in the morning they had been roused from their beds with notice that four churches and two ministers' homes had been bombed in Montgomery during the night. Taking the next plane for Montgomery, they left word that they would return as soon as possible.

Meanwhile, as the hour approached for opening the conference, the streets adjacent to Ebeneezer Baptist Church, site of the meeting, bristled with city police and plainclothesmen. Five minutes before the scheduled beginning, Detective Clarence M. Nelms gave me an urgent message at the door of the church, then rushed away to supervise the deployment of two carloads of newly arrived detectives. As the men disappeared within a few seconds into side streets and alleys, I stood for a moment in the doorway and pondered the words he had just spoken:

"Be careful. We got word that a carload of white men has started up from Florida to break up your meeting and raise hell in general. If you see anything suspicious, call this number and be damn quick about it."

By 2:30 that afternoon, no hell had been raised, but something of greater significance had happened. Sixty Negro leaders had come from 29 localities of 10 Southern states for the first session of the Negro Leaders Conference on Nonviolent Integration.

Every major protest leader was present. Leaders struggling with economic boycotts and reprisals in South Carolina were standing in a corner exchanging views with the "strong men" from the Mississippi Delta, who are forced to carry on their work at night, underground. The first person to take the floor was a man who had been shot because he had dared to vote. Some had come for technical advice, others to find out more about the spirit and practice of nonviolence. But all of them were determined to respond to the call "to delve deeper into the struggle."

The next day King returned. He reported that there had been great damage in the six bombings at Montgomery but that no one had been hurt. He told how, at a sympathetic white minister's home, twelve sticks of dynamite had failed to go off and had been found on the lawn near a window, in the morning. Then he said: "Let this be a sign unto you. God is truly our protector. He permits men the freedom to do evil. He also has His way to protect His children."

For a time there was a great silence. Then a minister began to pray. At the end of the prayer, King spoke movingly on the power of nonviolence. After this the session broke up in silence.

The final meeting of the conference may go down in history as one of the most important meetings that have taken place in the United States. Sixty beleaguered Negro leaders from across the South voted to establish a permanent Southern Negro Leaders Conference on Nonviolent Integration.

This was the beginning of a South-wide nonviolent resistance campaign against all segregation.

The leaders indicated the price they themselves might have to pay:

> We must continue to stand firm for our right to be first-class citizens. Even in the face of death, we have no other choice. If in carrying out this obligation we are killed, others more resolute will rise to continue.

They then made the following appeal to Negroes in both North and South:

> We call upon all Negroes . . . to assert their human dignity. . . . We know that such an assertion may cause them persecution; yet no matter how great the obstacles and suffering, we urge all Negroes to reject all segregation.

They expressed their realization that "equality" is not enough if it merely means Negroes' fighting for equality of opportunity within a corrupt and competitive social order. Time and again, speakers said that they must struggle against the things in their own hearts that might breed future violence and inequality.

> We ask them to seek justice and to reject all injustice, *especially that in themselves.* We pray that they will refuse further cooperation with the evil elements which invite them to collude against themselves in return for bits of patronage.

Perhaps the most moving part of the statement is that which urged the Negro people to adhere to nonviolence "in word, thought and deed":

> We call upon them to accept Christian Love in full knowledge of its power to defy evil. . . . Nonviolence is not a symbol of weakness or cowardice, but, as Jesus and Gandhi demonstrated, nonviolent resistance transforms weakness into strength and breeds courage in face of danger.

It was at this point that the conference voted to accept as the slogan of the broader movement the motto:

> Not one hair of one head of one white person shall be harmed.

At the press conference that followed, representatives of all the press services and many of the major papers raised questions for more than an hour. The Negro leaders explained how they had called upon white Southerners to realize that the treatment of Negroes is a basic spiritual problem, and how they had urged Southern Christians to speak out with conviction. They reminded the South that the major choice may no longer be between segregation and integration, but between chaos and law.

> People control their destinies only when order prevails. Disorder places all major decisions in the hands of state or federal police. We do not prefer this, for our ultimate aim is to win understanding with our neighbors.

King read a telegram that the conference had sent to President Eisenhower, asking him to "come South immediately to make a major speech in a major Southern city urging all Southerners to accept and to abide by the Supreme Court's decisions as the law of the land." He referred to another telegram sent to Vice-President Nixon urging him "to make a tour of the South similar to the one he made on behalf of Hungarian refugees."

Every major paper in the country carried references to these telegrams, but did not point up the real significance of the conference. The press did not seem to realize that this conference, which solidified the Southern Negroes on the twin platforms of freedom and nonviolence, gave impetus to a movement which will help change the economic and social structure of Southern culture.

As King and I left, we discussed a prophetic statement made by Gandhi. In 1935, Dr. Howard Thurman of Howard University had asked him to come to America—not for white America, he said, but to help the American Negro in his fight for civil rights.

"How I wish I could," Gandhi said, "but I must make good the message here before I bring it to you.

"It may be that through the American Negro the unadulterated message of nonviolence will be delivered to the world."

3
THE SIXTIES

THE MEANING OF BIRMINGHAM

As this pamphlet goes to press, the civil rights movement has reached yet a new step in its development. For the first time a thoroughgoing revolution is occurring in the South. From progressive Greensboro, to industrial Birmingham, to semi-rural Jackson the movement includes all levels of the Negro community. It is a movement that consciously intends to transform the white power structure in this country; a movement that has taken the initiative away from the Kennedy administration (and the forces that would contain the movement with moderate concessions); a movement that will not be satisfied with integrated lunch counters and promises but that is demanding jobs and freedom now.

Birmingham has taught white America many lessons—not the least of them that Negroes were serious when they said they would fill the jails until Southern cities were impoverished and that social dislocation is a reality that confronts all segregated institutions. It ought now to be perfectly clear that Negroes will not wait another twenty-five years. No longer can white liberals merely be proud of those well-dressed students, who are specialists in non-violent action; now they are confronted by a Negro working class that is demanding equal opportunity and full employment.

The Negro community is now fighting for total freedom. It took three million dollars and a year of struggle simply to convince the powers that be that one has the right to ride in the front of a bus. If it takes this kind of pressure to achieve a single thing, then one can just as well negotiate fully for more—for every economic, political, and social right that is presently denied. That is what is important about Birmingham: tokenism is finished.

The Negro masses are no longer prepared to wait for anybody: not for elections, not to count votes, not to wait on the Kennedys or for legislation, nor, in fact, for Negro leaders themselves. They are going to move. Nothing can stop them from moving. And if that Negro leadership does not move rapidly enough and effectively enough they will take it into their own hands and move anyhow.

From an introduction written for a pamphlet, *Civil Rights: The True Frontier*, June 18, 1963.

And out of this we can see a new phase for the civil rights movement. It is the phase of the use of mass action—nonviolent disobedience and nonviolent noncooperation.

Birmingham has proved that no matter what you're up against, if wave after wave of black people keep coming prepared to go to jail, sooner or later there is such confusion, such social dislocation, that white people in the South are faced with a choice: either integrated restaurants or no restaurants at all, integrated public facilities or none at all. And the South then must make its choice for integration, for it would rather have that than chaos.

This struggle is only beginning in the North, but it will be a bitter struggle. It will be an attack on business, on trade unions, and on the government. The Negro will no longer tolerate a situation where for every white man unemployed there are two or three Negroes unemployed. In the North, Negroes present a growing threat to the social order that, less brutally and more subtly than the South, attempts to keep him "in his place." In response, moderates today warn of the danger of violence and "extremism" but do not attempt to change conditions that brutalize the Negro and breed racial conflict. What is needed is an ongoing massive assault on racist political power and institutions.

The mood of the black community is one of anger and confidence of total victory. The victories to date have given added prestige to nonviolent resistance as a method. One can only hope that the white community will realize that the black community means what it says: jobs and freedom now!

IN ANSWER TO SENATOR THURMOND

We organized the 1963 March on Washington in less than eight weeks. In the midst of our somewhat frantic preparations, Senator Strom Thurmond denounced me on the floor of the Senate for being, among other things, a Communist and a draft dodger. His attack not only failed to hurt the March on Washington, but it rallied many new supporters to our side, including a number of Senators. I issued the following statement to the press on August 12, 1963.—B. R.

I wish to comment on two charges leveled against me by Senator Strom Thurmond.

The first charge is that I was a draft dodger during World War II. This is demonstrably false. As a Quaker, I refused to participate in World War II on grounds of conscientious objection. I notified my draft board accordingly. When I was sentenced to twenty-eight months in prison, the judge was sufficiently impressed with the sincerity of my pacifist convictions to allow me three weeks, without bail, to complete my work for the Congress of Racial Equality (CORE) before serving my sentence.

My activities in the pacifist and Quaker organizations are well known. My adherence to nonviolence in the civil rights movement is an outgrowth of the philosophical pacifism I came to accept in the course of those activities. One may quarrel with the conscientious objector, but it is neither fair nor accurate to call him a draft dodger. I did not dodge the draft. I openly and vigorously opposed it. Twenty-eight months' imprisonment was the price I willingly paid for my convictions.

Senator Thurmond charges me with communism. I am not now and never have been a member of the Communist party. More than twenty years ago, while a student at the City College of New York, I was a member of the Young Communist League. I joined the YCL in 1938, just prior to the Hitler-Stalin pact, when communist organizations appeared genuinely interested in peace and in racial justice, and, as a consequence, pacifists could feel relatively comfortable in the YCL. In 1941, after Hitler attacked the Soviet Union, the YCL line changed overnight. The fight for peace and for civil rights was declared subordinate to the defense of the Soviet Union. The league instructed me to stop agitating for integration of the armed forces on the grounds that this impaired the war effort.

I have never been willing to subordinate the just demands of my people to the foreign or domestic policy of any nation. I did not then, and I do not now, consider acquiescence in injustice the road to any kind of true democracy. Accordingly, I left the YCL in 1941.

Even before that year, my Quaker beliefs had conflicted with the basic aims and practices of the YCL. Those beliefs, strengthened over the years, remain incompatible with communism. In recent years I have served as executive secretary of the War Resisters' League, of which Albert Einstein was honorary chairman. I am also an editor of a monthly magazine, *Liberation*. In both positions I have given abundant and public demonstration of my opposition to totalitarianism and undemocratic elements everywhere—in Russia as well as in South Carolina.

The Senator alleges that I visited the Soviet Union. In fact, I have never been to the Soviet Union in my life. Mr. Thurmond stated that my imaginary visit to Moscow occurred in connection with the famous San Francisco to Moscow Peace Walk. He forgot to mention that the participants went to Red Square and distributed leaflets, in Russian, condemning nuclear testing by the Soviet government. He also failed to mention that the leaders of the walk spoke at the University of Moscow, where they denounced the absence of political democracy in the Soviet Union. When Communist politicians tried to halt the meeting, the students' heated protests prolonged it for another hour.

I would have been proud to have participated in both incidents, whose extraordinary effect in reaching the Russian people with the message of democracy was amply described in the *New York Times* and other publications with which members of the United States Senate are presumed to be familiar. As it was, my role in the project was confined to London, from which city I negotiated with various European governments for passage for the walkers.

I am not the first of my race to have been falsely attacked by spokesmen of the Confederacy. But even from them a minimal regard for the facts should be expected. Senator Thurmond's remarks were a disgrace to the United States Senate and a measure of the desperation of the segregationist cause.

With regard to Senator Thurmond's attack on my morality, I have no comment. By religious training and fundamental philosophy, I am disinclined to put myself in the position of having to defend my own moral character. Questions in this area should properly be directed to those who have entrusted me with my present responsibilities.

FROM PROTEST TO POLITICS: THE FUTURE OF THE CIVIL RIGHTS MOVEMENT

The decade spanned by the 1954 Supreme Court decision on school desegregation and the Civil Rights Act of 1964 will undoubtedly be recorded as the period in which the legal foundations of racism in America were destroyed. To be sure, pockets of resistance remain; but it would be hard to quarrel with the assertion that the elaborate legal structure of segregation and discrimination, particularly in relation to public accommodations, has virtually collapsed. On the other hand, without making light of the human sacrifices involved in the direct-action tactics (sit-ins, Freedom Rides, and the rest) that were so instrumental to this achievement, we must recognize that in desegregating public accommodations we affected institutions which are relatively peripheral both to the American socioeconomic order and to the fundamental conditions of life of the Negro people. In a highly industrialized twentieth-century civilization, we hit Jim Crow precisely where it was most anachronistic, dispensable, and vulnerable—in hotels, lunch counters, terminals, libraries, swimming pools, and the like. For in these forms, Jim Crow does impede the flow of commerce in the broadest sense; it is a nuisance in a society on the move (and on the make). Not surprisingly, therefore, the most mobility-conscious and relatively liberated groups in the Negro community—lower-middle-class college students—launched the attack that brought down this imposing but hollow structure.

The term "classical" appears especially apt for this phase of the civil rights movement. But in the few years that have passed since the first flush of sit-ins, several developments have taken place that have complicated matters enormously. One is the shifting focus of the movement in the South, symbolized by Birmingham; another is the spread of the revolution to the North; and the third, common to the other two, is the expansion of the movement's base in the Negro community. To attempt to disentangle these three strands is to do violence to reality. David Danzig's perceptive article, "The Meaning of Negro Strategy" (*Commentary*, February 1964), correctly saw in the Birmingham events the victory of the concept of collective strug-

From *Commentary*, February 1964.

gle over individual achievement as the road to Negro freedom. And Birming-ham remains the unmatched symbol of grass-roots protest involving all strata of the black community. It was also in this most industrialized of Southern cities that the single-issue demands of the movement's classical stage gave way to the "package deal." No longer were Negroes satisfied with integrating lunch counters. They now sought advances in employment, housing, school integration, police protection, and so forth.

Thus the movement in the South began to attack areas of discrimination which were not so remote from the Northern experience as were Jim Crow lunch counters. At the same time, the interrelationship of these apparently distinct areas became increasingly evident. What is the value of winning access to public accommodations for those who lack money to use them? The minute the movement faced this question, it was compelled to expand its vision beyond race relations to economic relations, including the role of education in modern society. And what also became clear is that all these interrelated problems, by their very nature, are not soluble by private, volun-tary efforts but require government action—or politics. Already Southern demonstrators had recognized that the most effective way to strike at the po-lice brutality they suffered from was to get rid of the local sheriff. That meant political action, which in turn meant, and still means, political action within the Democratic party, where the only meaningful primary contests in the South are fought.

And so in Mississippi, thanks largely to the leadership of Bob Moses, a turn toward political action has been taken. More than voter registration is involved here. A conscious bid for *political power* is being made, and in the course of that effort a tactical shift is being effected. Direct-action techniques are being subordinated to a strategy calling for the building of community institutions or power bases. Clearly, the implications of this shift reach far beyond Mississippi. What began as a protest movement is being challenged to translate itself into a political movement. Is this the right course? And if it is, can the transformation be accomplished?

The very decade which has witnessed the decline of legal Jim Crow has also seen the rise of *de facto* segregation in our most fundamental socioeconomic institutions. More Negroes are unemployed today that in 1954, and the un-employment gap between the races is wider. The median income of Negroes has dropped from 57 per cent to 54 per cent of that of whites. A higher per-centage of Negro workers is now concentrated in jobs vulnerable to auto-mation than was the case ten years ago. More Negroes attend *de facto* segregated schools today than when the Supreme Court handed down its famous decision; while school integration proceeds at a snail's pace in the South, the number of Northern schools with an excessive proportion of minority youth proliferates. And behind this is the continuing growth of racial slums, spreading over our central cities and trapping Negro youth in a milieu which, whatever its legal definition, sows an unimaginable demoralization. Again, legal niceties aside, a resident of a racial ghetto lives in segregated housing, and more Negroes fall into this category than ever before.

These are the facts of life which generate frustration in the Negro community and challenge the civil rights movement. At issue, after all, is not *civil rights*, strictly speaking, but social and economic conditions. Last summer's riots were not race riots; they were outbursts of class aggression in a society where class and color definitions are converging disastrously. How can the (perhaps misnamed) civil rights movement deal with this problem?

Before trying to answer, let me first insist that the task of the movement is vastly complicated by the failure of many whites of good will to understand the nature of our problem. There is a widespread assumption that the removal of artificial racial barriers should result in the automatic integration of the Negro into all aspects of American life. This myth is fostered by facile analogies with the experience of various ethnic immigrant groups, particularly the Jews. But the analogies with the Jews do not hold for three simple but profound reasons. First, Jews have a long history as a literate people, a resource which has afforded them opportunities to advance in the academic and professional worlds, to achieve intellectual status even in the midst of economic hardship, and to evolve sustaining value systems in the context of ghetto life. Negroes, for the greater part of their presence in this country, were forbidden by law to read or write. Second, Jews have a long history of family stability, the importance of which in terms of aspiration and self-image is obvious. The Negro family structure was totally destroyed by slavery and with it the possibility of cultural transmission (the right of Negroes to marry and rear children is barely a century old). Third, Jews are white and have the *option* of relinquishing their cultural-religious identity, intermarrying, passing, etc. Negroes, or at least the overwhelming majority of them, do not have this option. There is also a fourth, vulgar reason. If the Jewish and Negro communities are not comparable in terms of education, family structure, and color, it is also true that their respective economic roles bear little resemblance.

This matter of economic role brings us to the greater problem—the fact that we are moving into an era in which the natural functioning of the market does not by itself ensure for every man with will and ambition a place in the productive process. The immigrant who came to this country during the late nineteenth and early twentieth centuries entered a society which was expanding territorially and/or economically. It was then possible to start at the bottom, as an unskilled or semi-skilled worker, and move up the ladder, acquiring new skills along the way. Especially was this true when industrial unionism was burgeoning, giving new dignity and higher wages to organized workers. Today the situation has changed. We are not expanding territorially, the western frontier is settled, labor organizing has leveled off, our rate of economic growth has been stagnant for a decade. And we are in the midst of a technological revolution which is altering the fundamental structure of the labor force, destroying unskilled and semi-skilled jobs—jobs in which Negroes are disproportionately concentrated.

Whatever the pace of this technological revolution may be, the *direction* is clear: the lower rungs of the economic ladder are being lopped off. This means that an individual will no longer be able to start at the bottom and work his way up; he will have to start in the middle or on top, and hold on tight. It will not even be enough to have certain specific skills, for many skilled jobs are also vulnerable to automation. A broad educational background, permitting vocational adaptability and flexibility, seems more imperative than ever. We live in a society where, as Secretary of Labor Willard Wirtz puts it, machines have the equivalent of a high school diploma. Yet the average educational attainment of American Negroes is 8.2 years.

Negroes, of course, are not the only people being affected by these developments. It is reported that there are now 50 per cent fewer unskilled and semi-skilled jobs than there are high school dropouts. Almost one-third of the 26 million young people entering the labor market in the 1960's will be dropouts. But the proportion of Negro dropouts nationally is 57 per cent, and in New York City, among Negroes twenty-five years of age or over, it is 68 per cent. They are without a future.

To what extent can the kind of self-help campaign recently prescribed by Eric Hoffer in the *New York Times Magazine* cope with such a situation? I would advise those who think that self-help is the answer to familiarize themselves with the long history of such efforts in the Negro community, and to consider why so many foundered on the shoals of ghetto life. It goes without saying that any effort to combat demoralization and apathy is desirable, but we must understand that demoralization in the Negro community is largely a common-sense response to an objective reality. Negro youths have no need of statistics to perceive, fairly accurately, what their odds are in American society. Indeed, from the point of view of motivation, some of the healthiest Negro youngsters I know are juvenile delinquents. Vigorously pursuing the American dream of material acquisition and status, yet finding the conventional means of attaining it blocked off, they do not yield to defeatism but resort to illegal (and often ingenious) methods. They are not alien to American culture. They are, in Gunnar Myrdal's phrase, "exaggerated Americans." To want a Cadillac is not un-American; to push a cart in the garment center is. If Negroes are to be persuaded that the conventional path (school, work, etc.) is superior, we had better provide evidence which is now sorely lacking. It is a double cruelty to harangue Negro youth about education and training when we do not know what jobs will be available for them. When a Negro youth can reasonably foresee a future free of slums, when the prospect of gainful employment is realistic, we will see motivation and self-help in abundant enough quantities.

Meanwhile, there is an ironic similarity between the self-help advocated by many liberals and the doctrines of the Black Muslims. Professional sociologists, psychiatrists, and social workers have expressed amazement at the Muslims' success in transforming prostitutes and dope addicts into respectable citizens. But every prostitute the Muslims convert to a model of Calvinist virtue the ghetto replaces with two more. The Muslims, dedicated as they are to maintenance of the ghetto, are powerless to affect substantial moral reform. So too with every other group or program which is not aimed at the destruction of slums, their causes and effects. Self-help efforts must be geared, directly or indirectly, to mobilizing people into power units capable of effecting social change. That is, their goal must be genuine self-help, not merely self-improvement. Obviously, where self-improvement activities succeed in imparting to their participants a feeling of some control over their environment, those involved may find their appetites for change whetted; they may move into the political arena.

Let me sum up what I have thus far been trying to say. The civil rights movement is evolving from a protest movement into a full-fledged *social movement*—an evolution calling its very name into question. It is now concerned not merely with removing the barriers to full *opportunity* but with achieving the fact of *equality*. From sit-ins and Freedom Rides we have gone into rent strikes, boycotts, community organization, and political action. As a consequence of this natural evolution, the Negro today finds himself stymied by obstacles of far greater magnitude than the legal barriers he was attacking before: automation, urban decay, *de facto* school segregation. These are problems which, while conditioned by Jim Crow, do not vanish upon its demise. They are more deeply rooted in our socioeconomic order; they are the result of the total society's failure to meet not only the Negro's needs but human needs generally.

These propositions have won increasing recognition and acceptance, but with a curious twist. They have formed the common premise of two apparently contradictory lines of thought which simultaneously nourish and antagonize each other. On the one hand, there is the reasoning of the *New York Times* moderate who says that the problems are so enormous and complicated that Negro militancy is a futile irritation, and that the need is for "intelligent moderation." Thus, during the first New York school boycott, the *Times* editorialized that Negro demands, while abstractly just, would necessitate massive reforms, the funds for which could not realistically be anticipated; therefore the just demands were also foolish demands and would only antagonize white people. Moderates of this stripe are often correct in perceiving the difficulty or impossibility of racial progress in the context of present social and economic policies. But they accept the context as fixed. They ignore (or perhaps see all too well) the potentialities inherent in linking Negro demands to broader pressures for radical revision of existing policies. They apparently see nothing strange in the fact that in the last twenty-five years we have spent nearly a trillion dollars fighting or preparing for wars, yet we throw up our hands before the need to overhaul our schools, clear the slums, and really abolish poverty. My quarrel with these moderates is that they do not even envision radical changes; their admonitions of moderation are, for all practical purposes, admonitions to the Negro to adjust to the status quo, and are therefore immoral.

The more effectively the moderates argue their case, the more they convince Negroes that American society will not or cannot be reorganized for full racial equality. Michael Harrington has said that a successful war on poverty might well require the expenditure of a $100 billion. Where, the Negro wonders, are the forces now in motion to compel such a commitment? If the voices of the moderates were raised in an insistence upon a reallocation of national resources at levels that could not be confused with tokenism (that is, if the moderates stopped being moderates), Negroes would have greater grounds for hope. Meanwhile, the Negro movement cannot escape a sense of isolation.

It is precisely this sense of isolation that gives rise to the second line of thought I want to examine—the tendency within the civil rights movement to pursue, despite its militancy, what I call a "no-win" policy. Sharing with many moderates a recognition of the magnitude of the obstacles to freedom, spokesmen for this tendency survey the American scene and find no forces prepared to move toward radical solutions. From this they conclude that the only viable strategy is shock; above all, the hypocrisy of white liberals must be exposed. These spokesmen are often described as the radicals of the movement, but they are really its moralists. They seek to change white hearts —by traumatizing them. Frequently abetted by white self-flagellants, they may gleefully applaud (though not really agreeing with) Malcolm X because, while they admit he has no program, they think he can frighten white people into doing the right thing. To believe this, of course, you must be convinced, even if unconsciously, that at the core of the white man's heart lies a buried affection for Negroes—a proposition one may be permitted to doubt. But in any case, hearts are not relevant to the issue; neither racial affinities nor racial hostilities are rooted there. It is institutions—social, political, and economic institutions—which are the ultimate molders of collective sentiments. Let these institutions be reconstructed *today*, and let the ineluctable gradualism of history govern the formation of a new psychology.

My quarrel with the "no-win" tendency in the civil rights movement (and the reason I have so designated it) parallels my quarrel with the moderates outside the movement. As the latter lack the vision or will for fundamental change, the former lack a realistic strategy for achieving it. For such a strategy they substitute militancy. But militancy is a matter of posture and volume and not of effect.

I believe that the Negro's struggle for equality in America is essentially revolutionary. While most Negroes—in their hearts—unquestionably seek only to enjoy the fruits of American society as it now exists, their quest cannot *objectively* be satisfied within the framework of existing political and economic relations. The young Negro who would demonstrate his way into the labor market may be motivated by a thoroughly bourgeois ambition and thoroughly "capitalist" considerations, but he will end up having to favor a great expansion of the public sector of the economy. At any rate, that is the position the movement will be forced to take as it looks at the number of jobs being generated by the private economy and if it is to remain true to the masses of Negroes.

The revolutionary character of the Negro's struggle is manifest in the fact that this struggle may have done more to democratize life for whites than for Negroes. Clearly, it was the sit-in movement of young Southern Negroes which, as it galvanized white students, banished the ugliest features of McCarthyism from the American campus and resurrected political debate. It was not until Negroes assaulted *de facto* school segregation in the urban centers that the issue of quality education for *all* children stirred into motion. Finally, it seems reasonably clear that the civil rights movement, directly and through the resurgence of social conscience it kindled, did more to initiate the war on poverty than any other single force.

It will be—it has been—argued that these by-products of the Negro struggle are not revolutionary. But the term revolutionary, as I am using it, does not connote violence; it refers to the qualitative transformation of fundamental institutions, more or less rapidly, to the point where the social and economic structure which they comprised can no longer be said to be the same. The Negro struggle has hardly run its course; and it will not stop moving until it has been utterly defeated or won substantial equality. But I fail to see how the movement can be victorious in the absence of radical programs for full employment, the abolition of slums, the reconstruction of our educational system, new definitions of work and leisure. Adding up the cost of such programs, we can only conclude that we are talking about a refashioning of our political economy. It has been estimated, for example, that the price of replacing New York City's slums with public housing would be $17 billion. Again, a multibillion-dollar federal public works program, dwarfing the currently proposed $2-billion program, is required to reabsorb unskilled and semi-skilled workers into the labor market—and this must be done if Negro workers in these categories are to be employed. "Preferential treatment" cannot help them.

I am not trying here to delineate a total program, only to suggest the scope of economic reforms which are most immediately related to the plight of the Negro community. One could speculate on their political implications— whether, for example, they do not indicate the obsolescence of state government and the superiority of regional structures as viable units of planning. Such speculations aside, it is clear that Negro needs cannot be satisfied unless we go beyond what has so far been placed on the agenda. How are these radical objectives to be achieved? The answer is simple, deceptively so: *through political power.*

There is a strong moralistic strain in the civil rights movement which would remind us that power corrupts, forgetting that the absence of power also corrupts. But this is not the view I want to debate here, for it is waning. Our problem is posed by those who accept the need for political power but do not understand the nature of the object and therefore lack sound strategies for achieving it; they tend to confuse political institutions with lunch counters.

A handful of Negroes, acting alone, could integrate a lunch counter by strategically locating their bodies so as *directly* to interrupt the operation of the proprietor's will; their numbers were relatively unimportant. In politics, however, such a confrontation is difficult because the interests involved are merely *represented.* In the execution of a political decision a direct confrontation may ensue (as when federal marshals escorted James Meredith into the University of Mississippi—to turn from an example of nonviolent coercion to one of force backed up with the threat of violence). But in arriving at a political decision, numbers and organizations are crucial, especially for the economically disenfranchised. (Needless to say, I am assuming that the forms of political democracy exist in America, however imperfectly, that they are valued, and that elitist or putschist conceptions of exercising power are beyond the pale of discussion for the civil rights movement.)

Neither that movement nor the country's twenty million black people can win political power alone. We need allies. The future of the Negro struggle depends on whether the contradictions of this society can be resolved by a coalition of progressive forces which becomes the *effective* political majority in the United States. I speak of the coalition which staged the March on Washington, passed the Civil Rights Act, and laid the basis for the Johnson landslide—Negroes, trade unionists, liberals, and religious groups.

There are those who argue that a coalition strategy would force the Negro to surrender his political independence to white liberals, that he would be neutralized, deprived of his cutting edge, absorbed into the Establishment. Some who take this position urged last year that votes be withheld from the Johnson-Humphrey ticket as a demonstration of the Negro's political power. Curiously enough, these people who sought to demonstrate power through the non-exercise of it also point to the Negro "swing vote" in crucial urban areas as the source of the Negro's independent political power. But here they are closer to being right: the urban Negro vote will grow in importance in the coming years. If there is anything positive in the spread of the ghetto, it is the potential political power base thus created, and to realize this potential is one of the most challenging and urgent tasks before the civil rights movement. If the movement can wrest leadership of the ghetto vote from the machines, it will have acquired an organized constituency such as other major groups in our society now have.

But we must also remember that the effectiveness of a swing vote depends solely on other votes. It derives its power from them. In that sense, it can never be independent, but must opt for one candidate or the other, even if by default. Thus coalitions are inescapable, however tentative they may be. And this is the case in all but those few situations in which Negroes running on an independent ticket might conceivably win. Independence, in other words, is not a value in itself. The issue is which coalition to join and how to make it responsive to your program. Necessarily there will be compromise. But the difference between expediency and morality in politics is the difference between selling out a principle and making smaller concessions to win larger ones. The leader who shrinks from this task reveals not his purity but his lack of political sense.

The task of molding a political movement out of the March on Washington coalition is not simple, but no alternatives have been advanced. We need to choose our allies on the basis of common political objectives. It has become fashionable in some no-win Negro circles to decry the white liberal as the main enemy (his hypocrisy is what sustains racism); by virtue of this reverse recitation of the reactionary's litany (liberalism leads to socialism, which leads to communism), the Negro is left in majestic isolation, except for a tiny band of fervent white initiates. But the objective fact is that Eastland and Goldwater are the main enemies—they and the opponents of civil rights, of the war on poverty, of medicare, of social security, of federal aid to education, of unions, and so forth. The labor movement, despite its obvious faults, has been the largest single organized force in this country pushing for progressive social legislation. And where the Negro-labor-liberal axis was weak, as in the farm belt, it was the religious groups that were most influential in rallying support for the Civil Rights Bill.

The durability of the coalition was interestingly tested during the election. I do not believe that the Johnson landslide proved the "white backlash" to be a myth. It proved, rather, that economic interests are more fundamental than prejudice: the backlashers decided that loss of social security was, after all, too high a price to pay for a slap at the Negro. This lesson was a valuable first step in reeducating such people, and it must be kept alive, for the civil rights movement will be advanced only to the degree that social and economic welfare gets to be inextricably entangled with civil rights.

The 1964 elections marked a turning point in American politics. The Democratic landslide was not merely the result of a negative reaction to Goldwaterism; it was also the expression of a majority liberal consensus. The near unanimity with which Negro voters joined in that expression was, I am convinced, a vindication of the July 25 statement by Negro leaders calling for a strategic turn toward political action and a temporary curtailment of mass demonstrations. Despite the controversy surrounding the statement, the instinctive response it met with in the community is suggested by the fact that demonstrations were down 75 per cent as compared with the same period in 1963. But should so high a percentage of Negro voters have gone to Johnson, or should they have held back to narrow his margin of victory and thus give greater visibility to our swing vote? How has our loyalty changed things? Certainly the Negro vote had higher visibility in 1960, when a switch of only 7 per cent from the Republican column of 1956 elected President Kennedy. But the slimness of Kennedy's victory—of his "mandate"—dictated a go-slow approach on civil rights, at least until the Birmingham upheaval.

Although Johnson's popular majority was so large that he could have won without such overwhelming Negro support, that support was important from several angles. Beyond adding to Johnson's total national margin, it was specifically responsible for his victories in Virginia, Florida, Tennessee, and Arkansas. Goldwater took only those states where fewer than 45 per cent of eligible Negroes were registered. That Johnson would have won those states had Negro voting rights been enforced is a lesson not likely to be lost on a man who would have been happy with a unanimous electoral college. In any case, the 1.6 million Southern Negroes who voted have had a shattering impact on the Southern political party structure, as illustrated in the changed composition of the Southern congressional delegations. The "backlash" gave the Republicans five house seats in Alabama, one in Georgia, and one in Mississippi. But on the Democratic side, seven segregationists were defeated while all nine Southerners who voted for the Civil Rights Act were reelected. It may be premature to predict a Southern Democratic party of Negroes and white moderates and a Republican party of refugee racists and economic conservatives, but there certainly is a strong tendency toward such a realignment; and an additional 3.6 million Negroes of voting age in the eleven Southern states are still to be heard from. Even the *tendency* toward disintegration of the Democratic party's racist wing defines a new context for presidential and liberal strategy in the congressional battles ahead. Thus the Negro vote (North as well as South), while not *decisive* in the presidential race, was enormously effective. It was a dramatic element of a historic mandate which contains vast possibilities and dangers that will fundamentally affect the future course of the civil rights movement.

The liberal congressional sweep raises hope for an assault on the seniority system, Rule Twenty-two, and other citadels of Dixiecrat-Republican power. The overwhelming of this conservative coalition should also mean progress on much bottlenecked legislation of profound interest to the movement (e.g., bills by Senators Clark and Nelson on planning, manpower, and employment). Moreover, the irrelevance of the South to Johnson's victory gives the President more freedom to act than his predecessor had and more leverage to the movement to pressure for executive action in Mississippi and other racist strongholds.

None of this *guarantees* vigorous executive or legislative action, for the other side of the Johnson landslide is that it has a Gaullist quality. Goldwater's capture of the Republican party forced into the Democratic camp many disparate elements which do not belong there, big business being the major example. Johnson, who wants to be President "of all the people," may try to keep his new coalition together by sticking close to the political center. But if he decides to do this, it is unlikely that even his political genius will be able to hold together a coalition so inherently unstable and rife with contradictions. It must come apart. Should it do so while Johnson is pursuing a centrist course, then the mandate will have been wastefully dissipated. However, if the mandate is seized upon to set fundamental changes in motion, then the basis can be laid for a new mandate, a new coalition including hitherto inert and dispossessed strata of the population.

Here is where the cutting edge of the civil rights movement can be applied. We must see to it that the reorganization of the "consensus party" proceeds along lines which will make it an effective vehicle for social reconstruction, a role it cannot play so long as it furnishes Southern racism with its national political power. And nowhere has the civil rights movement's political cutting edge been more magnificently demonstrated than at Atlantic City, where the Mississippi Freedom Democratic party not only secured recognition as a bona fide component of the national party, but in the process routed the representatives of the most rabid racists—the white Mississippi and Alabama delegations. While I still believe that the FDP made a tactical error in spurning the compromise, there is no question that they launched a political revolution whose logic is the displacement of Dixiecrat power. They launched that revolution within a major political institution and as part of a coalitional effort.

The role of the civil rights movement in the reorganization of American political life is programmatic as well as strategic. We are challenged now to broaden our social vision, to develop functional programs with concrete objectives. We need to propose alternatives to technological unemployment, urban decay, and the rest. We need to be calling for public works and training, for national economic planning, for federal aid to education, for attractive public housing—all this on a sufficiently massive scale to make a difference. We need to protest the notion that our integration into American life, so long delayed, must now proceed in an atmosphere of competitive scarcity instead of in the security of abundance which technology makes possible. We cannot claim to have answers to all the complex problems of modern society. That is too much to ask of a movement still battling barbarism in Mississippi. But we can agitate the right questions by probing at the contradictions which still stand in the way of the Great Society. The questions having been asked, motion must begin in the larger society, for there is a limit to what Negroes can do alone.

THE INFLUENCE OF THE RIGHT AND LEFT IN THE CIVIL RIGHTS MOVEMENT

THE AMERICAN RIGHT

In the early twentieth century, Southern racism was quite distinct from Northern ultraconservatism with its rightist economics. Many a Dixiecrat—the virulent race hater Bilbo among them—championed both white supremacy and positive social welfare programs. During the postwar years, this traditional pattern broke down. In the 1964 elections the new trend came to a head with the coalition of racist politics and rightist economics under the banner of Barry Goldwater. The Goldwaterites now claim that 26 million Americans proved themselves ideological conservatives on Election Day. That, as the various polls have demonstrated, is untrue. Yet the fact remains that the rightist-racist coalition succeeded in capturing one of the two major political parties in America.

Moreover, the racist political appeal is greater than appears at first glance. Nationally, the voter was given a choice between Johnson and Goldwater. If an individual shared Goldwater's hostility to the Civil Rights Act of 1964, or feared a Negro moving into the neighborhood or getting a job, he could vote for Goldwater and express these sentiments, *but at a price:* i.e., he would be casting his ballot for a man who was also utterly irresponsible on the question of war and peace; whose primitive, contradictory economics threatened economic crisis and depression; and whose mental powers seemed to be those of an amiable incompetent. Thus, many Americans suppressed, but did not give up, their "backlash" feelings and voted for Johnson. This can be clearly seen in California where, though Johnson scored a notable victory, Proposition 14 repealing a portion of the state's anti-discrimination laws for housing was carried and Pierre Salinger lost the election—in part because of his stand on the referendum.

The rightist threat basically comes from outside the movement. As the November elections demonstrated, Negro voters and organizations were

A paper prepared by Bayard Rustin for the Negro Leadership Conference held in New York City on January 30–31, 1965.

overwhelmingly anti-Goldwater. Taking "rightist" in this Goldwaterite-ultra sense, we see there is no internal threat within the movement, but a most serious, and in many ways new, rightist challenge to the nation as a whole.

Where on the old right-left spectrum does one place the nationalist trends in the civil rights movement? In one sense, the anti-integrationist ideology of some of the nationalists has led to a programmatic agreement between them and some of the segregationists. There have even been occasional public alliances of black and white race separatists. On the other hand, many nationalists insist that they are much more radical than the "middle-class" leadership of the established organizations, and they attack from the "left." So it is necessary to see the new reality which redefines the old left-and-right terms.

Let me distinguish four different strands in the phenomenon of Negro nationalism. First, there is a healthy race pride, a total psychological rejection of white supremacy, which expresses itself in hair styles, African art and history, and in a new elan. It is positive and it is good. Second, there is a kind of nationalism which seeks to build black, middle-class enclaves and to solve the issue of race by avoiding it. It amounts to an abstention from the struggle and is a negative, if not too widespread, strategy for withdrawal. Third, there is a literary nationalism, often expressed in neo-Marxist terminology, which has captured a section of the Negro intelligentsia. It is intense, contradictory (some of its best-known advocates have interracial marriages), and of considerable importance because it involves some of the most talented Negroes whose intellectual abilities are needed by the movement. Fourth, and finally, there is the organized nationalist movement in all its various forms. The programs of these groups are often confused, yet certain themes persist: "Buy Black"; a black state or enclave; an identification with the new African nations; a hatred of the "white devil." Underlying all these points is the conviction that there are no present alternatives, within a framework of democracy, nonviolence, and integration, for the Negro. Out of this despair comes an identification with the most violent and extreme tendencies of African nationalism, like the Mau Mau. Sometimes even African history is distorted, as in the assertion that Jomo Kenyatta was exactly the kind of brutal terrorist that his British persecutors and their perjured witnesses said he was when they jailed him. But, more important, the nationalists advocate guerrilla strategies which may have made sense when a 90 or 95 per cent African majority was seeking national liberation from a colonial minority but have little relevance to the plight of that 10 per cent of America which is black.

Clearly, this fourth type of organized nationalism poses a problem to the movement. Yet the source of its strength is not conspiratorial or foreign. The nationalist emotion first really appeared right after World War I when Negro migrants from the South found in northern cities not a promised land, but a *de facto* racist economy and society. Similarly today the influence of the various forms of organized nationalism is greatest among the ghetto poor and workers who experience the contradiction between the talk of a "Negro Revolution" and the reality of Negro unemployment, housing, and schools in their daily lives.

The nationalists will not be won to our cause because we maneuver shrewdly. Neither will they be convinced by scholarly analyses of their errors. As long as the intolerable conditions of ghetto life continue and worsen, the nationalists cannot be written off. Conversely, the minute we begin really to move on the issues of unemployment, slum housing, and slum schools, we have the most powerful anti-nationalist argument in the world.

Let us turn now to the "left." I put the term in quotation marks because it has been used to mean so many things. And I think it important that we distinguish between three phenomena which are often carelessly lumped together under the single label of "left." There is, first of all, the traditional Communist left; second, the ultra left; third, the unaffiliated left.

THE TRADITIONAL COMMUNIST LEFT

Since the end of World War I, the most successful organization proclaiming itself to be part of the left was the Communist party. By "left," the Communists meant unquestioning subservience to the Soviet Union. In domestic American political terms, the Communist party was fairly early transformed from a revolutionary and insurrectionary movement into the American propaganda agent for Moscow's line of the movement. In pursuit of this aim, Communists acted as disciplined, and often secret, members of a party "fraction" within other organizations. They took the civil rights cue not from the situation of the Negro, but according to the needs of Moscow. So it was that the Communists attacked the March on Washington movement of 1941 and charged those who sought the "double V" of victory over racism at home and abroad with being disrupters; so it was that they fought against the struggle for fair employment practice legislation during the war.

Since this mode of operation posed the problem of an organized, coherent group taking orders from outside, many civil rights, liberal, and labor organizations were forced to build counter-fractions to deal with the situation.

The basic tactic was that of infighting, and usually no holds were barred on either side.

In 1956, a Communist party which had already lost three-fourths of its peak (1944) membership was shattered by the Khrushchev revelations about Stalin and by the Polish October Revolution and the Hungarian Revolution. Entire sections of the party quit in disgust, including almost the entire staff of the *Daily Worker*. More recently, the orthodox Moscow Communists expelled supporters of the Chinese Communist position and further weakened themselves. As a result, the Communist party is now at an historic low point within the civil rights movement.

Therefore the problem of the traditional Communist left is not that of combating a disciplined fraction by organizational means. And, as will be seen, such a strategy would not only ignore the real problem, but would exacerbate it.

THE ULTRA LEFT

There are other organizations—"Chinese" Communists, Trotskyists, etc.—which criticize the Communist party for being too moderate and which retain the Communist mode of factional struggle within other organizations. However, these groups do not have a significant following among Negroes. They are even smaller than the Communist party, and they do not occupy any positions of organizational power within the civil rights mainstream. By and large, such groups have concentrated on an appeal to nationalist sentiment among Negroes.

The foregoing analysis of the traditional Communist and the ultra left does not mean that there are *no* Communists of any kind infiltrating the movement. There are. But it does mean that people like J. Edgar Hoover, who have a vested political interest in maximizing the strength of the Communists, have distorted the problem. I suspect the complex reality can best be put in terms of the Harlem riot last summer.

As even the FBI admitted, no group, not the Communists or anyone else, organized that upheaval. It grew out of the intolerable conditions of the ghetto and the hatred of police brutality; it involved many socially desperate youth who, as dropouts, are without a future at the age of sixteen or seventeen. Various elements attempted to seize on the situation, among them criminals whose main concern was looting and some ultra left organizations. The latter organizations could not start the riots or control them. They could only seek to fan existing emotions. If, once again, there were an adequate program and struggle against the ghetto conditions, such groups would become utterly irrelevant; and if there is not, there is no way of stopping them from trying to capitalize on the situation.

THE UNAFFILIATED LEFT

By the "unaffiliated left" I mean groups of people within the movement who are bound together not by membership in an organization but by sharing common experiences, emotions, and politics. There are two types of thinking of this unaffiliated left that are most important.

THE THIRTIES VETERANS

One encounters people who went through the thirties together (or sometimes their children), who were in or around the Communist or fellow-traveling movements but who no longer belong to any organization. These people often act in common, yet they are not under orders from any central committee. They usually regard Communist totalitarianism as progressive, but proselytizing this point of view is not their main activity. They believe that white liberals, the Negro middle class, the union bureaucrats, and many other participants in the movement can and should be bluntly criticized; but to talk of "Communist" or "ultra" tendencies within the movement is "red baiting." Thus anyone with Communist or pro-Communist leanings is granted a privileged sanctuary where, immune from criticisms, he can criticize everyone else.

The distinguishing political characteristic of the thirties veterans is that they have no concept of coalition and alliance with the major forces in the society. Most of them did not understand, for instance, that Johnson, for all his faults, was infinitely better than Goldwater. In their America, there is nothing to choose between LBJ and Goldwaterism, which means that the overwhelming majority of the American people are politically hopeless. From this despairing vantage point, the thirties veterans come to think of a genocide resolution at the UN as more important than the Civil Rights Act and to engage in an elitist politics of maneuver.

The thirties veterans are not a numerically large group in the movement. But they are sophisticated, organizationally skilled, and their significance is in terms of their influence rather than their strength. They obviously cannot be dealt with by any organizational means, since they are not themselves formally organized. The problem which they represent can best be confronted by dealing with those to whom they attach themselves: the "spontaneous left."

127

THE SPONTANEOUS LEFT

This is perhaps the most important group and the hardest to define. It is not organized and it contains considerable differences within itself. The spontaneous left is critical of white liberalism and the established civil rights leadership, and prides itself on "militancy," which is defined as intransigence and the refusal of all compromise. While calling for a mass movement, the spontaneous left tends to isolate itself because of its rejection of all possible allies: labor, the churches, the liberals, etc. On many issues the political positions it has taken are the same as those urged by the ultra left, by the thirties veterans, or even by the nationalists. This has led many people who are familiar with the facts of life in the thirties and forties to assume that the group must be the result of conspiratorial, Communist-type infiltration. This is not the case.

The spontaneous left appeals to young people who, first of all, are convinced that civil rights and genuine equality will require significant changes, not simply in Southern prejudice or bigotry generally but in American society and the American economy. I share this point of view.

But then these people go on to despair—and they themselves sometimes do not know that this is what they are doing. They reject all allies, black and white, within and outside the movement. Racism, they say, is not a negotiable issue; it is absolutely wrong and therefore any compromise, any demand short of total and immediate freedom, is a sellout. Of course racism is absolutely wrong, but the effective implementation of the moral rights of a 10 per cent minority requires allies and politics. The spontaneous left does not see the necessities and complexities of the struggle. It therefore accentuates the negative, social dislocation, as the *only* tactic. (Social dislocation is, as I have so often pointed out, one of the most important tactics, but not a panacea.) It refuses partial and limited victory. Sometimes a positive program is put forward, but it is usually a fantasy about guerrilla strategies, or a revolutionary upsurge of the black and white poor against the whole society, the civil rights and labor movements included.

As critical as I am of this point of view, I insist that we distinguish its extreme, and oversimplified, abstractions from its genuine insights. This is necessary because the spirit and the people of the spontaneous left are very important to the movement. Our progress is slow; sometimes our allies drag their feet; and sometimes we ourselves fail in leadership and imagination. What is not true is that democracy and nonviolence have irrevocably failed. If they have, so then has the Negro failed, for there is no other way to win. And the only way to prove that democracy and nonviolence still have meaning is to demonstrate their effectiveness in action by achieving significant change.

The key to the phenomenon of the spontaneous left is not in Moscow, Peking, or Havana. It is in Harlem and Mississippi. And the only effective answer to blind-alley approaches is solid progress which makes a tangible difference in the daily lives of Negro citizens.

That the Civil Rights Act [of 1964] was an historic step forward is undeniable. Indeed, historians will record that the decade between the Supreme Court school decision and the Civil Rights Act witnessed the destruction of the legal foundation of Jim Crow. This achievement, of course, has been registered in response to the massive pressures generated by the Negro and his white allies. I am not in sympathy with those who would decry the Civil Rights Act as an opiate, ignoring the possibilities it opens up for us—possibilities of shifting our focus to new problem areas. The Act has been rightly described as a prologue; it sets the stage.

But we must be ready for the first act, ready with the program and the actors. Here I want to be brief, but it is pointless to outline the problems posed by the right and the left without suggesting solutions.

POSSIBLE SOLUTIONS

THE CIVIL RIGHTS MOVEMENT ALONE

1. Throughout the country, but particularly in the South, *massive voter registration campaigns* must be mounted. An estimated 3.6 million Negroes of voting age remain to be heard from in Dixie. Their potential political power must be mobilized through a variety of techniques: demonstrations, litigation, or whatever seems appropriate in given situations. Above all, I am convinced, the civil rights organizations must be *unified in this effort*—in Mississippi and elsewhere—combining our various specialized skills and techniques. We simply cannot afford disunity and divisiveness in this critical area.

2. I believe we must begin *now* to prepare the Negro community for vigorous *enforcement of the fair employment section of the Act*, which will take effect in July. I understand that the civil rights department of the AFL-CIO has already begun to prepare local labor bodies for full compliance. We have an obligation to educate and mobilize our community on this issue, so that it will be ready to demand its rights—again through a variety of techniques.

3. Police brutality, Northern and Southern, is another area in which the

civil rights movement as such can make progress. We must everywhere be part of the cry for civilian review boards, not in the naive belief that they are a panacea but in the conviction that police conduct is not the exclusive responsibility of commissioners and politicians. Police must be answerable to the citizenry they presumably protect, and if they have been educated to any other concept of their role, now is the time to reeducate them.

THE CIVIL RIGHTS MOVEMENT AND ITS ALLIES

These, then, are some of the major areas in which the Negro community, relying on a diversity of means, can push forward. Let us frankly admit, however, that there are limits to the progress that the civil rights movement can achieve on its own. After all, the fundamental limitation of the Civil Rights Act is precisely that it is a *civil rights* act, whereas the most serious problems confronting the Negro community today are not, strictly speaking, civil rights problems. They are social and economic problems deeply rooted in our economic life. *They are problems of employment, housing, and education.* The Civil Rights Act does not abolish slums, create jobs, or provide decent housing.

To achieve these goals requires an alliance between Negroes and organized, progressive forces in the white community. This principle governs the second group of programs I would advocate.

1. We have to develop employment policies which go beyond the placing of individual Negroes in professional jobs. It is not enough to exhort Negro youth to stay in school. We must insist on a sufficient degree of economic planning to enable us to know what jobs will be available for them upon graduation. We must have answers for the mass of unskilled and semi-skilled Negroes who are imperiled by structural changes in the labor market as a result of the technological revolution.

2. Full and fair employment and the upgrading of wages are essential if civil rights are to be meaningful. The voice of our movement should be loud in demanding implementation of the proposals of the Senate Subcommittee on Manpower and Employment for an additional $5 billion in social investment per year as a means of creating jobs and beginning the elimination of slums.

3. We should be joining with labor, liberals, and others in a campaign *to extend coverage of the Fair Labor Standards Act to all workers*, and to increase the *minimum wage to $2.00 per hour.*

4. We should be demanding immediate passage of an accelerated public works program and repeal of Section 14 b of the Taft-Hartley Act.

5. We should be in the front ranks of the fight for Medicare and medical programs for poverty-stricken children as steps toward a national health plan.

6. We should be mobilizing support for the expansion of the Economic Opportunity Act, insisting on the right of the poor, black and white, to be involved in the decision-making process.

7. We must be open to new ideas—to the proposal, for example, that *youngsters be paid to go to school.*

8. Finally, we need to be demanding of government, at all levels, a *serious timetable for the elimination of slums.*

CONCLUSION

Automation and the like are not exclusively Negro problems. Nor is the educational crisis, nor the growth of slums. Of course, we cannot take all society's burdens on our shoulders. On the other hand, enlightened self-interest dictates that we come up with some far-reaching answers or find ourselves stymied. For in a modern, automating society there are limits to self-help.

And in such a society, the economic realities are such that, in seeking answers for the Negro, we will in fact be refashioning national policies for the benefit of the white dispossessed as well. We can help stimulate motion in sections of the white population: in the labor movement, among liberals, religious groups, and so forth. Whoever doubts this need only ask why we have a "war on poverty" today if not for the civil rights movement and its reverberations throughout the country.

We need to stimulate such motion for still another reason. We cannot talk about the democratic road to freedom unless we are talking about building a majority movement in America. This means we need white allies. It means we must be united with them in demanding a program for reconstructing American life.

Such a program, in my view, will not only answer the frustrations which breed no-win policies; it will also undercut the danger on the right—or at least its political potency. We must create a situation in which backlashers are politically neutralized by having to pay too high a price for the exercise of racist impulses. The program for racial equality must be so intertwined with progressive economic and social policies as to make it impossible to choose one without the other. I know of no better educational technique.

MAKING HIS MARK

THE AUTOBIOGRAPHY OF MALCOLM X. With the assistance of Alex Haley. Illustrated. Grove Press. 455 pp. $7.50.

This odyssey of an American Negro in search of his identity and place in society really begins before his birth forty years ago in Omaha, Nebraska. He was born Malcolm Little, the son of an educated mulatto West Indian mother and a father who was a Baptist minister on Sundays and a dedicated organizer for Marcus Garvey's Back-to-Africa movement the rest of the week.

The first incident Malcolm recounts, as if it were his welcome to white America, occurred just before he was born. A party of Ku Klux Klanners galloped up to his house, threatened his mother, and left a warning for his father to "stop spreading trouble among the good [Negroes]" and get out of town. They galloped into the night after smashing all the windows. A few years later, the Klan was to make good its threat by burning down the Littles' Lansing, Michigan, home because Malcolm's father refused to become an Uncle Tom. These were the first in a series of incidents of racial violence . . . that were to haunt the nights of Malcolm and his family and hang like a pall over the lives of Negroes in the North and South. Five of Reverend Little's six brothers died by violence—four at the hands of white men, one by lynching, and one shot down by Northern police officers. When Malcolm was six, his father was found cut in two by a trolley car with his head bashed in. Malcolm's father had committed "suicide," the authorities said. Early in his life Malcolm concluded that "I too would die by violence. . . . I do not expect to live long enough to read this book."

Malcolm's early life in the Midwest was not wholly defined by race. Until he went to Boston when he was fourteen, after his mother suffered a mental breakdown from bringing up eight children alone, his friends were often white; there were few Negroes in the small Midwestern towns where he grew up. He recounts with pride how he was elected president of his eighth-grade class in an almost totally white school.

From the *Sunday Herald Tribune* "Book Week," November 14, 1965.

But the race problem was always there, although Malcolm, who was light-skinned, tried for a time to think of himself as white or just like anyone else. Even in his family life, color led to conflict that interfered with normal relationships. The Reverend Little was a fierce disciplinarian, but he never laid a hand on his light-skinned son, because unconsciously, according to Malcolm, he had developed respect for white skin. On the other hand, Malcolm's mother, whose father was a white man, was ashamed of this and favored Malcolm's darker brothers and sisters. Malcolm wrote that he spent his life trying to purge this tainted white blood of a rapist from his veins.

Race also set the limits on his youthful ambitions during what he describes as his "mascot years" in a detention home run by whites with mixed feelings of affection and superiority toward him. One of the top students in his school and a member of the debating club, Malcolm went to an English teacher he admired and told him of his ambition to become a lawyer. "Mr. Ostrowsky looked surprised and said, 'Malcolm, one of life's first needs is for us to be realistic . . . a lawyer, that's no realistic goal for a nigger . . . you're good with your hands . . . why don't you plan on carpentry?'" How many times has this scene been repeated in various forms in schoolrooms across the country? It was at this point, Malcolm writes, "that I began to change—inside. I drew away from white people."

Too many people want to believe that Malcolm, "the angry black man, sprang full grown from the bowels of the Harlem ghetto." These chapters on his childhood are essential reading for anyone who wants to understand the plight of American Negroes.

Malcolm Little was fourteen when he took the Greyhound to Boston to live with his half-sister, Ella, who had fought her way into the Boston "black bourgeoisie." The "400," as they were called, lived on "the Hill," only one step removed socially, economically, and geographically from the ghetto ("the Town"). Malcolm writes that "a big percentage of the Hill dwellers were in Ella's category—Southern strivers and scramblers and West Indian Negroes, whom both the New Englanders and Southerners called 'Black Jews.'" Ella owned some real estate and her own home, and like the first Jews who arrived in the New World, she was determined to shepherd new immigrants and teach them the strange ways of city life. There were deep bonds between Ella and her younger brother, and she tried to help him live a respectable life on the Hill.

But for Malcolm the 400 were only "a big-city version of those 'successful' Negro bootblacks and janitors back in Lansing . . . 8 out of 10 of the Hill Negroes of Roxbury . . . actually worked as menials and servants. . . . I don't know how many 40- and 50-year-old errand boys went down the Hill dressed as ambassadors in black suits and white collars to downtown jobs 'in government,' 'in finance,' or 'in law.' " Malcolm instead chose "the Town," where for the first time he felt he was part of a people.

Unlike the thousands of Negro migrants who poured into the Northern ghettos, Malcolm had a choice. But from the moment he made it, the options narrowed. He got a job at the Roseland Ballroom, where all the jazz greats played. His title was shoeshine boy but his real job was to hustle whiskey, prophylactics, and women to Negroes and whites. He got his first conk and zoot suit and a new identity, "Red," and his secondary education began before he was fifteen. "I was . . . schooled well, by experts in such hustles as the numbers, pimping, con games of many kinds, peddling dope, and thievery of all sorts, including armed robbery."

It is significant that it was Malcolm's good qualities—his intelligence, integrity, and distaste for hypocrisy—as well as his sickness that made him choose crime rather than what passed in the Negro community for a respectable bourgeois life. Later he moved on to bigger things in Harlem, became "Detroit Red," went on dope, and at one time carried three guns.

His description of the cutthroat competition between the hustlers and their fraternity is both frightening and moving. "As in the case of any jungle," he writes, "the hustler's every waking hour is lived with both the practical and the subconscious knowledge that if he ever relaxes, if he ever slows down, the other hungry, restless foxes, ferrets, wolves, and vultures out there with him won't hesitate to make him their prey." He summed up his morality at the time: "The only thing I considered wrong was what I got caught doing wrong . . . and everything I did was done by instinct to survive." As a "steerer" of uptown rich whites to Harlem "sex specialties," he recounts perversions with racial overtones, of white men begging to be beaten by black women or paying large amounts to witness interracial sex that make Genet's *The Balcony* seem inhibited by comparison.

"Detroit Red" was a limited success in his trade for four years. But even in this business, success was limited by race. The big operators, the successful, respectable, and safe executives of policy, dope, and prostitution rackets, were white and lived outside the ghetto.

Malcolm left Harlem to return to Boston, and a few months later was caught as the head of a burglary gang. In February 1946, not quite twenty-one, he was sentenced to ten years in prison, though the average sentence for burglary was about two years—the price for his being caught with his white girl friend and her sister.

Most of the first year in prison, Malcolm writes, he spent in solitary confinement, cursing: "My favorite targets were the Bible and God." Malcolm got a new name from the other prisoners—"Satan"—and plenty of time to think. He went through what he described as a great spiritual crisis, and, as a result, he, the man who cursed God, bowed down and prayed to Allah. It will be difficult for those readers who have never been in prison to understand the psychological torment that prisoners experience, their feelings of isolation, their need to totally commit their minds to something outside of themselves. Men without any of the external economic symbols of status seek security in a religion, philosophy, or ideology. Malcolm particularly, with his great feelings of rebelliousness, hatred, and internal conflict, turned to books and ideas for relief. When his brothers and sisters wrote to him that they had become followers of Elijah Muhammad and sent him Elijah's teachings, Malcolm seized on the tracts. Stimulated, he read other books on religion and philosophy voraciously. In his spiritual and psychological crisis he underwent religious conversion.

He took on a new identity and became Malcolm X, a follower of Elijah Muhammad. Now he had a God to love and obey and a white devil responsible for his plight. Many Negro prisoners accepted the "Messenger," Elijah Muhammad, for similar reasons. Excluded from American society, they were drawn to another one, the Nation of Islam. (This analysis of why Malcolm joined the Muslims is mine, for although Malcolm writes about Muslim ideas, nowhere does he discuss the reasons for his conversion beyond a surface level.)

Out of prison, Malcolm, while remaining religious, arrived at a balanced view of the more fantastic elements of Elijah's teachings and at a deeper understanding of one of the driving forces: "So many of the survivors whom I knew as tough hyenas and wolves of the streets in the old days now were so pitiful. They had known all the angles, but beneath that surface they were poor, ignorant, untrained men; life had eased up on them and hyped them. . . . I was thankful to Allah that I had become a Muslim and escaped their fate."

Alex Haley, who assisted Malcolm with the book, rightly commends him for deciding not to rewrite the first parts of the book and make it a polemic against his old leader, although in the interim they had broken and now were in competition with each other. As a result, the book interestingly shows changes in Malcolm's thinking.

After seven years in prison, Detroit Red emerged as Malcolm X and was soon to be the brightest star of the Nation of Islam. But as in every conversion, the man himself was not entirely reborn. Malcolm brought with him his traits of the past—the shrewd and competitive instincts learned on the ghetto streets, combined now with the language and thoughts of the great philosophers of Western culture he applied from reading Hegel, Kant, and Nietzsche, and great Negro intellectuals like Du Bois. Remaining, too, with his burning ambition to succeed, was the rebellious anger of his youth for being denied a place in society commensurate with his abilities. But on the other side of the coin was a desire for fraternity, family, and respectability.

Because of his ability, he was sent to New York, where he struck a responsive chord with a great many Harlem Negroes. The Nationalist sects provided an arena of struggle for power and status denied lower-class Negroes in the outside world.

But the same qualities that made him a successful ghetto organizer soon brought him into conflict with other Muslim leaders, especially Elijah's children and prospective heirs. They saw Malcolm as a threat to their domain and apparently were able to convince Elijah that there was a threat to himself as well. For although Malcolm always gave corollary credit to Elijah—and the limits set upon him by Elijah's demands made many underestimate the exceptional nature of his mind—he could not totally constrain his brilliance, pride, or ambition. "Only by being two people could I have worked harder in the service of the Nation of Islam. I had every gratification that I wanted. I had helped bring about the progress and additional impact such that none could call us liars when we called Mr. Muhammad the most powerful black man in America."

As Malcolm's star rose higher in the western sky, Mr. Muhammad saw his eastern star setting and grew jealous. The conflict grew, although Malcolm made efforts toward conciliation. Finally, there was a total break that could be fatal to the erring Muslim who was cast away. Malcolm was aware of the dangers. "I hadn't hustled in the streets for nothing. I knew I was being set up. . . . As any official in the Nation of Islam would instantly have known, any death-talk for me could have been approved of—if not actually initiated—by only one man." Later, just before his death, Malcolm said the attempt to murder him would come from a much greater source than the Muslims; he never revealed about whom he was talking.

Under a death sentence and without money or any substantial organization, Malcolm opted for action, although it was unclear whether he was running away from or toward something as he began another phase of his odyssey—a pilgrimage to Mecca, where he became El-Hajj Malik El-Shabazz. Throughout his many conversions and transformations, he never was more American than during his trip to Mecca. Because his ankles were not flexible enough, he was unable to sit properly cross-legged on the traditional Muslim rug with the others, and at first he shrank from reaching into the common food pot. Like many American tourists, he projected desires for hospitality and fraternity, frustrated at home, on the Muslims he met, most of whom he could not communicate with because of the language barrier. Back in America, he acknowledged that it would be a long time before the Negro was ready to make common struggle with the Africans and Arabs.

In Mecca, Malcolm also dramatically announced that he had changed his view on integration, because he had seen true brotherhood there between black and white Muslims. In reality he had begun changing his attitude on integration and the civil rights movement many months before, as the divisions between him and Elijah Muhammad widened. Partway through the book his attacks on the movement became muted, and in the epilogue Haley concludes that Malcolm "had a reluctant admiration for Dr. Martin Luther King."

The roots of Malcolm's ambivalence were much more profound than personal opportunism. In a touching confession of dilemma he told Haley, " 'the so-called moderate' civil rights organizations avoided him as 'too militant' and the 'so-called militants' avoided him as 'too moderate.' 'They won't let me turn the corner!' he once exclaimed. 'I'm caught in a trap!' " Malcolm was moving toward the mainstream of the civil rights movement when his life was cut short, but he still had quite a way to go. His anti-Semitic comments are a symptom of this malaise.

Had he been able to "turn the corner," he would have made an enormous contribution to the struggle for equal rights. As it was, his contribution was substantial. He brought hope and a measure of dignity to thousands of despairing ghetto Negroes. His extremism made the mainstream civil rights groups more respectable by comparison and helped them wrest substantial concessions from the power structure. Malcolm himself clearly understood the complicated role he played. At a Selma rally, while Dr. King was in jail, Malcolm said, "Whites better be glad Martin Luther King is rallying the people because other forces are waiting to take over if he fails." Of course, he never frightened the racists and the reactionaries as much as he made liberals feel uncomfortable, and moderates used his extremism as an excuse for inaction.

Behind the grim visage on television that upset so many white Americans there was a compassionate and often gentle man with a sense of humor. A testament to his personal honesty was that he died broke and money had to be raised for his funeral and family.

Upset by the comments in the African and Asian press criticizing the United States government for Malcolm's fate, Carl T. Rowan, director of the United States Information Agency, held up some foreign papers and told a Washington audience, according to Alex Haley, ". . . All this about an ex-convict, ex–dope peddler, who became a racial fanatic." Yes, all this and more, before we can understand. Malcolm's autobiography, revealing little-known aspects of his life and character, makes that tortured journey more understandable.

One of the book's shortcomings is that M. S. Handler and Haley, in their sensitive and insightful supplementary comments, make no comprehensive estimate of Malcolm X as a political leader. His often conflicting roles in the civil rights movement are described rather than analyzed. Perhaps this couldn't be helped, for Haley writes that Malcolm wanted a chronicler, not an interpreter. Obviously, Malcolm was not ready to make a synthesis of his ideas and an evaluation of his political role.

Shortly after Malcolm's death Tom Kahn and I wrote in *New America* and *Dissent*: "Now that he is dead, we must resist the temptation to idealize Malcolm X, to elevate charisma to greatness. History's judgment of him will surely be ambiguous. His voice and words were cathartic, channeling into militant verbiage emotions that otherwise might have run a violently destructive course. But having described the evil, he had no program for attacking it. With rare skill and feeling he articulated angry subterranean moods more widespread than any of us like to admit. But having blown the trumpet, he could summon, even at the very end, only a handful of followers."

Of course we cannot judge political effectiveness by numbers alone, but we cannot ignore his inability to build a movement. As a spokesman for Negro anger and frustration, he left his mark on history, but as a militant political leader he failed—and the Negro community needed both. Till the end, his program was a maze of contradictions. He was a brilliant psychologist when it came to articulating the emotions and thoughts of ghetto Negroes, but he knew virtually nothing about economics and, more important, his program had no relevance to the needs of lower-class Negroes. His conception of the economic roots of the problem is reflected in such remarks as "it is because black men do not own and control their community retail establishments that they cannot stabilize their own communities." And he advocates, as a solution, that Negroes who buy so many cars and so much expensive whiskey should own automobile franchises and distilleries. Malcolm was urging Negroes to pool their resources into small business establishments at a time when small businesses were declining under the pressure of big business and when an unplanned technological revolution was creating massive unemployment for unskilled Negroes. Malcolm's solutions were in fact almost a mirror image of many proposals made by white

economic moderates; those advocates of "self-help" without a massive program for jobs remind me of no one so much as those black nationalist sects
and their "build it yourself" black economy without capital. In short, Malcolm's economic program was not radical. It was, in fact, petty bourgeois.

Malcolm got a wide hearing in the ghetto because large sections of the
Negro working class were being driven into the "underclass" and made
part of the rootless mass by the vicissitudes of the economy. He articulated
the frustration and anger of these masses, and they admired his outspoken
attack on the racists and white hypocrites. But while thousands came to his
funeral (I was there, too, to pay my respects), few joined his organization.
Nor should it be surprising that the Negro masses did not support his proposed alliance of black Americans, Africans, and Arabs, including such leaders as Prince Faisal. For what did a Harlem Negro, let alone an Arab Bed-
ouin, have in common with a feudal prince like Faisal? And at home
Malcolm maintained an uneasy coexistence with the Harlem political machine. Today Malcolm's organization, the OAAU, hardly exists. In addition,
he never clearly understood that, as progress was made toward social integration, the problem for America's Negroes would become just as much one of
class as of race.

Malcolm was with the Negro masses, but he was not of them. His experience and ambitions separated him from working-class Negroes. But to say
this is not enough. In a sense Malcolm's life was tragic on a heroic scale.
He had choices but never took the easy or comfortable ones. If he had, he
might today be, as he said, a successful lawyer, sipping cocktails with other
members of the black bourgeoisie. He chose instead to join the Negro
masses who never had this freedom of choice. And before his death he
was working toward a more creative approach to the problems of the ghetto.
Perhaps he might have been successful in turning this corner.

After reflecting on the old days at Mosque 7, shortly before he was killed,
Malcolm told Haley, "That was a bad scene, brother. The sickness and mad-
ness of those days—I'm glad to be free of them. It's a time for martyrs now.
And if I'm to be one, it will be in the cause of brotherhood."

Our journey through the madness of racism continues, and there is much
we can learn about both the sickness and the cure from Malcolm X.

THE WATTS "MANIFESTO" AND
THE McCONE REPORT

The riots in the Watts section of Los Angeles last August continued for six days, during which 34 persons were killed, 1,032 were injured, and 3,952 were arrested. Viewed by many of the rioters themselves as their "manifesto," the uprising of the Watts Negroes brought out in the open, as no other aspect of the Negro protest has done, the despair and hatred that continue to brew in the Northern ghettos despite the civil rights legislation of recent years and the advent of the war on poverty. With national attention focused on Los Angeles, Governor Edward P. Brown created a commission of prominent local citizens, headed by John A. McCone, to investigate the causes of the riots and to prescribe remedies against any such outbreaks in the future. Just as the violent confrontation on the burning streets of Watts told us much about the underlying realities of race and class relations in America—summed up best, perhaps, by the words of Los Angeles Police Chief William Parker, "We're on top and they're on the bottom"—so does the McCone Report, published under the title *Violence in the City—An End or a Beginning?*, tell us much about the response of our political and economic institutions to the Watts "manifesto."

Like the much-discussed Moynihan Report, the McCone Report is a bold departure from the standard government paper on social problems. It goes beyond the mere recital of statistics to discuss, somewhat sympathetically, the real problems of the Watts community—problems like unemployment, inadequate schools, dilapidated housing—and it seems at first glance to be leading toward constructive programs. It never reaches them, however, for, again like the Moynihan Report, it is ambivalent about the basic reforms that are needed to solve these problems and therefore shies away from spelling them out too explicitly. Thus, while it calls for the creation of 50,000 new jobs to compensate for the "spiral of failure" that it finds among the Watts Negroes, the McCone Report does not tell us how these jobs are to be created or obtained and instead recommends existing

From *Commentary*, March 1966.

programs which have already shown themselves to be inadequate. The Moynihan Report, similarly, by emphasizing the breakdown of the Negro family, also steers clear of confronting the thorny issues of Negro unemployment as such.

By appearing to provide new viewpoints and fresh initiatives while at the same time repeating, if in more sophisticated and compassionate terms, the standard white stereotypes and shibboleths about Negroes, the two reports have become controversial on both sides of the Negro question. On the one hand, civil rights leaders can point to the recognition in these reports of the need for jobs and training, and for other economic and social programs to aid the Negro family, while conservatives can find confirmed in their pages the Negro penchant for violence, the excessive agitation against law and order by the civil rights movement, or the high rates of crime and illegitimacy in the Negro community; on the other hand, both sides have criticized the reports for feeding ammunition to the opposition. Unfortunately, but inevitably, the emphasis on *Negro* behavior in both reports has stirred up an abstract debate over the interpretation of data rather than suggesting programs for dealing with the existing and very concrete situation in which American Negroes find themselves. For example, neither report is concerned about segregation and both tacitly assume that the Civil Rights Acts of 1964 and 1965 are already destroying this system. In the case of the McCone Report, this leaves the writers free to discuss the problems of Negro housing, education, and unemployment in great detail without attacking the conditions of de facto segregation that underlie them.

The errors and misconceptions of the McCone Report are particularly revealing because it purports to deal with the realities of the Watts riots rather than with the abstractions of the Negro family. The first distortion of these realities occurs in the opening chapter—"The Crisis: An Overview" —where, after briefly discussing the looting and beatings, the writers conclude that "the rioters seem to have been caught up in an insensate rage of destruction." Such an image may reflect the fear of the white community that Watts had run amok during six days in August, but it does not accurately describe the major motive and mood of the riots, as subsequent data in the report itself indicate. While it is true that Negroes in the past have often turned the violence inflicted on them by society in upon themselves— "insensate rage" would perhaps have been an appropriate phrase for the third day of the 1964 Harlem riots—the whole point of the outbreak in Watts was that it marked the first major rebellion of Negroes against their own masochism and was carried on with the express purpose of asserting that they would no longer quietly submit to the deprivation of slum life.

This message came home to me over and over again when I talked with the young people in Watts during and after the riots, as it will have come home to those who watched the various television documentaries in which the Negroes of the community were permitted to speak for themselves. At a street corner meeting in Watts when the riots were over, an unemployed youth of about twenty said to me, "We won." I asked him: "How have you won? Homes have been destroyed, Negroes are lying dead in the streets, the stores from which you buy food and clothes are destroyed, and people are bringing you relief." His reply was significant: "We won because we made the whole world pay attention to us. The police chief never came here before; the mayor always stayed uptown. We made them come." Clearly it was no accident that the riots proceeded along an almost direct path to City Hall.

Nor was the violence along the way random and insensate. Wherever a store owner identified himself as a "poor working Negro trying to make a business" or as a "blood brother," the mob passed the store by. It even spared a few white businesses that allowed credit or time purchases, and it made a point of looting and destroying stores that were notorious for their high prices and hostile manners. The McCone Report itself observes that "the rioters concentrated on food markets, liquor stores, clothing stores, department stores, and pawnshops." The authors "note with interest that no residences were deliberately burned, that damage to schools, libraries, public buildings was minimal and that certain types of business establishments, notably service stations and automobile dealers, were for the most part unharmed." It is also worth noting that the rioters were much more inclined to destroy the stock of the liquor stores they broke into than to steal it and that, according to the McCone Report, "there is no evidence that the rioters made any attempt to steal narcotics from pharmacies . . . which were looted and burned."

This is hardly a description of a Negro community that has run amok. The largest number of arrests were for looting—not for arson or shooting. Most of the people involved were not habitual thieves; they were members of a deprived group who seized a chance to possess things that all the dinning affluence of Los Angeles had never given them. There were innumerable touching examples of this behavior. One married couple in their sixties was seen carrying a couch to their home, and when its weight became too much for them, they sat down and rested on it until they could pick it up again. Langston Hughes tells of another woman who was dragging a sofa through the streets and who stopped at each intersection and waited for the traffic light to turn green. A third woman went out with her children to get a kitchen set, and after bringing it home, she discovered they needed one more chair in order to feed the whole family together; they went back to get the chair and all of them were arrested.

If the McCone Report misses the point of the Watts riots, it shows even less understanding of their causes. To place these in perspective, the authors begin by reviewing the various outbursts in the Negro ghettos since the summer of 1964 and quickly come up with the following explanations: "Not enough jobs to go around, and within this scarcity not enough by a wide margin of a character which the untrained Negro could fill. . . . Not enough schooling to meet the special needs of the disadvantaged Negro child whose environment from infancy onward places him under a serious handicap." Finally, "a resentment, even hatred, of the police as a symbol of authority."

For the members of the special commission these are the fundamental causes of the current Negro plight and protest, which are glibly summed up in the ensuing paragraph by the statement that "Many Negroes moved to the city in the last generation and are totally unprepared to meet the conditions of city life." I shall be discussing these "causes" in detail as we go along, but it should be noted here that the burden of responsibility has already been placed on these hapless migrants to the cities. There is not one word about the conditions, economic as well as social, that have pushed Negroes out of the rural areas; nor is there one word about whether the cities have been willing and able to meet the demand for jobs, adequate housing, proper schools. After all, one could as well say that it is the *cities* which have been "totally unprepared" to meet the "conditions of *Negro* life," but the moralistic bias of the McCone Report, involving as it does an emphasis on the decisions of men rather than the pressure of social forces, continually operates in the other direction.

The same failure of awareness is evident in the report's description of the Los Angeles situation (the Negro areas of Los Angeles "are not urban gems, neither are they slums," the Negro population "has exploded," etc.). The authors do concede that the Los Angeles transportation system is the "least adequate of any major city," but even here they fail to draw the full consequences of their findings. Good, cheap transportation is essential to a segregated working-class population in a big city. In Los Angeles a domestic worker, for example, must spend about $1.50 and one and one-half to two hours to get to a job that pays $6 or $7 a day. This both discourages efforts to find work and exacerbates the feeling of isolation.

A neighborhood such as Watts may seem beautiful when compared to much of Harlem (which, in turn, is an improvement over the Negro section of Mobile, Alabama)—but it is still a ghetto. The housing is run-down, public services are inferior, the listless penned-in atmosphere of segregation is oppressive. Absentee landlords are the rule, and most of the businesses are owned by whites: neglect and exploitation reign by day, and at night, as one Watts Negro tersely put it, "There's just the cops and us."

The McCone Report, significantly, also ignores the political atmosphere of Los Angeles. It refers, for example, to the repeal in 1964 of the Rumford Act—the California fair housing law—in these words: "In addition, many Negroes here felt and were encouraged to feel that they had been affronted by the passage of Proposition 14." Affronted, indeed! The largest state in the Union, by a three-to-one majority, abolishes one of its own laws against discrimination and Negroes are described as regarding this as they might the failure of a friend to keep an engagement. What they did feel—and without any need of encouragement—was that while the rest of the North was passing civil rights laws and improving opportunities for Negroes, their own state and city were rushing to reinforce the barriers against them.

The McCone Report goes on to mention two other "aggravating events in the twelve months prior to the riot." One was the failure of the poverty program to "live up to [its] press notices," combined with reports of "controversy and bickering" in Los Angeles over administering the program. The second "aggravating event" is summed up by the report in these words:

> Throughout the nation unpunished violence and disobedience to the law were widely reported, and almost daily there were exhortations, here and elsewhere, to take the most extreme and illegal remedies to right a wide variety of wrongs, real and supposed.

It would be hard to frame a more insidiously equivocal statement of the Negro grievance concerning law enforcement during a period that included the release of the suspects in the murder of the three civil rights workers in Mississippi, the failure to obtain convictions against the suspected murderers of Medgar Evers and Mrs. Violet Liuzzo, the Gilligan incident in New York, the murder of Reverend James Reeb, and the police violence in Selma, Alabama—to mention only a few of the more notorious cases. And surely it would have been more to the point to mention that throughout the nation Negro demonstrations have almost invariably been nonviolent, and that the major influence of the civil rights movement on the Negro community has been the strategy of discipline and dignity. Obsessed by the few prophets of violent resistance, the McCone Commission ignores the fact that never before has an American group sent so many people to jail or been so severely punished for trying to uphold the law of the land.

It is not stretching things too far to find a connection between these matters and the treatment of the controversy concerning the role of the Los Angeles police. The report goes into this question at great length, finally giving no credence to the charge that the police may have contributed to the spread of the riots through the use of excessive force. Yet this conclusion is arrived at not from the point of view of the Watts Negroes, but from that of the city officials and the police. Thus, the report informs us, in judicial hearings that were held on 32 of the 35 deaths which occurred, 26 were ruled justifiable homicides; but the report—which includes such details as the precise time Mayor Yorty called Police Chief Parker and when exactly the National Guard was summoned—never tells us what a "justifiable homicide" is considered to be. It tells us that "of the 35 killed, one was a fireman, one was a deputy sheriff, and one was a Long Beach policeman," but it does not tell us how many Negroes were killed or injured by police or National Guardsmen. (Harry Fleischman of the American Jewish Committee reports that the fireman was killed by a falling wall; the deputy sheriff, by another sheriff's bullet; and the policeman, by another policeman's bullet.) We learn that of the 1,032 people reported injured, 90 were police officers, 36 were firemen, 10 were National Guardsmen, 23 were from government agencies. To find out that about 85 per cent of the injured were Negroes, we have to do our own arithmetic. The report contains no information as to how many of these were victims of police force, but one can surmise from the general pattern of the riots that few could have been victims of Negro violence.

The report gives credence to Chief Parker's assertion that the rioters were the "criminal element in Watts," yet informs us that of the 3,438 adults arrested, 1,164 had only minor criminal records and 1,232 had never been arrested before. Moreover, such statistics are always misleading. Most Negroes, at one time or another, have been picked up and placed in jail. I myself have been arrested twice in Harlem on charges that had no basis in fact: once for trying to stop a police officer from arresting the wrong man, the second time for asking an officer who was throwing several young men into a paddy wagon what they had done. Both times I was charged with interfering with an arrest and kept overnight in jail until the judge recognized me and dismissed the charges. Most Negroes are not fortunate enough to be recognized by judges.

Having accepted Chief Parker's view of the riots, the report goes on to absolve him of the charge of discrimination: "Chief Parker's statements to us and collateral evidence, such as his fairness to Negro officers, are inconsistent with his having such an attitude ['deep hatred of Negroes']. Despite the depth of feeling against Chief Parker expressed to us by so many witnesses, he is recognized even by many of his vocal critics as a capable Chief who directs an efficient police force and serves well this entire community."

I am not going to stress the usual argument that the police habitually mistreat Negroes. Every Negro knows this. There is scarcely any black man, woman, or child in the land who at some point or other has not been mistreated by a policeman. (A young man in Watts said, "The riots will continue because I, as a Negro, am immediately considered to be a criminal by the police and, if I have a pretty woman with me, she is a tramp even if she is my wife or mother.") Police Chief Parker, however, goes beyond the usual bounds. He does not recognize that he is prejudiced, and being both naive and zealous about law and order, he is given to a dangerous fanaticism. His reference to the Negro rioters as "monkeys" and his "top . . . and bottom" description of the riots speak for themselves, and they could only have further enraged and encouraged the rioters. His insistence on dealing with the outbreak in Watts as though it were the random work of a "criminal element" threatened to lead the community, as Martin Luther King remarked after the meeting he and I had with Chief Parker, "into potential holocaust." Though Dr. King and I have had considerable experience in talking with public officials who do not understand the Negro community, our discussions with Chief Parker and Mayor Samuel Yorty left us completely nonplused. They both denied, for example, that there was any prejudice in Los Angeles. When we pointed to the very heavy vote in the city for Proposition 14, they replied, "That's no indication of prejudice. That's personal choice." When I asked Chief Parker about his choice of language, he implied that this was the only language Negroes understood.

The impression of "blind intransigence and ignorance of the social forces involved" which Dr. King carried away from our meeting with Chief Parker is borne out by other indications. The cast of his political beliefs, for example, was evidenced during his appearance last May on the Manion Forum, one of the leading platforms of the radical right, in which (according to newspaper reports) he offered his "considered opinion that America today is in reality more than half pagan" and that "we have moved our form of government to a socialist form of government." Such opinions have a good deal of currency today within the Los Angeles police department. About a month before the riots, a leaflet describing Dr. King as a liar and a Communist was posted on the bulletin board of a Los Angeles police station, and only after the concerted efforts of various Negro organizations was this scurrilous pamphlet removed.

Certainly these were "aggravating factors" that the McCone Report should properly have mentioned. But what is more important to understand is that even if every policeman in every black ghetto behaved like an angel and were trained in the most progressive of police academies, the conflict would still exist. This is so because the ghetto is a place where Negroes do not want to be and are fighting to get out of. When someone with a billy club and a gun tells you to behave yourself amid these terrible circumstances, he becomes a zoo keeper, demanding of you, as one of "these monkeys" (to use Chief Parker's phrase), that you accept abhorrent conditions. He is brutalizing you by insisting that you tolerate what you cannot, and ought not, tolerate.

In its blithe ignorance of such feelings, the McCone Report offers as one of its principal suggestions that speakers be sent to Negro schools to teach the students that the police are their friends and that their interests are best served by respect for law and order. Such public relations gimmicks, of course, are futile—it is hardly a lack of contact with the police that creates the problem. Nor, as I have suggested, is it only a matter of prejudice. The fact is that when Negroes are deprived of work, they resort to selling numbers, women, or dope to earn a living; they must gamble and work in poolrooms. And when the policeman upholds the law, he is depriving them of their livelihood. A clever criminal in the Negro ghettos is not unlike a clever "operator" in the white business world, and so long as Negroes are denied legitimate opportunities, no exhortations to obey the rules of the society and to regard the police as friends will have any effect.

This is not to say that relations between the police and the Negroes of Watts could not be improved. Mayor Yorty and Police Chief Parker might have headed off a full-scale riot had they refrained from denouncing the Negro leaders and agreed to meet with them early on. Over and over again—to repeat the point with which we began—the rioters claimed that violence was the only way they could get these officials to listen to them. The McCone Commission, however, rejects the proposal for an independent police review board and instead recommends that the post of inspector general be established—under the authority of the chief of police—to handle grievances.

The conditions of Negro life in Watts are not, of course, ignored by the McCone Report. Their basic structure is outlined in a section entitled "Dull,

Devastating Spiral of Failure." Here we find that the Negro's "homelife destroys incentive"; that he lacks "experience with words and ideas"; that he is "unready and unprepared" in school; and that, "unprepared and unready," he "*slips* into the ranks of the unemployed" (my italics).

I would say *is shoved*. It is time that we began to understand this "dull, devastating spiral of failure" and that we stopped attributing it to this or that characteristic of Negro life. In 1940, Edward Wight Bakke described the effects of unemployment on family structure in terms of the following model: The jobless man no longer provides, credit runs out, the woman is forced to take a job; if relief then becomes necessary, the woman is regarded even more as the center of the family; the man is dependent on her, the children are bewildered, and the stability of the family is threatened and often shattered. Bakke's research dealt strictly with white families. The fact that Negro social scientists like E. Franklin Frazier and Kenneth Clark have shown that this pattern is typical among the Negro poor does not mean, then, that it stems from some inherent Negro trait or is the ineluctable product of Negro social history. If Negroes suffer more than others from the problems of family instability today, it is not because they are Negro but because they are so disproportionately unemployed, underemployed, and ill paid.

Anyone looking for historical patterns would do well to consider the labor market for Negroes since the Emancipation. He will find that Negro men have consistently been denied the opportunity to enter the labor force in anything like proportionate numbers, have been concentrated in the unskilled and marginal labor and service occupations, and have generally required wartime emergencies to make any advances in employment, job equality, and security. Such advances are then largely wiped out when the economy slumps again.

In 1948, for example, the rates of Negro and white unemployment were roughly equal. During the next decade, however, Negro unemployment was consistently double that of whites, and among Negro teenagers it remained at the disastrously high figure which prevailed for the entire population during the depression. It is true that the nation's improved economic performance in recent years has reduced the percentage of jobless Negroes from 12.6 per cent, which it reached in 1958 (12.5 per cent in 1961), to roughly 8.1 per cent today. Despite this progress, the rate of Negro unemployment continues to be twice as high as white (8.13 per cent as against 4.2 per cent). In other words, job discrimination remains constant. These statistics, moreover, conceal the persistence of Negro youth unemployment: in 1961, 24.7 per cent of those Negro teenagers not in school were out of work and it is estimated that in 1966 this incredible rate will only decline to 23.2 per cent. What this figure tells us is that the rise in Negro employment has largely resulted from the calling of men with previous experience back to work. This is an ominous trend, for it is estimated that in the coming year 20 per cent of the new entrants into the labor force will be Negro (almost twice as high as the Negro percentage of the population). Approximately half of these young Negroes will not have the equivalent of a high school education and they will be competing in an economy in which the demand for skill and training is increasing sharply.

Thus there is bound to be a further deterioration of the Negro's economic —and hence social—position, despite the important political victories being achieved by the civil rights movement. For many young Negroes, who are learning that economic servitude can be as effective an instrument of discrimination as racist laws, the new "freedom" has already become a bitter thing indeed. No wonder that the men of Watts were incensed by reports that the poverty program was being obstructed in Los Angeles by administrative wrangling. (As I write this, the *New York Times* reports that political rivalries and ambitions have now virtually paralyzed the program in that area.)

How does the McCone Report propose to halt this "dull, devastating spiral of failure"? First, through education—"our fundamental resource." The commission's analysis begins with a comparison of class size in white and Negro areas (the latter are referred to throughout as "disadvantaged areas" and Negro schools as "disadvantaged schools"). It immediately notes that classes in the disadvantaged schools are slightly smaller; on the other hand, the more experienced teachers are likely to be found in the *non*-disadvantaged areas, and there is tremendous overcrowding in the disadvantaged schools because of double sessions. The buildings in the "disadvantaged areas are in better repair"; on the other hand, there are "cafeterias in the advantaged schools" but not in the disadvantaged schools, which also have no libraries. This random balance sheet of "resources" shows no sense of priorities; moreover, despite the alarming deficiencies it uncovers in the "disadvantaged schools," the McCone Report, in consistent fashion, places its emphasis on the Negro child's "deficiency in environmental experiences" and on "his homelife [which] all too often fails to give him incentive. . . ."

The two major recommendations of the commission in this area will hardly serve to correct the imbalances revealed. The first is that elementary and junior high schools in the "disadvantaged areas" which have achievement levels substantially below the city average should be designated

"Emergency Schools." In each of these schools an emergency literacy program is to be established with a maximum of twenty-two students in each class and an enlarged and supportive corps of teachers. The second recommendation is to establish a permanent preschool program to help prepare three- and four-year-old children to read and write.

W. T. Bassett, executive secretary of the Los Angeles AFL-CIO, has criticized the report for its failure to deal with education and training for adolescents and adults who are no longer in school. Another glaring omission is of a specific plan to decrease school segregation. While most of us now agree that the major goal of American education must be that of quality integrated schools, we cannot, as even the report suggests, achieve the quality without at the same time moving toward integration. The stated goal of the McCone Commission, however, is to "reverse the trend of de facto segregation" by improving the quality of the Negro schools: in short, separate but equal schools that do not disturb the existing social patterns which isolate the Negro child in his "disadvantaged areas."

That the commission's explicit concern for Negro problems falls short of its implicit concern for the status quo is also evident in its proposals for housing. It calls for the liberalization of credit and FHA-insured loans in "disadvantaged areas," the implementation of rehabilitation measures and other urban-renewal programs, and, as its particular innovation, the creation of a "wide area data bank." Meanwhile it refuses to discuss, much less to criticize, the effect of Proposition 14 or to recommend a new fair housing code. To protect the Negro against discrimination, the McCone Report supports the creation of a commission on human relations, but does not present any proposals that would enable it to do more than collect information and conduct public relations campaigns.

The most crucial section of the report is the one on employment, and, not unexpectedly, it is also the most ignorant, unimaginative, and conservative —despite its dramatic recommendation that 50,000 new jobs be created. On the matter of youth unemployment, the report suggests that the existing federal projects initiate a series of "attitudinal training" programs to help young Negroes develop the necessary motivation to hold on to these new jobs which are to come from somewhere that the commission keeps secret. This is just another example of the commission's continued reliance on public relations, and of its preoccupation with the "dull, devastating spiral" of Negro failure. The truth of the matter is that Negro youths cannot change their attitudes until they see that they can get jobs. When what they see is unemployment and their economic opportunity programs being manipulated in behalf of politicians, their attitudes will remain realistically cynical.

Once again, let me try to cut through the obscurantism which has increasingly come to cloud this issue of Negro attitudes. I am on a committee which administers the apprenticeship training program of the Workers Defense League. For many years the league had heard that there were not enough Negro applicants to fill the various openings for apprenticeship training and had also repeatedly been told by vocational school counselors that Negro students could not pay attention to key subjects such as English and mathematics. The league began its own recruitment and placement program two years ago and now has more than 500 apprentice applicants on file. When, last fall, Local 28 of the Sheetmetal Workers Union—to take one example—announced that a new admission test for apprentices was to be given soon, the league contacted those applicants who had indicated an interest in sheet-metal work. The young men came to the office, filled out a ten-page application form, filed a ten-dollar fee, and returned it to the Local 28 office. Then, five nights a week for three weeks, they came to Harlem, in many cases from Brooklyn and Queens, to be tutored. Most of the young men showed up for all fifteen sessions, and scored well on the test. At their interviews they were poised and confident. Eleven of these men finally were admitted to a class of thirty-three. The WDL doesn't attribute this success to a miraculous program; it merely knows that when young people are told that at the end of a given period of study those who perform well will obtain decent work, then their attitudes will be markedly different from those who are sent off to a work camp with vague promises.

To cut the cost of job training programs, the McCone Commission avers that compensation "should not be necessary for those trainees who are receiving welfare support." Earlier in the report the authors point out that welfare services tend to destroy family life by giving more money to a woman who lives alone; yet they have the audacity to ask that the practice of not allowing men who are on family relief to earn an additional income be maintained for young men who are working and being trained. How is a young man to be adequately motivated if he cannot feel that his work is meaningful and necessary? The McCone Report would have us say to him, "There, there, young man, we're going to keep you off the streets—just putter around doing this make-work." But the young man knows that he can collect welfare checks and also hustle on street corners to increase his earnings. A man's share of a welfare allotment is pitifully small, but more than that, he should be paid for his work; and if one is interested in his morale, he should not be treated as a charity case.

Continuing with the problem of employment, the report recommends that "there should immediately be developed in the affected area a job training and placement center through the combined efforts of Negroes, employers, labor unions and government." In the absence of actual jobs, this would mean merely setting up a new division, albeit voluntary, of the unemployment insurance program. "Federal and state governments should seek to insure, through development of new facilities and additional means of communication, that advantage is taken of government and private training programs and employment opportunities in our disadvantaged communities." Perhaps the only thing the Job Corps program doesn't lack is publicity: last summer it received ten times as many applications as it could handle. Nor can new types of information centers and questionnaires provide 50,000 new jobs. They may provide positions for social workers and vocational counselors, but very few will be unemployed Negroes.

The report goes on: "Legislation should be enacted requiring employers with more than 250 employees and all labor unions to report annually to the state Fair Employment Practices Commission the racial composition of the work force and membership." But an FEP Commission that merely collects information and propaganda is powerless. And even with the fullest cooperation of labor and management to promote equality of opportunity, the fact remains that there are not enough jobs in the Los Angeles area to go around, even for those who are fortunate enough to be included in the retraining programs. As long as unions cannot find work for many of their own members, there is not much they can do to help unemployed Negroes. And the McCone Report places much of its hope in private enterprise, whose response so far has been meager. The highest estimate of the number of jobs given to Los Angeles Negroes since the Watts crisis is less than 1,000.

The Negro slums today are ghettos of despair. In Watts, as elsewhere, there are the unemployable poor: the children, the aging, the permanently handicapped. No measure of employment or of economic growth will put an end to their misery, and only government programs can provide them with a decent way of life. The care of these people could be made a major area of job growth. Los Angeles officials could immediately train and put to work women and unemployed youths as school attendants, recreation counselors, practical nurses, and community workers. The federal government and the state of California could aid the people of Watts by beginning a massive public works program to build needed housing, schools, hospitals, neighborhood centers, and transportation facilities; this, too, would create new jobs. In short, they could begin to develop the $100 billion Freedom Budget advocated by A. Philip Randolph.

Such proposals may seem impractical and even incredible. But what is truly impractical and incredible is that America, with its enormous wealth, has allowed Watts to become what it is and that a commission empowered to study this explosive situation should come up with answers that boil down to voluntary actions by business and labor, new public relations campaigns for municipal agencies, and information-gathering for housing, fair employment, and welfare departments. The Watts manifesto is a response to realities that the McCone Report is barely beginning to grasp. Like the liberal consensus which it embodies and reflects, the commission's imagination and political intelligence appear paralyzed by the hard facts of Negro deprivation it has unearthed, and it lacks the political will to demand that the vast resources of contemporary America be used to build a genuinely great society that will finally put an end to these deprivations. And what is most impractical and incredible of all is that we may very well continue to teach impoverished, segregated, and ignored Negroes that the only way they can get the ear of America is to rise up in violence.

"BLACK POWER" AND
COALITION POLITICS

There are two Americas, black and white, and nothing has more clearly revealed the divisions between them than the debate currently raging around the slogan of "black power." Despite—or perhaps because of —the fact that this slogan lacks any clear definition, it has succeeded in galvanizing emotions on all sides. Many whites see it as the expression of a new racism, and many Negroes take it as a warning to white people that Negroes will no longer tolerate brutality and violence. But even within the Negro community itself, "black power" has touched off a major debate— the most bitter the community has experienced since the days of Booker T. Washington and W. E. B. Du Bois, and one which threatens to ravage the entire civil rights movement. Indeed, a serious split has already developed between advocates of black power like Floyd McKissick of CORE and Stokely Carmichael of SNCC, on the one hand, and Dr. Martin Luther King of SCLC, Roy Wilkins of the NAACP, and Whitney Young of the Urban League, on the other.

There is no question, then, that great passions are involved in the debate over the idea of black power; nor, as we shall see, is there any question that these passions have their roots in the psychological and political frustrations of the Negro community. Nevertheless, I contend not only that black power lacks any real value for the civil rights movement, but that its propagation is positively harmful. It diverts the movement from a meaningful debate over strategy and tactics, it isolates the Negro community, and it encourages the growth of anti-Negro forces.

In its simplest and most innocent guise, black power merely means the effort to elect Negroes to office in proportion to Negro strength within the population. There is, of course, nothing wrong with such an objective in itself, and nothing inherently radical in the idea of pursuing it. But in Stokely Carmichael's extravagant rhetoric about "taking over" in districts of the South where Negroes are in the majority, it is important to recognize that Southern Negroes are in a position to win a maximum of only two

From *Commentary*, February 1965.

congressional seats and control of eighty local counties. (Carmichael, incidentally, is in the paradoxical position of screaming at liberals—wanting only to "get whitey off my back"—and simultaneously needing their support. After all, he can talk about Negroes taking over Lowndes County only because there is a fairly liberal federal government to protect him should Governor Wallace decide to eliminate this pocket of black power.) Now there might be a certain value in having two Negro congressmen from the South, but obviously they could do nothing by themselves to reconstruct the face of America. Eighty sheriffs, eighty tax assessors, and eighty school board members might ease the tension for a while in their communities, but alone they could not create jobs and build low-cost housing; alone they could not supply quality integrated education.

The relevant question, moreover, is not whether a politician is black or white, but what forces he represents. Manhattan has had a succession of Negro borough presidents, and yet the schools are increasingly segregated. Adam Clayton Powell and William Dawson have both been in Congress for many years; the former is responsible for a rider on school integration that never gets passed, and the latter is responsible for keeping the Negroes of Chicago tied to a mayor who had to see riots and death before he would put eight-dollar sprinklers on water hydrants in the summer. I am not for one minute arguing that Powell, Dawson, and Mrs. Motley should be impeached. What I am saying is that if a politician is elected because he is black and is deemed to be entitled to a "slice of the pie," he will behave in one way; if he is elected by a constituency pressing for social reform, he will, whether he is white or black, behave in another way.

Southern Negroes, despite exhortations from SNCC to organize themselves into a Black Panther party, are going to stay in the Democratic party—to them it is the party of progress, the New Deal, the New Frontier, and the Great Society—and they are right to stay. For SNCC's Black Panther perspective is simultaneously utopian and reactionary—utopian for the by now obvious reason that one-tenth of the population cannot accomplish much by itself; reactionary because such a party would remove Negroes from the main area of political struggle in this country (particularly in the one-party South, where the decisive battles are fought out in Democratic primaries), and would give priority to the issue of race precisely at a time when the fundamental questions facing the Negro and American society alike are economic and social. It is no accident that the two main proponents of black power, Carmichael and McKissick, should now be co-sponsoring a conference with Adam Clayton Powell and Elijah Muhammad, and that the leaders of New York CORE should recently have supported the machine candidate for surrogate—because he was the choice of a Negro boss—rather than the candidate of the reform movement. By contrast, Martin Luther King is working in Chicago with the industrial union department of the AFL-CIO and with religious groups in a coalition which, if successful, will mean the end, or at least the weakening, of the Daley-Dawson machine.

The winning of the right of Negroes to vote in the South ensures the eventual transformation of the Democratic party, now controlled primarily by Northern machine politicians and Southern Dixiecrats. The Negro vote will eliminate the Dixiecrats from the party and from Congress, which means that the crucial question facing us today is who will replace them in the South. Unless civil rights leaders (in such towns as Jackson, Mississippi; Birmingham, Alabama; and even to a certain extent Atlanta) can organize grass-roots clubs whose members will have a genuine political voice, the Dixiecrats might well be succeeded by black moderates and black Southern-style machine politicians, who would do little to push for needed legislation in Congress and little to improve local conditions in the South. While I myself would prefer Negro machines to a situation in which Negroes have no power at all, it seems to me that there is a better alternative today—a liberal–labor–civil rights coalition which would work to make the Democratic party truly responsive to the aspirations of the poor, and which would develop support for programs aimed at the reconstruction of American society in the interests of greater social justice. The advocates of black power have no such programs in mind. What they are in fact arguing for (perhaps unconsciously) is the creation of a *new black establishment*.

Nor, it might be added, are they leading the Negro people along the same road which they imagine immigrant groups traveled so successfully in the past. Proponents of black power—accepting a historical myth perpetrated by moderates—like to say that the Irish and the Jews and the Italians, by sticking together and demanding their share, finally won enough power to overcome their initial disabilities. But the truth is that it was through alliances with other groups (in political machines or as part of the trade union movement) that the Irish and the Jews and the Italians acquired the power to win their rightful place in American society. They most certainly did not make isolation their primary tactic.

In some quarters, black power connotes not an effort to increase the number of Negroes in elective office, but rather a repudiation of nonviolence in favor of Negro "self-defense." Actually this is a false issue, since no one has ever argued that Negroes as individuals should not defend themselves from attack.* Nonviolence has been advocated as a *tactic* for organized demonstrations in a society where Negroes are a minority and where the majority controls the police. Proponents of nonviolence do not, for example, deny that James Meredith has the right to carry a gun for protection when he visits his mother in Mississippi; what they question is the wisdom of his carrying a gun while participating in a demonstration.

There is, as well, a tactical side to the new emphasis on self-defense and the suggestion that nonviolence be abandoned. The reasoning here is that turning the other cheek is not the way to win respect, and that only if the Negro succeeds in frightening the white man will the white man begin taking him seriously. The trouble with this reasoning is that it fails to recognize that fear is more likely to bring hostility to the surface than respect. Far from prodding the "white power structure" into action, the new militant leadership, by raising the slogan of black power and lowering the banner of nonviolence, has obscured the moral issue facing this nation, and permitted the President and Vice-President to lecture us about "racism in reverse" instead of proposing more meaningful programs for dealing with the problems of unemployment, housing, and education.

"Black power" is, of course, a somewhat nationalistic slogan, and its sudden rise to popularity among Negroes signifies a concomitant rise in nationalist sentiment (Malcolm X's autobiography is quoted nowadays in Grenada, Mississippi, as well as in Harlem). We have seen such nationalistic turns and withdrawals back into the ghetto before. When we look at the conditions which brought them about, we find that they have much in common with the conditions of Negro life at the present moment—conditions which lead to despair over the goal of integration and to the belief that the ghetto will last forever.

In the light of the many juridical and legislative victories which have been achieved in the past few years, it may seem strange that despair should be so widespread among Negroes today. But anyone to whom it seems strange should reflect on the fact that despite these victories *Negroes today are in worse economic shape, live in worse slums, and attend more highly segregated schools than in 1954.* Thus—to recite the appalling and appallingly familiar statistical litany once again—more Negroes are unemployed today than in 1954; the gap between the wages of the Negro worker and the white worker is wider; while the unemployment rate among white

* As far back as 1934, A. Philip Randolph, Walter White, then executive secretary of the NAACP, Lester Granger, then executive director of the Urban League, and I joined a committee to try to save the life of Odell Waller, a sharecropper who had murdered his white boss in self-defense.

youths is decreasing, the rate among Negro youths has increased to 32 *per cent* (and among Negro girls the rise is even more startling). Even the one gain which has been registered, a decrease in the unemployment rate among Negro adults, is deceptive; for it represents men who have been called back to work after a period of being laid off. In any event, unemployment among Negro men is still twice that of whites, and no new jobs have been created.

So too with housing, which is deteriorating in the North; and yet the housing provisions of the 1966 civil rights bill are weaker than the anti-discrimination laws in several states which contain the worst ghettos even with these laws on their books. And so too with schools. According to figures issued recently by the Department of Health, Education and Welfare, 65 per cent of first-grade Negro students in this country attend schools that are from 90 to 100 per cent black. If in 1954, when the Supreme Court handed down the desegregation decision, you had been the Negro parent of a first-grade child, the chances are that this past June you would have attended that child's graduation from a segregated high school.

To put all this in the simplest and most concrete terms: the day-to-day lot of the ghetto Negro has not been improved by the various judicial and legislative measures of the past decade.

Negroes are thus in a situation similar to that of the turn of the century, when Booker T. Washington advised them to "cast down their buckets" (that is to say, accommodate to segregation and disfranchisement) and when even his leading opponent, W. E. B. Du Bois, was forced to advocate the development of a group economy in place of the direct-action boycotts, general strikes, and protest techniques which had been used in the 1880's, before the enactment of the Jim Crow laws. For all their differences, both Washington and Du Bois then found it impossible to believe that Negroes could ever be integrated into American society, and each in his own way therefore counseled withdrawal into the ghetto, self-help, and economic self-determination.

World War I aroused new hope among Negroes that the rights removed at the turn of the century would be restored. More than 360,000 Negroes entered military service and went overseas; many left the South seeking the good life in the North and hoping to share in the temporary prosperity created by the war. But all these hopes were quickly smashed at the end of the fighting. In the first year following the war, more than seventy Negroes were lynched, and during the last six months of that year, there were twenty-four riots throughout America. White mobs took over whole cities, flogging, burning, shooting, and torturing at will, and when Negroes tried to defend themselves, the violence only increased. Along with this, Negroes were excluded from unions and pushed out of jobs they had won during the war, including federal jobs.

In the course of this period of dashed hope and spreading segregation—the same period, incidentally, when a reorganized Ku Klux Klan was achieving a membership which was to reach into the millions—the largest mass movement ever to take root among working-class Negroes, Marcus Garvey's "Back to Africa" movement, was born. "Buy Black" became a slogan in the ghettos. Faith in integration was virtually snuffed out in the Negro community until the 1930's, when the CIO reawakened the old dream of a Negro-labor alliance by announcing a policy of nondiscrimination and when the New Deal admitted Negroes into relief programs, WPA jobs, and public housing. No sooner did jobs begin to open up, and Negroes begin to be welcomed into mainstream organizations, than "Buy Black" campaigns gave way to "Don't Buy Where You Can't Work" movements. A. Philip Randolph was able to organize a massive March on Washington demanding a wartime FEPC; CORE was born and with it the nonviolent sit-in technique; the NAACP succeeded in putting an end to the white primaries in 1944. Altogether, World War II was a period of hope for Negroes, and the economic progress they made through wartime industry continued steadily until about 1948 and remained stable for a time. Meanwhile, the nonviolent movement of the 1950's and '60's achieved the desegregation of public accommodations and established the right to vote.

Yet at the end of this long fight, the Southern Negro is too poor to use those integrated facilities and too intimidated and disorganized to use the vote to maximum advantage, while the economic position of the Northern Negro deteriorates rapidly.

The promise of meaningful work and decent wages once held out by the antipoverty programs has not been fulfilled. Because there has been a lack of necessary funds, the program has in many cases been reduced to wrangling for positions on boards or for lucrative staff jobs. Negro professionals working for the program have earned handsome salaries—ranging from $14,000 to $25,000—while young boys have been asked to plant trees at $1.25 an hour. Nor have the Job Corps camps made a significant dent in unemployment among Negro youths; indeed, the main beneficiaries of this program seem to be the private companies who contract to set up the camps.

Then there is the war in Vietnam, which poses many ironies for the Negro community. On the one hand, Negroes are bitterly aware of the fact that more and more money is being spent on the war, while the antipoverty program is being cut. On the other hand, Negro youths are enlisting in great numbers, as though to say that it is worth the risk of being killed to learn a trade, to leave a dead-end situation, and to join the only institution in this society which seems to be really integrated.

The youths who rioted in Watts, Cleveland, Omaha, Chicago, and Portland are the members of a truly hopeless and lost generation. They can see the alien world of affluence unfold before them on the TV screen. But they have already failed in their inferior segregated schools. Their grandfathers were sharecroppers, their grandmothers were domestics, and their mothers are domestics too. Many have never met their fathers. Mistreated by the local storekeeper, suspected by the policeman on the beat, disliked by their teachers, they cannot stand more failures and would rather retreat into the world of heroin than risk looking for a job downtown or having their friends see them push a rack in the garment district. Floyd McKissick and Stokely Carmichael may accuse Roy Wilkins of being out of touch with the Negro ghetto, but nothing more clearly demonstrates their own alienation from ghetto youth than their repeated exhortations to these young men to oppose the Vietnam war, when so many of them tragically see it as their only way out. Yet there is no need to labor the significance of the fact that the rice fields of Vietnam and the Green Berets have more to offer a Negro boy than the streets of Mississippi, or the towns of Alabama, or 125th Street in New York.

The Vietnam war is also partly responsible for the growing disillusion with nonviolence among Negroes. The ghetto Negro does not in general ask whether the United States is right or wrong to be in Southeast Asia. He does, however, wonder why he is exhorted to nonviolence when the United States has been waging a fantastically brutal war, and it puzzles him to be told that he must turn the other cheek in our own South while we fight for freedom in South Vietnam.

Thus, as in roughly similar circumstances in the past—circumstances, I repeat, which in the aggregate foster the belief that the ghetto is destined to last forever—Negroes are once again turning to nationalistic slogans. And "black power" affords the same emotional release as "Back to Africa" and "Buy Black" did in earlier periods of frustration and hopelessness. This is not only the case with the ordinary Negro in the ghetto; it is also the case with leaders like McKissick and Carmichael, neither of whom began as a nationalist or was at first cynical about the possibilities of integration. It took countless beatings and twenty-four jailings—and the absence of strong and continual support from the liberal community—to persuade Carmichael that his earlier faith in coalition politics was mistaken, that nothing was to be gained from working with whites, and that an alliance with the black nationalists was desirable. In the areas of the South where SNCC has been working so nobly, implementation of the Civil Rights Acts of 1964 and 1965 has been slow and ineffective. Negroes in many rural areas cannot walk into the courthouse and register to vote. Despite the voting rights act, they must file complaints and the Justice Department must be called to send federal registrars. Nor do children attend integrated schools as a matter of course. There, too, complaints must be filed and the Department of Health, Education and Welfare must be notified. Neither department has been doing an effective job of enforcing the acts. The feeling of isolation increases among SNCC workers as each legislative victory turns out to be only a token victory—significant on the national level, but not affecting the day-to-day lives of Negroes. Carmichael and his colleagues are wrong in refusing to support the 1966 act, but one can understand why they feel as they do.

It is, in short, the growing conviction that the Negroes cannot win—a conviction with much grounding in experience—which accounts for the new popularity of black power. So far as the ghetto Negro is concerned, this conviction expresses itself in hostility, first toward the people closest to him who have held out the most promise and failed to deliver (Martin Luther King, Roy Wilkins, etc.), then toward those who have proclaimed themselves his friends (the liberals and the labor movement), and finally toward the only oppressors he can see (the local storekeeper and the policeman on the corner). On the leadership level, the conviction that the Negroes cannot win takes other forms, principally the adoption of what I have called a "no-win" policy. Why bother with programs when their enactment results only in sham? Why concern ourselves with the image of the movement when nothing significant has been gained for all the sacrifices made by SNCC and CORE? Why compromise with reluctant white allies when nothing of consequence can be achieved anyway? Why indeed have anything to do with whites at all?

On this last point, it is extremely important for white liberals to understand what, one gathers from their references to "racism in reverse," the President and the Vice-President of the United States do not: that there is all the difference in the world between saying, "If you don't want me, I don't want you" (which is what some proponents of black power have in effect been saying), and the statement, "Whatever you do, I don't want you" (which is what racism declares). It is, in other words, both absurd and immoral to equate the despairing response of the victim with the contemptuous assertion of the oppressor. It would, moreover, be tragic if white liberals allowed verbal hostility on the part of Negroes to drive them out of the movement or to curtail their support for civil rights. The issue was injustice before black power became popular, and the issue is still injustice.

In any event, even if black power had not emerged as a slogan, problems would have arisen in the relation between whites and Negroes in the civil rights movement. In the North, it was inevitable that Negroes would eventually wish to run their own movement and would rebel against the presence of whites in positions of leadership as yet another sign of white supremacy. In the South, the well-intentioned white volunteer had the cards stacked against him from the beginning. Not only could he leave the struggle any time he chose to do so, but a higher value was set on his safety by the press and the government—apparent in the differing degrees of excitement generated by the imprisonment or murder of whites and Negroes. The white person's importance to the movement in the South was thus an ironic outgrowth of racism and was therefore bound to create resentment.

But again: however understandable all this may be as a response to objective conditions and to the seeming irrelevance of so many hard-won victories to the day-to-day life of the mass of Negroes, the fact remains that the quasi-nationalist sentiments and no-win policy lying behind the slogan of "black power" do no service to the Negro. Some nationalist emotion is, of course, inevitable, and black power must be seen as part of the psychological rejection of white supremacy, part of the rebellion against the stereotypes which have been ascribed to Negroes for three hundred years. Nevertheless, pride, confidence, and a new identity cannot be won by glorifying blackness or attacking whites; they can only come from meaningful action, from good jobs, and from real victories such as were achieved on the streets of Montgomery, Birmingham, and Selma. When SNCC and CORE went into the South, they awakened the country, but now they emerge isolated and demoralized, shouting a slogan that may afford a momentary satisfaction but that is calculated to destroy them and their movement. Already their frustrated call is being answered with counterdemands for law and order and with opposition to police review boards. Already they have diverted the entire civil rights movement from the hard task of developing strategies to realign the major parties of this country, and embroiled it in a debate that can only lead more and more to politics by frustration.

On the other side, however—the more important side, let it be said—it is the business of those who reject the negative aspects of black power not to preach but to act. Some weeks ago President Johnson, speaking at Fort Campbell, Kentucky, asserted that riots impeded reform, created fear, and antagonized the Negro's traditional friends. Mr. Johnson, according to the *New York Times*, expressed sympathy for the plight of the poor, the jobless, and the ill housed. The government, he noted, has been working to relieve their circumstances, but "all this takes time."

One cannot argue with the President's position that riots are destructive or that they frighten away allies. Nor can one find fault with his sympathy for the plight of the poor; surely the poor need sympathy. But one can question whether the government has been working seriously enough to eliminate the conditions which lead to frustration-politics and riots. The President's very words, "all this takes time," will be understood by the poor for precisely what they are—an excuse instead of a real program, a cover-up for the failure to establish real priorities, and an indication that the administration has no real commitment to create new jobs, better housing, and integrated schools.

For the truth is that it need take only ten years to eliminate poverty—ten years and the $100 billion Freedom Budget recently proposed by A. Philip Randolph. In his introduction to the budget, which was drawn up in consultation with the nation's leading economists, Mr. Randolph points out: "The programs urged in the Freedom Budget attack all of the major causes of poverty—unemployment and underemployment, substandard pay, inadequate social insurance and welfare payments to those who cannot or should not be employed; bad housing; deficiencies in health services, education, and training; and fiscal and monetary policies which tend to redistribute income regressively rather than progressively. The Freedom Budget leaves no room for discrimination in any form because its programs are addressed to all who need more opportunity and improved incomes and living standards, not to just some of them."

The legislative precedent Mr. Randolph has in mind is the 1945 Full Employment Act. This bill, conceived in its original form by Roosevelt to prevent a postwar depression, would have made it public policy for the government to step in if the private economy could not provide enough employment. As passed finally by Congress in 1946, with many of its teeth removed, it had the result of preventing the Negro worker, who had finally reached a pay level of about 55 per cent that of the white wage, from making any further progress in closing that discriminatory gap; instead, he was pushed back by the chronically high unemployment rates of the '50's. Had the original bill been passed, the public sector of our economy would have been able to insure fair and full employment. Today, with the spiraling thrust of automation, it is even more imperative that we have a legally binding commitment to this goal.

Let me interject a word here for those who say that Negroes are asking for another handout and are refusing to help themselves. From the end of the nineteenth century up to the last generation, the United States absorbed and provided economic opportunity for tens of millions of immigrants. These people were usually uneducated and a good many could not speak English. They had nothing but hard work to offer and they labored long hours, often in miserable sweatshops and unsafe mines. Yet in a burgeoning economy with a need for unskilled labor, they were able to find jobs, and as industrialization proceeded, they were gradually able to move up the ladder to greater skills. Negroes who have been driven off the farm into a city life for which they are not prepared, and who have entered an economy in which there is less and less need for unskilled labor, cannot be compared with these immigrants of old. The tenements which were jammed by newcomers were way stations of hope; the ghettos of today have become dead ends of despair. Yet just as the older generation of immigrants—in its most decisive act of self-help—organized the trade union movement and then in alliance with many middle-class elements went on to improve its own lot and the condition of American society generally, so the Negro of today is struggling to go beyond the gains of the past and, in alliance with liberals and labor, to guarantee full and fair employment to all Americans.

We must see, therefore, in the current debate over black power, a fantastic challenge to American society to live up to its proclaimed principles in the area of race by transforming itself so that all men may live equally and under justice. We must see to it that in rejecting black power we do not also reject the principle of Negro equality. Those people who would use the current debate and/or the riots to abandon the civil rights movement leave us no choice but to question their original motivation.

If anything, the next period will be more serious and difficult than the preceding ones. It takes very little imagination to understand that the Negro should have the right to vote, but much creativity, patience, and political stamina are demanded to plan, develop, and implement programs and priorities. It is one thing to organize sentiment behind laws that do not disturb consensus politics, and quite another to win battles for the redistribution of wealth. Many people who marched in Selma are not prepared to support a bill for a two-dollar minimum wage, to say nothing of supporting a redefinition of work or a guaranteed annual income.

It is here that we who advocate coalitions and integration and who object to the black-power concept have a massive job to do. We must see that the liberal–labor–civil rights coalition is maintained and indeed strengthened, so that it can fight effectively for a Freedom Budget. We are responsible for the growth of the black-power concept because we have not used our own power to ensure the full implementation of the bills whose passage we were strong enough to win, and we have not mounted the necessary campaign for winning a decent minimum wage and extended benefits. "Black power" is a slogan directed primarily against liberals by those who once counted liberals among their closest friends. It is up to the liberal movement to prove that coalition and integration are better alternatives.

GUNS, BREAD, AND BUTTER

Public organizations in the United States tend, by and large, to be monistic in their interests—that is, they tend to function on behalf of specific causes. However, for some the task of concentrating attention on their special interests is more difficult than it is for others. For instance, it may not be too difficult for the AMA to concern itself exclusively with problems affecting the medical profession. But particularly for politically oriented organizations, the problem is somewhat different. On the one hand, they recognize their obligation to focus upon their stated objective; on the other, they are forced to deal with the fact that marginal issues impinge upon and affect the attainment of their own objectives. Thus we find liberal and civil rights organizations keeping attuned to and in touch with the diverse political, economic, and ideological sounds of the society. And we find the peace movement engaging at times in dialogue over what ought or ought not to be its singular area of interest.

Since for most of my life I have been engaged in peace and civil rights activities, I know something about these problems and conflicts. In my years with the War Resisters League, there were frequent discussions about the amount of time I was spending with the civil rights movement. It was not so much a debate over my personal right to participate in civil rights activities, but rather over my own view that nonviolence was not simply a philosophical stance for the peace movement, but was indeed a fundamental way of life. The implication of this view, therefore, was that wherever there was a possibility of violence, the War Resisters League had some obligation to work against that violence. Many of my colleagues were inclined to agree with me, but many others remained convinced that nonviolence was the exclusive strategy of the peace movement.

The question is a very difficult one that becomes even more meaningful in the context of a broad and engaged conscience in our time: How can we continue to pay tender and exclusive attention to shoring up our own special furrow when the rest of the field is eroding all around us?

From *War/Peace Report*, March 1967. Reprinted with permission.

It is somewhere in this context that we must examine the problem of what is the responsibility of the civil rights movement to the peace movement, or whether the civil rights movement, per se, has any official responsibility in the peace movement at all.

When all is said and done, we are all citizens of a world in crisis. The universe of human suffering is everybody's universe. Moreover, it may well be that the solution of one problem has implications for the solution of another. This being so, there is a role for citizens to play in the solution of different problems that converge and impinge upon their personal situation. All of which means that if there is not a part for the civil rights movement to play in the peace struggle, there is certainly a part for Negroes to play, by joining peace groups all around the country.

What's more, many Negroes do take a deep and genuine interest in the problems of war and peace, and are trying to find some ground on which they can make a contribution. As I travel across the country, speaking before religious, liberal, civil rights, trade union, and campus groups, I am invariably asked by a large number of Negroes what they can do for peace. On such occasions, I always advise them to become members of peace organizations. When young Negro boys come up to me and say they are conscientiously opposed to war, I advise them to contact the War Resisters League, the Central Committee for Conscientious Objectors, or the American Friends Service Committee.

Of course I am aware that there is not going to be a tremendous onrush of Negroes into the peace movement. The immediate problems of Negroes' lives in America are so vast as to allow them very little time or energy to focus upon international crises. What is still crucial in the thinking and experience of Negroes in our society is that even in some of the most liberal cities they have a hard time finding a job, living in a decent neighborhood, sending their children to quality integrated schools, or even getting a taxi. We have also got to realize that politically Negroes have carried a great national burden for the past 10 years. Almost all of the progressive developments during this period have been the result of Negroes' marching in the streets, demonstrating for equal treatment under the law. Negroes helped end McCarthyism on U.S. campuses because the freedom struggle attracted and awakened the best moral instincts of our college youth. An American ecumenical movement came into being primarily because the religious conscience had to respond to the struggle for human rights in our country. Therefore, one must be careful, while examining the extent of Negro involvement in causes beyond civil rights, not to demand that they ought, with equal ardor, to be catalysts in the struggle for social and human rights at home and the quest for peace abroad.

The peace movement finds itself in a peculiar position. On the one hand, it would like to protect the integrity of its activities and objectives; on the other, it is somewhat unhappy over the fact that the civil rights movement does not openly ally itself with peace efforts. The answer to the latter problem is for Negroes to ally themselves individually with the peace struggle without committing the civil rights movement. And if this is true, then members of the peace movement have an obligation to ally themselves with certain objectives of the civil rights struggle without committing their organizations to any official involvement.

There is one other problem, with relation to war, that Negroes find difficult to resolve. Traditionally Negroes have made some of their more significant strides in American society during periods of military crisis. During World War I, hundreds of thousands of Negroes migrated out of the oppressed conditions of the South to find jobs in the North. During World War II, tremendous employment opportunities opened up for them in Detroit and other large industrial centers. And even during this horrible Vietnam war, many Negro young men who would have no alternative but to stand on street corners in Mississippi, Alabama, or New York are convinced that by joining the armed forces they can learn a trade, earn a salary, and be in a position to enter the job market on their return.

All this means that thousands of Negroes, in order to rehabilitate themselves, are forced to take a stand beyond morality and exploit the opportunities presented to them by their country's military involvement. I myself can afford the luxury of drawing those moral lines, but it is more difficult to suggest to people who are hungry, jobless, or living in slums that they turn their backs on opportunities that promise them a measure of economic betterment.

If this attitude on the part of thousands of Negroes horrifies the peace movement, then perhaps the peace movement might well conclude that it must give a large part of its energy to the struggle to secure the social and economic uplift of the Negro community. Needless to say, that is not what peace workers conclude, and this fact reveals the problem. I am not saying that they must, but if they object to what Negroes are forced to do in this situation, then they should follow the clear implication of their objection.

DR. KING'S PAINFUL DILEMMA

One of the undertones of the attacks in the white press on Dr. Martin Luther King's recent statements on Vietnam may well reveal that America really does not believe that Negroes, as citizens, have yet come of age. Like children, we should be seen but not heard.

I say this because the criticism of Dr. King was not limited to an evaluation of his proposals and his strategy for ending the war. It was, by and large, an attack on his right to debate, or even to discuss, Vietnam. In substance, many editorials seemed to be asking, "What is Dr. King doing discussing Vietnam?" or "Who gave him the right to make proposals about our [meaning white America's] foreign policy?"

In a democracy all citizens have not only a right but also a solemn duty to vote, to advise on domestic affairs, and to address themselves to all aspects of foreign policy. As Americans, Dr. King and all other Negroes have such a duty. First, it is their duty as citizens. Second, it is their duty as black citizens, considering that twice as many Negroes proportionately are fighting and dying in Vietnam.

Equally compelling, for Dr. King, is the fact that he is a Nobel Peace Prize winner. As such he has a moral obligation to speak out for peace according to his insight as a man of God and in keeping with his conscience as a free man.

On the other hand, however, if Dr. King makes proposals that others disagree with, they have the duty to differ with him on the merits or demerits of his proposals. Dr. King knows this, and he will expect no less. Such honest differences may encourage Dr. King to embark upon a reexamination of his position. Such honest discussion will encourage all of us to keep the vexing problem of Vietnam in constant review.

This process might very well turn out to be as illuminating for Dr. King as for the rest of us. But to assume that any individual (particularly any civil rights worker) does not have the right to discuss any problem that

From the *New York Amsterdam News*, March 3, 1967. This and subsequent columns from the *News* appeared in twenty-five Negro newspapers as well.

affects his nation is to propose that such an individual is still a second-class citizen.

The Negro community should, and I hope will, continue to enter all discussions relative to their experience as Americans. We must, of course, be prepared to accept the political consequences and responsibilities that result from taking such a position.

Perhaps the real question is this: How should Negroes who have a concern for peace organize to express these sentiments? Should they organize through the existing peace organizations, or should they organize within the civil rights movement? I must say that I would consider the involvement of the civil rights organizations as such in peace activities distinctly unprofitable and perhaps even suicidal.

Yet there must be an opportunity for Negroes to work for peace. For many Negroes do take a deep and genuine interest in the problems of war and peace, if for no other reason than because of the disproportionate number of Negroes in Vietnam.

This is not to say that there is going to be any tremendous onrush of Negroes into the peace movement. The immediate problems facing Negroes are so vast and crushing that they have little time or energy to focus upon international crises.

Nevertheless, when Dr. King speaks out as he recently did, we are forced to recognize and clarify the problems of strategy, tactics, and philosophy that confront the Negro freedom movement in a time of war. Dr. King is, no doubt, more aware today of the subtleties of these conflicts than he was before he made his statement.

THE PREMISE OF THE STEREOTYPE

The resort to stereotype is the first refuge and chief strategy of the bigot. Though this is a matter that ought to concern everyone, it should be of particular concern to Negroes. For their lives, as far back as we can remember, have been made nightmares by one kind of bigotry or another.

This urge to stereotype groups and deal with them accordingly is an evil urge. Its birthplace is in that sinister back room of the mind where plots and schemes are hatched for the persecution and oppression of other human beings.

It comes out of many things, but chiefly out of a failure or refusal to do the kind of tough, patient thinking that is required of difficult problems of relationship. It comes, as well, out of a desire to establish one's own sense of humanity and worth upon the ruins of someone else's. Nobody knows this, or should know it, better than Negroes and Jews.

Bigots have, for almost every day we have spent out of Africa or out of Palestine, invented a whole catalogue of Negro and Jewish characteristics, invested these characteristics with inferior or undesirable values, and, on the basis of these fantasies, have engaged in the most brutal and systematic persecution.

It seems to me, therefore, that it would be one of the great tragedies of Negro and Jewish experience in a hostile civilization if the time should come when either group begins using against the other the same weapon which the white majorities of the West used for centuries to crush and deny them their sense of humanity.

All of which is to say that we ought all to be disturbed by a climate of mutual hostility that is building up among certain segments of the Negro and Jewish communities in the ghettos.

Jewish leaders know this and are speaking to the Jewish conscience about it. So far as Negroes are concerned, let me say that one of the more unprofitable strategies we could ever adopt is now to join in history's oldest and most shameful witch hunt, anti-Semitism. This attitude, though not

---

From the *New York Amsterdam News*, April 8, 1967.

typical of most Negro communities, is gaining considerable strength in the ghetto. It sees the Jew as the chief and only exploiter of the ghetto, blames the ghetto on him, and seems to suggest that anything Jews do is inherent in the idea of their Jewishness.

I believe, though, that this attitude has two aspects—one entirely innocent of anti-Semitic animus. The first is that the Negro, in responding justifiably to bitterness and frustration, blames the plight of the ghetto on any visible reminder or representative of white America. . . .

Since in Harlem Jews happen to be the most immediate reminders of white American oppression, they naturally inherit the wrath of black frustration. And I don't believe that the Negroes who attack out of this attitude are interested in the subtleties of ethnic, cultural, and religious distinction, or that they would find any such distinction emotionally or intellectually useful.

It is the other aspect of the attitude that is more dangerous, that is consciously anti-Semitic, and that mischievously separates Jews from other white Americans and uses against them the old stereotypes of anti-Semitic slander and persecution. It is outrageous to blame Harlem on Jewishness. Harlem is no more the product of Jewishness than was American slavery and the subsequent century of Negro oppression in this country.

In the ghetto everybody gets a piece of the action: those who are Jews and those who are Christians; those who are white and those who are black; those who run the numbers and those who operate the churches; those—black and white—who own tenements and those—black and white—who own businesses.

Harlem is exploited by American greed. Even those who are now stirring up militant anti-Semitic resentments are exploiting the ghetto—the ghetto's mentality, its frustration, and its need to believe anything that brings it a degree of psychological comfort.

The Jews are no more angels than we are—there are some real grounds for conflict and contention between us as minority groups—but it is nonsense to divert attention from who it is that really oppresses Negroes in the ghetto. Ultimately the real oppressor is white American immorality and indifference, and we will be letting off the real oppressor too easily if we now concentrate our fulminations against a few Jews in the ghetto.

The premise of the stereotype is that everything that a man does defines his particular racial and ethnic morality. The people who say that about Jews are the same people who say it about Negroes. If we are now willing to believe what that doctrine says about Jews, then are we not obligated to endorse what it says about us?

I agree with James Baldwin entirely. I agree with him that we should "do something unprecedented: to create ourselves without finding it necessary to create an enemy . . . the nature of the enemy is history; the nature of the enemy is power; and what every black man, boy, woman, girl is struggling to achieve is some sense of himself or herself which this history and this power have done everything conceivable to destroy."

To engage in anti-Semitism is to engage in self-destruction—man's most tragic state.

ON LANGSTON HUGHES

There was in Langston Hughes's face a resemblance to the character of his work. His face had a warm, dreamlike, and sardonic quality. It was full of secret and secure wisdom: the face of a man who knew the score and who, rather than shouting it, would whisper it with a smile—a smile that made you feel the secrets he knew about himself were exactly the secrets he knew about you.

To know the score as a Negro American is to know a lot about pain and denial and the antidotes for these that one needs if one is not to be defeated. If at least two of those antidotes are smiles and dreams, then Hughes was their preeminent poet. He was not a political thinker. He did well enough what he had to do, lived well enough what he had to be. He looked at life not with piousness or didacticism but with eyes that caught experience in all its dimensions, suffering in all its ambiguities, without ever reducing in his own mind the particularity of Negro identity and experience.

It is being increasingly recommended that Negroes should not look at life, certainly not American life, that way. However, Hughes remains a representative writer of that period of Negro American thinking when the attack upon America was grounded in an affirmation of common humanity, when humor and optimism survived as necessary accompaniments to the freedom struggle. His "Simple," a man who used smiles and humor as a weapon against adversity, remains the "homespun existentialist" archetype of the Negro streets.

He was a leading figure of the Negro renaissance of the 1920's. As an artist he could well afford to contemplate the special pleasures and advantages of this movement for the Negro creative spirit. Nevertheless, he brought to it the same sardonic criticism that was his characteristic weapon: "I was there, I had a swell time while it lasted. But I thought it would not last long. . . . For how could a large enthusiastic number of people be crazy Negroes forever? . . . They thought the race problem had at last been solved by art. . . .

From the *New York Amsterdam News*, May 25, 1967.

I don't know what made many Negroes think that—except that they were mostly intellectuals doing the thinking. The ordinary Negroes hadn't heard about the Negro renaissance. And if they had, it hadn't raised their wages any."

IN DEFENSE OF MUHAMMAD ALI

Though we may not agree with the politics of the Black Muslims, we cannot contest their right to consider themselves a genuine religious group. In any case, our belief in the principles of individual and religious liberty should be of more importance than any disagreements we might have with the Muslims. That is the basis on which all religious differences ought to be approached, for the more one disagrees with people, the more tempting it becomes to violate their privileges. This has not been sufficiently recognized in the case of Muhammad Ali. His efforts to seek deferment from the armed services are being judged less on their legitimate merits than on the basis of personal and religious animosity.

The most fundamental example of this concerns his application to be deferred on the grounds of his Muslim ministry. There are many precedents for this in our society; hundreds of other ministers have sought deferment on the same grounds and have not been denied it. Because one of our traditions guarantees the separation of church and state, the authorities do not usually seek to determine for themselves the credentials of any Baptist, Presbyterian, or other minister. They recognize not only the definitions supplied by these religions, but also the autonomous privilege of these religions to make their own determinations. In the case of Ali and the Muslims, the authorities seem to be insisting on the right to make their own determination. The Constitution clearly warns against any official establishment of religion, but it would seem that the authorities, by now insisting on the right to determine what is or isn't a legitimate minister, or what is or isn't a legitimate religion, are taking a clear position on the establishment of religion.

Another reason for public hostility toward Muhammad Ali is that he changed his name. The great majority of the press and public have refused to respect his wishes or his right. This is rather strange, considering that no one refers to Cary Grant as "Archibald Alexander Leach who wants to be called Cary Grant" or to Billy Graham as "William Franklin alias Billy Graham." Nor did anyone contest the right of Norma Jean Baker to be known as Marilyn Monroe. The fact that neither the press nor the society

From the *New York Amsterdam News*, June 3, 1967.

shares a belief in Muhammad Ali's way of life is hardly a sufficient excuse for them to violate his personal privilege.

Considering how lucrative it would have been for him to become a "playboy boxer," and the great losses and penalties he now faces by deciding to confront the convictions in himself, his courage is more to be admired than vilified—particularly in a period when there is so little consistency between belief and action.

Finally, the boxing authorities, because of their contempt for due process, have further prejudiced the entire proceedings against Ali by depriving him of his heavyweight championship even while his case is still being determined in the courts. All this aside, we must be horrified, and to some extent amused, that the men who control a sport that is not notable for its abundance of ethical scruples should now rush so quickly to cloak it in the mantle of piety and morality.

A WAY OUT OF THE EXPLODING GHETTO

There is no longer any denying that this country is in the throes of a historic national crisis. Its ramifications are so vast and frightening that even now, shocked into numbness and disbelief, the American people have not yet fully grasped what is happening to them.

The grim data are clear enough and still coming in. Since this summer began, thirty of our cities, big and small, have been wracked by racial disorder; scores of citizens, almost all of them black, have been killed, thousands injured, and even more arrested. Property damage has exceeded a billion dollars; total income loss is incalculable.

As a people, we are not unaccustomed to violence. Frontier lawlessness, Southern vigilante-ism, Chicago gangsterism: these are images and themes embedded in the American tradition. We have only just lost a President to an assassin's bullet. But, having escaped the bombs of two world wars, we are not familiar with the horror of burned-out buildings, smoking rubble, tanks in our streets, the blasts of Molotov cocktails, the ring of snipers' bullets from rooftops. Today we look at sections of Detroit and think of war-torn Berlin. We see rampaging, looting mobs and think of the unstable politics of underdeveloped countries. A nation's identity has been overturned.

In our own history we can find no precedent in this century for the massive destruction the past three years have brought to our cities—no precedent since the Civil War. But the greatest toll is not in property damage or even in lives lost. Nor is the greatest danger that the violence will go on indefinitely, any more than the Civil War did. It is that the aftermath of that war will be repeated, that as in the Compromise of 1877 the country will turn its back on the Negro, on the root causes of his discontent, on its own democratic future.

Not since the Great Depression have social policy, our national institutions, our political order been more severely tested than at present. The coming months will shape the character of America in the remainder of

---

the twentieth century—and I am trying to speak with the utmost sobriety, precision, and restraint.

Why does the republic find itself at a crossroads? What has actually happened?

The term "race riot" is unilluminating and anachronistic. It describes the Detroit disorders of 1943, when the Negro and white communities were locked in combat. White mobs invaded the ghetto. Negroes forayed downtown. Men were beaten and murdered for the color of their skins. In the upheavals of the last four summers, destruction has been confined to the ghetto; nor, discounting the police, were black and white citizens fighting each other. In fact, in Detroit whites joined in the looting and sniping. And I am told that whites were free to walk through the embattled ghetto without fear of violence from Negroes.

This is not to deny the importance of anti-white hostility. One has only to hear the sick racial epithets "honkey" and "whitey" to recognize the deep and bitter hatred that is loose on the streets of the ghettos. But if white blood was what the rioters thirsted for, they didn't go very far to get it. What they assaulted were the symbols of white power—police and property, the latter embracing the entire ghetto. These are traditional targets of rebellions and in that sense the riots can be called rebellions.

That sense, however, must be sharply qualified. Is it correct to speak of "race rebellion" or "Negro rebellion"? Are America's Negroes on the verge of revolution? More than one newspaper and television commentator has already begun to draw comparisons between the ghetto uprisings and the French, Russian, Algerian, Irish, and Black African independence revolutions. Some black power advocates have proclaimed the beginnings of guerrilla warfare and see the urban Negro as a counterpart to the Viet Cong. And in Paris it has become fashionable to speak of the *"révolution des noires"* in the U.S.

The reality is that the revolutionary rhetoric now employed by some young Negro militants cannot create the preconditions for successful, or even authentic, revolution. The independence movements in colonial territories provide no model for the simple reason that American Negroes can have no geographical focus for nationalist sentiment.

Moreover, American Negroes do not constitute a popular majority struggling against a relatively small white colonial ruling group—the ideal condition for guerrilla warfare. Whatever separatist impulses exist among American Negroes cannot find appropriate models in the colonial world.

If independence revolutions are no model, what of social revolutions? This is a more interesting subject because the phrase "social revolution" has been widely used by the civil rights and liberal movements generally. But in this sense—and the sense in which I have been using it for thirty years—the phrase designates fundamental changes in social and economic class relations resulting from mass political action. Such action would be democratic. That is, it would aim to create a new majority coalition capable of exercising political power in the interest of new social policies. By definition the coalition has to be interracial.

As a minority, Negroes by themselves cannot bring about such a social revolution. They can participate in it as a powerful and stimulating force, or they can provoke a counterrevolution. In either case the decisive factor will be the political direction in which the majority will move.

Numbers are not the only issue. Also important is the class content of revolt. At least in the French and Russian revolutions, revolutionary leaders and parties sought to mobilize fairly definable and cohesive socioeconomic classes—workers, peasants, the middle class—which, though oppressed or aggrieved, were part of the society they sought to transform. Upon what classes do the advocates of rioting, the voices of the apocalypse, base their revolutionary perspective? This is another way of posing the question I left hanging earlier: Who is rioting?

Daniel Patrick Moynihan is correct in locating the riots in the "lower class" or, in the words of another controversial man, Karl Marx, in the "*lumpenproletariat*" or "slum proletariat." Lower class does not mean working class; the distinction is often overlooked in a middle-class culture that tends to lump the two together.

The distinction is important. The working class is employed. It has a relation to the production of goods and services; much of it is organized in unions. It enjoys a measure of cohesion, discipline, and stability lacking in the lower class. The latter is unemployed or marginally employed. It is relatively unorganized, incohesive, unstable. It contains the petty criminal and antisocial elements. Above all, unlike the working class, it lacks the sense of a stake in society. When the slum proletariat is black, its alienation is even greater.

From the revolutionist point of view, the question is not whether steps could be taken to strengthen organization among the *lumpenproletariat* but whether that group could be a central agent of social transformation. Generally, the answer has been no.

The black slum proletariat has been growing in numbers and density. As agricultural mechanization and other factors continue pushing Negroes out of the South, the urban ghettos expand each year by half a million; only

40,000 Negroes annually find their way into the suburbs. This trend has not been affected at all by any antipoverty or Great Society programs.

When the migration of Negroes to Northern and Western cities was at its height during World War II, factory jobs were available at decent wages. With the advent of advanced technology eliminating many semi-skilled and unskilled jobs, and with the movement of plants from the central cities to the suburbs (New York lost 200,000 factory jobs in a decade), urban Negroes suffered rising joblessness or employment in low-paying service jobs.

The depth of the unemployment problem in the slum ghettos is indicated in a recent U.S. Department of Labor report on "subemployment" in cities and slums. While the traditional unemployment rate counts only those "actively looking" but unable to find work, the subemployment index reflects in addition: (1) those who have dropped out of the labor market in despair, (2) those who are working part time but want full-time jobs, (3) heads of households under sixty-five working full time but earning poverty wages (less than $60 a week), (4) individuals under sixty-five who are not heads of households and earn less than $56 a week in full-time jobs, and (5) a conservatively estimated portion of males known to be living in the slums but who somehow do not show up in employment or unemployment counts.

The report states: "If the traditional statistical concept of 'unemployment' (which produced the nationwide average of 3.7 per cent unemployment rate for January, 1967) is applied to the urban slum situation, the *'unemployment rate' in these areas is about 10 per cent . . . three times the average for the rest of the country*." [Original italics.] The figure for Detroit's Central Woodward area, incidentally, is 10.1 per cent.

The subemployment rate in the 10 cities surveyed yields an average figure of almost 35 per cent. Though possibly in need of further refining, the subemployment rate is the more meaningful figure. Not only does it include the categories listed above, but it also tends to reflect the number of people who experience unemployment over a period of time. By contrast, the official rate counts those unemployed at a point in time (i.e., the time the survey is taken).

High unemployment and low income are not the only problems afflicting the black slum proletariat, but they are the crucial ones. Without adequate income, there is no access to the decent housing market, educational opportunity, even proper health care. (In 1964, East and Central Harlem, comprising 24 per cent of Manhattan's population, accounted for 40 per cent of its TB deaths, 33 per cent of its infant deaths; in Bedford-Stuyvesant, which contains 9 per cent of Brooklyn's population, the respective figures were 24 and 22 per cent.)

The tendency of much current antipoverty rhetoric to create a multitude of disparate problems out of a central multifaceted one is a mistake. It is precisely in the expansion of public facilities and social services that new employment opportunities can be generated, at varying skill levels. High sub-employment rates and the lack of decent housing in the slums are two sides of the same coin.

Meanwhile, within the slum proletariat, youth constitutes a subdivision of increasing economic and political importance. While according to the official unemployment rates the joblessness gap between Negro and white men over twenty has been narrowing since 1961, even this official rate records a widening of the gap between Negro and white teen-agers since 1957. Right now the Negro unemployment rate is 25 per cent nationally, but for sixteen-to-nineteen-year-olds in the ten slum areas surveyed, it is over 38 per cent! Moreover, this rate was unaffected by the downward trend of the nation's overall unemployment rate late last year. For white teen-agers, on the other hand, unemployment since 1957 never went beyond 15 per cent and is now at 10 per cent.

Nor is there any evidence that Negro teen-agers do not want to work. Whenever job programs have been announced, they have turned out in large numbers, only to find that the jobs weren't there. In Oakland, a "Job Fair" attracted 15,000 people; only 250 were placed. In Philadelphia, 6,000 were on a waiting list for a training program.

What Negro teen-agers are not inclined to accept are dead-end jobs that pay little and promise no advancement or training. Many would prefer to live by their wits as hustlers or petty racketeers, their version of the self-employed businessman or salesman. That their pursuit of this distorted entrepreneurial ideal only mires them deeper in the slum proletariat is not the point. They want to be part of the white-collar organization man's world that is America's future, not trapped behind brooms and pushcarts.

Nor can they fairly be blamed by a society which has itself produced these yearnings, reveled in its affluence, encouraged the consumption of trivia, and proclaimed the coming of computerized utopias. The middle classes may nostalgically extol their immigrant parents' fortitude and perseverance in manual labor, but they do not steer their own children toward the construction gang or the garment district. They show them the push buttons, not the pushcart. Might they not then show some compassionate understanding of black youngsters who dream of better things, even when crippled by poor education, broken families, and the disabilities bred by slum life? If it is true that a Negro boy is nobody unless he owns alligator shoes and an alpaca sweater, who created these symbols? Who whetted this appetite? Who profited from the sale of these commodities, and who advertised them? And who is victimized?

The ghetto youth who is out of school, unemployed, and rejected even by the draft (as 52 per cent are in Harlem) is the extreme embodiment of the bitter frustration in the slum proletariat. He is utterly propertyless, devoid of experience in the productive process, and without a stake in existing social arrangements. At the same time, because he is young and not beaten down, he is irreverent, filled with bravado, hostile to the alien authority of the police, and determined to "make it" in any way that he can. He is at the core of the rioting.

In Detroit, the riot begins when pimps and prostitutes taunt police who are raiding a "blind pig" at 5 A.M. In Minneapolis, two women fight over a wig, the police try to break it up, and a riot erupts in an atmosphere already charged by delays in the mailing of Federal Youth Opportunity Program pay checks to youths in the ghetto area. In Cairo, Illinois, a Negro soldier dies in the city jail; police say it was suicide but order the body embalmed without an autopsy, and fire bombings and shooting follow.

In these cases, the police figure prominently in the incidents that triggered the rioting. Sometimes they are not directly involved, but rumors of police brutality flood through the ghetto. Although it may be of some interest to search for a pattern, no very profound purpose is served by concentrating on who struck the match. There are always matches lying around. We must ask why there was also a fuse and why the fuse was connected to a powder keg.

To pursue this analogy: Whether the match is struck by police misconduct or by an "extremist" exhorting his listeners to violence, the fuse is the condition of life among the black slum proletariat—hostile, frustrated, and with nothing to lose. The powder keg is the social background against which the riots break out and which extends their scope. They become more than riots pure and simple, yet less than politically coherent rebellions. They are *riotous manifestations of rebellion.*

The social background is defined by the fact that the black slum proletariat is part of a larger community of oppressed and segregated citizens—the overwhelming majority of the Negro population. Were it not for this the riots could be dismissed merely as wild, inchoate sprees of looting and violence, the expressions of criminal greed, a carnival of destruction to be suppressed by police force. Such actions, detached from political policies, programs, and goals—and, make no mistake about it, the riots were not on behalf of the black power ideology; the latter is an after-the-fact justification employed by people in search of a constituency—do not properly constitute a rebellion.

But because of the social background, the riots, while not *the rebellion* of the Negro people, are charged with manifestations of rebellion.

It is because of this background that the riots can set off a chain reaction, fan out from the slum proletariat and, as Detroit showed, involve people who ordinarily would not be found looting stores. It is because of this background that snipers and the most violent elements can feel that their actions are in some sense heroic. And it is because of this background that the riots have enormous implications for the future of all Negroes.

As Martin Luther King, A. Philip Randolph, Roy Wilkins, and Whitney Young pointed out in their recent statement, the most severe and immediate damage has been to the Negro community itself. In addition to those who lost their lives, thousands lost their homes, food supplies, access to schools. There is danger of a counterreaction enlisting the most bigoted, vigilante-minded elements in the white community. Ammunition has been given to the reactionaries in an already backlash-dominated Congress. Many whites sincerely in favor of integration will be silenced out of fear and confusion. Riots do not strengthen the power of black people; they weaken it and encourage racist power.

But why, asks white America, do the Negroes riot now—not when conditions are at their worst but when they seem to be improving? Why now, after all of the civil rights and antipoverty legislation? There are two answers.

First, progress has been considerably less than is generally supposed. While the Negro has won certain important legal and constitutional rights (voting, desegregation of public accommodations, etc.), his relative socio-economic position has scarcely improved. There simply has not been significant, visible change in his life.

Second, if a society is interested in stability, it should either not make promises or it should keep them. Economic and social deprivation, if accepted by its victims as their lot in life, breeds passivity, even docility. The miserable yield to their fate as divinely ordained or as their own fault. And, indeed, many Negroes in earlier generations felt that way.

Today, young Negroes aren't having any. They don't share the feeling that something must be wrong with them, that they are responsible for their own exclusion from this affluent society. The civil rights movement—in fact, the whole liberal trend beginning with John Kennedy's election—has told them otherwise.

Conservatives will undoubtedly seize the occasion for an attack on the Great Society, liberalism, the welfare state, and Lyndon Johnson. But the young Negroes are right: the promises made to them were good and necessary and long, long overdue. The youth were right to believe in them. The only trouble is that they were not fulfilled. Prominent Republicans and Dixiecrats are demanding not that the promises be fulfilled, but that they be revoked.

What they and the American people absolutely must understand now is that the promises cannot be revoked. They were not made to a handful of leaders in a White House drawing room; they were made to an entire generation, one not likely to forget or to forgive. If Republican leaders Everett Dirksen and Gerald Ford, hand in glove with the diehards of the Confederacy, continue their contemptible effort to exploit the nation's tragedy for partisan political advantage, they will sow the dangerous seeds of race hate and they will discredit themselves morally in the eyes of the coming generations and of history. This is not a wise policy for a party that only yesterday reduced itself to a shambles by catering to the most backward and reactionary elements in the country.

It is ironic that in a nation which has not undertaken a massive social and economic reform since the New Deal one now hears even liberal voices asking: "Don't the causes of the riots go deeper than economics, than jobs, housing, schools? Aren't there profound moral, cultural, psychological, and other factors involved—powerlessness, an identity crisis?"

Of course, but in the present context such questions smack of a trend toward mystification which, if it gains ascendancy, will paralyze public policy. Then, too, I cannot help suspecting that they are rationalizations for the yearning of some white liberals to withdraw. "Obviously," they are saying, "there seems to be nothing we can do. We're not even wanted. Why not give the ghettos over to the black power people?"

I have no hesitation in saying that this recommendation simply aids and abets the Congressional reactionaries, who would have no objection to letting Negroes run their own slum tenements, dilapidated schools, and tax-starved communities. Isn't this in the best tradition of rugged self-help, Horatio Alger and all that? Haven't Barry Goldwater and William F. Buckley endorsed this notion of black power? Just so long as white people are left alone. Just so long as the total society is not forced to examine its own inner contradictions. Just so long as the federal government isn't challenged to launch radical and massive programs to rebuild our cities, end poverty, guarantee full employment at decent wages, clear our polluted air and water, and provide mass transportation.

This is just the challenge posed by A. Philip Randolph's $185 billion "Freedom Budget for All Americans"—a carefully designed, economically feasible program for the obliteration of poverty in 10 years. Unless the nation is prepared to move along these lines—to rearrange its priorities, to set a timetable for achieving them, and to allocate its resources accordingly—it will not be taking its own commitments seriously. Surely it cannot then turn amazedly to responsible Negro leaders, whose pleas for large-scale programs it has failed to heed, for an explanation of the consequences.

The present administration has a grave responsibility. It is very well for it to proclaim that we can have guns *and* butter, that we can pursue our course in Vietnam and still make progress at home. We do have the economic capacity for both, as the Freedom Budget itself shows. But we are not doing both. Let us stop proclaiming that we *can* do what we *don't* do and start *doing* it.

If administration actions are not to mock its own rhetoric, the President must now take the lead in mobilizing public opinion behind a new resolve to meet the crisis in our cities. He should now put before Congress a National Emergency Public Works and Reconstruction bill aimed at building housing for homeless victims of the riot-torn ghettos, repairing damaged public facilities, and in the process generating maximum employment opportunities for unskilled and semiskilled workers. Such a bill should be the first step in the imperative reconstruction of all our decaying center cities.

Admittedly, the prospects for passage of such a bill in the present Congress are dismal. Congressmen will cry out that the rioters must not be rewarded, thereby further penalizing the very victims of the riots. This, after all, is a Congress capable of defeating a meager $40 million rat extermination program the same week it votes $10 million for an aquarium in the District of Columbia!

But the vindictive racial meanness that has descended upon this Congress, already dominated by the revived coalition of Republicans and Dixiecrats, must be challenged—not accommodated. The President must go directly to the people, as Harry Truman did in 1948. He must go to them, not with slogans, but with a timetable for tearing down every slum in the country.

There can be no further delay. The daydreamers and utopians are not those of us who have prepared massive Freedom Budgets and similar programs. They are the smugly "practical" and myopic philistines in the Congress, the state legislatures, and the city halls who thought they could sit it out. The very practical choice now before them and the American people is whether we shall have a conscious and authentic democratic social revolution or more tragic and futile riots that tear our nation to shreds.

THE LESSONS OF THE
LONG HOT SUMMER

Toward the end of the long hot summer of 1967—a summer which saw riots in more than thirty-two cities and the deaths of nearly one hundred Negroes—Vice-President Humphrey was asked to comment on the assertion that the United States had spent $904 billion (or 57 per cent of the nation's budget) on military power since 1946, while spending only $96 billion (or 6 per cent) on social programs in the same period. "The fact is," he said, "there has been a 'sickness' in the world in these post–World War II years which we have not had the luxury of ignoring." Apparently, however, we *have* had the luxury of ignoring the sickness created by the simultaneous growth and decay of our central cities. The question posed for us by the events of this past summer is whether we can now afford the price.

In 1910, a large majority of our population lived in rural areas; today, about three-fourths of our population lives in urban areas (and since 1950, 1.5 million Negroes have moved to Northern ghettos). Yet the United States Congress remains a basically rural body. In the House, 225 out of 435 members come from towns with populations of 50,000 or less, and in the Senate the ratio is 56 to 44. It is, therefore, no great cause for wonder that the needs of our cities should simultaneously have increased and been neglected. Until recently, indeed, we did not even possess a precise inventory of those needs. Largely through the efforts of the AFL-CIO, however, the Joint Economic Committee of Congress has now drawn up such an inventory, projected to 1975.

The study, entitled "State and Local Public Facility Needs and Financing," is not the product of academics removed from reality, utopian civil rights activists, or labor leaders with a vested interest in higher wages; it represents the findings of experts in the various fields surveyed. The projected costs it estimates do not include the cost of the additional teachers, doctors, policemen, etc., who will have to staff the new facilities once they are built. Nevertheless, these estimates do give us a rough idea of our unmet needs,

From *Commentary*, October 1967.

some notion of what it will take to meet them, and the benefits, in terms of long-range employment opportunities, of doing so.

To begin with education: based on the U.S. Office of Education's figure of 27 pupils per classroom, 107,000 new classrooms are needed to handle present overcrowding, and another 200,000 to replace existing facilities that ought to be abandoned because they are unfit. Altogether, 750,000 new classrooms will have to be built over the next ten years if we are to cope with the present backlog, future deterioration, and expected increase in enrollment. This means an expenditure by 1975 of $5.3 billion, as compared with $3.7 billion in 1965—and for elementary education alone the cost over the entire ten years totals $42 billion. So far as higher educational opportunities are concerned, if the growing demand for them is to be met, state and local governments will have to spend $13.9 billion for academic facilities during the next decade, and another $6.1 billion to provide housing and related facilities for the students. Thus outlays in this area will have to climb from approximately $1.2 billion in 1964 to nearly $2.5 billion in 1975.

Then there is housing. The federal government's major vehicle for providing multi-family moderate income housing is Sec. 221(d)(3) of the National Housing Act. Under this program nonprofit sponsors receive 100 per cent mortgages at low interest rates, and yet in the six years since the passage of that bill only 40,000 units have flowed from it. If we were to build 40,000 units per year in New York City alone, it would take more than twenty years to reach the number of deteriorating buildings occupied at this moment.

Next, transportation. Congress finally recognized the problems created by mass transportation in 1964, when it adopted the Mass Transportation Act. As a result, grants are now available to state and local governments in connection with capital outlays for mass transit facilities. But in order to meet the needs estimated for 1975, spending for highways, roads, streets, bridges, tunnels, airports, marine facilities, mass transit, etc., will have to climb to nearly $18 billion in that year.

Similarly with health facilities. In 1965 we spent $500 million on them; in the next decade $13 billion will be required if the health needs of our people are to be adequately managed. Moreover, in such public health areas as sewage and waste disposal, capital outlays will have to rise from $385 million and $625 million respectively in 1965 to $1.1 billion and $1.2 billion respectively in 1975. So too with public water supply systems. In 1965, state and local governments spent just over a billion dollars in capital outlays on such systems. The needs estimated for 1975 will require $2.25 billion.

Writing in the March 1967 issue of the *Federationist*, AFL-CIO economist Nathaniel Goldfinger cogently sums up the significance of this inventory of American needs. Pointing out that the labor force will increase at the rate of 1.5 million per year in the next decade, Goldfinger goes on:

> A logical policy would be to see to it that these two needs—the growing need for jobs and the pressing need for public facilities—are brought together in a planned program.
>
> The employment impact of these construction activities is substantial. The U.S. Bureau of Labor Statistics has estimated that each million dollars spent in this way creates approximately one hundred jobs for the year—about forty jobs at the construction site and about sixty jobs in industries supplying building material, equipment and services, including unskilled and semiskilled jobs badly needed in an automated economy.
>
> Moreover, to this must be added the indirect impact—that is, the impact felt as the result of the wages and salaries paid to these workers. As these wages and salaries are spent, retail sales are increased and still more jobs are created—in stores and warehouses and in companies producing consumer goods. This adds another 50 to 100 full-time jobs.
>
> *This would mean that a billion dollars spent on public facility construction is worth 100,000 jobs directly created on the construction site and in the production and distribution of equipment and material, plus somewhere between 50,000 to 100,000 more jobs as the result of increased sales to consumers.* [Italics mine—B. R.]

Here, then, is what the AFL-CIO rightly calls "the foundation for a nationwide program . . . based on federal financial and technical assistance to the state and local governments, including federal grants-in-aid and guaranteed loans, as well as direct federal aids."

Not the least important consequence of such a program would be to make jobs available to the unemployed poor. Thanks largely to the agitation of the civil rights movement and a book by Michael Harrington called *The Other America*, this nation instituted a war on poverty several years ago. It would seem only reasonable that the first task of an assault on poverty would be to create jobs for all those who are able to work. This apparently self-evident proposition was not, however, one of the assumptions behind the Johnson war on poverty. *That* war was implicitly based on the notion that poor people are poor because there is something wrong with them, and it has accordingly proceeded to set up a bedlam of community-action programs under the delusion that the poor can be helped to organize themselves out of poverty. (Even if this were possible, it is hard to see how it could be accomplished at an expenditure of fifty dollars per poor person—which is all the Office of Economic Opportunity has been allocated by Congress after administrative costs are subtracted.)

To be sure, community-action programs have their value, but they do not employ the unemployed; nor do job-training camps do any good when they train young people for jobs which simply do not exist. On top of all this, the war on poverty as presently conceived involves no strategy for lifting the *employed* poor out of poverty—those, that is, who are so underpaid that they live in poverty even while working; nor can it help the 13 per cent of the poor who live in families headed by women who should not work, or the 25 per cent of the poor who, being over sixty-five, cannot work. Only a high minimum wage and some form of guaranteed income can help people in those three categories.

Let me emphasize that I am here suggesting not that the war on poverty be scrapped, but that it be widened and intensified so that it may more adequately attack the problems it now claims to be attacking. And I want to stress the problems of Negroes, for it is no secret that the inadequacy of our programs for dealing with the needs of our urban population, and of the poor among them in particular, places a special burden on the American Negro. One grows weary of citing the same hideous figures time and time again—figures which show that life in the ghetto has been getting worse rather than better in the last ten years, that housing is worse, that schooling is worse, that the job situation is worse. I will try on this occasion to bring it all home through a less familiar set of horrifying statistics.

In 1930, according to analyses made by Drs. Paul M. Vincent and James D. Haughton of the New York City Board of Health, pregnant Negro women were twice as likely to die in childbirth as pregnant white women. In 1964 the mortality rate of Negro women in childbirth was *more than three times* that of white women.

In 1940, fourteen times as many non-white mothers had their babies delivered by midwives as white mothers. In 1960 the figure was *twenty-three times* as many.

In 1950, the infant mortality rate for non-whites was 66 per cent higher than for whites, but in 1964 it was *90 per cent* higher.

Thus we are confronted in 1967 by a nation which has neglected to meet the basic needs of its entire population and which has most grievously failed in providing for the needs of Negroes. It is beyond the resources neither of human ingenuity nor of the national treasury to formulate and act upon a plan for doing what is necessary. It remains to be seen whether it is beyond the resources of the national will.

The goals are clear. First: full employment. Second: a $2 minimum wage.

Third: a guaranteed annual income for those now dependent, through no fault of their own, on welfare.

Everyone pays lip service to the goal of full employment, but the fact is that there is much resistance to it in Washington. Oscar Gass has succinctly described the thinking behind that resistance in "The Political Economy of the Great Society" (*Commentary*, October 1965):

> American public men are quite united in concern to avoid a depression of 10 to 15 million unemployed. But they are almost equally united in sharing a leery attitude toward full employment. ... Under full employment, wages are pushed up; prices are pushed up; the value of fixed income declines; profits come easily; businessmen lose their sobriety; innovation is neglected; the international competitive position is weakened. . . . Consequently, . . . men of authority in Washington take only a limited interest in the reduction of unemployment below the present 4½ per cent. They are more concerned with the danger of "overheating" the economy.

The problem of changing such attitudes poses an enormously important challenge to economists who disagree with that line of reasoning. A non-economist may, however, be permitted to observe that if the long hot summer of 1967 proves anything, it is that "the danger of 'overheating' the economy" may turn out to be as nothing compared with the dangers of our present employment policies. For those latter dangers include not only violence but an answering repressiveness that could end by threatening the very fabric of American liberties.

A series of federally financed public works programs for the creation of the physical facilities detailed by the Joint Economic Committee would be an obvious step in the direction of full employment. In helping to build these facilities, the poor would be working at something that would enlist their seriousness and their hope; the young would be trained for jobs that actually existed, and they would know they had a chance to grow and improve with those jobs. (Another step toward full employment would be the creation of a whole new hierarchy of nonprofessional workers to help the professional perform some of the services he now performs by himself. Social work aides could, for example, act as companions to older people, and could interpret the need for family planning to overburdened mothers.)

The immediate passage of a $2 minimum wage would do as much as the entire poverty program in helping the poor to rehabilitate themselves. Yet even a $2 minimum wage would only guarantee an income of $4,160 for a year's work—roughly $2000 less than what the government has computed to be a "modest but adequate" urban family budget. We should not be satisfied until every American family has at least that "modest but adequate" income. For now, however, increasing the minimum wage to $2 an hour would be a responsible and reasonable step in the right direction. There are those who say that doing so would result in the elimination of precisely those jobs which now provide at least some opportunity for unskilled Negroes, young people, and others who are not qualified to compete in an automated economy. This is true, and it explains why the proposal makes sense only within the framework of a national commitment to generate a large number of new jobs.

In our culture, a man's judgment of himself is inevitably related to his role in the production of goods and services. He is someone because he does something on which society sets a value. So the idea of a guaranteed annual income is a good one only for people who are incapacitated from working either by age or physical disability. Full employment is the answer for everyone else.

In the meantime, there are the burnt-out neighborhoods of Detroit and Newark to be dealt with. In a recent article in *Newsday*, Daniel Patrick Moynihan calls for the immediate rebuilding of those neighborhoods—an action that in my view should be taken by means of a National Emergency Public Works and Reconstruction Act which would not only be a good thing in itself but would create employment for unskilled and semiskilled workers living in the riot-torn ghettos.

We do, then, have a fairly good idea of what our national needs are; we have the makings of a viable program for dealing with them; and we have the financial resources. But do we have the final, and indispensable, element —the political will?

The administration proclaims that we can continue to pursue the war in Vietnam and still make progress at home. Yet the President asks for an across-the-board tax increase of 10 per cent to pay for the Vietnam war—an increase which will exacerbate the injustices of an already regressive tax structure, and which bespeaks a twisted idea of our national priorities. Reporting on the atmosphere in Washington in the aftermath of the Detroit and Newark riots, Daniel Patrick Moynihan writes:

> The mood of the administration in Washington is one of paralysis. There is no political will for the Executive Branch to move in any direction and nothing but fear as to what direction Congress will take if it should seize the initiative. . . . The result has been a curious process of backward reasoning. First: "We can't do anything

[for lack of money]." Second: "We don't do anything." Third: "We shouldn't do anything."

And Moynihan adds: "We cannot do anything without the President, and the President seems determined to do nothing. Worse, he is denying it."

The surprising fact of the matter, however is that the President's paralysis and the Congressional backlash do not seem to represent the prevailing national mood. The August Harris Poll on post-riot attitudes found that while a few more white people (between 5 and 8 per cent) were resorting to racial stereotypes than in 1966, a large majority (more than 60 per cent) of whites supported federal programs to tear down the urban ghettos (84 per cent of the Negroes favored this) and wanted large-scale government works projects to provide jobs for all the unemployed (91 per cent of the Negroes favored this proposal).

But even if the political support is there, only political organization can activate and make it effective. The Negroes are the only group in our population that is presently in significant motion. This poses serious problems because Negroes by themselves do not have sufficient political power to bring about a social revolution. As a minority, they can participate in it as a powerful and stimulating force; or they can provoke a counterrevolution. In either case the decisive factor will be the political direction in which the majority decides to move. Thus, as I have argued many times before, Negroes have no constructive alternative to acting in concert with other minority groups, with liberals, with intellectuals, and with the labor movement. In other words, there is no alternative to coalition politics.

"Twice in this generation," William V. Shannon recently observed in the *New York Times,*

> the leaders of American life outside Washington reached agreement on a major issue and forced the federal government to act. In 1947–48 the issue was the Marshall Plan. Business and civic leaders rallied to support the rebuilding of Western Europe submitted by a Democratic President to a conservative and potentially balky Republican Congress. In 1963–64, religious leaders of all faiths powerfully reinforced the civil-rights movement and compelled President Kennedy [and Johnson] to ask for a far-reaching civil-rights bill and Congress to enact it.

The catalyst behind the passage of the Civil Rights Act of 1964 and the Voting Rights Act of 1965 was, of course, the civil rights movement. That movement, despite the malaise and shenanigans of the past year, remains the prime force for democratic social change in this country. It is true that we have not recently been witnessing the kind of excitement stirring within it that we were accustomed to for almost ten years. What we have been witnessing instead are rioting and demagogic ranting. But we tend to see only what the mass media permit us to see, and the mass media consistently tend to a preference for the dramatic over the real.

They do not, for example, stress the fact that in almost every city across the country scores of community groups are working on the problems of housing, schools, jobs, health, and police relations (in New York City alone over three hundred such groups are now active). From New York to Los Angeles, vigorous and often successful work is being done to get Negro youngsters into the building trades. And the South is honeycombed with voter-registration groups that have emerged—largely under the leadership of the Southern Regional Council and the NAACP—since the passage of the 1965 Voting Rights Act.

While a number of organizations that were concerned between 1955 and 1965 with direct mass action now show evidence of decline, the two oldest members of the civil rights movement, the NAACP and the National Urban League, have been growing steadily since 1965. The NAACP has just had one of the largest national conventions in its history. Last year it raised $686,786 in new life memberships, a considerable increase over 1965; in the last two years, it has added eighty-seven new branches and sixty youth councils; and its membership in Mississippi alone has doubled. In the last three years, similarly, the National Urban League has added to its affiliates by a third, doubled its budget, and greatly increased its staff. The Scholarship Defense Fund, formerly affiliated with CORE, conducts workshops throughout the South. The Legal Defense Fund of the NAACP has opened new offices and expanded its services. In Mississippi the NAACP, the Mississippi Freedom Democratic Party, and former SNCC activists like Fannie Lou Hamer have banded together to elect at least sixteen Negro local officials.

But if the civil rights movement is far from dead, it most certainly is in a crisis. Having come to the end of one historical phase of activity, it must readapt its tactics to confront a new one, and the crisis is a reflection of the uncertainties of the transition.

Let me try to compare some of the new problems with those of the preceding period.

1. From 1955 to 1965 the objectives of the movement were chiefly to secure the Negro's right to vote and to integrate public accommodations. Those issues affected Negroes almost exclusively and could be attacked simply as civil rights problems. Secondly, because they were matters of sim-

ple dignity, of getting what the Constitution clearly said everybody ought to have, and because they yielded spectacular and emotional victories, they could sustain the interest of people who were becoming attracted to the movement. In the present period we confront the more complex problems of housing, education, and jobs, which affect not only Negroes but also whites. And, in attacking them, we are not merely raising questions about the Constitution; we are also stimulating a great national debate over economics, priorities, and planning.

2. In the previous period the unity of the Negro community cut across class lines. Most Negroes, regardless of their economic or social station, were subject to the same discrimination in public places. Ralph Bunche was as likely to be refused service in a restaurant or a hotel as any illiterate sharecropper in Mississippi. This common bond prevented latent class differences and resentments from being openly expressed. But the people who have benefited most from the Negro revolution are middle-class Negroes (whose sons and daughters actually created and led the sit-in movement). The economic status of the black middle class now makes it possible for them to utilize integrated public accommodations, and American industry has stimulated middle-class progress by upgrading the educated Negro—a fact which is simultaneously appreciated, scorned, and exaggerated by unemployed Negroes. The resentment felt by this new underclass of Negroes is likely to show itself in frustration behavior—such as riots—and in other forms of hostility, not only toward whites who "have it" but also toward Negroes who have "made it."

3. In the previous period, the only expenditure the federal government was called upon to make involved the cost of police protection and enforcement. It is much easier to issue moral proclamations when there is no need to back them up with congressional appropriations. Many white Americans who joined the March on Washington and applauded Martin Luther King's dream of freedom seem far less enthusiastic about helping us realize that dream when it means altering our economic structure.

4. In the 1955–65 period, though it was the quest for voting rights and desegregation that constituted the main objectives, the dynamic around the campaign to secure them was provided by racist brutality. Nothing that any Negro leader did or said stiffened the will of the mass movement quite so much as Bull Connor's policemen, dogs, fire hoses, and cattle prods, or the bombing of churches, or the murder of children and civil rights workers. All this both strengthened the Negro will and created a consensus of conscience in the white community. When Mayor Daley failed to respond cre-

atively to some of Martin Luther King's demands in Chicago last year, he proved that the dynamic of the fight for the objectives of the new period—better housing, jobs, and education—is political, not moral.

5. Because of the drama of the previous period, the movement received a great deal of help from the mass media; almost every day for ten years newspapers all across the nation carried news of civil rights activity on their front pages. In the present period, however, the slow, irksome, and unspectacular work being done does not draw headlines. Much of our present activity is either ignored or relegated to small items on back pages. Perhaps this is why so many people consider the movement dead. In any case, this adds to our problem of developing and sustaining momentum.

6. In the previous period, most people, if asked to identify the nation's most compelling social problem, would have said "civil rights." Today the answer is more likely to be "Vietnam." This means that whereas before we were being carried along by a forward psychological thrust, we are now trying to progress against a stream of psychological withdrawal. The Vietnam war has created disunity in the civil rights movement; it has caused many liberals to abandon the movement and concentrate their energies in antiwar activities; it has permitted reactionaries, in the guise of super-patriots, to cut back funds urgently needed for social change on the home front.

7. In the 1955–65 period, a young civil rights worker needed only two qualities to function effectively: bravery and perseverance. With those qualities alone, he could sit-in at hostile lunch counters, throw his body across the streets, integrate buses and bus terminals, and march in the teeth of police brutality and power. The questions he raised were questions of clear principle—the right to vote, free access to public accommodations, etc. Today the young civil rights worker needs more than just courage and perseverance. The strategies of social reconstruction, of reordering national priorities, and of social planning require more than "soul." They require an ability to organize, an understanding of political power and action, and an insight into the processes of social change.

8. Because the chief strategy in the period just past centered on nonviolent mass action, the movement tended to congeal. While there was some debate surrounding strategy and tactics, it was limited solely to the areas of public accommodations and voting. But once the questions become, as they now have, questions of economics, a wider dialogue also becomes inevitable; and there can be no meaningful discussion of such matters without basic philosophical differences emerging.

9. The previous period was one of nonviolence. Even those Negroes who

were not persuaded of nonviolence as a moral principle practiced it as a viable tactic. Today, many younger Negroes are convinced that a violent confrontation is both necessary and inevitable. While I myself do not believe that violence can play a constructive role in solving the problems that face Negroes, society keeps providing the ghetto communities with evidence that unless they riot, they will get nothing. Yet there is also the danger that rioting will produce repressive action. This is in the nature of the very reluctant and token concessions that are being made to the Negro. Beyond a certain point there will be no token concessions left to be made, and since the larger and more basic victories will not have been won through violence, rioting will almost certainly come to reap only resistance and repression. On the other side, very little short of constructive programs for better jobs, housing, and education will prevent Negroes from expressing the rage that has been repressed for so long.

10. We are no longer in a period of civil rights revolt as such. We are now in the midst of a struggle to wrest human and economic rights out of the basic contradictions of American society. I am convinced that unless we establish social and economic priorities and organize politically in their behalf, nothing will happen. Protest demonstrations alone will not arouse the financial or moral commitment to solve the problems of poverty. To get the necessary money out of Congress for the necessary programs, we must organize within the broad coalition of American need and American social and political concern.

In sum, to reiterate a point I have made in these pages on more than one occasion in the past, the previous period was a period of protest; the present period must be one of politics.

Although the civil rights movement cannot by itself activate the American political will, it can, if it succeeds in readjusting itself to the realities of the new period, take the lead in stirring us all into motion. To that end it will have to concentrate on three major objectives: (1) the implementation of existing laws; (2) voter registration and education; and (3) the development of an economic strategy that will unite blacks and whites in a new majority.

The segregationists have taught us a bitter lesson in the importance of the way laws are applied. For several years now, Negroes have been winning legislative victories, while racists have been subverting these victories by their relentless pressure on the bureaucracy in Washington. Thus the black man who first was forced to master the secrets of the judicial and then the legislative process in America is now being forced to learn how to deal with the bureaucratic apparatus and get it to enforce existing laws.

The movement has made enormous strides in securing the Negro's right to vote in the South. By taking full advantage of opportunities won at great cost, the movement can now help to change not simply the plight of the Southern Negro but the shape of American politics as well. Only half the eligible black voters below the Mason-Dixon line are registered. However, they have already begun to exercise an impact on their region, as Negroes sit in state legislatures and city councils for the first time since Reconstruction. An increase in Negro registrants will inevitably mean a growth of Negro political power.

But voter education is no less essential than registration. In Alabama last year it might have been possible to defeat the Wallaces if there had been unity between Negroes and the liberal-labor bloc. In the absence of such unity, black voting strength was dissipated and a racist presidential candidacy was furthered. To avert any recurrence of such a situation, Southern Negroes, once they have registered and organized themselves politically, will have to seek out allies with whom they can form a new majority. This tactic has already borne some fruit in states like Tennessee, Texas, and Florida. Now it must be applied to the racist heartland itself.

The consequences of such an integrated political coalition would extend far beyond the South. There are, as James MacGregor Burns has shown, four parties in the United States: liberal Presidential Democrats, moderate Presidential Republicans, conservative congressional Democrats, and Republicans. It was, of course, the cooperation between the congressional Democrats and the Republicans which frustrated any basic social change from 1938 until the Johnson landslide in 1964. And one of the main bulwarks of this reactionary alliance was the one-party South, which provided a bloc of safe conservative seats and through the seniority system guaranteed the Southern caucus disproportionate power on congressional committees.

In 1964, Barry Goldwater forced a temporary realignment from the right, and following the Johnson landslide Congress passed more social legislation than at any time since the New Deal. But the defeat of many liberal freshmen in 1966 changed all that. The ruling alliance of the conservative congressional Democrats and Republicans was reconstituted, albeit circumspectly. It is a fairly good bet that the practical reactionaries will not again follow a Goldwater tactic in this generation. That could mean a new "deadlock of democracy," to use Professor Burns's phrase. Negroes would suffer, of course, since they are the first and worst victims of every social problem in this country. But so would whites. There would be no political dynamic capable of responding to the challenge of the city, of transportation, of air pollution, and so on.

If, however, Southern Negroes were to register, organize themselves, and enter into alliance with the white liberal and labor movements of the region, there could be a realignment from the Democratic left rather than from the Goldwater right. The effect of such a strategy would be the creation of a two-party South and a consequent erosion of one of the main sources of conservative strength in the United States. Viewed in this perspective, a dynamic Negro political movement in the old Confederacy would make an enormous contribution to solving the problems of the black ghettos of the North and, indeed, of the entire society.

This leads directly to my third point: the importance of an economic program. As long as white workers think that the Negro demand for employment is an attempt to steal their jobs, or that the Negro insistence upon decent housing is a conspiracy to destroy the property values so laboriously accumulated by the white lower-middle class, just so long will there be no progress in these areas. In each case, the posing of the issue inevitably divides people who could, under other circumstances, act as allies. Put more generally, there can be no such thing as an exclusively Negro economic program, for that would counterpose the interests of a little more than ten per cent of the society to those of the overwhelming majority. The action urged by the civil rights movement will either be integrated or else it will be a failure. Black people must indeed organize black people, and assert their rightful power. But this power will avail them little in the absence of a political strategy and a viable social and economic program.

I do not see the civil rights movement in the period immediately ahead scoring dramatic victories, such as those scored in the struggle to end segregation in public accommodations and to get Negroes into the voting booths. Rather, I see a process of reorganization and regrouping which may well appear tedious and gradualist but which is even more revolutionary in its implications than the Montgomery bus boycott of 1955, the sit-ins of 1960, or the March on Washington of 1963. For the movement is now faced with the task of challenging not just the prejudices of the white community, but some of the basic injustices and contradictions woven into the political and economic fabric of American society.

MINORITIES:
THE WAR AMIDST POVERTY

The dissension and hostility among some of the Negro and Spanish-speaking poverty groups in New York City underscore once again both the problems and the necessity of building and maintaining alliances.

If, as I believe, combined political action is the key to the solution of the economic and social problems that plague racial minorities, then we will not be able to engage in this kind of action without alliances between our own groups and other forces in the society that are committed to social change. But most certainly the first need is for the racial minority groups to establish alliances among themselves.

I have said in the past that we need to establish alliances with progressive trade union groups, progressive religious groups, and progressive liberal and political groups. And to those who resist this kind of alliance on the basis that they can find no love in their hearts for these groups, my reply is that political alliances are not built on love but on mutual interests and common goals.

Now, concerning the need for alliances among the minority groups themselves: In this society, as it presently exists, all economically oppressed minority groups have a common cause, though some of the details of their common problems may differ. If we create a situation where Negroes are working for themselves, we will be destroying that potential common front that is necessary to bring about massive federal programs.

Anything short of this will be crumbs of programs thrown here and there, and the minority groups will end up scrambling indecently for them among themselves.

While I am well aware of the long and historic grievances that exist in the Negro community, I can still understand the problems of the Spanish Americans. In addition to being victimized by some of the same problems from which we suffer, they have the further problems of language and cultural differences. But we cannot expect a people to submerge their cul-

From the *New York Amsterdam News*, December 30, 1967.

tural individuality simply because they are engaged in a common struggle for social justice.

Therefore, in attempting to unify around common objectives, neither we nor they should allow cultural differences to stand in the way. There are deep and beautiful forms that the Spanish-speaking Americans hold dear, just as there are deep and beautiful cultural forms that we hold dear.

True, our cultural differences are within the framework of American culture, whereas theirs are not. But there is one important contribution which their differences can make. Spanish Americans bring from their own historical backgrounds a tradition of revolutionary action against injustice which we can share.

It is very easy for us to get bogged down in separate struggles. The relevant question is not whether an oppressed ethnic group is Negro or Spanish, but what problems it confronts or what problems the groups must confront together.

We cannot afford to give priority to these differences at a time when our urgent need is social and economic justice. We have a much bigger job to do. We need to be calling for public works, job training, national economic planning, quality education, and attractive public housing.

We must clearly see that our inclusion in the full benefits of American life, delayed for so long, cannot come about in an atmosphere of competitive bitterness. Negroes and Spanish-speaking Americans must work together.

MEMO ON THE SPRING PROTEST IN WASHINGTON, D.C.

Several years before he died, Martin Luther King, Jr., established a re-search committee which met when he had certain questions he wanted to discuss. This is a paper I prepared at his request on January 1, 1968, when the Poor People's Campaign was first suggested.—B. R.

TO: Martin Luther King
FROM: Bayard Rustin
RE: Strategy and Tactics

I. AIMS AND OBJECTIVES

I submit that the aims and objectives should center on economic questions, since I believe that the lack of income is the most serious problem for Negroes. The aim should be stated as twofold: (1) goals not necessarily expected to be achieved now, such as guaranteed income for those who cannot work, and public works at decent wages with possibility of upgrading for those who can work (emphasis on the passing of the O'Hara bill; (2) realizable demands for jobs, housing, welfare, and passage of a strong civil rights bill.

A failure to achieve some major victories in the nation's capital at this time will, I believe, increase frustration nationally. Thus, demands should be broad enough to make sure some of them will be won soon.

II. BASIC APPROACH

Given the mood in Congress, given the increasing backlash across the nation, given the fact that this is an election year, and given the high visibility of a protest movement in the nation's capital, I feel that in this atmosphere any effort to disrupt transportation, government buildings, etc., can only lead to further backlash and repression.

Such tactics will, I believe, not only fail to attract persons dedicated to nonviolence, but attract elements that cannot be controlled and that, on the contrary, will converge on the project with a variety of objectives in mind other than those of civil rights.

Given this position, I would hope that the spring protest will be limited to constitutional, nonviolent protest.

III. THE STATEMENT OF AIMS AND OBJECTIVES

I do not believe it is possible to attract sufficient numbers to the nation's capital unless, far in advance, the strategy and tactics have been made fully clear to all concerned. We are not now in the period of 1963, at the time of Selma, Birmingham, and the March on Washington. Then there was absolute clarity in everyone's mind as to objectives. Under those circumstances, people were willing to come when they were called because they did have a clear conviction that public accommodations and voting rights were of utmost importance. Today's confusion about economic questions and the splintering in the movement requires, I am convinced, a clear statement as to objectives, strategy, and tactics.

If nonviolent protest within the law is to be used exclusively, or if disruption is to be used, most people not only have a moral right to clarification of this point but will insist on having it before they come. The alternative to this clarification is to attract the most irresponsible and uncontrollable elements.

IV. STEPS PRIOR TO THE WASHINGTON DEMONSTRATION

Not only do I feel it is essential that those being called into Washington know precisely what they are being called into, but I believe it is important that those in government should have a very clear picture of aims, strategy, and tactics. I would therefore propose the following steps prior to the Washington demonstration:

1. Since Walter Washington is a Negro and has had limited time to bring about a number of the changes he has in mind, I believe it is imperative for you to meet with him and to discover where there can be cooperation around certain of his objectives.

2. As in the March on Washington, I believe you and your staff should have a conference on strategy, tactics, and aims with the heads of those departments in government such as Health, Education and Welfare, Labor,

etc., laying before them the demands and making quite clear the nature of the protest.

3. Again, as in the March on Washington, I believe you should present the entire program to the leaders of Congress. You will recall that a Republican from the Senate and a Democrat from the House invited liberal congressmen to the Senate Caucus Room. There A. Philip Randolph had the opportunity to explain the aims and objectives of the March on Washington some six weeks in advance. That meeting had a very creative effect on the situation.

4. I believe you should address a series of mass meetings across the country outlining clearly your plans, in order to set the tone for the Washington demonstration. Then certain elements would have no excuse for converging on Washington without clear reasons. I sincerely believe that unless this is done many individuals could become severe problems once they are in Washington.

5. I am convinced that you should spend at least ten days in Washington itself, walking the streets, talking with people, and clarifying the strategy and tactics.

V. A POSSIBLE FIRST PROJECT

In order to ensure a disciplined and massive first project, I would propose that your staff seek out across the country five hundred ministers who are prepared to come to Washington for the first project. Each minister should be responsible for bringing with him ten persons whom he can control and who, thus, will be responsive to the discipline that SCLC establishes.

I believe that the first concentration should not be upon government agencies but upon Congress itself, and that the slogans and approach should be directed toward the failure of Congress to be sensitive to, and to meet, our needs. I say this since no city in the country, including Washington, has the funds, without Congressional assistance, to deal with the problems of housing, education, and jobs.

VI. CONCLUSION ON OVERALL STRATEGY

There is in my mind a very real question as to whether SCLC can maintain control and discipline over the April demonstration, even if the methods used are limited to constitutional and nonviolent tactics.

The SCLC essentially lost control over the Mississippi March, when the splintering and confusion were quite simple as compared with the current mood.

I therefore feel the statement attributed to you—that in the event of violence on the part of your participants you would call off the demonstration—represents an exceedingly wise decision.

THE MIND OF THE BLACK MILITANT

The problems of the school, we have been told, are intimately related to those of the city. Commissioner [of Education Harold] Howe said that we cannot have good schools if we have bad cities. I would agree with this statement, but I would carry it a step further: We cannot have good cities unless we have a good nation. And to have a good nation, we must face, once and for all, the problems of poverty and race. Only through the formulation of a national program to eliminate poverty and racial discrimination can we lay the basis for a good, let alone a great, society.

There is no longer any denying that this country is in the throes of a historic national crisis. Its implications for education are so frightening that even now the American people have not yet fully grasped what is happening to them.

The grim data are still coming in. In the summer of 1967, thirty of our cities, big and small, were wracked by racial disorder. Scores of citizens, almost all of them black, were killed; thousands were injured and even more arrested. Property damage exceeded a billion dollars; total income loss is incalculable.

The greatest toll, however, is not in property damage or even in lives lost. Nor is the greatest danger that the violence will go on indefinitely, any more than the Civil War did. It is that the aftermath of that war will be repeated —that, as in the Compromise of 1877, the country will turn its back on the Negro, on the root causes of his discontent, on its own democratic future.

Why does the republic find itself at a crossroads? What is actually happening?

Several newspaper columnists and television commentators have already begun to draw comparisons between the ghetto uprisings and the French, Russian, Algerian, Irish, and Black African independence revolutions. Some black power advocates have proclaimed the beginnings of guerrilla warfare and see the urban Negro as a counterpart to the Viet Cong. And in Paris it

A speech delivered at the Conference on the Schoolhouse in the City sponsored by the Educational Facilities Laboratory, Stanford University, July 10, 1967.

has become fashionable to speak of the *révolution des noires* in the United States.

The preconditions for an authentic independence revolution are completely lacking, however. American Negroes have no geographical focus for nationalist sentiment, nor do they constitute a popular majority struggling against a relatively small, white colonial group. More aptly, the situation can be described as a form of social revolution. The phrase "social revolution"—widely used by civil rights leaders—designates fundamental changes in social and economic class relations resulting from mass political action. Such action would be democratic. That is, it would aim to create a new majority coalition capable of exercising political power in the interest of new social policies. By definition, the coalition must be interracial.

As a minority, Negroes by themselves cannot bring about such a social revolution. They can participate in it as a powerful and stimulating force, or they can provoke a counterrevolution.

If, however, the comparison between Harlem and Algeria is misleading, the term "race riot" is similarly unilluminating and anachronistic.

Any real effort to understand the educational meaning of these events must begin with an examination of the mentality of the black activist and the psychological factors that will inevitably face those who attempt to do anything constructive about ghetto conditions and specifically ghetto schools. The mentality of the activist influences—both those who, by their constructive, concrete behavior, are attempting to influence the schools in a positive direction and those who, by virtue of their militancy, exercise a substantial veto over anyone else who attempts to act in the community.

At the outset, it is essential to understand that Negroes are not only "exaggerated Americans," as Gunnar Myrdal said; they are also inevitably ambivalent. A good illustration of this is the total confusion surrounding my friend Stokely Carmichael, who has been accused of being a racist. I happen to disagree with Mr. Carmichael's strategy and tactics, but he is not a racist. He is *ambivalent*, and so appears to be fostering a new form of black nationalist racism.

The racist says, "No matter who you are, what you have done, what your capabilities are, what you have accomplished, you are like that and I am like this. Stay away from me. I do not choose to recognize you as a man."

This is not what Stokely Carmichael says about white people. You have to know him and to know the dynamics of ambivalence to understand what he is saying. Actually, he is saying, "I recognize you for your accomplishments and for what you really are, but, knowing from experience that you are not going to recognize me, I cannot endure another injury from you. Therefore, before you have an opportunity to injure me, get the hell out of my way. I hate you. I do not want to have anything to do with you." This is protective negativism, but it is not racism.

Unless one understands that this basic negativism is an effort to be loved, one cannot understand ghetto psychology. Those who are teachers will understand this, and so will those who are mothers, because ghetto rioting can be compared, fundamentally, to a child's tantrum. The child in tantrum ought not to be slapped by his mother, for the child is simply saying, "Mother, something hurts. You do not understand me. I need to be loved. There is something wrong and I need your help." And so he kicks and screams in order to get the attention he needs.

The "tantrums" of the underprivileged are caused by a series of problems. Ghetto people, for example, feel that they have been boxed in by other people—not because they deserve it but because other people disrespect them. Consider Harlem. With wealthy Westchester to the north, Central Park to the south, the East River on one side, and the Hudson River on the other, there is no way for the community to expand. Already overcrowded, its population continues to grow. The same is true elsewhere as well. In fact, the population of our urban ghettos is increasing by half a million each year. Within these tightly confined areas, the whites—whether they are wanted, loved, or loathed—must fight the ghetto's sense of compression.

So long as people lack mobility—economically, socially, and politically —intruders from the outside world will be regarded ambivalently. Police, teachers, and small businessmen comprise the fundamental outside groups that the Negro community depends on and, therefore, in a certain sense, likes. Resentment at being boxed in, however, turns this liking into loathing:

- Resentment of the policeman—because telling a man in a box to behave is tantamount to telling him to accept his unemployment, his lack of education, and his slum housing.
- Resentment of the teacher—because, no matter how great his or her contribution, the ghetto child still lags years behind in reading and mathematics.
- Resentment of the white small businessman, Jewish or otherwise, because, no matter how good a man he may be, his installment selling (which makes buying possible for the poor) also means an overall higher price.

All such resentments stem from, and contribute to, this boxed-in feeling from which the Negro in the ghetto can find no escape. The constriction, the sense of no place to go, the lack of outlet, sharpen resentment and amplify every petty dislike into instant hate.

Black activists know, too, that the problems in education are staggering, and they see still less progress in coping with them. The fact is that the educational system is no longer as capable as it once was when it comes to preparing ordinary, uneducated citizens for productive roles in society. People from Eastern Europe who came here in 1900 could, when given a minimal public education, find jobs and become part of the productive system. Today, however, people coming out of Mississippi, even though they know the language and the culture of the United States, need more than a minimal education to take their place in the advanced technological society. The present automation revolution is so pervasive and complex as to leave no room for the uneducated or the semiskilled. A once-over-lightly education is not enough.

Technology, in short, demands a higher level of competence from both schools and people than it did a mere generation ago. Activists know this, and for that reason they recognize that ordinary measures to improve the schooling of ghetto children are not enough. This accounts for the intensity of their concern with education. This is why the schools have become a primary target of the ghetto activist.

The black militants, looking at housing, looking at employment, looking at health care, looking at education, also understand something else that many whites do not. They recognize that in the great period of civil rights struggle, between 1955 and 1965, all efforts were directed toward the Negroes in the South—that the 1963 March on Washington, the 1964 civil rights bill, and the 1965 civil rights bill were all directed toward the Southern Negro. In fact, there has not been a single victory for ghetto Negroes in the past fifteen years, not a single thing they might point to that makes the ghetto look different, that means more money is coming in or that their children are being better educated. Is it surprising, then, that activists in the ghetto are thoroughly convinced our society does not intend to do away with racism and economic disadvantage?

From this conviction flows a series of corollaries. First, the Negro sees this society as one that responds only to violence. The chief lesson that young Negroes are learning today in the ghetto is to achieve, create violence.

To illustrate their contention, they point to A. Philip Randolph, a most respected Negro, who for five years headed a committee in New York for upgrading the police in the Harlem and Bedford-Stuyvesant areas. For five years, I was secretary to that committee and nothing happened. However, two weeks after the riot in Harlem, a Negro, Lloyd Sealey, was promoted to police captain.

Or they cite the situation in Chicago, where Negroes rioted because they wanted to use the fire hydrants to keep cool. Dr. Martin Luther King had been in Chicago two years. He had won not a single concession, except a housing commitment on paper, which was subsequently not honored. But, less than twenty-four hours after the Negroes rioted, Mayor Daley was traipsing through the ghetto, distributing eight-dollar sprinklers and promising two new swimming pools.

Again, they mention Watts. There, a bus line had been sought for many years because there was no decent transportation system. After the rioting, the Establishment rushed in, talking about building a hospital and a decent transportation system. One of the young men said to me at the end of the riot, "Mr. Rustin, I don't know what you have been here for. You should go back to New York because we won, and, if you don't believe me, go out into that street. There are so many sociologists, educators, and economists here, you will trip over them." I would certainly not have tripped over them before the riot.

What is happening is simple. Society, by waiting for riots to occur before responding to needs, deprives the more responsible Negro leaders of any possibility of leadership. Why should anyone join the NAACP or the Southern Christian Leadership Conference? Society has systematically taught ghetto people that the methods used by Roy Wilkins and the late Martin Luther King, Jr., are useless.

Reduced to violence and robbed of leadership, the Negro activist is struck by still another reality—the shift of public attention away from these problems. White America, instead of turning its energies toward a solution of these problems, has turned away. After about 1965, most intelligent Americans would have argued that civil rights represented America's most pressing problem. Today, however, attention has shifted to Vietnam. Here again the Negro finds himself the victim of discrimination, for the war has diverted more than attention—it has diverted resources that might have been used to eliminate the ghetto from American life.

Worse yet, the Negro activist looks at Vietnam and finds proportionally more Negro Americans there than whites. He sees society, which is unwilling or incapable of dealing with racism and unwilling or incapable of dealing with poverty, pouring its youth and its money into war. The activist concludes that this society is dirty and rotten and that it ought to be wiped from the face of the earth—a drastic conclusion, which results finally in what might be called "frustration politics."

Those who are frustrated, who feel they cannot free themselves and cannot escape from the box in which they find themselves, turn on those who visibly represent the outside world. Since teachers are, in fact, among the most visible representatives of the outside world, they often bear the brunt of the attack. Pressure tactics will not solve unemployment or eradicate slums, but they can give the local board of education and the teachers a hard time—a substitute satisfaction. It may be impossible to get at those in the Pentagon who are sending the boys to Vietnam, but it is relatively easy to strike back at those who run the schools. Thus frustration politics results in such demands as:

Get rid of all white teachers in the ghetto.

Employ only Negro principals in the ghetto.

Win the right to establish the curriculums in ghetto schools.

Take over the ghetto schools completely, and destroy all central control over urban school systems.

I do not agree with all these demands, particularly the last; if control of ghetto schools can be captured by a local group of Negroes, the same sort of thing could be done by any other minority group. What would some other groups that I can think of do if they gained control of the schools? Put in a John Birch curriculum? Insist on only white principals who are Catholic or Protestant, but not Jewish? I cannot agree with this in principle.

Even if one did, however, there is an even more fundamental problem with the politics of frustration—a sense of the hopelessness of it all. Ghetto radicals see the problems of housing, schools, jobs, health, and police as so interrelated and so complex that it appears to them that *no* program is, in fact, workable.

In New York, for example, this negativism is based on the history of the local school situation over the past ten years. Every year there has been a new gimmick. First it was buses; the next year it was the Allen Plan. Now these are forgotten. The following year it was talk about education parks. Last year it was the More Effective Schools program. This year it's decentralization. Next year it will be still another gimmick. The fundamental reason educators have become involved in this gimmickry is that they do not seem to understand that unless there is a *master plan* to cover housing, jobs, and health, every plan for the schools will fall on its face. No piecemeal strategy can work.

There must be a diversion of federal funds simultaneously to schools, housing, jobs, and health. We must eradicate our worst poverty—not the poverty in Harlem or Watts, but the poverty in men's imaginations. The middle classes who think that string, Scotch tape, and spit will get us out of our present dilemma must be convinced otherwise. Even compensatory education, isolated from adequate housing, decent living conditions, and good neighborhoods, is useless.

What is needed is something more far-reaching, more imaginative. We must begin by accepting the idea of a *national plan to eradicate the ghetto.* We must have national priorities and we must adjust the scale of our thinking to the scale of the problem.

Economic and social deprivation, if accepted by its victims as their lot in life, breeds passivity, even docility. The miserable yield to their fate as divinely ordained or as their own fault. And, indeed, many Negroes in earlier generations felt that way.

Today young Negroes aren't having any of this. They don't share the feeling that something must be wrong with them, that they are responsible for their own exclusion from this affluent society. The civil rights movement —in fact, the whole liberal trend beginning with John Kennedy's election— has told them otherwise.

These young Negroes are right. The promises made to them were good and necessary and long, long overdue. The youth were right to believe in them. The only trouble is that the promises were not fulfilled.

What they and the American people absolutely must understand now is that these promises cannot be revoked. They were not made to a handful of leaders in a White House drawing room; they were made to an entire generation, one not likely to forget or to forgive.

Unless the nation is prepared to rearrange its priorities, to set a timetable for achieving them, and to allocate its resources accordingly, it will not be taking its own commitments seriously. Surely it cannot then turn in amazement to responsible Negro leaders, whose pleas for large-scale programs it has failed to heed, for an explanation of the consequences.

INTEGRATION WITHIN
DECENTRALIZATION

I do not know of a more important figure in the development of an American philosophy of education than John Dewey. I do not know of anyone whose ideas have played a more crucial part in shaping the theory and practice of American public school education. And though the response of the society does not always bear this out, I do not think there is a group of public servants who share a heavier responsibility for protecting Dewey's vision of a democratic education, or for nourishing the old roots of a democratic ethic in our society, than our public school teachers.

Unfortunately, the work of matching dream to fulfillment is not always easy and has not always been successful. But there are few of us here whose lives have not, in one constructive form or another, been shaped at that point where a democratic educational theory converges most happily with the creative labors of the American teacher.

I happen to have grown up in a town where Negroes had few rights, where they could not safely walk through certain streets, where they could not go to certain schools, where they were condemned to certain menial jobs, where they were barred from public facilities, and where the only certain view of them was that they were worth nothing—and that they had an unlimited capacity for amounting to precisely what they were worth.

I happen also—partly in consequence of that view—to have grown up in a house where there was no father, where the burdens for feeding and rearing young children were borne mainly by grandparents. Theirs was no easy task, and they might well have failed, were it not for the help, guidance and inspiration of an old public school teacher in Pennsylvania by the name of Miss Maria Brock.

Miss Brock did, and did well, what we have come to expect good and creative teachers to do: She not only stimulated in me a great desire to learn, but also introduced me to the possibilities that education had for lib-

This is Bayard Rustin's acceptance speech to the United Federation of Teachers on being presented with the 1968 John Dewey Award "in recognition of his courage, his wisdom, and his unconquerable zeal," April 6, 1968.

erating one from the prison of one's inherited circumstances. And she taught me to transcend those ugly passions and rationales by which one group of people maintain such prisons for others.

She also did, and did well, what teachers are not normally expected to do: She took deep personal interest in our social upbringing. And it was due largely to her help that four young people, without a father in the house, and with a minimum of economic resources, were able to go through public school, through high school, and into college.

I have no doubt that the life and labors of Miss Brock made all the difference to mine. I have no hesitation in crediting her for the directions of public service in which my life has proceeded ever since. And I have no reservation about sharing with her whatever satisfaction I have derived from a life devoted to the creation of a more democratic society for all Americans.

For Miss Brock, and for the many other excellent teachers who influenced me, I am honored to receive the John Dewey Award. And I accept it with pride, with pleasure, and with deep humility.

We find ourselves today in perilous and rapidly changing times, times which demand of us that we reexamine and even give up some of our old and obsolete rigidities. But, far more important, they are times that test the seriousness of our attachment to those values which are indispensable to the survival of a civilized and democratic tradition.

We are neither the first people nor the first generation to have been so confronted. In fact, it is the habit of most generations to see themselves in crisis, and to imagine that their experience is without precedent in history.

On the other hand, it is sometimes useful and instructive to seek parallels in other times. And a period I am reminded of today is mid-nineteenth-century Europe—her traditional certainties shattering in the face of revolutionary discoveries and ideologies in science, industry, religion, and politics.

It was a time in England that led Matthew Arnold—himself, like Dewey, an educational theorist and man of letters—to view the crisis of his old order as "a darkling plain, swept with confused alarms of struggle and flight, where ignorant armies clash by night."

Today, and certainly in present company, we can afford to hold Arnold's poetry in higher regard than his aristocratic premonitions of doom. For though he was considered a humanist and liberal thinker of his time, by the standards of our time he was a conservative. He would certainly have collapsed at the thought of a trade union movement existing in England. His sympathies remained closer to the genteel agonies of the classes than to the dreadful problems of the masses. And, like some of the strange liberals of our own day, he could attack with equal passion the excesses of his country's colonial administrators in the West Indies and the passage of the Reform Bill at home.

Nor can we share the distress he felt at the advance of new styles of thought and belief upon his tradition-bound society. For many of those ideological innovations have since nourished the growth of a radical humanism and made possible a greater measure of social justice and progress in our own time.

But if we cannot sympathize with the politics of Arnold's judgment, neither can we ignore the human quality of his anguish. The connection he felt to values of his time was perhaps as close as the connection we feel to some of ours. And the visions he entertained of "ignorant armies clashing by night" are precisely the fears that are racking our society today. However, I think that *our* fears are more real and more justified—because the values for whose survival we are now concerned spring from a more democratic tradition; a tradition which, though imperfect, we cannot afford to scrap; a tradition much closer to the egalitarian sentiments of John Dewey than to the qualified and genteel liberalism of Matthew Arnold.

Leaving aside those differences, one thing that both Arnold and Dewey would agree upon is the importance of the role teachers play in ensuring the survival of the more attractive traditions of their society. And I cannot underestimate the seriousness of the challenge now faced by schools, not only in ensuring the survival of a democratic education, but also in fertilizing the growth of a democratic citizenship among all Americans.

It is a challenge that arises out of racial, political, technological, economic, and social demands more serious than any Dewey was ever asked to contemplate. Yet, it is precisely at this time that we can seek and perhaps find guidance in the example of Dewey—a tireless experimenter, and a man who was neither rigid in his determinations nor determined to be rigid.

The chief task now, it seems to me, is for teachers and educationists to ensure quality education, to foster the ideal of communication and compassion among all the young people of our society, and to view the teaching process as an integral part of the effort to bring about social change and social justice in our society. All this can be done only when the educational community is prepared, like Dewey, to innovate, to be flexible, and to be imaginative in the application of educational philosophy.

More concretely, I would like to touch upon a few realities and strategies that must be of serious concern to teachers and teachers' unions if they are to help keep Arnold's "ignorant armies" apart, and if they are to be more responsive and relevant to the complex demands of our society at the present time.

1. The teachers' union is more than just an instrument through which to seek and obtain redress of professional grievances. It happens also to belong to the American labor movement, and therefore it becomes a part of that tradition in America which has historically been committed to the cause of social and economic justice.

I would be the first to admit that, as in all American institutions, discrimination continues to exist in the trade union movement. Nevertheless it has made outstanding contributions to the economic upliftment of millions of blacks and whites in this country. The trade union movement was an indispensable part of that coalition which helped shape and achieve the New Deal—which transformed this nation at an earlier period, and made safe the continued right of both blue- and white-collar workers to organize. In spite of its remaining vestiges of injustice, it is more integrated than our schools, our churches, and American industry. The trade union movement was one of the vital elements of the civil rights coalition of the early 1960's —the most vigorous lobbyists in behalf of civil rights and voting rights legislation. And even now, the trade union movement is the only mass institution in our society that is making the social and economic demands which, if enacted, will eradicate poverty.

Therefore, no arm of the trade union movement, whether it be teachers or office workers, can disassociate itself from that tradition of social concern or from the activities being carried out to win new objectives.

What are some of these new objectives? We need a two-dollar minimum wage, a guaranteed income, public works for socially urgent institutions, free medical care, destruction of slums, creation of new towns, increased federal aid, and reorganization of the school system. These are basic demands of the trade union movement, and no religious group, no business group—in fact, no other group in the society—is as dedicated to this program.

Moreover, there is a direct relationship between our social and economic problems and the inability of our teachers to teach or to achieve the best results. Therefore, teachers cannot avoid the struggle to achieve more decent communities, better housing, full employment, a higher minimum wage, and a generally more humane environment. It is only when these problems are solved—or begin to appear soluble—that teachers will be able to achieve their full effectiveness and their full potential as professionals.

2. Across this nation, in every city and state, teachers are underpaid; the educational bureaucracy is cumbersome; classes are too large; parents are

complaining; children are not learning as well as they should; and their teachers are being reduced to clerks, baby-sitters, and cops.

While these problems arise out of the social and economic nature of the society, they are exacerbated by the sterile bureaucracy of boards of education and the refusal of the state and federal governments to appropriate enough money, and to introduce enough facilities, into the school systems. All this illustrates how adept the educational bureaucracy is at applying the strategy of "divide and rule."

In a situation where children are not learning, parents and teachers enter into a vendetta, whereas they are precisely the ones who should be in a powerful coalition against the educational bureaucracy to demand the facilities they need. This, therefore, is a new imperative: No effort should be spared to create a coalition between teachers, trade unions, and parent groups to make the educational authorities more accountable and responsive to the needs of students, the demands of parents, and the problems of teachers.

3. Having said that, I am still aware that there are limits to what coalitions can do in the struggle to bring about quality integrated education and a better school system. But it is at those limits that teachers unions are called upon to introduce certain revolutionary strategies in their collective bargaining arrangements—in order to literally wrest concessions from the dead hands of the authorities.

Let me try to illustrate. In 1964, a coalition of Negro and Puerto Rican parents, along with a number of liberal groups, made a strong and bold demand for quality integrated education for their children. The first dramatic expression of that demand came in the form of the 1964 school boycott which the Reverend Milton Galamison and I organized. Half a million children stayed home, and shut down the New York City school system. A few months later, the Reverend Galamison led another boycott, in which some 40 per cent of the children stayed out of school. Subsequently, the NAACP, CORE, and other civil rights organizations sponsored a march on City Hall, in which, once again, the demand was for quality integrated education.

Well, what did we get? Nothing, really. Only a series of meaningless plans and statements from the board of education aimed simply at catching and deceiving public attention. In addition to that we also got spectacular sounding proposals for busing, pairing, 4-4-4, etc. But all this did nothing. The inadequacies of the school system remained fundamentally unmet and unchanged. Classes were still overcrowded. Teachers were still overburdened and, in many instances, untrained and unprepared. The curriculums were still defective and inappropriate to the needs of thousands of Negro and Puerto Rican children. We were, in fact, no closer to quality integrated education than we were when the great civil rights effort began.

The lessons—at least, to me—were clear. Public protest alone would not get us anywhere. We needed a silent partner in this effort—the teachers' union. And the teachers' union's role in that partnership would be of mutual benefit to parents, children, and the teachers themselves. What would the union do? Just this: Make the issue of quality educational facilities one of the major bargaining points at contract negotiations. In other words, get the demands written into their contracts.

That was precisely the point I made in 1966 when I addressed the annual convention of the American Federation of Teachers. Therefore, I was glad when the UFT, the largest affiliate of the AFT, did just that in their negotiations with the New York Board of Education and achieved a significant measure of success. The point having been made, all teachers' unions should now move to incorporate demands for quality educational facilities into their basic negotiating strategies.

4. I spoke earlier of the need for flexibility and imagination: of the courage to give up rigid postures which, though they might be comforting, are no longer attractive, creative, or feasible and which, in fact, now merely hinder rather than advance progress. And I spoke, on the other hand, of the courage to defend and maintain those principles which are indispensable to the survival of civility and a democratic texture in our relationships.

There are now a number of demands being made on teachers which challenge both your courage to be flexible and your courage to remain faithful to ideals which are good.

I will try to deal with just two of these demands. The first one demands flexibility. It asks you to recognize that Negro children in this society—and white children also—are being taught biased, edited, and ultimately racist versions of American history and culture. It is not enough to pay lip service to the idea of racial harmony and equality. We must refuse any longer to accept the distorted view of our roots and our past in this country.

As taught in our textbooks, this history reinforces in white children the notion that they are superior and the only creators of this country, and it reinforces in black children the notion that they are inferior and made no contributions.

It may be true that most blacks came here as slaves, but the first of them were here as free men, and gave their lives in the struggle to win independence for this nation. They fought as well as any one else during the civil war; they played their part in the opening of the American West; they helped plan and lay out some of our major American cities; they developed the only indigenous form of American music; they made notable contributions to scientific research; they are to be found in the growth and development of the American musical and dramatic stage; and the best of their writing ranks with the best that has been done in America. This is by no means all, but then I am by no means an historian. In any case, the question is not whether they should have done more. The miracle is that in the circumstances of their history here they could have done so much.

It is because of racism, it is because the dominant value judgments in this society are white, and it is because a consistently poor estimate has been placed on the quality and extent of Negro effort—it is for all these reasons that the true story of the Negro in America is not told in our history books. And it is for all these reasons that historians continue to tell lies, continue to avert their eyes, and continue to retard the progress of civility, decency, and human dignity in our society.

It is time, then, to give up that old rigid stance. For, however comforting it may be to some, it is a delusion, and it is a violation of the right of all young minds to know the truth and to be free.

Organized teachers can play a major role in the effort to liberate American history books. They can join those who are making an effort to bring truth into the schools through a total revision of the textbooks. Where good texts are not in existence, teachers must bring in supplementary material to their classes. And they themselves can make studies of Negro history and culture.

The second great demand now being made by both white and black extremists is that we surrender our time-honored dedication to the idea of integration and substitute various forms of separation.

I do not have to detail the reasons for this demand. It is being made in the name of community participation, in the name of community control, in the name of quality education, and in the name of several other interests—but ultimately, whether the groups mean it or not, it is in fact a demand for segregation.

Therefore, regardless of some of the good arguments in favor of such concepts as decentralization, that concept cannot be discussed independent of the implications it has for institutionalizing one of the worst evils in the history of this society—segregation.

While I am prepared to recognize that some measure of decentralization is feasible and perhaps desirable, I would proceed very carefully, because we may end up creating and worsening more problems than those we solve.

Some of the positive aspects of the proposal to decentralize are (1) that it reflects a concern for the present state of education in our public schools; (2) that it promises to bring parents in closer touch with the process in which their children are being educated; (3) that it could foster closer unity between teachers and parents in some communities, and enable them to-gether to affect educational programs and policies; and (4) that it could make teachers more responsive to some of the special needs and special problems of certain communities.

But there are also some real dangers. *First,* the proposal seems concerned more with political self-determination in education than with quality in education. *Second,* it is meaningless to promise communities control with-out also promising them the funds to make this control effective. If political control is not complemented by financial control, then it may ultimately lead merely to an increase in community frustrations. *Third,* there is a real danger of community school boards being taken over by extremist groups—black and white, on the right and on the left—who are less interested in education than in racial and community politics. The education of children is much too important to be subverted to such interests. *Fourth,* after all the years of our struggle, we are now being asked to accept the idea that segregated education is in fact a perfectly respectable, perfectly desirable, and perfectly viable way of life in a democratic society.

Needless to say, I do not accept this. Therefore, that measure of decen-tralization that I support is one in which the school districts should be suffi-ciently broad to include as wide a degree of quality integrated education as possible. In other words: *integration within decentralization.*

I know that taking such a position leaves me open to harsh criticism from the segregationists both black and white. And to the degree that the UFT holds similar views, it will also come in for criticism.

It is at this point, however, that the second kind of courage I spoke of comes into play: the courage to remain faithful to those ideals which are good and which are indispensable to the kind of society we want to create. Teachers must therefore stand firmly on the principle that America is a democratic pluralist society. Teachers must reject all forms of educational separatism and elitism; teachers must become militant integrationists.

In closing, let me quote from the Report of the National Advisory Commis-sion on Civil Disorders, one of the most serious pronouncements ever made on the state of American society. On the question of public education, the report states:

We have cited the extent of racial isolation in our urban schools. It is great and it is growing. It will not easily be overcome. Nonetheless, we believe school integration to be vital to the well-being of this country. We have seen in this last summer's disorders the consequences of racial isolation, at all levels, and of attitudes toward race, on both sides, produced by three centuries of myth, ignorance and bias. It is indispensable that opportunities for inter-action between races be expanded. The problems of this society will not be solved unless and until our children are brought into a common encounter and encouraged to forge a new and more viable design for life.

The problems in our schools and the problems in our society will ulti-mately be solved through political action. Therefore, teachers have no choice but to organize and join the coalition of forces necessary to get programs and money out of Congress.

Teachers are uniquely qualified to be part of this coalition, because they know the problems as well as any other group in our society, and better than most.

This means that teachers must play something other than a 9–3 role; that they must have empathy with the problems and conditions of the communities in which they serve. Finally, if they have faith in the ability of children to learn, then those children, whatever their background and cir-cumstance, will in fact learn. It calls for the willingness to be compassionate, to innovate, to experiment, and to be imaginative. It is a willingness which John Dewey, were he among us today, would have welcomed as an endorse-ment and an enlargement of his pragmatic and democratic educational philosophy.

REFLECTIONS ON THE DEATH OF
MARTIN LUTHER KING, JR.

The murder of Dr. Martin Luther King, Jr., has thrust a lance into the soul of America. The pain is most shattering to the Negro people. We have lost a valiant son, a symbol of hope, and an eloquent spirit that inspired masses of people. Such a man does not appear often in the history of social struggle. When his presence signifies that greatness can inhabit a black skin, those who must deny this possibility stop at nothing to remove it. Dr. King now joins a long list of victims of desperate hate in the service of insupportable lies, myths, and stereotypes.

For me, the death of Dr. King brings deep personal grief. I had known and worked with him since the early days of the Montgomery bus protest in 1955, through the founding of the Southern Christian Leadership Conference, the Prayer Pilgrimage in 1957, the youth marches for integrated schools in 1958 and 1959, and the massive March on Washington in 1963.

Though his senior by twenty years, I came to admire the depth of his faith in nonviolence, in the ultimate vindication of the democratic process, and in the redeeming efficacy of social commitment and action. And underlying this faith was a quiet courage grounded in the belief that the triumph of justice, however long delayed, was inevitable. Like so many others, I watched his spirit take hold in the country, arousing long-slumbering consciences and giving shape to a new social movement. With that movement came new hopes, aspirations, and expectations. The stakes grew higher.

At such a time, so great a loss can barely be sustained by the Negro people. But the tragedy and shame of April 4 darken the entire nation as it teeters on the brink of crisis. And let no one mistake the signs: our country is in deadly serious trouble. This needs to be said because one of the ironies of life in an advanced industrialized society is that many people can go about their daily business without being directly affected by the ominous rumblings at the bottom of the system.

Yet we are at one of the great crossroads in our history, and the alternatives before us grow more stark with every summer's violence. In moments

From the *AFL-CIO American Federationist*, May 1968.

like these there is a strong temptation to succumb to utter despair and help-less cynicism. It is indeed hard to maintain a clear perspective, a reliable sense of where events are heading. But this is exactly what we are called upon to do. Momentous decisions are about to be made—consciously or by default—and the consequences will leave not one corner of this land, nor any race or class, untouched.

Where, then, do we go from here?

We are a house divided. Of this Dr. King's murder is a stunning reminder. Every analysis, strategy, and proposal for a way out of the American di-lemma must begin with the recognition that a perilous polarization is taking place in our society. Part of it is no doubt due to the war in Vietnam, part to the often remarked generation gap. But generations come and go and so do foreign policies. The issue of race, however, has been with us since our earliest beginnings as a nation. I believe it is even deeper and sharper than the other points of contention. It has bred fears, myths, and violence over centuries. It is the source of dark and dangerous irrationality, a current of social pathology running through our history and dimming our brighter achievements.

Most of the time the reservoir of racism remains stagnant. But—and this has been true historically for most societies—when major economic, social, or political crises arise, the backwaters are stirred and latent racial hostility comes to the surface. Scapegoats must be found, simple targets substituted for complex problems. The frustration and insecurity generated by these problems find an outlet in notions of racial superiority and inferiority. Very often we find that the most virulent hostility to Negroes exists among eth-nic groups that only recently "made it" themselves or that are still near the bottom of the ladder. They need to feel that somebody is beneath them. (This is a problem which the labor movement has had to face more acutely perhaps than any comparable institution in American life. And it's a prob-lem which some of labor's middle-class critics have not had to cope with at all.)

Negroes are reacting to this hostility with a counter-hostility. Some say the white man has no soul; others say he is barbaric, uncivilized; others pro-claim him racially inferior. As is so often the case, such a *reaction* is the exaggerated obverse of the original *action*.

And in fact it incorporates elements of white stereotypes of Negroes. ("Soul," for example, so far as it is definable, seems to consist in part of rhythm, spontaneity, pre-industrial sentimentality, a footloose antiregimentation, etc.—qualities attributed to Negroes by many whites, though in different words.)

This reaction among Negroes is not so new as many white people think. What is new is the intensity with which it is felt among some Negroes and the violent way it has been expressed in recent years. For this, the conservatives and reactionaries would blame the civil rights movement and the federal government. And in the very specific sense, we must conclude that they are right.

One effect of the civil rights struggle in the past ten years has been to convince a generation of young Negroes that their place in society is no longer predetermined at birth. We demonstrated that segregationist barriers could be toppled, that social relations were not fixed for all time, that change was on the agenda. The federal government reinforced this new consciousness with its many pronouncements that racial integration and equality were the official goals of American society.

The reactionaries would tell us that these hopes and promises were unreasonable to begin with and should never have been advanced. They equate stability with the preservation of the established hierarchy of social relations, and chaos with the reform of that unjust arrangement. The fact is that the promises were reasonable, justified, and long overdue. Our task is not to rescind them—how do you rescind the promise of equality?—but to implement them fully and vigorously.

This task is enormously complicated by the polarization now taking place on the race issue. We are caught in a vicious cycle: inaction on the poverty and civil rights fronts foments rioting in the ghettos; the rioting encourages vindictive inaction. Militancy, extremism, and violence grow in the black community; racism, reaction, and conservatism gain ground in the white community.

Personal observation and the law of numbers persuade me that a turn to the right comprises the larger part of the polarization. This, of course, is a perilous challenge not only to the Negro but also to the labor movement, to liberals and civil libertarians, to all of the forces for social progress. We must meet that challenge in 1968.

Meanwhile, a process of polarization is also taking place within the Negro community and, with the murder of Dr. King, it is likely to be accelerated.

Ironically and sadly, this will occur precisely because of the broad support Dr. King enjoyed among Negroes. That support cut across ideological and class lines. Even those Negro spokesmen who could not accept, and occasionally derided, Dr. King's philosophy of nonviolence and reconciliation, admired and respected his unique national and international position. They were moved by his sincerity and courage. Not, perhaps, since the days of Booker T. Washington—when 90 per cent of all Negroes lived in the South and were occupationally and socially more homogeneous than today—had any one man come so close to being *the* Negro leader. He was a large unifying force and his assassination leaves an enormous vacuum. The diverse strands he linked together have fallen from his hands.

The murder of Dr. King tells Negroes that if one of the greatest among them is not safe from the assassin's bullet, then what can the least of them hope for? In this context, those young black militants who have resorted to violence feel vindicated. "Look what happened to Dr. King," they say. "He was nonviolent; he didn't hurt anybody. And look what they did to him. If we have to go down, let's go down shooting. Let's take whitey with us."

Make no mistake about it: a great psychological barrier has now been placed between those of us who have urged nonviolence as the road to social change and the frustrated, despairing youth of the ghettos. Dr. King's assassination is only the latest example of our society's determination to teach young Negroes that violence pays. We pay no attention to them until they take to the streets in riotous rebellion. Then we make minor concessions—not enough to solve their basic problems, but enough to persuade them that we know they exist. "Besides," the young militants will tell you, "this country was built on violence. Look at what we did to the Indians. Look at our television and movies. And look at Vietnam. If the cause of the Vietnamese is worth taking up guns for, why isn't the cause of the black man right here in Harlem?"

These questions are loaded and oversimplified, to be sure, and they obscure the real issues and the programmatic direction we must take to meet them. But what we must answer is the bitterness and disillusionment that give rise to these questions. If our answers consist of mere words, they will fall on deaf ears. They will not ring true until ghetto-trapped Negroes experience significant and tangible progress in the daily conditions of their lives—in their jobs, income, housing, education, health care, political representation, etc. This must be understood by those often well-meaning people who, frightened by the polarization, would retreat from committed action into homilies about racial understanding.

We are indeed a house divided. But the division between race and race, class and class, will not be dissolved by massive infusions of brotherly sentiment. The division is not the result of bad sentiment and therefore will not be healed by rhetoric. Rather the division and the bad sentiments are both reflections of vast and growing inequalities in our socioeconomic system—inequalities of wealth, of status, of education, of access to political power. Talk of brotherhood and "tolerance" (are we merely to "tolerate" one another?) might once have had a cooling effect, but increasingly it grates on the nerves. It evokes contempt not because the values of brotherhood are wrong—they are more important now than ever—but because it just does not correspond to the reality we see around us. And such talk does nothing to eliminate the inequalities that breed resentment and deep discontent.

The same is true of most "black power" sloganeering, in which I detect powerful elements of conservatism. Leaving aside those extremists who call for violent revolution, the black power movement embraces a diversity of groups and ideologies. It contains a strong impulse toward withdrawal from social struggle and action, a retreat back into the ghetto, avoidance of contact with the white world. This impulse may, I fear, be strengthened by the assassination of Dr. King.

This brand of black power has much in common with the conservative white American's view of the Negro. It stresses self-help ("Why don't those Negroes pull themselves up by their own bootstraps like my ancestors did?"). It identifies the Negro's main problems in psychological terms, calls upon him to develop greater self-respect and dignity by studying Negro history and culture and by building independent institutions.

In all of these ideas there is some truth. But taken as a whole, the trouble with this thinking is that it assumes that the Negro can solve his problems by himself, in isolation from the rest of the society. The fact is, however, that the Negro did not create these problems for himself and he cannot solve them by himself.

Dignity and self-respect are not abstract virtues that can be cultivated in a vacuum. They are related to one's job, education, residence, mobility, family responsibilities, and other circumstances that are determined by one's economic and social status in the society. Whatever deficiencies in dignity and self-respect may be laid to the Negro are the consequence of generations of segregation, discrimination, and exploitation. Above all, in my opinion, these deficiencies result from systematic exclusion of the Negro from the economic mainstream.

This exclusion cannot be reversed—but only perpetuated—by gilding the ghettos. A "separate but equal" economy for black Americans is impossible. In any case, the ghettos do not have the resources needed for massive programs of abolishing poverty, inferior education, slum housing, and the other problems plaguing the Negro people. These resources must come primarily from the federal government, which means that the fate of the Negro is unavoidably tied to the political life of this nation.

It is time, therefore, that all of us, black and white alike, put aside rhetoric that obscures the real problems. It is precisely because we have so long swept these incendiary problems under the rug that they are now exploding all around us, insisting upon our attention. We can divert our eyes no longer.

The life and death of Martin Luther King are profoundly symbolic. From the Montgomery bus protest to the Memphis sanitation workers strike, his career embodies the internal development, the unfolding, the evolution of the modern civil rights struggle.

That struggle began as a revolt against segregation in public accommodations—buses, lunch counters, libraries, schools, parks. It was aimed at ancient and obsolete institutional arrangements and mores left over from an earlier social order in the South, an order that was being undermined and transformed by economic and technological forces.

As the civil rights movement progressed, winning victory after victory in public accommodations and voting rights, it became increasingly conscious that these victories would not be secure or far-reaching without a radical improvement in the Negro's socioeconomic position. And so the movement reached out of the South into the urban centers of the North and West. It moved from public accommodations to employment, welfare, housing, education—to find a host of problems the nation had let fester for a generation.

But these were not problems that affected the Negro alone or that could be solved easily with the movement's traditional protest tactics. These injustices were imbedded not in ancient and obsolete institutional arrangements but in the priorities of powerful vested interests, in the direction of public policy, in the allocation of our national resources. Sit-ins could integrate a lunch counter, but massive social investments and imaginative public policies were required to eliminate the deeper inequalities.

Dr. King came to see that this was too big a job for the Negro alone, that it called for an effective coalition with the labor movement. As King told the AFL-CIO convention in 1961:

> Negroes are almost entirely a working people. There are pitifully
> few Negro millionaires and few Negro employers. Our needs are

identical with labor's needs—decent wages, fair working conditions, livable housing, old age security, health and welfare measures, conditions in which families can grow, have education for their children and respect in the community.

That is why Negroes support labor's demands and fight laws which curb labor.

That is why the labor-hater and labor-baiter is virtually always a twin-headed creature spewing anti-Negro epithets from one mouth and anti-labor propaganda from the other mouth.

The duality of interest of labor and Negroes makes any crisis which lacerates you, a crisis from which we bleed. As we stand on the threshold of the second half of the twentieth century, a crisis confronts us both. Those who in the second half of the nineteenth century could not tolerate organized labor have had a rebirth of power and seek to regain the despotism of that era while retaining the wealth and privileges of the twentieth century.

. . . The two most dynamic and cohesive liberal forces in the country are the labor movement and the Negro freedom movement.

. . . I look forward confidently to the day when all who work for a living will be one, with no thought to their separateness as Negroes, Jews, Italians, or any other distinctions.

This will be the day when we shall bring into full realization the American dream—a dream yet unfulfilled. A dream of equality of opportunity, of privilege and property widely distributed; a dream of a land where men will not take necessities from the many to give luxuries to the few; a dream of a land where men will not argue that the color of a man's skin determines the content of his character; a dream of a nation where all our gifts and resources are held not for ourselves alone but as instruments of service for the rest of humanity; the dream of a country where every man will respect the dignity and worth of human personality —that is the dream.

And so Dr. King went to Memphis to help 1,300 sanitation workers—almost all of them black—to win union recognition, dues checkoff, higher wages, and better working conditions. And in the midst of this new phase of his work he was assassinated. Since then, the sanitation workers have won their fight. But the real battle is just beginning.

The Report of the National Advisory Commission on Civil Disorders is the latest in a series of documents—official, semiofficial, and unofficial— that have sought to arouse the American people to the great dangers we face and to the price we are likely to pay if we do not multiply our efforts to eradicate poverty and racism.

The recent recommendations parallel those urged by civil rights and labor groups over the years. The legislative work of the Leadership Conference on Civil Rights, of the National Association for the Advancement of Colored People, and of the AFL-CIO has been vital to the progress we have made so far. This work is now proceeding effectively on a broad coordinated basis. It has pinpointed the objectives for which the entire nation must strive.

We have got to provide meaningful work at decent wages for every employable citizen. We must guarantee an adequate income for those unable to work. We must build millions of low-income housing units, tear down the slums, and rebuild our cities. We need to build schools, hospitals, mass transit systems. We need to construct new, integrated towns. As President Johnson has said, we need to build a "second America" between now and the year 2000.

It is in the context of this national reconstruction that the socioeconomic fate of the Negro will be determined. Will we build into the second America new, more sophisticated forms of segregation and exploitation or will we create a genuine open, integrated, and democratic society? Will we have a more equitable distribution of economic resources and political power, or will we sow the seeds of more misery, unrest, and division?

Because of men like Martin Luther King, it is unlikely that the American Negro can ever again return to the old order. But it is up to us, the living, black and white, to realize Dr. King's dream.

This means, first of all, to serve notice on the 90th Congress that its cruel indifference to the plight of our cities and of the poor—even after the martyrdom of Dr. King—will not be tolerated by the American people. In an economy as fabulously productive as ours, a balanced budget cannot be the highest virtue and, in any case, it cannot be paid for by the poor.

Next, I believe, we must recognize the magnitude of the threat we face in an election year from a resurgence of the rightwing backlash forces. This threat will reach ever greater proportions if this summer sees massive violence in the cities. The Negro-labor-liberal coalition, whatever differences now exist within and among its constituent forces, must resolve to unite this fall in order to defeat racism and reaction at the polls. Unless we so resolve, we may find ourselves in a decade of vindictive and mean conservative domination.

We owe it to Martin Luther King not to let this happen. We owe it to him to preserve and extend his victories. We owe it to him to fulfill his dreams. We owe it to his memory and to our futures.

THE ANATOMY OF FRUSTRATION

The United States is in a deep moral crisis—and I speak with a heavy heart. Many younger Negroes today, in deep frustration, sincerely, gropingly, tragically, have adopted some of the negative and degrading concepts which have brutalized and enslaved them, believing somehow that these concepts can bring them freedom.

We must try to analyze the problem.

We would be mistaken to think that the only desires of young Negroes today are to have a job, to have a decent house, to be well educated, to have medical care. All these things are very important, but deeper and more profound is the feeling of young Negroes today—through all classes, from the *lumpenproletariat* to the working poor, the working classes, the middle classes, and the intelligentsia—that the time has come when they must demand recognition of their dignity and when they should have power, a voice in the solution of problems which affect them.

The tragedy is that those who are in deepest revolt are not only reponding to the frustrations of their objective situation, but more fundamentally to the morality of a society which is teaching them that violence is the only effective force for social change. This society is systematically teaching them that it will respond only to tactics of desperation and violence.

This is not only true for Negroes. Many of us have been concerned for years about Columbia University taking all the land around its Harlem site and running people out of their homes to build high-rise structures exclusively for white people. We warned Columbia officials that a problem would occur. But the great educators at Columbia did not respond to our pleas. They waited until two hundred students, using the tactics of desperation, closed down the university. Then they were ready to talk. Then they were ready to discuss whether there ought to be a building where Columbia students, predominantly white, would enter from the top into one gym and where Negroes from Harlem would enter at the bottom of the same structure into a separate gym. They should have known that such separated facilities would create problems.

From an address to the Anti-Defamation League of B'nai B'rith, given on May 6, 1968.

In New York, A. Philip Randolph and I had for five years tried to get the police department to upgrade Negro patrolmen. We urged that a Negro be made head of the police force in Harlem for psychological reasons. It was not done. But two weeks after the riot in 1964, they upgraded a Negro lieutenant, made him a captain, and put him in charge of the Central Harlem precinct. I then received a letter from a youth group saying, "You and Randolph failed. You should roll over and get the hell out of the way for your methods don't work. *We* upgraded a Negro policeman with sticks and stones and Molotov cocktails."

So this is the lesson we are teaching—that when the liberal forces of this nation join in coalition and urge that something be done, they are ignored; but when people riot, something is done. Basic needs may not be met, yet minor and often insignificant concessions are made.

Negro women in Watts making fifty-five and sixty dollars a week as maids were spending up to twenty-six of those dollars on taxis from the Negro ghetto to the white homes where they worked, all because no one had provided a transportation system for Watts. When Martin Luther King and I went to Watts and told the young Negroes they must put an end to rioting, that it was destroying their own community, they said, "Go back where you came from. We are winning." One of them lit a match, held it up, and said, "This is our manifesto and it's winning." And he went on to say that if you went out into the streets you would find sociologists, economists, city planners, hospital experts, transportation experts, "all there because of our manifesto." The fact is that before the riot there were groups in Watts which urged the city to do something about conditions. They were ignored.

The action for dealing with the problem of justice must come quickly, and before more rioting, lest we further teach people that the only viable method of social change is an act of desperation.

What I know, and what you ought to know, is the tragedy of a society which will not make basic changes but will make promises and token concessions—so long as the rioting goes to point X. But when it reaches X plus one, we are all in trouble, for then there will be the most vigorous repression. Then there will be vigilantism. Even more important, you cannot repress one-tenth of the population, no matter how badly elements of it behave, without threatening the civil liberties of everyone in the nation. Where there are not civil liberties, we cannot make social progrsss.

What must be understood is the anatomy of frustration, and here is where the Jewish problem can be put into focus. I am not one who goes around apologizing for or explaining away Negro anti-Semitism. It is here, it is dangerous, it must be rooted out. We cannot say it is somehow different or not really important. We cannot sweep it under the rug. What we can and had better do is understand it if we are to deal with it.

The first thing about those who are frustrated is that their frustration causes them to adopt a psychology, an economics, and a sociology based on the thinking of the frustrated. It goes like this: The United States is no longer viable. Negroes are never going to get their rights. All institutions must be destroyed and new ones established.

The death of Dr. Martin Luther King spurred that philosophy to its logical conclusion. Stokely Carmichael is reported to have said: "If they wanted to brutalize a black man, why didn't they get me or Rap Brown? We're the really dangerous ones to this social order. The fact that they got King indicates that Negroes will never get anything in this society and they are out to exterminate us all."

So the first point of the frustrated is that the society is not viable. Second, if the society is not viable, then no program needs to be projected because to project a program is to fool the masses of Negroes. So they viciously attack the Freedom Budget put forth by A. Philip Randolph. To them Randolph and I became the major enemies because we were putting forth a program, and to put forth a program, when you know nothing will move, is dishonest.

Third, if the nation is not viable and no program is needed, then all those people who have worked over the years for civil rights, and are still working for integration into this society, become the enemy. Not the Ku Klux Klan, not the John Birch Society, but those closest to you.

This is what Jews need to understand: that in the list of whom you attack, those you love come first. You attack those you have expected something from. You attack those who have in fact carried the banner. Before King's death, he and his nonviolence were the first enemy precisely because he had done the most. The argument went that if, after all the bloodshed, the bombings, the tear-gas, the water-hosings, and the dogs, King could not produce real victories, then he had fooled his people, exposed them to useless sacrifice. After his death, of course, a new situation was created. Now they had the opportunity to shift gears, to say that the greatest Negro was killed by a white. But when King was alive, it was a different story.

Next in the list of enemies of the frustrated come Roy Wilkins, Whitney Young, A. Philip Randolph. They are now the traitors to the cause. Listed too are the liberal community, which has fought side by side with us, and the Jews, who have made greater contributions than anybody else in the liberal community. Because of this reverse hate-affection syndrome, Martin

Luther King, Roy Wilkins, Whitney Young, A. Philip Randolph, the liberals, the Jews, the labor leaders who lifted almost two million Negroes out of the *lumpenproletariat* into the working classes are all bastards now.

The point is that if Jews are under attack by the extreme left in the Negro community, they are in the same basket with Negro leaders and even the most progressive political leadership. Jews are not likely to feel better simply because others are also under attack; nevertheless there ought to be an understanding of what the problem really is.

In the anatomy of frustration, the long-time leadership is rejected. But heroes must be found somewhere, and so the frustrated adopt heroes of foreign revolutions—not because they believe in their philosophy but because they want to adopt the extreme tactics that they believe have worked for those heroes. Thus Che Guevara, Mao Tse-tung, Castro, and Fanon become heroes. This doesn't make the militants Communists. It means, rather, that they are so desperate for new methods that they reach into completely different kinds of situations, hoping that those tactics can be applied here. Of course, they cannot be, but the frustrated, by the anatomy of frustration, are convinced that the only thing left to do is to give everybody hell, to denounce everybody, and to call for revolt.

Consider the question of the Jew in the ghetto. Nothing that I say is justification for anti-Semitism, for I know that in a situation where anti-Semitism exists none of us is safe. Anti-Semitism must be rooted out. We have, however, an obligation to try to understand Negro anti-Semitism without excusing it.

If you happen to be an uneducated, poorly trained Negro living in the ghetto, and particularly if you live by your wits selling numbers, selling dope, engaging in prostitution, then you only see four kinds of white people: the policeman, the businessman, the teacher, and the welfare worker. In many cities, three of those four are predominantly Jewish. Except for the policeman, the majority of the businessmen, teachers, and welfare workers are Jewish. Here again is the hate-love syndrome.

Ninety per cent of the crimes that Negroes commit are against other Negroes in the ghetto. Negroes, therefore, both hate and depend on policemen. To have to depend on someone whom you dislike and who often brutalizes you is ghastly.

Then comes the businessman. Many ghetto Negroes know nothing about capitalization. The fact is, if you walk up 125th Street you will see what Negroes say you will see: a television set that sells in department stores for $79.50 costs $132 in Harlem. But the ghetto dweller does not know that the department store is able to sell the TV set at $79.50 because the buyer makes a considerable down payment and is required to finish payments within one year, while the ghetto buyer is often given, with no down payment, three or four years in which to pay. He may not understand that as the length of time for payment is increased, the interest is increased. He does not always understand that only such long-term capitalization makes it possible for him to have a TV set at all.

Many people are kept alive for three and four weeks at a time by local businessmen who let them pile up a debt until they hit the numbers or something and can pay for what they bought. But if you hit the numbers once in a year and have to give most of the money to the grocer for things you have already eaten, when there are still more things you need, you hate him for taking your money even though you know it belongs to him.

The chief characteristic of every ghetto and of every major poor area is that people operate on the principle of immediate gratification. If you have little money, you operate on immediate gratification. You don't buy a new sheet until the old sheet is in shreds. You don't buy salt until you're at dinner and the salt runs out. Nobody can save up enough money to take advantage of a sale; you've got to buy things when you need them. The tragedy is that the need to live always on the principle of immediate gratification can sometimes be frightening.

A young fellow I got a job for came to see me a week after receiving his first two weeks' pay—$125. He came to thank me for the job and to show me what he had bought for himself. He had gone into a store on 125th Street and paid $67.50 for a pair of alligator shoes.

Now, this may shock you, unless you never had anything but sneakers, usually with holes in them, and day after day you had been walking past the shoestore seeing something beautiful there. To pay $67.50 for shoes may be uneconomical, but it is psychologically understandable. He held those shoes to his breast waiting for me to rave about them. And I did. I knew that at a later time I would have to talk to him about the wise use of money, but I wasn't going to destroy his moment of immediate gratification—for him a moment of great beauty.

Next comes the teacher. In the ghetto one does not lay the blame on the board of education and the whole corrupt system or realize that no matter how much a teacher wants to teach she cannot in those conditions. One does not realize that it is not the teacher's fault that a child has no breakfast and may not have lunch, that he may have to go to the poolroom to bum money for potato chips and an orange soda, which may be all he eats that day. How can you teach such a child? How can you teach children when you have forty in a class and two disruptive children who need psychiatric care? The ghetto mother knows only that the teacher is there and is Jewish. And she does not think the Jewish teacher cares whether her child learns or not.

Then comes the welfare worker. If you know anything about welfare you know that spying is part of the system. Sneaking around on weekends to find out if there are men's shoes or pants hanging in the closet, or whether a man has been in the house for the weekend, is part of the job. One method by which the relief rolls are decreased is finding a man in the house.

We must get at these problems not on the basis of urging people merely to change their attitudes or of misinterpreting the Kerner Report on civil disorders. That report does not say that Americans are racist. If it did, the only answer would be to line everybody up, all 200 million of us, then line up 200,000 psychiatrists, and have us all lie on couches for ten years trying to understand the problem and for ten years more learning how to deal with it. All over the country people are beating their breasts crying *mea culpa*— "I'm so sorry that I am a racist"—which means, really, that they want to cop out because if racism is to be solved on an individual psychological basis, then there is little hope.

What the Kerner Report is really saying is that the *institutions* of America brutalize not only Negroes but also whites who are not racists but who in many communities have to use racist institutions. When it is put on that basis, we know we cannot solve the fundamental problem by sitting around examining our innards, but by getting out and fighting for institutional change.

I am all in favor of Jewish businessmen's doing what they can to find jobs here and there for Negroes. But if the choice were between putting energy into that effort and putting the weight of affluent Jewish businessmen behind fundamental social change—in which the government becomes the employer of first and last resort for the hard-core poor—then I would propose the latter choice. Neither individuals nor the private sector of the economy has, or can take, responsibility for full employment in American society. This is the responsibility of all segments of the society and thus, finally, of the government.

The Negro and the poor can be lifted out of poverty only when the government takes the responsibility of creating work for those whom the private sector can no longer use, given the impact of automation and cybernation. American business will not buy sheer muscle power. The sale of muscle power began to diminish when sweatshops began to disappear. American capital is not going to put the undereducated back to work; the society must collectively do that. Private enterprise should do what it can, but there are extreme limitations.

For example, we are not going to find homes for the poor until we have a national land-use policy, as well as a national migration policy. We talk about the urban crisis while Negroes in Mississippi, Georgia, and Alabama are being run off the farms and forced by our present farm policy to Chicago, St. Louis, and New York. One-half million Negroes are leaving the South annually, coming to New York, Chicago, and other ghettos—one-half million coming in while only about 30,000 a year are going out of the ghettos into the suburbs. For those who don't take the trouble to find out, that is how the ghettos grow larger, with more frustration and more despair.

Here are some of the things we are going to have to do in order to deal with white fear and Negro frustration. We must have a two-dollar minimum wage in this country. And small businessmen who cannot afford to pay this wage should be subsidized by the government, just as it subsidizes millionaire railway men and millionaire farmers with price supports.

We are going to have to have public works programs to put these people back to work and to do it without a lot of talk about pre-training. These people don't have to be pre-trained. All they need is to know that there are jobs. John Dewey said that a man learns by doing. I want to go Dewey one better: we must put these people to work learning *while* doing, and while being paid. In World War II we did not ask whether people were too black, or too old, or too young, or too stupid to work. We simply said to them this is a hammer, this is a tool, this is a drill. We built factories and sent these people into the factories. We paid them extraordinarily good wages and in two months they created the miracle of making planes that flew. We can find a peacetime method for doing this—public works for schools, hospitals, psychiatric clinics, new modes of transportation, of cleaning the air, of cleaning the rivers. All of these improvements would benefit not only the poor but also the affluent.

Furthermore, those who cannot work because they are too young, too old, or too sick or who are female heads of large families must have guaranteed incomes. In addition, we must supply free medical care, and we must pay a salary to those capable of going through school. Beyond this we must realize that the ghettos, with their high density of people per room, cannot be improved. We must create new towns and destroy the ghettos, providing work through construction projects and human services to human beings. Nothing short of this will be effective.

These programs will cost us $18.5 billion a year beyond the present level of expenditure and that money can come from the gross national product. But I want to assure businessmen that the people who benefit from the programs are not going to sit on the money when they get it. They are going to act like Americans. They are going to buy all the junk that is advertised, thereby raising the GNP, raising the economic production and growth of the country, and fundamentally adding to its economic stability.

The way things are now, we are twice damned. We are paying $15 billion a year for the support and misdeeds of those who cannot find work and end up in prison or on welfare. If they are provided with work and improve the economy, then we have additional growth plus the $15 billion we are now paying for keeping them on welfare and in jail.

For the things which must be done, I request the understanding, the cooperation, and the aid of Jews. I do so knowing that there is Negro anti-Semitism and knowing how Jews must feel when they hear some Negro extremists talk. To hear these young Negroes spouting material directly from *Mein Kampf* must bring terrible memories, shocking inner turmoil. But in times of confusion, I recommend to Jews what I do for myself in times of confusion. I go back and read the Jewish prophets, mainly Isaiah and Jeremiah. Isaiah and Jeremiah have taught me to be against injustice wherever it is, and first of all in myself. There is a moral problem in abandoning the fight against injustice merely because less than 2 per cent of the Negroes in this country are engaging in anti-Semitism. It is a problem which Isaiah and Jeremiah would be the first to point out. The issue never was, and never can be, simply a problem of Jew and gentile or black and white. The problem is man's inhumanity to man and must be fought from that basic principle regardless of race or creed. We must get on with the fight for a coalition of labor forces, of religious forces, of businessmen, of liberal and civil rights groups standing together. White fear, Negro frustration, and anti-Semitism will disappear not because we rail against them but because we bring about a social and economic program to neutralize them.

What is truly at stake is whether we can band together in a great political movement to bring about the socialization of this nation where it needs to be socialized, or whether we are going to permit the nation we love to be torn asunder in a race war in which people who don't want to be on either side may be forced to take sides. That is our problem. That is our challenge.

SOUL SEARCHING VS. SOCIAL CHANGE

The traditional reluctance in this country to confront the real nature of racism is once again illustrated by the manner in which the majority of American whites interpreted what the Kerner Commission had to say about white racism.

It seems that they have taken the Kerner Report as a call merely to examine their individual attitudes. The examination of individual attitudes is, of course, an indispensable requirement if the influence of racism is to be neutralized, but it is neither the only nor the basic requirement.

The Kerner Report took great pains to make a distinction between racist attitudes and racist behavior. In doing so, it was trying to point out that the fundamental problem lies in the racist behavior of American institutions toward Negroes, and that the behavior of these institutions is influenced more by overt racist actions of people than by their private attitudes. If so, then the basic requirement is for white Americans, while not ignoring the necessity for a revision of their private beliefs, to concentrate on actions that can lead to the ultimate democratization of American institutions.

By focusing upon private attitudes alone, white Americans may come to rely on token individual gestures as a way of absolving themselves personally of racism, while ignoring the work that needs to be done within public institutions to eradicate social and economic problems and redistribute wealth and opportunity.

I mean by this that there are many whites sitting around in drawing rooms and board rooms discussing their consciences and even donating a few dollars to honor the memory of Dr. King. But they are not prepared to fight politically for the kind of liberal Congress the country needs to eradicate some of the evils of racism, or for the massive programs needed for the social and economic reconstruction of the black and white poor, or for a revision of the tax structure whereby the real burden will be lifted from the shoulders of those who don't have it and placed on the shoulders of those who can afford it.

From the *New York Amsterdam News*, May 18, 1968.

Our time offers enough evidence to show that racism and intolerance are not unique American phenomena. The relationship between the upper and lower classes in India is in some ways more brutal than the operation of racism in America. And in Nigeria black tribes have recently been killing other black tribes in behalf of social and political privilege.

But it is the nature of the society which determines whether such conflicts will last, whether racism and intolerance will remain as proper issues to be socially and politically organized. If the society is a just society, if it is one which places a premium on social justice and human rights, then racism and intolerance cannot survive—will, at least, be reduced to a minimum.

While working with the NAACP some years ago to integrate the University of Texas, I was assailed with a battery of arguments as to why Negroes should not be let in. They would be raping white girls as soon as they came in; they were dirty and did not wash; they were dumb and could not learn; they were uncouth and ate with their fingers.

These attitudes were not destroyed because the NAACP psychoanalyzed white students or held seminars to teach them about black people. They were destroyed because Thurgood Marshall got the Supreme Court to rule against and destroy the institution of segregated education. At that point, the private views of white students became irrelevant.

So while there can be no argument that progress depends both on the revision of private attitudes and a change in institutions, the onus must be placed on institutional change.

If the institutions of this society are altered to work for black people, to respond to their needs and legitimate aspirations, then it will ultimately be a matter of supreme indifference to them whether white people like them, or what white people whisper about them in the privacy of their drawing rooms.

NOW KENNEDY: THE BILL MOUNTS HIGHER

Within two months two Americans who exemplified the best their country stands for—or should stand for—and who worked to create a climate of justice, civility, and moral sanity in the world have been brutally destroyed by one of the very evils they sought to eradicate.

Much of the moral upheaval and restlessness now going on in the world and in America is a justified revolt against conditions which are no longer acceptable. It is a revolt against certain outmoded authorities that are no longer either relevant to the realities of the new age or responsive to the aspirations of a young generation which has every right to be considered a vital and legitimate constituency of the age.

Robert Kennedy and Martin Luther King understood this deeply, and gave responsible, inspiring, and high moral leadership to the new feeling and the new aspiration, as well as to the demand in our own country for a just, non-violent, and open society for all.

The tragic removal of these two men, at this time, from the American scene reveals in starkest relief the problems and crisis that plague our society. Both men were deeply committed to the elimination of poverty in a land of plenty. Both men were dedicated to peace and to the restrained and moral exercise of American power abroad.

Both men understood the human wastefulness of violence and the folly of utilizing violence in a democratic and humane society as the chief instrument for social and moral change. Both understood and supported the absolute necessity for the total freedom of black Americans. Both were in touch with the alienation of American youth, black and white, and its demand to be involved in the shaping of a new and more just society. Both were fully aware of the risks they ran and the penalties they faced for trying to work against the current American moral grain.

And yet both men, believing as Kennedy did that "man was not made for

From the *New York Amsterdam News*, June 15, 1968.

safe havens," accepted the risks and paid the penalties as a price for trying to make a difference in their time and for striving to show mankind that it can be better than it is.

We do not have enough of such men. And one wonders whether a country in which it cost so many decades to rear such affirmative and humane spirits can afford the destruction of two of the best of them within the short span of sixty days. Either answer to this question is frightening, and that may well be one of the truest measures of the crisis we are in.

But while these were men for all good seasons and all moral causes, their loss will be felt most severely by the new young American generation, struggling to forge a more satisfying relationship with American values and institutions; by the Negroes struggling to win their total freedom and privileges as American citizens; and by the black and white poor who at this very moment are petitioning the President and Congress for an equitable share in the great affluence of American society.

To feel and express a deep fear for the future of our democracy is not to sound a melodramatic alarm. For if all those who represent the hope and the chance for moral and racial reconciliation as well as the demand for social justice in America, if all these men are removed, then we are creating a no man's land which the armies of extreme reaction and extreme despair may well rush in to fill.

With each assassination, the bill for moral and social change in America mounts higher and higher. The question is when America will be ready to make good on this debt. And a far more serious question is whether it will make good before the bill mounts still higher, and before the armies move into the no man's land from which men like Robert Kennedy and Martin Luther King have been violently eliminated.

THE CHOICE IS CLEAR

When I was young my grandmother used to ask me, "If you're so smart, why aren't you rich?" I'd like to ask a similar question of those who are now saying to the black community: "Don't bother to vote. It makes no difference who wins." If this advice made sense, then after all the years we didn't (couldn't) vote, we should be fully free.

Who are the nonvoters? By and large, they are poor and low-income people, including Negroes. They are the people who get the worst deal in this society. On the other hand, those who vote generally have higher incomes and better educations. They get the best deal—which is why they vote. They have their stake and they mean to keep it.

That's why there's nothing radical (or very smart) about the so-called radicals who are telling us to "go fishing" on election day. Their line sounds tough and cynical, but it's just a hot-air prescription for another expensive round of white power by default. Maybe some of the soap-boxers can afford a four-year dose of conservative rule, but the man in the street cannot.

The circumstances surrounding Richard Nixon's nomination prove that the Republican party is firmly in the hands of its right wing—a coalition of conservative business interests and Southern reactionaries à la Strom Thurmond. Nixon confided to his Southern supporters that he opposes open housing legislation. He has also said that we can forget about spending any more money on city problems if he's elected.

Despite the clashes between brutal police and provocative demonstrators in Chicago—and I witnessed some of those horrifying confrontations—the Negro-labor-liberal forces are clearly on top in the Democratic party.

The victory of the integrated Mississippi delegation, the seating of Julian Bond, the routing of the regular Alabamians—all indicate that the days of the Dixiecrats in the majority party are numbered. They are fleeing to Wallace and Nixon. With their departure, there is a vacuum which the black community can help to fill, thus radically changing the structure of the party.

From the *New York Amsterdam News*, September 21, 1968.

Without minimizing the conflicts that raged among the McCarthy, Mc-Govern, and Humphrey backers, it is interesting to note that all these men are more liberal on the basic issues than any candidate ever nominated by a major party.

The Democrats' final choice, Hubert Humphrey, has a civil rights record unmatched by any national political figure. His championship of the workingman—and black Americans are mainly workers—has earned him the enthusiastic support of the labor movement. His efforts on behalf of disarmament are acknowledged even by critics of the Vietnam War.

It would be a national tragedy if these assets were lost to us because of the divisions among the progressive forces over Vietnam—especially when the alternative is a Republican "solution" in Southeast Asia. The war in Vietnam will end before long, but our problems at home will haunt us for generations if we do not act now.

Not since 1876 have the stakes been so high for the black community. With the polls predicting a close race, our vote can elect the next President. So there's nothing Wallace and his ilk would like better than for us to "go fishing" on Election Day.

The choice is clear and simple. A Nixon victory will be a victory for the white backlash and the forces of repression. A Humphrey victory will be a victory for the Negro and a defeat for the racists of this country.

NEGROES AND THE 1968 ELECTIONS

1968 is now part of history, and those of us dedicated to democratic social change in America can only hope that we shall never have to live through such a year again. The assassination of Dr. Martin Luther King, Jr., has left a vacuum in the civil rights movement that until now shows no sign of being filled. And the assassination of Senator Robert Kennedy not only dealt a serious blow to our struggle but also further embittered and disillusioned our young people, black and white. Moreover, we witnessed the ominous growth of both racial and political polarization which threatened the stability of our social order and brought on a powerful right-wing reaction that ultimately led to a conservative victory in the presidential election. That year is over—and now we must suffer its consequences.

Yet there is by no means cause for *total* despair. We must remember that while conservative forces triumphed nationally in 1968, they suffered a defeat within the Democratic party so great that they may never recover the influence they once held in that sphere. This is a subject that will occupy us at a later point, but for the present let it be noted that all of the major contenders for the Democratic presidential nomination—Hubert Humphrey, the late Robert Kennedy, George McGovern, and Eugene McCarthy —were strong liberals committed to social justice. Humphrey, the man finally chosen by the party, had the finest civil rights and labor record of any presidential candidate of a major party in the history of the United States. This powerful liberal movement within the Democratic party may eventually prove to be far more significant than the election of Richard Nixon that today weighs so heavily upon our minds.

The most pressing task of the moment is to analyze the factors that permitted the conservatives to triumph in 1968, so that we can develop a political strategy which will insure that their ascendancy will be short-lived. The most visible, yet perhaps the most misunderstood, of these factors is the racial polarization which reached its peak during the presidential campaigns of Eldridge Cleaver and George Wallace. No two individuals, it would seem,

---

A working paper prepared in December 1968 for the use of A. Philip Randolph Institute affiliated groups.

could be further apart politically than Cleaver and Wallace. Cleaver, on the one hand, embodies and articulates the rage that has gripped large segments of the black community in recent years. Born of desperation and despair, this rage has produced burnings and lootings in the ghetto as well as a philosophy of black separatism that represents more a withdrawal from an intimidating and unresponsive white society than a positive program for political action. This rage was also the source of Cleaver's influence. He could ride its powerful currents to fame and notoriety—which the mass media were more than willing to heap upon him—but he could not begin to propose a solution to the injustices that had produced it. Indeed, to assuage the anger and frustration in the black community would have threatened his own base of power.

Wallace, on the other hand, has often been called the embodiment of white racism and reaction. That he is, but, more precisely, his preeminence was a result of the fear which gripped large sections of the white community throughout the country. The Wallace movement grew to frightening proportions not because of anything that Wallace did but because the politically polarized atmosphere in the country called forth the need for a man who would represent the fears and the very worst instincts of millions of people.

While Cleaver and Wallace seem on the surface to be so very different, they are both simply the manifestations of the same social evils. Black rage and burnt-out ghettos are the product of the economic deprivation of Negro Americans; and white fear and the Wallace vote are the result of the economic scarcity that motivates whites, particularly those in the lower middle class, to feel that they must protect the little they have against the rising demands of blacks. The conditions of deprivation and scarcity, and the consequent growth of racial hostility and political polarization, formed the context within which the events of 1968 unfolded.

Ask any American to name the event that most stands out in his mind in relation to the election-year activities, and chances are he will cite the violence which took place in the streets of Chicago during the Democratic national convention. It is true that the police in Chicago were brutal. But it is also true that they were provoked into violence by demonstrators whose program of confrontation politics demanded a brutal police response. This is not to justify that response—nothing could—but let us not forget that Negroes have been aware of that brutality now for hundreds of years. They were aware of it when they saw their brothers and sisters being lynched in the South and beaten and clubbed at Selma Bridge. They were also aware of it during the Republican convention when three Negroes were killed by the police in the streets of Miami. The news media, which were largely for Nixon, let the loss of these three lives go nearly unmentioned while they transformed the beatings in Chicago into an event of international magnitude. Those beatings are to be abhorred, perhaps as much as the killings in Miami, but one must also deplore the failure of the media to give a balanced portrayal of the events.

The real tragedy of Chicago was not that the police were brutal but that the violence obscured the truly creative things that happened inside the Democratic convention. It obscured the tremendous importance of the fact that the Loyal Democrats of Mississippi, an integrated and progressive delegation, was seated, and not the Eastland crowd. There was also the partial seating of the challenge delegation from Georgia, led by Julian Bond, which compelled the Maddox forces to leave the convention. The right to vote in the South, which we struggled and suffered so long to achieve, made these things possible in Chicago. We can now look forward to a time in the not too distant future when Negroes in the South and their white allies will have the strength to drive the racists out of the Democratic party and out of the Congressional committees which they now control.

These changes are part of a general realignment that is now going on within the Democratic party. This realignment will take place all the more swiftly now that the unit rule has been done away with. The Democratic party will not only become more democratic but, by genuinely representing the people (the labor movement, Negroes, liberals) who compose its coalition, it will be the vehicle through which American society itself can be politically and economically democratized.

In light of these events, it is difficult to understand why so many liberals have bitterly condemned the convention for being "totalitarian." Many liberals came to Chicago hoping to nominate a peace candidate, or at least to have a strong anti-Vietnam plank adopted as part of the party platform. In neither of these efforts did they succeed, yet nonetheless they participated in the most thorough, substantive debate on a political issue that has ever taken place at a major party convention. This debate over the American involvement in Vietnam was at once a confrontation of opposing views and a judicious dialogue among reasonable men. It was a vindication of the democratic process. Certainly no such debate took place in Miami, where there was only fanfare and balloons. When one hears the word "totalitarian" applied to the Chicago convention, one can only be reminded of George Orwell's famous warning that the consequence of the debasement of language is the destruction of truth.

One final word on the Democratic convention. When it came time to choose a candidate for the presidency of the United States, the name of Channing Phillips, a Negro, was placed in nomination. He was the first Negro ever to receive such an honor, and we should not overlook the symbolic significance of that event. It is possible that historians may some day regard the 1968 Democratic convention as a watershed in the history of the Negro in America.

During the presidential campaign defeatism and indifference were popular attitudes among some Democrats. As was expected and forewarned, these attitudes contributed in part to Humphrey's defeat. Nor is it surprising that they have now found in that defeat a source of justification. In brief, the defeatist argument claims that the Democratic coalition of Negroes, labor, and liberals which was forged during the New Deal is now a thing of the past and no longer exists as a coherent political force.

My analysis of the election, however, concludes with the exact opposite judgment—that continuity with the past was the most striking feature of the Democratic performance in 1968. The coalition of the minorities, the trade union movement, and, to a degree, the liberal forces that in the past elected Roosevelt, Truman, Kennedy, and Johnson by and large stood firm in November. Given the difficult nature of our time, the fact of this continuity is that much more impressive.

In the first place, the Negro integrationist forces voted overwhelmingly for Humphrey. There has been much talk of black separatism, and it has been said that we are moving toward two societies—one black, one white. I do not mean to deal lightly with this tragic and dangerous trend. Nor do I mean to imply that there is not tremendous disaffection, alienation, and despair in the Negro community. But in 1968 there were two black militant candidates running against Humphrey—Cleaver and Dick Gregory. And they received less than 86,000 votes nationally, many of them, I am sure, cast by white people.

The point is that while many Negroes may sympathize with some of the ideas and the feelings of the militants and the separatists, the vast majority realize that the course they are proposing is politically disastrous. Negroes may listen to Cleaver and even agree with him in some respects, but they will vote for Hubert Humphrey, for they realize that separatism and violence are equivalent to suicide.

But they will not vote for Richard Nixon. Except in the unusual election of 1964, when almost every Negro was opposed to Goldwater, the Democrats have never received a larger percentage of the black vote. A sampling taken by the National Broadcasting Company found that the vote for Humphrey in all-black precincts averaged over 90 per cent. A higher percentage voted for Humphrey in 1968 than for Kennedy in 1960. But it is also important to point out that numerically *fewer* Negroes voted for Nixon in 1968 than in 1960 all over the country in state after state. Figures produced by the COPE research department show that in the Negro precincts of Atlanta, the Democrats received 41.9 per cent in 1960 and 98 per cent in 1968. Similar figures for Negro precincts in Baltimore are 74.8 per cent and 92.6 per cent, and in Boston, 61.4 per cent and 90.9 per cent. To go on would be tedious. It is clear that Negroes are not deserting the Democratic party but, on the contrary, are giving it their ever-increasing support.

The trade union movement was confronted with a double threat in 1968—from Nixon and from Wallace. Nixon saw a great irony in the strength of the labor movement. The tremendous organization of blue- and white-collar workers, he felt, had benefited them economically to the point where they had become members of the middle classes, which traditionally vote Republican. Nixon hoped to capture that part of the working-class vote, and he did receive some of it, but nothing like what he thought he would get.

The Wallace threat was far more formidable, and the trade union movement met it head on to achieve one of the most brilliant triumphs in its history. In the months preceding the election one could not pick up a newspaper without reading of the deep inroads that Wallace had cut into the working class. That many workers were leaning toward Wallace is beyond doubt. So too were farmers and professionals. But while all Americans of good will took fright at this fascistic trend, the trade union movement was the only major institution in America that did anything to counter it. It undertook a fantastic educational job among its members, distributing over fifty million pieces of literature which attacked Wallace not only for his anti-labor record in Alabama but for his racism and bigotry as well. The result was that in the last weeks of the campaign thousands of workers rejected Wallace's disastrous course and returned to the Democratic fold. The effect of this shift was almost enough to give Humphrey the election.

Finally, a word must be said about the liberals, especially those who, as A. Philip Randolph has said, "urged black Americans to 'go fishing' on Election Day" as they themselves were determined to do. These liberals were opposed to our involvement in Vietnam. As we live in a democratic society, they had every right to express that opposition. But they also wanted to "teach the Democratic party a lesson." They wanted to do this even if it meant the election of Richard Nixon, an event which is potentially equivalent to the national tragedy of 1876, when the federal government abandoned its responsibility for the rights of black Americans. They were so preoccupied with Vietnam that they failed to consider that, as President, Nixon might choose as many as five Supreme Court Justices and thus determine the character and decisions of the Court for the remainder of this century; that he would name the Attorney General and the head of the Civil Rights Division; that he would staff and determine the policies and the budget of our federal welfare system; and that he would influence the composition, structure, and politics of the 91st and 92nd Congress. In all fairness, it should be said that at the midnight hour of the campaign many of these liberals confronted for the first time the implications of a Nixon victory, but this realization came to too few and at too late a time. Given the extraordinary closeness of the election, one cannot help thinking that herein lies the reason for Humphrey's defeat.

What the turbulent months of the campaign and the election revealed most of all, I think, was that the American people were voicing a profound demand for change. On the one hand, the Humphrey people were demanding a Marshall Plan for our diseased cities and an economic solution to our social problems. The Nixon and Wallace supporters, on the other hand, were making their own limited demands for change. They wanted more "law and order," to be achieved not through federal spending but through police, Mace, and the National Guard. We must recognize and accept the demand for change, but now we must struggle to give it a progressive direction.

For the immediate agenda, I would make four proposals. *First*, the Electoral College should be eliminated. It is archaic, undemocratic, and potentially very dangerous. Had Nixon not achieved a majority of the electoral votes, Wallace might have been in the position to choose and influence our next President. A shift of only 46,000 votes in the states of Alaska, Delaware, New Jersey, and Missouri would have brought us to that impasse. We should do away with this system, which can give a minority and reactionary candidate so much power and replace it with one that provides for the popular election of the President. It is to be hoped that a reform bill to this effect will emerge from the hearings that will soon be conducted by Senator Birch Bayh of Indiana.

Second, a simplified national registration law should be passed that provides for universal permanent registration and an end to residence requirements. Our present system discriminates against the poor who are always underregistered, often bcause they must frequently relocate their residence, either in search of better employment and living conditions or as a result of such poorly planned programs as urban renewal (which has been called Negro removal).

Third, the cost of the presidential campaigns should come from the public treasury and not from private individuals. Nixon, who had the backing of wealthy corporate executives, spent $21 million on his campaign. Humphrey's expenditures totaled only $9.7 million. A system so heavily biased in favor of the rich cannot rightly be called democratic.

And finally, we must maintain order in our public meetings. It was disgraceful that each candidate, for both the presidency and the vice-presidency, had to be surrounded by cordons of police in order to address an audience. And even then, hecklers were able to drown him out. There is no possibility for rational discourse, a prerequisite for democracy, under such conditions. If we are to have civility in our civil life, we must not permit a minority to disrupt our public gatherings.

If we confront the problem of fundamental social reforms, we should recognize the tremendous need for reorganization within the Democratic party. The races for the Senate and the House of Representatives in 1970 will be decisive for the reunification of the party and the reestablishment of the Democratic coalition as the dominant political force in the country. In this regard, there is little evidence that the McCarthy movement will be active at that time as an independent movement, though its participants should remain within the Democratic coalition. Its leader has already relinquished the moral authority he had over his followers by refusing to support Senator Edward Kennedy's bid for Senate whip and surrendering his seat on the Senate Foreign Relations Committee to Gale McGee, a supporter of the war effort. Beyond this, the movement itself showed only a limited interest in working politically to solve the persisting problems of poverty and segregation. With the election year excitement having subsided, the McCarthy movement already seems to be dissolving.

The Wallace phenomenon is another matter. As a candidate of fear and frustration, Wallace was essentially a prisoner of events. If in the next two years we have extreme disorder and social dislocation, we should expect that Wallace will be a significant factor in 1970. If, on the other hand, we have a return to social calm, his influence should be greatly reduced.

Evidently much depends on what Nixon does, and one can only speculate as to exactly what that will be. It is my own belief that Nixon will be neither violently conservative nor very ideological. While he will be pressed from the right by his Southern constituency, he must also respond to the left-of-center demands coming from the Atlantic seaboard. Beyond that, he must face the growing pressure from Negroes and other minority groups for real social change. As he will be pressed from different sides by these three elements, I do not think he can move decisively in any one direction. He should try to assume a generally centralist position and then hope that he can play it by ear.

As for his Negro policy, he has already stated that he supports a program of black capitalism. I am entirely in favor of Negroes running grocery stores, as long as they realize the danger that they will be out of business the moment the A and P decides to open a supermarket around the corner. But beyond that, it seems to me highly questionable to speak of black capitalism when 95 per cent of Negroes are workers and hundreds of thousands of them are unemployed. To talk to Negroes about becoming capitalists when masses of them are barely surviving in the *lumpenproletariat* is to substitute a mirage for social analysis.

There is a second reason why I have doubts about black capitalism. It is significant not because of what it proposes to do, but because of the social and political context in which it is put forth. Black capitalism today is part of a larger series of ideas, including community control, which claim the failure of the federal government to solve the problem of poverty and which accept racial segregation. These ideas are not progressive. They represent defeatism and despair, and they let both the federal government and the white community off the hook while the Negro community must bear the whole burden of society's injustices.

Many proponents of black capitalism are also highly critical of the labor movement. So are the growing numbers of liberals who say that the trade union movement is dead or at best reactionary. I find these attitudes hard to understand, for there is not a Jewish, Protestant, Catholic, corporate, or civil rights organization in the country that has a basic economic program equal to the one proposed by the trade union movement. It is a program that calls for the destruction of the ghetto and for the construction of decent homes for everybody, for full employment, a guaranteed income, and free medical care. Moreover, not a single bill affecting the poor in America would have got through Congress without the support of the labor lobby, and in this I include all the civil rights legislation that has been passed in recent years. And finally, I must emphasize that all of the war on poverty, were it multiplied a thousand times, could not do for the black *lumpenproletariat* what the trade union movement has done by organizing two million of them. I cannot conceive of an effective and progressive coalition which does not include the labor movement.

Richard Nixon has called for unity. I am sure his plea was heard by Eldridge Cleaver and George Wallace and all their supporters. But I doubt that it will be heeded. There cannot be unity while poverty exists, and certainly it cannot be achieved with billy clubs and Mace. What we need is a sound social and economic program that will do away with the distinction between the haves and the have-nots. Then we shall be together, and it is toward this end that we must now dedicate ourselves.

SEPARATE IS NOT EQUAL

There is a great irony in the demands now being made by black college students for separate black studies departments. In essence these students are seeking to impose upon themselves the very conditions of separatism and inequality against which black Americans have struggled since the era of Reconstruction.

The argument can of course be made that separate need not be unequal. But black people have heard this argument before—from Southern racists justifying Jim Crow and from Northern bigots rationalizing *de facto* segregation. They have heard it long enough to know that "separate but equal" will always be a form of exploitation and degradation. And it will continue to be such, whether it is demanded by whites out of malicious intent or by blacks out of the poignant need, born of fear and insecurity, to withdraw from competition with the larger society.

For if we are to face the truth, however painful this may be, we must recognize that black people have been brutalized in the past by inferior segregated education and economic deprivation to the point where they have been put at a disadvantage with whites. Consequently, when they are placed in a difficult competitive situation, such as obtains at predominantly white universities, their immediate impulse is to retreat into themselves and establish a black curriculum with separate—and lower—standards by which their performance shall be judged.

There are three great dangers here. First, if history and present circumstances are any indicators, as I think they are, separate black programs will be poorly financed, understaffed, and generally neglected. Second, rather than demanding a separate (and inferior) program of study, black students should be insisting on the best education that is possible to compensate for their brutalization in the past. They should be demanding access to the best professors, smaller classes, extra work during summer sessions, and more scholarships for other black students. Third, they must have these things because after graduation they will have to engage in free and open competi-

From the *New York Amsterdam News*, February 13, 1969.

tion for jobs in a marketplace where standards are universal. And black people must get the best jobs available if they are substantially to increase their economic and social power.

In this regard, I reserve my most severe criticism for those white students and faculty members who are aiding and abetting the separatist demands of black students, and for those frightened administrators who do not have the courage to reject the demands. They are not only telling young Negroes what is not true in real life—that a minority can influence social change through violent confrontation—but they are urging these blacks to do something which they themselves, discontented though they may be, don't have the courage to do: make a head-on attack on our social institutions. And while these whites enjoy their revolution by proxy, they are studying for the degrees that will give them soft jobs in universities and beautiful homes in the suburbs. It is only the blacks who will suffer.

So that I will not be misunderstood, I want to emphasize that I am whole-heartedly in support of black studies. The history of the Negro in America is an extraordinarily significant area of study for *all* Americans—one which has been mostly neglected or distorted in the past. It is a history that is both magnificent and tragic, and one can only become wiser from studying it. I fully commend the proposal of the Harvard faculty committee to offer a degree in Afro-American studies that will be open to all students.

What I fear is that black studies will be made a pretext for separatism, in which case they will become a means of escaping from reality, not of discovering it. If this comes to pass, I think that a great injustice will have been committed against black Americans.

HOW BLACK AMERICANS SEE BLACK
AFRICANS—AND VICE VERSA

The relationship between Africans and Afro-Americans is one of ambivalence. It is an ambivalence that derives from a great tension between, on the one hand, a shared ancient heritage and racial identification and, on the other, profound differences in the historical, cultural, and political circumstances of the two peoples which make them almost incomprehensible to each other. This tension has produced in the Negro a poignant desire to reach backward to Africa in search of his roots, and the forward-looking need to achieve full economic and social equality on his native soil—which is America.

The central experience that binds Africans and Negroes together is their common understanding of the brutality of racism. The difference here, however, is that while the African knowledge of racism has grown out of his experience with imperialism and colonialism, Afro-Americans have been concerned with it in the context of slavery, segregation, and social inequality. As a result, both have found it necessary to develop political strategies of opposition appropriate to the different circumstances surrounding the development of racism in their respective lands. The fact that they have had to employ different strategies in order to destroy the same evil has led to much confusion.

Africans, we must never forget, are the majority in societies which until very recently were dominated by a white minority. (In South Africa, Rhodesia, Mozambique, and Angola, the anachronistic injustice of white domination still persists.) Their fundamental concern, therefore, was to seize national power through violent or nonviolent revolutionary action. The African political context of imperialism, in other words, provided the conditions for a genuine revolution.

Many American Negroes have tried to use the independence movements in colonial territories as the model for their own political actions. Consequently, we have had black nationalist movements for "self-determination"

From *War/Peace Report*, March 1969. Reprinted with permission.

and "black power," which some people have called anti-imperialist and revolutionary. This revolutionary rhetoric is misplaced, however, and the movements have inevitably failed to achieve their goals for two simple reasons: Negroes can have no geographical focus for national sentiment and they do not constitute a majority of the population. They constitute but 11 per cent of the American people, and they are dispersed throughout every state in the nation. Negroes, therefore, must be concerned with obtaining that degree of power which one-ninth of the population should expect. They must do this through constitutional and democratic means, for to attempt a revolution would bring on a counterrevolution of the sort that I do not wish to contemplate.

Beyond these political distinctions, there are differences in cultural and social patterns of behavior that are so profound as to make it almost impossible for Africans and Negroes to understand one another. This situation is illustrated by a conversation I had with a seventeen-year-old boy during a recent visit to Nairobi, Kenya. He said to me, "Mr. Rustin, I am a Kenyan and I belong to the Kikuyu tribe. You are an American, and I would like to know what tribe you belong to."

Being taken aback, I replied, "I belong to the Negro tribe," upon which he asked me to speak some Negro to him. I tried to explain to him that Negroes had originally been Africans at which time they spoke their tribal languages, but that after 300 years in America we had forgotten our tribal tongue and now spoke the common American language of English. Incredulously, he asked, "How can you be of the Negro tribe if you do not speak the Negro language? I am a Kikuyu and I speak Kikuyu as my first language and Swahili as my second."

Our conversation lasted for over an hour, and though I made every effort to be explicit and explanatory, it was impossible for me to identify myself to him in any way that he could understand. He found me as strange a being as he might find a white American, a European, or an Asian.

Just as Africans have difficulty understanding Negroes, so many of our own people do not know that there is not *one* Africa but many, including many tribes that are now within the borders of African states. The extent of the American Negro's failure to understand Africa was articulately described in *Ebony* by Tom Mboya, Kenya's minister for economic planning and development:

> ...I find sometimes there is a complete misunderstanding of what
> African culture really means. For example, some people think that
> to identify as an African, one has to wear a shaggy beard or a piece

of cloth or skin on the head, or has to wear one's hair natural. These are conditions imposed on the African today by the circumstances of poverty, limitations in technical and educational and other resources. These must not be confused with culture.

An African walks barefoot or wears sandals made of old tires not because it is his culture, but because he lives in poverty. He lives in a mud or wattle hut, but these are signs of poverty which must not be mistaken for cultural heritage. Culture is something much deeper. It is the total sum of your personality, outlook, and attitude to life.

Mboya made these remarks as part of a larger statement discouraging American Negroes from expatriating to Africa "because they are black." His words are relevant today because there is again talk among some Negroes of going back to Africa. While relatively few Negroes realistically consider expatriation a possibility, the fact that it is being discussed is significant, for it is part of a much broader movement by black Americans to separate themselves from the mainstream of society.

There is a reason for this movement which has to do far less with the Negro's relation to Africa than to America. The "Back to Africa" and separatist tendencies are always strongest at the very time when the Negro is most intensely dissatisfied with his lot in America. It is when the Negro has lost hope in America—and lost his identity *as* an American—that he seeks to reestablish his identity and his roots as an African.

This period of despair has historically followed hard upon a period of hope and of efforts to become integrated—on the basis of full equality— into the economic, social, and political life of the United States. The present separatist mood, as we know, has come after a decade in which the Negro has achieved enormous and unprecedented gains through the civil rights struggle, and it has coincided with a right-wing reaction that has obstructed further measures toward equality. The combination of progress, aroused hopes, frustration, and despair has caused many Negroes to withdraw into separatism and to yearn for Africa.

Three times in the past the Negro has been similarly disenchanted. During the period of social stress following the founding of this nation, the humanitarian ardor which had been aroused by the independence movement disappeared. Negroes who had hoped for progress turned inward, and it was during this period that the African Church was formed. The separatism of Booker T. Washington rose upon the ruined expectations that had been aroused by the Civil War and its aftermath but dashed by the Compromise of 1876. And when Negroes expected but were denied justice after fighting for their country in World War I, Marcus Garvey organized a movement of over 2,000,000 blacks to buy ships that would carry them back to Africa.

Many who joined the Garvey movement, I believe, did not really wish to return to Africa. Rather, they wanted to express to other Americans their intense dissatisfaction with the injustices that they had been subjected to in this country. For to the Negro Africa is a vague memory and a misunderstood reality. He is an American. His ancestors have suffered here and have died here. He has roots in this country as deep as—or deeper than—any other American. However much the Negro searches for his African heritage, he can never escape his American identity. He has no choice, therefore, but to struggle for the establishment of the economic and social conditions that will enable him to realize fully his potential on this soil. Not until this struggle is successful will he entirely reject the illusion of Africa and accept the reality of his American selfhood.

WHAT ABOUT BLACK CAPITALISM?

There has been much talk recently about black capitalism as the new approach to solving the economic and social problems of Negro Americans. As this approach is gaining considerable support within the Nixon administration and in certain segments of the black community, I think that we must closely analyze whether or not it can make a contribution to the Negro struggle for equality.

I favor the notion of black people's owning and operating businesses, and I should add in this regard that I find particularly creative the efforts that some Negroes have made to form cooperatives. Yet I think that these enterprises have had more of a psychological than an economic effect on black Americans.

They have helped destroy the brutal stereotype that black people are not capable of engaging in entrepreneurial activity. But the economic impact of black capitalism has been—and can only be—marginal at best, and if we are not careful this approach may actually compound the injustices from which Negroes suffer.

We must not forget that businesses are in business not to attack social injustice but to make a profit, and that the ghetto represents a poor market to invest in because of its poverty and deprivation. Businesses will only, therefore, be attracted into the ghetto through tax incentives which guarantee them a high profit and which also insure that they themselves, and not the poor, will be the prime beneficiaries of their investments.

Of course some of these beneficiaries will be black capitalists, but these individuals are a very small and affluent section of the Negro community. It is the black working poor and the unemployed who constitute the mass of Negroes in need of economic uplift, and I think it is both foolish and misleading to speak to these people about becoming capitalists. Rather, our central objective must be to enable them to join their two million brothers and sisters who are part of the American trade union movement, which is

From the *New York Amsterdam News*, March 8, 1969.

the institution most responsible for the integration of the black poor into the economic life of our society.

I am also distressed by the separatist framework within which black capitalism is so often discussed. Many of its advocates employ black nationalist rhetoric in proposing the economic development of the ghetto, assuming, therefore, that the ghetto is a separate entity in American life that must be nurtured and made viable.

I understand that the ghetto will not disappear tomorrow, but we must not fall into the dangerous and divisive trap of abandoning the goals of integration and the elimination of a separatist social structure which has imposed such degradation and hardship upon black people and which today threatens to divide our nation.

And finally, I am most deeply concerned that black capitalism is projected by some of its proponents not as a marginal and supplementary program, but as an alternative to massive public expenditures for full employment and the reconstruction of our cities.

I can think of nothing more potentially harmful to black people than the substitution of the delusion of black capitalism for the absolute necessity for federal programs to provide all Negroes with dignified employment, decent housing, and quality-integrated schools. Black people cannot ignore these objectives without forsaking the ultimate goal of economic liberation.

THE TOTAL VISION OF
A. PHILIP RANDOLPH

Social struggle, if it is effectively to uplift masses of impoverished and exploited individuals, must articulate and satisfy their diverse needs as well as reconcile objectives that are often considered contradictory. A people degraded by poverty and a caste system of segregation, for example, will have the inchoate desire for dignity and liberation, but that desire will remain unfulfilled until it is given programmatic direction by a political movement. And in the course of fulfillment, there is always the danger that the felt need deriving from a perception of fundamental and historic injustices will conflict with the required political strategy, which by its nature must respond to circumstances of the moment.

I think it is part of the greatness of A. Philip Randolph that, throughout his sixty years as a leader of Negro Americans, he has maintained a total vision of the goal of freedom for his people and of the means for achieving it. From his earliest beginnings as a follower of Eugene V. Debs and a colleague of Norman Thomas, he has understood that social and political freedom must be rooted in economic freedom, and all his subsequent actions have sprung from this basic premise.

He has identified with the spiritual longings of black people, but has insisted that economic security is the precondition for pride and dignity. While he has felt that Negro salvation is an internal process of struggle and self-affirmation, he has recognized the political necessity of forming alliances with men of other races and the moral necessity of comprehending the black movement as part of a general effort to expand human freedom. Finally, as a result of his deep faith in democracy, he has realized that social change does not depend upon the decisions of the few, but on direct political action through the mobilization of masses of individuals to gain economic and social justice.

Randolph thus stands out among Negro leaders of the twentieth century as a man of both principled idealism and practical accomplishment. He has

From *The New Leader*, April 14, 1969. Reprinted with permission. Copyright © 1969 by The American Labor Conference on International Affairs.

stood firm against racial separatism—whether advocated in the 1920's by Marcus Garvey or in the 1960's by black nationalists—because of his belief in integration and his knowledge that separatism would mean the continued exploitation and degradation of black people. Again, he has rejected elitism —be it in the form of W. E. B. Du Bois's concept of "a talented tenth" or of a proposal for black capitalism—because of his democratic commitment and his opposition to programs that would economically benefit a minority at the expense of the majority. He has adhered to nonviolence as a moral principle and as the most effective means of political struggle.

Pursuing his conviction that the Negro can never be socially and politically free until he is economically secure, Randolph worked to build an alliance between black Americans and the trade union movement. His first efforts met with strong opposition from Southern oligarchs and powerful business leaders who had traditionally tried to use the Negro to subvert the labor movement. Their tactic was to exploit the Negro's grievous need for employment by inviting him to scab on unionized white workers striking for just demands. Realizing that the only beneficiaries of these practices were the exploiters themselves, Randolph embarked upon a crusade opposing any form of strikebreaking by Negroes, advocating instead their full integration into the American trade union movement. Today there are two million black trade unionists in America who have attained economic dignity, job security, and protection against racial discrimination.

Randolph's activities on behalf of black workers, however, did not stop with this broad crusade. In 1925, he began the long and arduous campaign to organize the Brotherhood of Sleeping Car Porters (BSCP). Despite fierce resistance from railway companies and the hardships of the depression, the BSCP eventually won certification in 1937.

This victory not only resulted in the first contract signed by a white employer with a Negro labor leader; it also became a symbol of what could happen if black people organized and bargained collectively. The BSCP en abled thousands of black workers to earn higher wages. What is more important, it became the central focus of the early civil rights protest movement. Brotherhood members, armed with the sophistication they had acquired through their economic battles and making use of the mobility provided by their jobs, carried the message of equality to Negroes in every state in the nation. They formed what was in effect a network for the distribution of political literature. It is hardly surprising, therefore, that E. D. Nixon, one of the main organizers of the 1955 Montgomery, Alabama, bus protest which marked the beginning of the modern civil rights movement, was the head of the local BSCP division and himself a porter.

Since the political strategy of mass protest has become commonplace during the last decade, it is all too often forgotten that this was developed by Randolph at a time when the use of such tactics by Negroes was unheard of. He believed that Negroes could not achieve economic advancement without fighting for it, but he was no less profoundly aware that as an oppressed people, the very act of struggling would confer upon them a dignity they had been denied.

Thus in 1941, with the advent of World War II, Randolph conceived the idea of a massive Negro March on Washington to protest the exclusion of black people from jobs in the defense industries. He wrote of the dramatic plan in the Negro press and agitated for it on the street corners of Harlem and elsewhere. The idea was scoffed at or scorned by most people in the white community, and it was so unprecedented that even many Negroes had difficulty believing it could be made into a reality.

Local March on Washington committees nevertheless began to spring up across the country, and as preparations assumed larger proportions, the pressure on President Roosevelt mounted. On June 20, 1941, less than two weeks before the scheduled date of the march, the President issued Executive Order 8802, banning discrimination in the war industries and setting up the Fair Employment Practices Committee. Once more, thousands of new jobs were opened up to Negroes through Randolph's efforts, and black people began to sense their power as an organized group and the effectiveness of nonviolent direct action tactics.

Even when his actions have seemed to be directed toward noneconomic ends, Randolph has been guided by a persistent concern for the Negro's economic welfare. In 1948, for instance, he traveled to Washington to speak with President Truman on the problem of segregation and discrimination in the armed forces. Although he was of course concerned that Negroes in the army be treated with dignity, the more fundamental difficulty he saw was that segregation would exclude them from high-paying officer positions as well as from training programs in skills they would need for post-service civilian employment. Such were Randolph's influence and authority that another executive order was issued to comply with his demands.

In 1955, when Randolph urged me to go South to help Dr. Martin Luther King organize the Montgomery bus boycott, he likewise had a dual objective in mind. He naturally felt that Negroes had a right to sit where they wanted to on public accommodations. But he also felt that if the boycott was successful and spread elsewhere, it would create jobs for Negroes as bus drivers and in restaurants, parks, and libraries. His conception was that where Negroes were free to come, they would be free to work; if this proved not to be the case, once having gained access to an institution, they would use the same techniques for obtaining employment that they had originally used to open it up. And this in fact is what has happened throughout the South.

His interest in educational desegregation, too, transcended the problem of dignity or of Negroes and whites attending the same schools together, for he was concerned with the growing threat posed to Negro employment by cybernetics and automation. Since education is the basis for economic advancement, he knew that access to all educational facilities and opportunities was vital to the Negroes. A decade later, we can see even more clearly the devastating effect the combination of automation and inferior segregated education has had on the employment of blacks.

It was Randolph's perception of the economic basis of Negro freedom that enabled him to grasp the unique significance of the 1963 March on Washington. He conceived of it as marking the termination of the mass protest period—during which Negroes had destroyed the Jim Crow institutions in the South—and the inauguration of an era of massive action at the ballot box designed to bring about new economic programs. Aware that the central problem Negroes faced was no longer simply one of *civil* rights but of *economic* rights—for the one would lack social substance without the other— he called for a March on Washington which brought a quarter of a million Americans to the nation's capital to demand *"Jobs* and Freedom."

At the same time President Kennedy introduced what was to become the 1964 Civil Rights Act, and in the minds of some people this became the main focus of the march. Randolph, however, refused to be misled by transient emotion and persisted in his demand for an economic program. At the 1966 White House conference, "To Fulfill These Rights," he proposed the Freedom Budget, calling for an annual federal expenditure of $18.5 billion for ten years to wipe out poverty.

Randolph was not speaking here of tax incentives for industry, voluntary assistance by private individuals, or community action programs. He was speaking of full employment and a guaranteed income, the rebuilding of our cities, the provision of superior schools for all of our children, and free medical care for all our citizens. He was speaking, very simply and without rhetoric, of achieving equality in America.

And he was not being unrealistic. He proposed, along with the Freedom Budget, a political strategy for achieving it that calls for building a coalition of Negroes, labor, liberals, religious organizations, and students. If these groups could unite, they would form a majority capable of democratizing the economic, social, and political power of this nation.

Today there are many Negroes and liberals who reject the idea of this coalition. The reason for this, I think, is that they have failed to view the problem of inequality in its totality. Unlike Randolph, their vision is fractured and constricted. Some Negroes, for example, are advocating racial separatism and black nationalism because they are engaged in a very significant psychological quest for identity.

I am in sympathy with this search to a degree, as was Randolph in 1940 when he wrote: ". . . the Negro and the other darker races must look to themselves for freedom. Salvation for a race, nation, or class must come from within. Freedom is never granted; it is won. Justice is never given; it is exacted. Freedom and justice must be struggled for by the oppressed of all lands and races, and the struggle must be continuous, for freedom is never a final act, but a continuing, evolving process to higher and higher levels of human, social, economic, political and religious relationships."

Randolph did not believe that blacks should isolate themselves, though, so he added: "But Negroes must not fight for their liberation alone. They must join sound, broad, liberal social movements that seek to preserve American democracy and advance the cause of social and religious freedom."

Randolph's position is not only morally correct but strategically necessary, for Negroes today are in danger of letting an emotional imperative destroy the possibility for social and economic liberation. They are emphasizing blackness to the point of isolating themselves from broad political movements for social justice—forgetting that, as one-tenth of the population, they cannot by themselves bring about necessary social changes such as those embodied in the Freedom Budget.

Indeed, many liberals have become obsessed with the psychological aspects of the racial problem to the point of neglecting its economic dimensions. During the early years of the civil rights movement these liberals, unlike Randolph, favored integration primarily as a means of fostering better relations between blacks and whites. Now that the cry of black nationalism has arisen from some Negroes, they have transferred their concern for brotherhood to the need for blacks to achieve pride and identity and for whites to purge themselves of guilt and racism. In both the earlier and the current cases there is a failure to confront the overriding fact of poverty. Most mistakenly, many have now abandoned the objective of building an integrated movement to achieve economic equality.

We are still very much in need of the guidance of A. Philip Randolph. As he reaches his eightieth birthday, this April 14, the freshness and the comprehensiveness of his vision remain evident. And by his presence, he poses a challenge to his followers: to build, through means that are democratic and nonviolent, a just society in which all men need not fear poverty and in which men of all races, graced with the dignity that comes from a full life, need not fear each other. In no other way can we at last become a nation that is at peace with itself.

NO MORE GUNS

Black people have known violence in America. They have known the Ku Klux Klan and the White Citizens Councils. They have seen the white mobs in Mississippi and in Cicero, Illinois. They have understood that violence is synonymous with oppression and destruction. Therefore, the use of guns on the Cornell University campus by a group of black students should come as a great shock—and a great sorrow—to all black Americans struggling for freedom and social justice.

Those black students who paraded so arrogantly with their guns will not bring progress to the black community or reform to the universities by imitating the tactics of the Klan. Nothing creative can emerge from their mindless use of force. Rifles will not enhance their education, nor will bullets enlighten their minds. And guns will not provide them with the knowledge and skills they need to help uplift their black brothers who are still suffering in the ghetto.

Those black students were not interested in reforming the university. Otherwise they would not have acted in such a way as to destroy the university. The fundamental cause of their actions lies not in the failure of the university to provide them with the means of obtaining an adequate education. I say this in full knowledge of the tremendous changes which must be made in policy and curriculum if universities are to meet the profound needs of black students—and white students—in our urban and technological society. In this regard Cornell is far ahead of most universities in responding to that challenge.

Those students acted as they did because they are under severe psychological stress. They have come to a predominantly white university from predominantly black high schools where they were brutalized by inferior, segregated education. They now not only find themselves in an alien social environment, but they are being asked to perform academically at a level they have not been prepared to reach. On top of this, they are undergoing a difficult quest for black identity which is aggravated by feelings of guilt at having deserted the ghetto.

From the *New York Amsterdam News*, April 24, 1969.

Caught in a strange and pressured environment and deprived of the psychological security they had in the ghetto, their impulse is to withdraw from the challenges of the university and establish a separate world for themselves. Once a situation of racial separatism has been established, racial hostility becomes inevitable. Mutual misunderstanding and fear predominate. A psychology of warfare develops, guns are procured, and the university is transformed into an armed camp.

The black students at Cornell only *displayed* their arms. They used them to intimidate the administration. But built into the situation is the logic of escalation. Violence that is threatened with bravado will become violence used with viciousness, and the main victims will not be the administration but the black students—and the university.

I therefore find those guilt-ridden and nihilistic white students who encouraged the blacks in this madness to be equally culpable. So too is the indecisive and flaccid administration, which has abdicated its responsibility to ensure that reason prevails in our institutions of higher learning. Cheap accommodationism will only bring greater violence in the future.

Moreover, by their irresponsible actions, these black students have strengthened the reactionary forces in the society which will obstruct any progress for black Americans. The fear in the white community which produced George Wallace has also been the source of resistance to programs to rebuild our cities, educate our youth, and employ all our adults. These students have increased that fear and have thus further obstructed efforts for real social progress. They have not done a service to their black brothers in the ghetto.

Finally, the central and most profound difficulty was well articulated by Kenneth Clark, who perceived in the confrontation tactics of these students "the destruction of the institutions and the total rejection of the rational and democratic process as a basis for redress of grievances." Thus it is not only the university which is being threatened by these students but all our democratic institutions. And if democracy is destroyed and violence prevails, those who will suffer most will be black Americans. This has been true in the past, and it remains true today. We must repudiate such violence if we are to achieve our liberation.

FEAR, DEMAGOGUES, AND REACTION

We have reached a point in the political development of America that can legitimately be called a crisis. Our country is in trouble, very severe trouble, and those who are most profoundly threatened by this unhappy situation are black Americans.

Recently we have seen a conservative appointed as Chief Justice of the Supreme Court. We have seen two integrationist candidates for the school board of Denver, Colorado, go down in a resounding defeat. We have seen an obscure police chief from Minneapolis run away with the mayoralty election on a platform of nothing more than "law and order." In Los Angeles we have witnessed the defeat of a talented and idealistic Negro candidate for mayor and the victory of an incompetent and unprincipled demagogue. And now in New York City we have seen both the Republican and the Democratic parties nominate right-wing candidates for mayor. As these developments have come in the wake of a Republican presidential victory and the racist Wallace movement whose size was unprecedented, we can understand the gravity of the present situation, and we must recognize the necessity to change the course of our common political destiny.

There are many reasons for this reaction that is victimizing all people concerned with social justice, but the fundamental reason lies in the dynamic of fear. There exists today a dangerous relationship between the extreme left and the extreme right, and between black rage and white fear. The confrontation tactics of the one evoke a reactionary response from the other. When the would-be revolutionaries of the new left manhandle professors, occupy buildings, and destroy property, the right wins new adherents. When sincere but misdirected young black people engage in violence in the name of justice, they are strengthening those very forces which in the past have inflicted violence and injustice upon the Negro community. Such acts of protest may be cathartic, may appear to be bold and militant; but let us be very clear— their primary effect is to bring about political reaction.

These acts have set loose a wave of panic in this country, and opportunistic right-wing demagogues understand the nature of that panic and are building

From the *New York Amsterdam News*, June 19, 1969.

their political futures upon it. These demagogues do not believe in meeting the black community's urgent needs for income and education. Indeed, social justice, by removing the cause of social unrest, would threaten the very base of fear upon which they stand. Their program is the billy club and their staunchest ally the police arm of the state. They believe in repression.

The lessons of these recent developments should be clear. An assault upon our democratic institutions will not reform them but destroy them. Violence will lead to more violence, not to social justice. And the fundamental tragedy is that the absence of justice will provoke more people to engage in violent acts. We must find a way out of this vicious cycle.

The needs of the black community for adequate jobs, housing, and education can be met only by developing a political strategy that will attract a majority of Americans to a program for social change. There are whites who are unemployed and white workers whose real income is steadily decreasing as the cost of living rises. Both these groups share with blacks the desire for increased and upgraded employment opportunities. Let us build a movement with them. There are whites living in substandard housing and paying exorbitant rents. Their children attend schools that are overcrowded and understaffed. They share with blacks the desire for massively funded programs of housing and education. Let us build a movement with them also. And there are those more affluent whites of liberal persuasion who sincerely desire social justice. They too should be our allies.

These are positive points around which a political majority can be built. Such a strategy is the only means by which black people will achieve social and economic equality within the context of contemporary American society. This strategy demands the repudiation of racial separatism which can only isolate Negroes. It demands the rejection of extremism and violence which increase fear and heighten animosities between groups that might otherwise be united.

Black people are enraged because there are social injustices which provoke rage. But if that rage is not expressed politically, if it is not directed toward achieving constructive goals, then it will be self-defeating and ultimately self-destructive. *Let us be enraged about injustice, but let us not be destroyed by it.* Let us act now with forcefulness but restraint, with militancy but wisdom, in the hope of liberating ourselves from rage and injustice and our white brothers from the fear which now enslaves them.

THE ROLE OF THE NEGRO
MIDDLE CLASS

The question of the role of the Negro middle class has been a persistent source of controversy and confusion since the time of Reconstruction. There have been some who have castigated this class and others who have glorified it, but few have been able to treat the subject with the objectivity they could call forth in discussing any other middle-class racial or ethnic group in America.

I think the confusion results from the fact that the Negro middle class behaves in a way that is characteristically middle class but uniquely Negro. The sociological distinction I am drawing between class and race is essential to a full understanding of the problem. But unfortunately it is a distinction rarely made, with the result that we are burdened with analyses of the Negro middle class that are superficial or misleading.

Some, for example, are asking the Negro to behave as if class were totally unimportant. By ignoring the class factor, they arrive at a sentimental notion of black solidarity if they are apologists for middle-class Negroes; and if they are their critics, they condemn them for deserting their poor black brothers. Both the apologists and the critics in this case fail to understand that there are serious class divisions in the Negro community which must be recognized for what they are. The apologist is blind to these divisions, the critic thinks that they should not exist, and both are bound by the feeling that race—and not class—is the force that motivates group behavior. Therefore they are caught by surprise when the Negro middle class acts in a typically middle-class way, and their response is either to close their eyes to this phenomenon or to become enraged about it. The fact is that conflicts of an economic nature have arisen within each minority group in America. At the turn of the century, for example, relations between the wealthy "lace curtain Irish" and the poor "shanty Irish" were anything but friendly. Moreover, Jewish organizations, which developed as a means of forwarding Jewish life and culture, emerged along class lines. The American Jewish Committee at-

From the *Crisis*, June–July 1969. Reprinted with the permission of the Crisis Publishing Co., Inc.

tracted the very wealthy, the middle classes were drawn to the American Jewish Congress, while the poor joined more orthodox groups.

Further evidence of these class divisions can be found in a pattern of be-havior known as "grasshopping," which describes the residential changes made by individuals during the process of upward mobility. As the poor Jew rose economically, he left the Lower East Side for the Upper West Side and eventually ended up in Scarsdale. And as the head of the Irish family accu-mulated capital he moved out of Hell's Kitchen into what is now Harlem. The Italian worker, when he was upgraded by the emergence of trade unions, left Mulberry Street for a six-room house in Queens. It is little won-der that the Negro should act similarly. The process of economic mobility, which carried him from Harlem to Jamaica and eventually to St. Albans, should not be ignored or condemned so much as analyzed as a sociological reality.

While it is true that this social process has created a distance between middle-class and lower-class Negroes, it has also enabled the former to be of great assistance to the latter. I am referring not only to the historical fact that it was middle-class Negroes who founded the universities, schools, churches, and newspapers which have helped unify and uplift all black people. I am also speaking of the political role they have played in the Negro struggle for equality.

Here again Negroes do not differ substantially from other groups. In times of cultural and political revolution, the money, the energy, and the leadership for a forward social thrust are provided by the class that is better off, in the in-terests of the poor. This has been true of independence movements in Africa and the West Indies and of the struggle for the extension of democracy in Latin America. It was also true of the American and French revolutions in the eighteenth century and, more recently, of the Russian and Chinese revolutions. And, finally, it is true all over the world today in coun-tries where there are minorities who have suffered from discrimination. This includes the untouchables in India, the French Canadians in Canada, the Walloons in Belgium, and the Welsh and the Scotch in the United Kingdom.

And it is true of the Negro movement in America. It was the predom-inantly middle-class NAACP that won all the great legal battles which gave rise to the period of protest and sit-ins. The greatest protestor of all was Martin Luther King, Jr., who came from the privileged upper middle class of Atlanta. Even the young SNCC people, who dramatized and accelerated the sit-ins and helped establish a high degree of political freedom in Mississippi, were children of middle-class parents.

Moreover, it was middle-class Negroes who provided the leadership and the initiative for the black struggle during its very early stages. Leaders like Frederick Douglass, W. E. B. Du Bois, and A. Philip Randolph were all men of immense learning. Their profound social vision was the result of long hours of study and reflection, which required certain advantages that have been denied the most brutalized segments of the black community.

We are thus dealing with a paradox. Those blacks who are most exploited are often least inclined to engage in political protest, while the greatest revolutionaries emerge from the wealthier classes and would thus seem to have least reason to revolt. I am aware that there are exceptions to this rule—that there were many slave revolts and that in our own time oppressed masses of black people have engaged in violent protest. Yet these protests have tended to be more spontaneous expressions of despair and frustration than disciplined political movements for social justice.

The psychological dynamic at work here is that oppression leads to despair, which will manifest itself in apathetic inactivity or sporadic outbursts of undirected rage. A more advantageous social condition, on the other hand, leads to hope and, therefore, to activity designed to improve one's situation. In his magnificent autobiography, Frederick Douglass recounts his transfer from an evil master to a relatively good one and the psychological effect this had upon him:

> The freedom from bodily torture and unceasing labor had given my mind an increased sensibility and imparted to it greater activity. . . . Beat and cuff the slave, keep him hungry and spiritless, and he will follow the chain of his master like a dog, but feed and clothe him well, work him moderately and surround him with physical comfort, and dreams of freedom will intrude. Give him a bad master and he aspires to a good master; give him a good master, and he wishes to become his own master. Such is human nature. You may hurl a man so low beneath the level of his kind, that he loses all just ideas of his natural position, but elevate him a little, and the clear conception of rights rises to life and power, and leads him onward.

While those who are better off are thus in a position to lead a social struggle, it is of course true that they do not always wish to do so. Their interest in their own welfare may cause them to exploit the lower classes or totally ignore their plight. Moreover, for reasons of status they may often try to dissociate themselves completely from those below them.

This is again a universal phenomenon, but it applies to middle-class Negroes in a unique way *because they are Negroes*. For example, they are in a weaker position in relation to the whole society than is the white middle-class, because of the historic exploitation of black people in this country. They have less capital than whites of the same class, and they have been adversely affected by segregated institutions, particularly in the fields of education and employment. Yet at the same time they are far more advantaged than the Negro lower class, which has suffered even greater damage from the evils of slavery and discrimination.

The middle-class Negro, therefore—trapped between privileged whites above him and exploited blacks below him—finds himself in a difficult and frustrating position. He does not have the full status attributable to him by virtue of his class, and he suffers from the indignities that have been committed against his race. Denied full access to the wider society, he has been forced to achieve wealth and status within a segregated context—and this has not been easy. Although the situation of the Negro middle class has changed appreciably since 1939, when E. Franklin Frazier wrote *The Negro Family in the United States*, his analysis sheds light even today on the hardships which segregation has caused middle-class blacks, and on the sometimes questionable activities which, out of their frustration, they have resorted to:

> . . . behind the walls of racial segregation, where they enjoy a sheltered and relatively secure position in relation to the lower economic classes, they look with misgivings upon a world where they must compete with whites for a position in the economic order and struggle for status. Hence much of their racial pride is bound up with their desire to monopolize the Negro market. They prefer the overevaluation of their achievements and position behind the walls of segregation to a democratic order that would result in economic and social devaluation for themselves.

This is, of course, not to say that the Negro middle class *in general* is guilty of the faults which Frazier has analyzed, but rather that the evil of segregation has made possible a situation in which some middle-class Negroes have been forced to seek economic and social advantage to the detriment of their poorer black brothers.

The gains made by the civil rights movement have substantially altered the conditions underlying the relationship of middle-class to lower-class blacks. As the struggle for equality continues the process of black liberation, the need of middle-class blacks to accumulate wealth within a segregated context should be reduced. And as the walls of segregation are broken down, there will be more healthy interaction between the races, which should enhance the development of a genuine sense of identity among middle-class Negroes. They will, therefore, no longer need the protection of segregation to insure a false sense of status.

But of course there are still problems. Today many blacks with master's degrees and Ph.D.'s cannot find employment that satisfies their aspirations. They rightly desire the same opportunities that whites of equal qualifications now have open to them. But because segregation and discrimination still exist, they are frustrated in their drive for advancement. Without a full outlet for their aspirations in the wider society, they are seeking to monopolize the avenues of advancement within the ghetto and are thus calling for all-black schools with black teachers and supervisors, black capitalism, and other forms of racial separatism. According to social psychologist Thomas F. Petti-grew, a study completed in 1968 shows that "college graduates tended to be the more separatist in those realms where their training gives them a vested interest in competition-free positions—Negro-owned stores for Negro neighborhoods and Negro teachers in mostly-Negro schools."

While some middle-class blacks may derive moderate economic benefits from this kind of separation, I doubt that they shall find total self-fulfillment. The ghetto does not have the economic resources sufficient to satisfy their demands, and they cannot achieve the status they desire if they avoid the challenges of free and open competition with the wider society. They may find temporary comfort in the ghetto, but ultimately confidence and self-realization come from leaving a protective environment, not by retreating into it.

The demand for black power made by many of these Negroes is, therefore, a demand for *black middle-class power,* and I fear that even if they achieve their goal it will not enhance the economic and political power of the lower- and working-class blacks. It is this latter group, however, that is most deprived and most numerous. Consequently, the energies of the black struggle for equality must be concentrated above all on improving its lot.

If these poor black people are to be uplifted we need an economic package —a comprehensive program designed to achieve full employment, a minimum wage, and a guaranteed income. In addition, our cities must be reconstructed; millions of new homes must be built so that people will no longer be forced to live in deteriorated housing. Funds must be provided so that each child can receive the superior education to which he is by rights entitled. And we must also have free medical care so that, among other things, the infant mortality rate among Negroes does not continue at its present catastrophic level.

It is obvious that an increase in black businesses or in the number of managerial positions open to Negroes will not bring us any nearer to the economic program I have described. The achievement of such an economic program will require a strong political movement, one which does not exist today.

It requires building a coalition of Negroes, the trade union movement, and liberals who together would constitute a political majority in America.

This coalition cannot sustain the loss or decimation of any of its component parts without suffering irreparable damage. It is here that the role of middle-class Negroes becomes so essential, for they must provide the leadership that will help make the black community a powerful element in this majority movement. The central question, therefore, is not so much whether these Negroes remain in the ghetto, but whether they will join in doing those things that will uplift the black poor.

Finally, in struggling for a program of integration and equality for poor black people, the Negro midde class will find that it has benefited itself as well. For the segregation of the black community will lead to the isolation of the black middle class, and the impoverishment of masses of Negroes will ultimately affect the conditions under which all Negroes must live. The primary role of middle-class blacks, therefore, is within a political movement for social justice. And by participating in the struggle to uplift their impoverished brothers, they will find their identity and become liberated as human beings.

NATURE, NURTURE, OR NONSENSE?

What is intelligence? How is it produced? And how can it be measured? These are questions of special interest to social scientists whose job it is to try to provide us with precise, quantifiable answers. They are also of general interest to all who are curious about the nature of human development. Historically, the debate has been between those who believe that the most important factor determining an individual's intelligence is his natural, genetic endowment and those who emphasize the supreme importance of environmental factors such as social class, family rearing, and the quality of schooling.

This nature-nurture debate is no doubt intellectually stimulating, and social scientists will continue to publish studies defending one side or the other. But there are times when the debate takes on an ugly racial character. One race is claimed to be inherently superior (Hitler's "Aryans," for example) or another is "proven" to be inherently inferior. I do not think it at all coincidental that in America such theories tend to appear during periods of intense racial conflict. Around the turn of the century, when the legal structure of segregation was being solidified in the South, numerous "studies" appeared, such as Robert W. Shufeldt's *The Negro: A Menace to American Civilization*, which rationalized popular racist attitudes. Today, when the consciousness of racial distinctions is unusually intense and racial antagonism is growing in the society, the same question is once again being debated: whether Negroes are inherently inferior to whites.

The focus of the debate is a study by Arthur Jensen which appeared in the *Harvard Educational Review* in 1968. It purported to prove, on the basis of IQ test scores, that intelligence and the ability to reason abstractly are overwhelmingly determined by genetic factors, and that blacks have less intelligence than whites. The study has aroused a furor, and justifiably so. Its conclusion violates the faith—shared by men of good will—in the possibility of a democratic, *racially equal* society. Worse, it provides grist for the bigot's mill. But what seems essential at the present time is less indignant emotion and more critical thought.

From the *New York Amsterdam News*, October 9, 1969.

In discussing the Jensen report, we must clearly distinguish between its intellectual legitimacy and its political effect. If Jensen is correct, we must accept his conclusions whether we like them or not. But I do not think he is correct. His study is based on IQ test scores, not on genetic data, and nobody has ever proved that IQ measures intelligence. (One person has sarcastically written that it measures only IQ.) True, the IQ measures the ability of a child to take an IQ test, but this ability depends upon the successful *learning* of certain psychological processes. Jensen assumes that all American children have an equal opportunity to learn these processes, but this assumption fails to take into consideration the terribly unequal *environmental* conditions under which children—particularly black and white children—are reared in America. IQ does, to a degree, predict achievement in school, but this may well be more an indication that children are treated according to their IQ, and produce what is expected of them, than that their achievement is genetically determined.

The psychologist Benjamin Bloom has responded to Jensen by pointing out the IQ scores of children living under the equal conditions of an Israeli kibbutz. There Jewish children of European origin, who normally have an IQ of 105, have a tested IQ of 115. Jewish children of Middle Eastern origin, who normally have an IQ of 85, also have a tested IQ of 115. Jensen does not consider this kind of data. Most of his conclusions are based on studies of identical twins with common genes who, reared apart in different families, still have fairly similar IQ scores. But even so, one-sixth of this group of identical twins have IQ's differing as much (fifteen points) as those of blacks and whites. Since the twins' genes are the same, this difference is entirely due to environment. I do not think it is too much to assume that the radically unequal conditions under which blacks and whites live might produce a similar difference in IQ.

Christopher Jencks, a social scientist, has argued persuasively in *The New Republic* that Jensen does not substantiate his claim that the IQ differences between blacks and whites are genetically determined. Jencks concludes that "Jensen's decision to reopen this ancient controversy without first gathering more evidence strikes me as a serious political blunder." Indeed it is, for whatever Jensen's intent in writing his report (and I doubt that it was racist), its effect has been to offend black people profoundly and to provide bigoted white people with a new argument with which to defend their racist beliefs and actions.

My own feeling is that the Jensen study is irrelevant and that we should dismiss it entirely. It is irrelevant because it tells us nothing we can believe and contributes nothing to our struggle for social equality. Rather than quibble over a study which suggests the permanence of inequality, we must work to change those social and economic conditions which have determined the nature of Jensen's conclusions. If we can change these conditions, not only can we make life livable for black people in America, but we can provide social scientists with new data to refute the theory of inherent racial inequality.

AN EXCHANGE WITH DANIEL MOYNIHAN AND THOMAS A. BILLINGS

August 12, 1969

Mr. Daniel P. Moynihan
Assistant to the President
The White House
Washington, D.C.

Dear Pat:

Enclosed is an "Open Letter" to me written by Thomas A. Billings, the Director of Upward Bound, and my reply. I have requested that he send my letter to the Upward Bound Project Directors and Consultants who have also received his original letter.

Best,
BAYARD RUSTIN
Executive Director
A. Philip Randolph Institute

June 16, 1969

To: Upward Bound Project Directors and Consultants

From: Thomas A. Billings, Director, Project Upward Bound

AN OPEN LETTER TO BAYARD RUSTIN

As a long-time admirer of yours, I am hesitant about challenging any of your remarks regarding the needs and aspirations of black youth in Amer-

From *The New Leader*, December 22, 1969. Reprinted with permission. Copyright © 1969 by The American Labor Conference on International Affairs.

ica. Certainly you should know more about those needs and aspirations than I do. A white man half your age should probably remain silent when you speak on racial matters.

But your recent remarks regarding "soul courses" and the "real world" went infinitely beyond mere instruction to black youth. Your remarks, among other things, strike at the very heart of "liberal education." Since I am persuaded that our current national tragedy reflects the eclipse of "liberal learning" and the bankruptcy of liberal knowledge in the nation, I am compelled to radically disagree with you about (1) the value of "soul courses" and, (2) their relevance to the "real world."

Because I want you to understand what I hope to say about the "real world," Mr. Rustin, I will avoid most of the technical language of philosophy normally connected with discussions of this sort. Part of our problem nowadays stems from our careless use of language on the one hand, and our use of pseudo-technical language on the other hand.

But before I get into a conversation with you about the "real world," Mr. Rustin, let me point out that there have been three great problems— or questions—or branches of philosophy. The three great questions have been: What is real? What is true? What is good? These remarkably durable human questions have given rise to three great areas of human inquiry. Generally, questions about "reality" fall to the *ontologists* for response. The scientific method is a natural outgrowth of man's concern for the "real world"; both the soft and hard sciences are stalwarts in the house of ontology.

Questions about "truth" gave rise to *epistemology* or, put another way, to that branch of philosophy which explores human comprehension of "the real," an inquiry into how man learns about "the real." Commonly, philosophy 101 attempts to reveal the complex and intimate relationship between "the real" and "the true." Let me assure you, epistemology is a veritable minefield of ancillary questions: If real, is it also true? Can something be true, but not real? Aren't reality and truth one? Is reality general, objective, and universal or is it specific, subjective, and particular? If you remove the human subject, does reality have "meaning"? If so, to whom? If not, does the "real world" depend upon human interpretation? Is the "real world" an invention or a discovery? Is the world of "ought" as "real" as the world of "is"? Is an idea "real"? As "real" as a rock? Are there modes of "reality"? Was Martin Luther King's dream real? Are social "realities" immutably decreed by the gods, or are they products of human imagination, hence subject to human revision?

The third great question—What is good?—gave rise to *ethics*, the consideration of human (interpersonal) relationships. The profound questions of "good" and "evil" appear here, inextricably bound up with questions about the "real" and the "true," that is, bound up with ontology and epistemology.

For at least 5,000 years, Mr. Rustin, men on this planet have been grappling with these great prime questions. I was startled, therefore, by the suddenness with which you closed out the dialogue and bolted the door of inquiry and revision. Obviously, at last we have it: "X has no meaning in the 'real world.' " What else, Mr. Rustin, beyond "soul courses," have [sic] "no meaning in the real world"? Is it possible that *souls* have no place in the "real world"? Are all the attributes and delights of the human soul equally untenable in "the real world"? What would nurture a *soul*, Mr. Rustin, but soul courses, *i.e.*, instruction? What place has poetry in your "real world," Mr. Rustin—or art or dance or drama? Aren't "soul courses," now urged by black youth, only a combination of the art, poetry, music, and literature of black people cast in the mold of the American black experience? Isn't that art and that poetry and that music and that literature "real" and hasn't the black experience in America been "real"? Isn't all poetry and all art and all music and all literature only the expression of a people's life experience whether it's the art and poetry and music and literature of American blacks or the art, poetry, music and literature of American Celts, Buriat Mongolians, Berber Tribesmen, Basque Shepherds, Mexican Villagers, Catholic Bavarians, Irish Republicans, Vietnamese Nationals, Buddhist Monks, Japanese Fishermen, Islandic Eskimos, Javanese Mountainmen, or Suburban Anglo-Saxon Executives?

Or is the "real world" only the world—objective and subjective—which the American marketing-military-industrial Establishment has fashioned? I think that I could agree with you that "soul courses" aren't going to be worth a dime in that world. But, Mr. Rustin, is that the "real world"? If so, is it at the same time "true" and "good"? If it is not true and good, do you suppose "soul courses" would help it become not only "real," but "true" and "good," or is it possible that truth and goodness have no meaning in the "real world"? My God, has it really come to that?

How long has it been, Mr. Rustin, since you took a long, hard look at the curriculum in the schools of America? What sense of pride, of cultural legacy, of self-confidence accrues to a Chicano child after twelve years in the public schools of El Paso, Texas? What sense of pride, of cultural legacy, of self-confidence accrues to a North Cheyenne child after twelve years in the public schools of Billings, Montana? What sense of pride, of cultural legacy, of self-confidence accrues to a black child after twelve years in the public schools of Montgomery, Alabama or Shreveport, Louisiana? What is the effect on a child's spirit when he finds that the language spoken in his home, the language of his mother's lullabies and his father's pride, is illegal, not the language spoken in the "real world"? What is the effect on a child's spirit when the sounds and sights and loves and hopes of his little world are systematically excluded from the "real world"? What mangling of the spirit must come, what breakage of the heart must follow the "realization," i.e., the desperate assimilation into the "real world" of these troubled centers of little worlds? Or worse, what rage must follow these violations of the little worlds of Ben Hernandez and John Has-Many-Horses and Joyce Lee and Johnny Old-Coyote?

If I understand anything about American youths it is that many of them are deeply unhappy about the "real world"; they are not at all sure that it is the world in which they want to live and work. Many of them—and God bless them for it—long for a better world, a more responsible world, a more humane world, a world in which the tears of children are as "real" as the rock of Gibraltar and ever much more alarming than the dips in the Dow-Jones Industrial Average. Most of them want desperately to believe in the human capacities of labor and intelligence and compassion. Most of them are sick to death of political chicanery, racial bigotry, religious hypocrisy, international looting and piracy disguised as the "national interest." Most of them are just tired of the champagne music of Lawrence Welk and the silly charade of manliness staged by America's business elite. It's this world, Mr. Rustin, that our young people are saying must go! The "real world"? Alas, of course it is! But not forever! Our young are part of the "real world," too, Mr. Rustin, as real as General Motors and Wall Street and Howard Hughes and American Airlines and Richard Nixon and J. Edgar Hoover and the United Fruit Company. And their hopes are real, and their dreams and tears. And their anger!

A last point. Technical skill is always an important thing to have. *Techne* —or "know-how," while highly prized among the Greeks, was rarely confused with either knowledge (*gnosis*)—or wisdom (*sophia*), both of which were infinitely more valuable than techne. *Techne* was techne—craftsmanship, skill, technique, an important attribute in the workaday world. But the Greek world was more than the workaday world. It included art and poetry and drama; indeed, much of the world's great soul food. Only among slaves was the workaday world the whole world, the "real world." For you not to know this would be an unbearable irony, Mr. Rustin, and a tragic paradox.

August 12, 1969

Mr. Thomas A. Billings
Director, Project Upward Bound
Office of Economic Opportunity
Washington, D.C. 20506

Dear Mr. Billings:

I found your open letter to me opposing my position on separatist black studies very interesting—not for anything it had to say about black studies or higher education, but for what it revealed about your own dilemma and, by extension, the dilemma of other similarly situated white liberals.

You are convinced "that our current national tragedy reflects the eclipse of 'liberal learning' and the bankruptcy of liberal knowledge in the nation. . . ." Since you are a liberal, I think this remark betrays an exquisite form of self-contempt, a self-contempt that is not entirely unrelated to the extraordinary guilt with which liberals like yourself are reacting to our racial crisis. If liberalism is bankrupt and in decline as you maintain, if it lacks any revitalizing tradition and system of values, then it follows that liberals must look beyond themselves for a new world view, a new source of vitality. They must look figuratively to the East, to African and Asiatic culture, which has always represented in Western consciousness the subjective urges of man, that which is primitive, irrational, vital; that, in other words, which they have repressed. And in America, alas, they look toward the Negro. Drawing unwittingly upon our country's racist heritage, they place the Negro in the role of the natural man come to revive the juices of white civilization.

A second aspect to the problem is relevant here. There is a psychological phenomenon occurring today among increasing numbers of affluent highly-educated Americans like yourself that has been variously described as anomie, alienation, identity crisis. These people suffer from a sense of dislocation and dispossession which has given rise to a political orientation that Arnold Toynbee has called "subjective proletarianism." It is a romantic form of politics rooted in guilt, acutely sensitive to problems concerning individuality and identity, and characterized by a peculiar combination of self-deprecation and snobbish patronization. Thus it is not surprising that this *lumpen* intelligentsia would react with unusual enthusiasm to the position of black nationalists, would romanticize their demands for separatism and self-determination, and would identify these demands as the position of the "black community," when, in fact, they represent the views of a small minority of Negroes. Negroes have been used and exploited in many ways by white Americans, but it is only recently that they have been asked to satisfy the masochistic craving of disenchanted liberals for flagellation and rejection.

Let me be quite explicit. There is today a legitimate and heated debate going on within the Negro community between separatists and integrationists. It is not a new debate, but one that has recurred repeatedly in the history of black Americans, particularly during periods of political reaction when many Negroes, out of despair, want to withdraw from the mainstream of our society. You are certainly free to take sides in this debate, even if in the process you must patronizingly indicate to Negroes their need for a "sense of pride, of cultural legacy, of self-confidence." I should think that you are far more lacking in these qualities, for you have nothing but disdain for your own cultural and intellectual tradition.

Let me remind you that my position in this debate derives from my experience as a black man in America (not as a "Suburban Anglo-Saxon Executive"), from my knowledge that separatism historically and presently for Negroes has been indistinguishable from inequality, exploitation, and poverty, and that despite all the romantic rhetoric used to make it appear respectable, separatism shall continue to be immoral and degrading. It was not out of any failure to perceive the nature of the "real world" that I spent twenty-eight months in a federal penitentiary for my pacifist beliefs, or thirty days on a chain-gang in North Carolina for trying to integrate a bus, or that I was arrested on twenty-one other occasions for opposing injustice. One can be aware that "the tears of children are as 'real' as the rock of Gibraltar" without indulging in sentimentality and self-righteousness.

Despite your entreaties, I shall continue to advocate those means by which Negroes can obtain the educational skills, as well as the political and economic power, that will enable them to achieve equality *within* the context of American society. And I shall oppose those strategies, whether motivated out of the desire to oppress or to patronize, which can only perpetuate and compound the injustices committed against black people in this nation.

I trust you will send my reply to all the Upward Bound project directors and consultants.

Sincerely,
BAYARD RUSTIN
Executive Director
A. Philip Randolph Institute

September 30, 1969

Mr. Bayard Rustin
Executive Director
A. Philip Randolph Institute
260 Park Avenue South
New York, N.Y. 10010

Dear Bayard:

I enclose a letter being sent to all Upward Bound directors and consultants by Mr. [Donald] Rumsfeld. This is, of course, in response to your letter to me of August 12 reporting the incredible and intolerable behavior of the former director of Upward Bound, and enclosing a reply by you to the attack which he had addressed to that group. Mr. Rumsfeld's letter will distribute your reply to all those who received the original letter from Billings.

In the nature of the situation this is, I suppose, all that can be done. An outrageous charge has been made and distributed, a reply is distributed in return. However, you and I know that the exchange is rarely an equal one. It is clear to me that you have been done an intolerable injury by an official of the United States government. I have established that Mr. Billings' letter is dated a day after his resignation from the government, and that it was sent without the knowledge of his superiors in the Office of Economic Opportunity. (Mr. Billings became deputy project manager of the Upward Bound Program in April 1967 and shortly thereafter became project manager, which post he left on June 15, 1969, on the occasion of the transfer of the program from OEO to HEW.) The fact remains that a government official, on stationery of the Executive Office of the President, directed an extended personal attack against a private citizen because of views expressed by that citizen on public issues. The letter was written and mailed at government expense, and sent to persons who in one form or another are recipients of public monies disbursed by the same public official.

As you will be the first to agree, the injury done you has nothing to do with the rightness or wrongness of your views. The issue is the intimidation by government of a private citizen because of his holding disapproved opinions.

This is the essence of thought control in a totalitarian state. Those who express thoughts disapproved of by those who control the government machinery are vilified and defamed; others who might be so tempted are warned of the consequences in the most vulgar terms. "You, too, can get in trouble."

286

I do not know which development appalls me more: that Billings sent the letter, or that no Project Upward director has apparently seen fit to protest it. Have Americans become so accustomed to seeing government abusing the rights of individuals and intimidating the recipients of government benefactions? I recall from my youth the observation that if fascism should ever come to the United States it would be in the guise of anti-fascism. I very much fear we see the tendency in this squalid enterprise.

Mr. Billings was clearly not appointed by this administration. His letter is as disrespectful to President Nixon as it is libelous of you. No persons of responsibility in the present administration even knew of the letter. But that, of course, is small consolation.

It should be clear from my letter how much I have been troubled by this event. If you should for any reason wish to make my letter public, do not hesitate to do so.

Sincerely,
DANIEL P. MOYNIHAN
Assistant to the President

4
1970-71

THE FAILURE OF BLACK SEPARATISM

We are living in an age of revolution—or so they tell us. The children of the affluent classes pay homage to their parents' values by rejecting them; this, they say, is a youth revolution. The discussion and display of sexuality increases—actors disrobe on stage, young women very nearly do on the street—and so we are in the midst of a sexual revolution. Tastes in music and clothing change, and each new fashion too is revolutionary. With every new social phenomenon now being dubbed a "revolution," the term has in fact become nothing more than a slogan which serves to take our minds off an unpleasant reality. For if we were not careful, we might easily forget that there is a conservative in the White House, that our country is racially polarized as never before, and that the forces of liberalism are in disarray. Whatever there is of revolution today, in any meaningful sense of the term, is coming from the right.

But we are also told—and with far greater urgency and frequency—that there is a black revolution. If by revolution we mean a radical escalation of black aspirations and demands, this is surely the case. There is a new assertion of pride in the Negro race and its cultural heritage, and although the past summer was marked by the lack of any major disruptions, there is among blacks a tendency more pronounced than at any time in Negro history to engage in violence and the rhetoric of violence. Yet if we look closely at the situation of Negroes today, we find that there has been not the least revolutionary reallocation of political or economic power. There is, to be sure, an increase in the number of black elected officials throughout the United States and particularly in the South, but this has largely been the result of the 1965 Voting Rights Act, which was passed before the "revolution" reached its height and the renewal of which the present administration has not advocated with any noticeable enthusiasm. Some reallocation of political power has indeed taken place since the presidential election of 1964, but generally its beneficiaries have been the Republicans and the anti-Negro forces. Nor does this particular trend show much sign of abating. Nixon's attempt to reverse the liberal direction of the Supreme Court has

---

From *Harper's Magazine*, January 1970.

just begun. Moreover, in the 1970 Senate elections, 25 of the 34 seats to be contested were originally won by the Democrats in the great liberal surge of 1964, when the political picture was quite different from that of today. And if the Democrats only break even in 1970, the Republicans will control the Senate for the first time since 1954. A major defeat would leave the Democrats weaker than they have been at any time since the conservative days of the 1920's.

There has been, it is true, some moderate improvement in the economic condition of Negroes, but by no stretch of the imagination could it be called revolutionary. According to Andrew Brimmer of the Federal Reserve System, the median family income of Negroes between 1965 and 1967 rose from 54 per cent to 59 per cent of that for white families. Much of that gain reflected a decrease in the rate of Negro unemployment. But between February and June of 1969, Negro unemployment rose again by 1.3 per cent and should continue to rise as Nixon presses his crusade against inflation. The Council of Economic Advisers reports that in the past eight years the federal government has spent $10.3 billion on metropolitan problems while it has spent $39.9 billion on agriculture, not to mention, of course, $507.2 billion for defense. In the area of housing, for instance, New York City needs at the present time as many new subsidized apartments—780,000— as the federal housing program has constructed *nationally* in its entire thirty-four years. The appropriations for model cities, rent supplements, the Job Corps, the Neighborhood Youth Corps, and other programs have been drastically reduced, and the Office of Economic Opportunity is being transformed into a research agency. Nixon's welfare and revenue-sharing proposals, in addition to being economically stringent, so that they will have little or no effect on the condition of the Northern urban poor, are politically and philosophically conservative.

Any appearance that we are in the grip of a black revolution, then, is deceptive. The problem is not whether black aspirations are outpacing America's ability to respond but whether they have outpaced her willingness to do so. Lately it has been taken almost as axiomatic that with every increase in Negro demands, there must be a corresponding intensification of white resistance. This proposition implies that only black complacency can prevent racial polarization, that any political action by Negroes must of necessity produce a reaction. But such a notion ignores entirely the question of what *kind* of political action, guided by what *kind* of political strategy. One can almost assert as a law of American politics that if Negroes engage in violence as a tactic they will be met with repression, that if they follow a strategy of racial separatism they will be isolated, and that if they engage in anti-democratic activity, out of the deluded wish to skirt the democratic process, they will provoke a reaction. To the misguided, violence, separatism, and minority ultimatums may seem revolutionary, but in reality they issue only from the desperate strivings of the impotent. Certainly such tactics are not designed to enhance the achievement of progressive social change. Recent American political history has proved this point time and again with brutal clarity.

The irony of the revolutionary rhetoric uttered in behalf of Negroes is that it has helped in fact to promote conservatism. On the other hand, of course, the reverse is also true: the failure of America to respond to the demands of Negroes has fostered in the minds of the latter a sense of futility and has thus seemed to legitimize a strategy of withdrawal and violence. Other things have been operating as well. The fifteen years since *Brown vs. Topeka* have been for Negroes a period of enormous dislocation. The modernization of farming in the South forced hundreds of thousands of Negroes to migrate to the North where they were confronted by a second technological affliction, automation. Without jobs, living in cities equipped to serve neither their material nor spiritual needs, these modern-day immigrants responded to their brutal new world with despair and hostility. The civil rights movement created an even more fundamental social dislocation, for it destroyed not simply the legal structure of segregation but also the psychological assumptions of racism. Young Negroes who matured during this period witnessed a basic challenge to the system of values and social relations which had presumed the inferiority of the Negro. They have totally rejected this system, but in doing so have often substituted for it an exaggerated and distorted perception both of themselves and of the society. As if to obliterate the trace of racial shame that might be lurking in their souls they have embraced racial chauvinism. And as if in reply to past exclusions (and often in response to present insecurities), they have created their own patterns of exclusiveness.

The various frustrations and upheavals experienced recently by the Negro community account in large part for the present political orientation of some of its most vocal members: seeing their immediate self-interest more in the terms of emotional release than in those of economic and political advancement. One is supposed to think black, dress black, eat black, and buy black without reference to the question of what such a program actually contributes to advancing the cause of social justice. Since real victories are thought to be unattainable, issues become important in so far as they can provide symbolic victories. Dramatic confrontations are staged which serve as outlets for radical energy but which in no way further the achievement of radical social goals. So that, for instance, members of the black community are mobilized to pursue the "victory" of halting construction of a state office building in Harlem, even though it is hard to see what actual economic or social benefit will be conferred on the impoverished residents of that community by their success in doing so.

Such actions constitute a politics of escape rooted in hopelessness and further reinforced by government inaction. Deracinated liberals may romanticize this politics, nihilistic new leftists may imitate it, but ordinary Negroes will be the victims of its powerlessness to work any genuine change in their condition.

The call for black power is now over three years old, yet to this day no one knows what black power is supposed to mean and therefore how its proponents are to unite and rally behind it. If one is a member of CORE, black power posits the need for a separate black economy based upon traditional forms of capitalist relations. For SNCC the term refers to a politically united black community. US would emphasize the unity of black culture, while the Black Panthers wish to impose upon black nationalism the philosophies of Marx, Lenin, Stalin, and Chairman Mao. Nor do these exhaust all the possible shades and gradations of meaning. If there is one common theme uniting the various demands for black power, it is simply that blacks must be guided in their actions by a consciousness of themselves as a separate race.

Now, philosophies of racial solidarity have never been unduly concerned with the realities that operate outside the category of race. The adherents of these philosophies are generally romantics, steeped in the traditions of their own particular clans and preoccupied with the simple biological verities of blood and racial survival. Almost invariably their rallying cry is racial self-determination, and they tend to ignore those aspects of the material world which point up divisions within the racially defined group.

But the world of black Americans is full of divisions. Only the most supine of optimists would dream of building a political movement without reference to them. Indeed, nothing better illustrates the existence of such divisions within the black community than the fact that the separatists themselves represent a distinct minority among Negroes. No reliable poll has ever identified more than 15 per cent of Negroes as separatists; usually the percentage is a good deal lower. Nor, as I have already indicated, are the separatists unified among themselves, the differences among them at times being so intense as to lead to violent conflict. The notion of the undifferentiated black community is the intellectual creation both of whites—liberals as well as racists to whom all Negroes are the same—and of certain small groups of blacks who illegitimately claim to speak for the majority.

The fact is that like every other racial or ethnic group in America, Negroes are divided by age, class, and geography. Young Negroes are at least as hostile toward their elders as white new leftists are toward their liberal parents. They are in addition separated by vast gaps in experience, Northern from Southern, urban from rural. And even more profound are the disparities in wealth among them. In contrast to the white community, where the spread of income has in recent years remained unchanged or has narrowed slightly, economic differentials among blacks have increased. In 1965, for example, the wealthiest 5 per cent of white and nonwhite families each received 15.5 per cent of the total income in their respective communities. In 1967, however, the percentage of white income received by the top 5 per cent of white families had dropped to 14.9 per cent while among nonwhites the share of income of the top 5 per cent of the families had risen to 17.5 per cent. This trend probably reflects the new opportunities which are available to black professionals in industry, government, and academia, but have not touched the condition of lower class and lower middle-class Negroes.

To Negroes for whom race is the major criterion, however, divisions by wealth and status are irrelevant. Consider, for instance, the proposals for black economic advancement put forth by the various groups of black nationalists. These proposals are all remarkably similar. For regardless of one's particular persuasion—whether a revolutionary or a cultural nationalist or an unabashed black capitalist—once one confines one's analysis to the ghetto, no proposal can extend beyond a strategy for ghetto development and black enterprise. This explains in part the recent popularity of black capitalism and, to a lesser degree, black cooperatives: once both the economic strategy and goal are defined in terms of black self-determination, there is simply not much else available in the way of ideas.

There are other reasons for the popularity of black capitalism, reasons having to do with material and psychological self-interest. E. Franklin Frazier has written that Negro business is "a social myth" first formulated toward the end of the nineteenth century when the legal structure of segregation was established and Negro hopes for equality destroyed. History has often shown us that oppression can sometimes lead to a rationalization of the unjust conditions on the part of the oppressed and, following this, to an opportunistic competition among them for whatever meager advantages are available. This is, according to Frazier, exactly what happened among American Negroes. The myth of Negro business was created and tied to a belief in the possibility of a separate Negro economy. "Of course," wrote Frazier, "behind the idea of the separate Negro economy is the hope of the black bourgeoisie that they will have the monopoly of the Negro market." He added that they also desire "a privileged status within the isolated Negro community."

Nor are certain Negro businessmen the only ones who stand to gain from a black economy protected by the tariff of separatism. There are also those among the white upper class for whom such an arrangement is at least as beneficial. In the first place, self-help projects for the ghetto, of which black capitalism is but one variety, are inexpensive. They involve no large-scale redistribution of resources, no "inflationary" government expenditures, and, above all, no responsibility on the part of whites. These same upper-class whites may have been major exploiters of black workers in the past, they may have been responsible for policies which helped to create ghetto poverty, but now, under the new dispensations of black separatism, they are being asked to do little more by way of reparation than provide a bit of seed money for a few small ghetto enterprises.

Moreover, a separate black economy appears to offer hope for what Roy Innis has called "a new social contract." According to Innis' theory, the black community is essentially a colony ruled by outsiders; there can be no peace between the colony and the "mother country" until the former is ruled by some of its own. When the colony is finally "liberated" in this way, all conflicts can be resolved through negotiation between the black ruling class and the white ruling class. Any difficulties within the black community, that is, would become the responsibility of the black elite. But since self-determination in the ghetto, necessitating as it would the expansion of a propertied black middle class, offers the advantage of social stability, such difficulties would be minimal. How could many whites fail to grasp the obvious benefit to themselves in a program that promises social peace without the social inconvenience of integration and especially without the burden of a huge expenditure of money? Even if one were to accept the colonial analogy—and it is in many ways an uninformed and extremely foolish one—the strategy implied by it is fatuous and unworkable. Most of the experiments in black capitalism thus far have been total failures, as, given the odds, they will continue to be. For one thing, small businesses owned and run by blacks will, exactly like their white counterparts, suffer a high rate of failure. In fact, they will face even greater problems than white small businesses because they will be operating in predominantly low-income areas where the clientele will be poor, the crime rate and taxes high, and the cost of land, labor, and insurance expensive. They will have to charge higher prices than the large chains, a circumstance against which "Buy Black" campaigns will in the long or even the short run have little force. On the other hand, to create large-scale black industry in the ghetto is unthinkable. The capital is not available, and even if it were, there is no vacant land. In Los Angeles, for example, the area in which four-fifths of the Negroes and Mexican-Americans live contains only 0.5 per cent of all the vacant land in the city, and the problem is similar elsewhere. Overcrowding is severe enough in the ghetto without building up any industry there.

Another current axiom of black self-determination is the necessity for community control. Questions of ideology aside, black community control is as futile a program as black capitalism. Assuming that there were a cohesive, clearly identifiable black community (which, judging by the factionalism in neighborhoods like Harlem and Ocean Hill–Brownsville, is far from a safe assumption), and assuming that the community were empowered to control the ghetto, it would still find itself without the money needed in order to be socially creative. The ghetto would still be faced with the same poverty, deteriorated housing, unemployment, terrible health services, and inferior schools—and this time perhaps with the exacerbation of their being entailed in local struggles for power. Furthermore, the control would ultimately be illusory and would do no more than provide psychological comfort to those who exercise it. For in a complex technological society there is no such thing as an autonomous community within a large metropolitan area. Neighborhoods, particularly poor neighborhoods, will remain dependent upon outside suppliers for manufactured goods, transportation, utilities, and other services. There is, for instance, unemployment in the ghetto while the vast majority of new jobs are being created in the suburbs. If black people are to have access to those jobs, there must be a metropolitan transportation system that can carry them to the suburbs cheaply and quickly. Control over the ghetto cannot build such a system nor can it provide jobs within the ghetto.

The truth of the matter is that community control as an idea is provincial and as a program is extremely conservative. It appears radical to some people because it has become the demand around which the frustrations of the Negro community have coalesced. In terms of its capacity to deal with the social and economic causes of black unrest, however, its potential is strikingly limited. The call for community control in fact represents an adjustment to inequality rather than a protest against it. Fundamentally, it is a demand for a change in the racial composition of the personnel who administer community institutions: that is, for schools, institutions of public and social service, and political organizations—as all of these are presently constituted—to be put into the keeping of a new class of black officials. Thus in a very real sense, the notion of community control bespeaks a fervent hope that the poverty-stricken ghetto, once thought to be a social problem crying for rectification, might now be deemed a social good worthy of acceptance. Hosea Williams of SCLC, speaking once of community control, unwittingly revealed the way in which passionate self-assertion can be a mask for accommodation: "I'm now at the position Booker T. Washington was about sixty or seventy years ago," Williams said. "I say to my brothers, 'Cast down your buckets where you are'—and that means there in the slums and ghettos."

There is indeed profound truth in the observation that people who seek social change will, in the absence of real substantive victories, often seize upon stylistic substitutes as an outlet for their frustrations.

A case in point is the relation of Negroes to the trade union movement. In their study *The Black Worker*, published in 1930, Sterling D. Spero and Abram L. Harris describe the resistance to separatism among economically satisfied workers during the heyday of Marcus Garvey:

> . . . spokesmen of the Garvey movement went among the faction-torn workers preaching the doctrine of race consciousness. Despite the fact that Garveyism won a following everywhere at this time, the Negro longshoremen of Philadelphia were deaf to its pleas, for their labor movement had won them industrial equality such as colored workers nowhere else in the industry enjoyed.

The inverse relation of black separatism and anti-unionism to the quality of employment available to Negroes holds true today also. In the May 1969 UAW elections, for example, black candidates won the presidency and vice-presidency of a number of locals. Some of the most interesting election victories were won at the Chrysler Eldon Gear and Axle Local 961 and at Dodge #3 in Hamtramck where the separatist Eldon Revolutionary Union Movement (ELRUM) and Dodge Revolutionary Union Movement (DRUM) have been active. At both locals the DRUM and ELRUM candidates were handily defeated by black trade unionists who campaigned on a program of militant integrationism and economic justice.

This is not to say that there are not problems within the unions which have given impetus to the separatist movements. There are, but in the past decade unions have taken significant steps toward eliminating discrimination against Negroes. As Peter Henle, the chief economist of the Bureau of Labor Statistics, has observed:

> Action has been taken to eliminate barriers to admission, abolish discrimination in hiring practices, and negotiate changes in senior-

ity arrangements which had been blocking Negro advances to higher-paying jobs. At the same time, unions have given strong support to governmental efforts in this same direction.

Certainly a good deal is left to be done in this regard, but just as certainly the only effective pressure on the unions is that which can be brought by blacks pressing for a greater role *within* the trade union movement. Not only is separatism not a feasible program, but its major effect will be to injure black workers economically by undermining the strength of the union. It is here that ignorance of the economic dimension of racial injustice is most dangerous, for a Negro, whether he be labeled a moderate or a militant, has but two alternatives open to him. If he defines the problem as primarily one of race, he will inevitably find himself the ally of the white capitalist against the white worker. But if, though always conscious of the play of racial discrimination, he defines the problem as one of poverty, he will be aligned with the white worker against management. If he chooses the former alternative, he will become no more than a pawn in the game of divide-and-conquer played by, and for the benefit of, management—the result of which will hardly be self-determination but rather the depression of wages for all workers. This path was followed by the "moderate" Booker T. Washington who disliked unions because they were "founded on a sort of enmity to the man by whom he [the Negro] is employed" and by the "militant" Marcus Garvey who wrote:

> It seems strange and a paradox, but the only convenient friend the Negro worker or laborer has in America at the present time is the white capitalist. The capitalist being selfish—seeking only the largest profit out of labor—is willing and glad to use Negro labor wherever possible on a scale reasonably below the standard union wage . . . but if the Negro unionizes himself to the level of the white worker, the choice and preference of employment is given to the white worker.

And it is being followed today by CORE, which collaborated with the National Right to Work Committee in setting up the Black Workers Alliance.

If the Negro chooses to follow the path of interracial alliances on the basis of class, as almost two million have done today, he can achieve a certain degree of economic dignity, which in turn offers a genuine, if not the only, opportunity for self-determination. It was this course which A. Philip Randolph chose in his long struggle to build a Negro-labor alliance, and it was also chosen by the black sanitation workers of Memphis, Tennessee, and the black hospital workers of Charleston, South Carolina.

Not that I mean here to exonerate the unions of their responsibility for discrimination. Nevertheless, it is essential to deal with the situation of the black worker in terms of American economic reality. And as long as the structure of this reality is determined by the competing institutions of capital and labor (or government and labor, as in the growing public sector of the economy), Negroes must place themselves on one side or the other. The idea of racial self-determination within this context is a delusion.

There are, to be sure, sources beyond that of economic discrimination for black separatism within the unions. DRUM, ELRUM, and similar groups are composed primarily of young Negroes who, like whites their age, are not as loyal to the union as are older members, and who are also affected by the new militancy which is now pervasive among black youth generally. This militancy has today found its most potent form of expression on campus, particularly in the predominantly white universities outside the South. The confusion which the movement for programs in black studies has created on campus almost defies description. The extremes in absurdity were reached this past academic year at Cornell, where, on the one hand, enraged black students were demanding a program in black studies which included Course 300c, Physical Education: "Theory and practice in the use of small arms and combat. Discussion sessions in the proper use of force," and where, on the other hand, a masochistic and pusillanimous university president placed his airplane at the disposal of two black students so that they could go to New York City and purchase, with $2,000 in university funds, some bongo drums for Malcolm X Day. The foolishness of the students was surpassed only by the public relations manipulativeness of the president.

The real tragedy of the dispute over black studies is that whatever truly creative opportunities such a program could offer have been either ignored or destroyed. There is, first, the opportunity for a vastly expanded scholastic inquiry into the contribution of Negroes to the American experience. The history of the black man in America has been scandalously distorted in the past, and as a field of study it has been relegated to a second-class status, isolated from the main themes of American history and omitted in the historical education of American youth. Yet now black students are preparing to repeat the errors of their white predecessors. They are proposing to study black history in isolation from the mainstream of American history; they are demanding separate black studies programs that will not be open to whites, who could benefit at least as much as they from a knowledge of Negro history; and they hope to permit only blacks (and perhaps some whites who toe the line) to teach in these programs. Unwittingly they are conceding

300

what racist whites all along have professed to believe, namely, that black history is irrelevant to American history.

In other ways black students have displayed contempt for black studies as an academic discipline. Many of them, in fact, view black studies as not an academic subject at all, but as an ideological and political one. They propose to use black studies programs to create a mythologized history and a system of assertive ideas that will facilitate the political mobilization of the black community. In addition, they hope to educate a cadre of activists whose present training is conceived of as a preparation for organizational work in the ghetto. The Cornell students made this very clear when they defined the purpose of black studies programs as enabling "black people to use the knowledge gained in the classroom and the community to formulate new ideologies and philosophies which will contribute to the development of the black nation."

Thus faculty members will be chosen on the basis of race, ideological purity, and political commitment—not academic competence. Under such conditions, few qualified black professors will want to teach in black studies programs, not simply because their academic freedom will be curtailed by their obligation to adhere to the revolutionary "line" of the moment, but because their professional status will be threatened by their association with programs of such inferior quality.

Black students are also forsaking the opportunity to get an education. They appear to be giving little thought to the problem of teaching or learning those technical skills that all students must acquire if they are to be effective in their careers. We have here simply another example of the pursuit of symbolic victory where a real victory seems too difficult to achieve. It is easier for a student to alter his behavior and appearance than to improve the quality of his mind. If engineering requires too much concentration, then why not a course in soul music? If Plato is both "irrelevant" and difficult, the student can read Malcolm X instead. Class will be a soothing, comfortable experience, somewhat like watching television. Moreover, one's image will be militant and, therefore, acceptable by current college standards. Yet one will have learned nothing, and the fragile sense of security developed in the protective environment of college will be cracked when exposed to the reality of competition in the world.

Nelson Taylor, a young Negro graduate of Morehouse College, recently observed that many black students "feel it is useless to try to compete. In order to avoid this competition, they build themselves a little cave to hide in." This "little cave," he added, is black studies. Furthermore, black students are encouraged in this escapism by guilt-ridden new leftists and faculty members who despise themselves and their advantaged lives and enjoy seeing young Negroes reject white middle-class values and disrupt the university. They are encouraged by university administrators who prefer political accommodation to an effort at serious education. But beyond the momentary titillation some may experience from being the center of attention, it is difficult to see how Negroes can in the end benefit from being patronized and manipulated in this way. Ultimately, their only permanent satisfaction can come from the certainty that they have acquired the technical and intellectual skills that will enable them upon graduation to perform significant jobs competently and with confidence. If they fail to acquire these skills, their frustration will persist and find expression in ever newer forms of antisocial and self-destructive behavior.

The conflict over black studies, as over other issues, raises the question of the function in general served by black protest today. Some black demands, such as that for a larger university enrollment of minority students, are entirely legitimate; but the major purpose of the protest through which these demands are pressed would seem to be not so much to pursue an end as to establish in the minds of the protesters, as well as in the minds of whites, the reality of their rebellion. Protest, therefore, becomes an end in itself and not a means toward social change. In this sense, the black rebellion is an enormously *expressive* phenomenon which is releasing the pent-up resentments of generations of oppressed Negroes. But expressiveness that is oblivious to political reality and not structured by instrumental goals is mere bombast.

James Forman's *Black Manifesto*, for instance, provides a nearly perfect sample of this kind of bombast combined with positive delusions of grandeur. "We shall liberate all the people in the U.S.," the introduction of the *Manifesto* declares, "and will be instrumental in the liberation of colored people the world around. . . . We are the most humane people within the U.S. . . . Racism in the U.S. is so pervasive in the mentality of whites that only an armed, well-disciplined, black-controlled government can insure the stamping out of racism in this country. . . . We say think in terms of the total control of the U.S."

One might never imagine from reading the *Manifesto* that Forman's organization, the National Black Economic Development Conference, is politically powerless, or that the institution it has chosen for assault is not the government or the corporation, but the church. Indeed, the exaggeration of language in the *Black Manifesto* is directly proportional to the isolation and impotence of those who drafted it. And their actual achievements provide an accurate measure of their strength. Three billion dollars in reparations was demanded—and $20,000 received. More important, the effect of this demand upon the Protestant churches has been to precipitate among them a conservative reaction against the activities of the liberal national denominations and the National Council of Churches. Forman's failure, of course, was to be expected: the only effect of an attack upon so organizationally diffuse and nonpolitical an institution as the church can be the deflection of pressure away from the society's major political and economic institutions and, consequently, the weakening of the black movement for equality.*

The possibility that his *Manifesto* might have exactly the opposite effect from that intended, however, was clearly not a problem to Forman, because the demands he was making upon white people were more moral than political or economic. His concern was to purge white guilt far more than to seek social justice for Negroes. It was in part for this reason that he chose to direct his attack at the church, which, as the institutional embodiment of our society's religious pretensions, is vulnerable to moral condemnation.

Yet there is something corrupting in the wholesale release of aggressive moral energy, particularly when it is in response to the demand for reparations for blacks. The difficulty is not only that as a purely racial demand its effect must be to isolate blacks from the white poor with whom they have common economic interests. The call for three billion dollars in reparations demeans the integrity of blacks and exploits the self-demeaning guilt of whites. It is insulting to Negroes to offer them reparations for past generations of suffering, as if the balance of an irreparable past could be set straight with a handout. In a recent poll, *Newsweek* reported that "today's proud Negroes, by an overwhelming 84 to 10 per cent, reject the idea of preferential treatment in hiring or college admissions in reparation for past injustices." There are few controversial issues that can call forth a greater uniformity of opinion than this in the Negro community.

I also question both the efficacy and the social utility of an attack that impels the attacked to applaud and debase themselves. I am not certain whether or not self-flagellation can have a beneficial effect on the sinner (I tend to

---

* Forman is not the only militant today who fancies that his essentially reformist program is revolutionary. Eldridge Cleaver has written that capitalists regard the Black Panther Breakfast for Children program (which the Panthers claim feeds 10,000 children) "as a threat, as cutting into the goods that are under their control." He also noted that it "liberates" black children from going to school hungry each morning. I wonder if he would also find public school lunch programs liberating.

doubt that it can), but I am absolutely certain that it can never produce anything politically creative. It will not improve the lot of the unemployed and the ill housed. On the other hand, it could well happen that the guilty party, in order to lighten his uncomfortable moral burden, will finally begin to rationalize his sins and affirm them as virtues. And by such a process, today's ally can become tomorrow's enemy. Lasting political alliances are not built on the shifting sands of moral suasion.

On his part, the breast-beating white makes the same error as the Negro who swears that "black is beautiful." Both are seeking refuge in psychological solutions to social questions. And both are reluctant to confront the real cause of racial injustice, which is not bad attitudes but bad social conditions. The Negro creates a new psychology to avoid the reality of social stagnation, and the white—be he ever so liberal—professes his guilt precisely so as to create the illusion of social change, all the while preserving his economic advantages.

The response of guilt and pity to social problems is by no means new. It is, in fact, as old as man's capacity to rationalize or his reluctance to make real sacrifices for his fellow man. Two hundred years ago, Samuel Johnson, in an exchange with Boswell, analyzed the phenomenon of sentimentality:

> Boswell: "I have often blamed myself, Sir, for not feeling for others, as sensibly as many say they do."
> Johnson: "Sir, don't be duped by them any more. You will find these very feeling people are not very ready to do you good. They *pay* you by *feeling*."

Today, payments from the rich to the poor take the form of "giving a damn" or some other kind of moral philanthropy. At the same time, of course, some of those who so passionately "give a damn" are likely to argue that full employment is inflationary.

We are living in a time of great social confusion—not only about the strategies we must adopt but about the very goals these strategies are to bring us to. Only recently whites and Negroes of good will were pretty much in agreement that racial and economic justice required an end to segregation and the expansion of the role of the federal government. Now it is a mark of "advancement," not only among "progressive" whites but among the black militants as well, to believe that integration is passé. Unintentionally (or as the Marxists used to say, objectively), they are lending aid and comfort to traditional segregationists like Senators Eastland and Thurmond. Another "advanced" idea is the notion that government has gotten too big and that what is needed to make the society more humane and livable is an enormous new move toward local participation and decentralization. One cannot question the value or importance of democratic participation in the government, but just as misplaced sympathy for Negroes is being put to use by segregationists, the liberal preoccupation with localism is serving the cause of conservatism. Two years of liberal encomiums to decentralization have intellectually legitimized the concept, if not the name, of states' rights and have set the stage for the widespread acceptance of Nixon's "New Federalism."

The new anti-integrationism and localism may have been motivated by sincere moral conviction, but hardly by intelligent political thinking. It should be obvious that what is needed today more than ever is a political strategy that offers the real possibility of economically uplifting millions of impoverished individuals, black and white. Such a strategy must of necessity give low priority to the various forms of economic and psychological experimentation that I have discussed, which at best deal with issues peripheral to the central problem and at worst embody a frenetic escapism. These experiments are based on the assumption that the black community can be transformed from within when, in fact, any such transformation must depend on structural changes in the entire society. Negro poverty, for example, will not be eliminated in the absence of a total war on poverty. We need, therefore, a new national economic policy. We also need new policies in housing, education, and health care which can deal with these problems as they relate to Negroes within the context of a national solution. A successful strategy, therefore, must rest upon an identification of those central institutions which, if altered sufficiently, would transform the social and economic relations in our society; and it must provide a politically viable means of achieving such an alteration.

Surely the church is not a central institution in this sense. Nor is Roy Innis' notion of dealing with the banking establishment a useful one. For the banks will find no extra profit—quite the contrary—in the kind of fundamental structural change in society that is required.*

Moreover, the recent flurry of excitement over the role of private industry in the slums seems to have subsided. A study done for the Urban Coalition has called the National Alliance of Businessmen's claim to have hired more than 100,000 hard-core unemployed a "phony numbers game." Normal hiring as the result of expansion or turnover was in some cases counted as re-

---

* Innis' demand that the white banks deposit $6 billion in black banks as reparations for past injustices should meet with even less success than Forman's ill-fated enterprise. At least Forman had the benefit of the white churchman's guilt, an emotion not known to be popular among bankers.

cruitment. Where hard-core workers have been hired and trained, according to the study, "The primary motivation . . . is the need for new sources of workers in a tight labor market. If and when the need for workers slackens, so will industry's performance." This has already occurred. The *Wall Street Journal* reported in July of 1969 that the Ford Motor Company, once praised for its social commitment, was forced to trim back production earlier in the year and in the process "quietly closed its two inner-city hiring centers in Detroit and even laid off some of the former hard-cores it had only recently hired." There have been similar retrenchments by other large companies as the result of a slackening in economic growth, grumblings from stockholders, and the realization by corporate executives that altruism does not make for high profits. Yet even if private industry were fully committed to attack the problem of unemployment, it is not in an ideal position to do so. Private enterprise, for example, accounted for only one out of every ten new jobs created in the economy between 1950 and 1960. Most of the remainder were created as the result of expansion of public employment.

While the church, private enterprise, and other institutions can, if properly motivated, play an important role, it is the trade union movement and the Democratic party which offer the greatest leverage to the black struggle. The serious objective of Negroes must be to strengthen and liberalize these. The trade union movement is essential to the black struggle because it is the only institution in the society capable of organizing the working poor, so many of whom are Negroes. It is only through an organized movement that these workers, who are now condemned to the margin of the economy, can achieve a measure of dignity and economic security. I must confess I find it difficult to understand the prejudice against the labor movement currently fashionable among so many liberals. These people, somehow for reasons of their own, seem to believe that white workers are affluent members of the Establishment (a rather questionable belief, to put it mildly, especially when held by people earning over $25,000 a year) and are now trying to keep the Negroes down. The only grain of truth here is that there *is* competition between black and white workers which derives from a scarcity of jobs and resources. But rather than propose an expansion of those resources, our stylish liberals underwrite that competition by endorsing the myth that the unions are the worst enemy of the Negro.

In fact it is the program of the labor movement that represents a genuine means of reducing racial competition and hostility. Not out of a greater tenderness of feeling for black suffering—but that is just the point. Unions organize workers on the basis of common economic interests, not by virtue of racial affinity. Labor's legislative program for full employment, housing, urban reconstruction, tax reform, improved health care, and expanded educational opportunities is designed specifically to aid both whites and blacks in the lower and lower middle classes where the potential for racial polarization is most severe. And only a program of this kind can deal simultaneously and creatively with the interrelated problems of black rage and white fear. It does not placate black rage at the expense of whites, thereby increasing white fear and political reaction. Nor does it exploit white fear by repressing blacks. Either of these courses strengthens the demagogues among both races who prey upon frustration and racial antagonism. Both of them help to strengthen conservative forces—the forces that stand to benefit from the fact that hostility between black and white workers keeps them from uniting effectively around issues of common economic interest.

President Nixon is in the White House today largely because of this hostility; and the strategy advocated by many liberals to build a "new coalition" of the affluent, the young, and the dispossessed is designed to keep him there. The difficulty with this proposed new coalition is not only that its constituents comprise a distinct minority of the population, but that its affluent and youthful members—regardless of the momentary direction of their rhetoric—are hardly the undisputed friends of the poor. Recent Harris polls, in fact, have shown that Nixon is most popular among the college educated and the young. Perhaps they were attracted by his style or the minimal concessions he has made on Vietnam, but certainly their approval cannot be based upon his accomplishments in the areas of civil rights and economic justice.

If the Republican ascendancy is to be but a passing phenomenon, it must once more come to be clearly understood among those who favor social progress that the Democratic party is still the only mass-based political organization in the country with the potential to become a majority movement for social change. And anything calling itself by the name of political activity must be concerned with building precisely such a majority movement. In addition, Negroes must abandon once and for all the false assumption that as 10 per cent of the population they can by themselves effect basic changes in the structure of American life. They must, in other words, accept the necessity of coalition politics. As a result of our fascination with novelty and with the "new" revolutionary forces that have emerged in recent years, it seems to some the height of conservatism to propose a strategy that was effective in the past. Yet the political reality is that without a coalition of Negroes and other minorities with the trade union movement and with liberal groups, the shift of power to the Right will persist and the democratic

Left in America will have to content itself with a well-nigh permanent minority status.

The bitterness of many young Negroes today has led them to be unsympathetic to a program based on the principles of trade unionism and electoral politics. Their protest represents a refusal to accept the condition of inequality, and in that sense it is part of the long, and I think, magnificent black struggle for freedom. But with no comprehensive strategy to replace the one I have suggested, their protest, though militant in rhetoric and intention, may be reactionary in effect.

The strategy I have outlined must stand or fall by its capacity to achieve political and economic results. It is not intended to provide some new wave of intellectual excitement. It is not intended to suggest a new style of life or a means to personal salvation for disaffected members of the middle class. Nor is either of these the proper role of politics. My strategy is not meant to appeal to the fears of threatened whites, though it would calm those fears and increase the likelihood that some day we shall have a truly integrated society. It is not meant to serve as an outlet for the terrible frustrations of Negroes, though it would reduce those frustrations and point a way to dignity for an oppressed people. It is simply a vehicle by which the wealth of this nation can be redistributed and some of its more grievous social problems solved. This in itself would be quite enough to be getting on with. In fact, if I may risk a slight exaggeration, by normal standards of human society I think it would constitute a revolution.

BENIGN NEGLECT: A REPLY
TO DANIEL MOYNIHAN

With the publication of his memo to the President urging "benign neglect" of the issue of race, Daniel P. Moynihan once again finds himself involved in a bitter controversy. We seem to be in the midst of a replay of what took place almost five years ago when his report on the Negro family was published. An internal government memo written by Moynihan and relating to Negroes is released to the public, the general reaction in the black community is outrage, recrimination and explanations follow, and Moynihan emerges a hero to some, a villain to many others.

Such at least are the similarities, but there are significant differences which must be seen if we are to understand the full meaning of Moynihan's recent message to the President.

Beyond the fact that he is likely to lose more friends this time around than the last, Moynihan is not in the same position today that he was in five years ago. At that time he was a member of a liberal administration. His report, whatever else might be said for or against it, was an attempt to draw attention to a social problem, to identify the social and economic causes of that problem, and to outline what he called "the case for national action." While there is reason to doubt the wisdom of some of Moynihan's formulations, at least he sensed the urgency of America's racial crisis. Today just the opposite is true. Moynihan is a member of a conservative administration, his memo is designed to draw attention away from a social problem, he places the blame for our racial crisis almost exclusively on the Negro, he offers no proposals for government action beyond some studies and conferences, and his tone is infused with complacency and self-congratulation.

The change cannot be explained away by observing that this is one liberal's way to adapt to the conservative period that we are in. Mr. Moynihan, to all intents and purposes, has become a conservative himself.

Let us first look at his "general assessment of the position of Negroes" at the end of Mr. Nixon's first year in office. As a sociologist Moynihan is aware

From the *Long Island Press*, March 15, 1970.

that statistics can be both used and misused with great effectiveness. I think it is fair to say that in his memo to the President, Moynihan is guilty of mis using statistics. His figures are correct, as far as I can judge, but he has been highly selective in choosing only those which give the impression that "the American Negro is making extraordinary progress." Important progress was made during the last decade. Everybody knows that. But as Andrew Brimmer and others have pointed out, the benefits of progress accrued largely to middle- and working-class blacks, while the social and economic condition of impoverished Negroes did not improve and, in fact, worsened.

We are beginning to see that Negroes in one area can bring problems to another. The improvement in the income and living standard of many black families enabled them to move out of the hard-core poverty areas of the cities. But they left behind them black communities that were worse off than before the onset of "progress," more homogeneously poor, with fewer stable middle-class elements, with schools, housing, and health-care facilities rapidly deteriorating, and with the population density as high as ever since the departing middle class was replaced by impoverished immigrants from the South.

During the last decade Negroes trapped in the inner-city ghettos became more desperate, more despairing, more subject to the vicious conditions of poverty and segregation.

My intention is not to demean the importance of the progress that was made during the last decade. But neither will I use superlatives, as does Moynihan, in describing what amounted to a first step in attacking the overwhelming and complex social problems of the nation. To point out improvements where they have been made, but not to couple this with an urgent call for more action is to provide an excuse for complacency and criminal inaction.

I also take issue with the interpretation, which is implicit in Moynihan's argument, of the origins of progress and poverty in the black community. His statistics on black progress all relate to "husband-wife Negro families," while, according to Moynihan, "Increasingly, the problem of Negro poverty is the problem of the female-headed family." Here we have it again, the same old argument about the Negro family, only this time Moynihan does not offer joblessness as a major cause, but rather as a major effect, of family instability. He has reversed the tables and in the process has placed the onus of blame for poverty on the black community, a characteristically conservative argument. He has also neglected to mention the real source of progress for blacks in the sixties—namely, the dramatic expansion of our economy with the accompanying reduction in unemployment and poverty.

It is true that many hard-core unemployed, because they lacked the proper training, were not prepared to benefit from the economic boom. But the very fact that there was a tight labor market motivated government and industry to initiate training programs to employ these individuals. Today, however, as a direct result of Nixon's regressive economic policies, we are moving into a recession. Unemployment is increasing as more and more workers are being laid off and training programs are closing down. Only last week the Department of Labor terminated a large contract to hire thousands of hard-core unemployed for production jobs in Chrysler plants. The progress some Negroes experienced during the last decade is thus being undermined, and whatever opportunity there was for the hard-core unemployed to escape from poverty has been crushed, at least for the present.

Moynihan has written a memo to the President on the condition of Negroes without mentioning the disastrous effect the administration's economic policies are having upon blacks. One can only conclude that either Moynihan is a partisan of those policies, or he just does not want to make waves within the administration. If the latter is true, he is guilty of gross irresponsibility. One can expect nothing less than outrage in the black community at Moynihan's statement that "apart from white racial attitudes . . . the biggest problem black Americans face is the anti-social behavior among black males."

Moynihan totally neglects social and economic injustice as he narrows the problems of the ghetto down to the simple and cruelly misleading remark, "Black Americans injure one another." Once again he is attempting to pin the blame for the racial crisis upon the Negro. Take his long digression on the fire problem in the ghetto, which amounts to over one-eighth of his memo. He admits that some fires result from population density, but the real cause, he says, is "social pathology." Slum residents "deliberately set" a large part of the fires in their communities. This is as far from the truth as it is contemptuous of the Negro community. There is no mention of the drastic housing shortage which has severely affected the whole society, and most of all the ghetto.

The problem is not simply that the population density in the ghetto has become unbearable, which it has. What is worse is that, in the absence of decent housing, blacks are crowded into old, dilapidated dwellings which have unvented heaters and faulty wiring and which, Mr. Moynihan, are nothing more than fire-traps. Not only is President Nixon doing nothing to alleviate this problem, he has actually aggravated it by cutting back on funds for Model Cities and urban renewal and, most important, by raising interest rates to the point where home-building has declined to its lowest level in more than twenty years.

There is an element of social pathology here, but it is not in the black community as much as it is in a society which permits a situation like this to continue.

All this is by way of introduction to the really controversial aspect of Moynihan's memo, his suggestion that "the time may have come when the issue of race could benefit from a period of 'benign neglect.'" Let us look closely at what this means, since we would not want to be accused of misunderstanding the President's counselor. Moynihan is not saying that we should neglect the problems of blacks but the issue of race. He wants to see tempers cooled and extremists of either race isolated.

Now all this is fine enough, but in the context of Moynihan's entire memo, not to speak of the political context in which the memo was written, these words take on a different meaning. Many civil rights leaders and spokesmen, myself included, have firmly opposed extremism of both races, black as well as white. But we have done so not simply to cool tempers but to build movements. We have seen that racial extremism is self-defeating, that it divides blacks from natural allies in the white community, and that it undermines the central objective of building a coalition of progressive forces which can become the political majority in America. We have seen that until such a coalition exists, our nation will not undertake a comprehensive program to wipe out poverty among blacks, Mexican Americans, Indians, Puerto Ricans, and whites.

But Moynihan has no such objective in mind when he urges "benign neglect" of racial issues. Indeed, he is an important member of an administration which is the major opposition to the coalition I just described. "Benign neglect," as Moynihan has used it, is consistent with the rest of his memo and, therefore, does not mean neglect of the issue of race but government neglect of the Negro.

It is significant that Moynihan borrowed the phrase "benign neglect" from a colonialist context. It was originally used in a report written in 1839 by the British Earl of Durham. According to Moynihan, the Earl recommended self-government for the British colony of Canada, which had grown self-reliant "through many years of benign neglect" by Britain. From our discussion of the other sections of Moynihan's memo, it should be clear that this phrase was carefully chosen to support the rest of his contentions. Whether he was discussing unemployment or social pathology, Moynihan took care to locate the source of the difficulty in Negroes themselves, in what he claims are our "female-headed families," our "anti-social behavior," our penchant for arson, and our "social alienation."

Like Canada in the early nineteenth century, Moynihan feels that today America would benefit from a policy of "benign neglect" toward Negroes, during which it could put its own house in order, tidy up its family life, and get its arsonists under control. His argument is fundamentally for a kind of black self-help and against a government role in solving the problems of the black poor. Moynihan's memo must have found a receptive audience in a conservative President who has done everything possible, in keeping with his philosophy of the "new federalism," to reduce the role of the federal government.

Moynihan's suggestions to the President on what he should do in relation to the black community make an excellent case for government inaction. Aside from urging "benign neglect," he suggests that administration officials get together to "talk out the subject a bit" in order to develop a "more coherent administration approach," and that the administration do more research on crime.

It is indeed remarkable that, after noting that the unemployment rate among black teen-agers is 24.4 per cent, Moynihan can only suggest that we need more studies on crime—as if we did not already know that there is a high correlation between poverty and crime, that unemployment is a leading indicator of criminal behavior. And the Nixon administration is hardly doing anything to reduce unemployment.

Finally, there is Moynihan's suggestion to give more recognition to the "silent black majority," the black working class. Nixon will have to give this group far more than recognition if he is to befriend it, for it has already been deeply offended by his economic policies and Southern strategy.

Moynihan urges a cooling of racial emotions, but the policies of the Nixon administration are making extremists out of moderates. The Black Panthers will not disappear if they are ignored, as Moynihan suggests. They will not disappear because the conditions which produced them continue to exist. And as long as this society fails to carry out a social and economic program which can attack those conditions at their roots, there will be extremists in the black community.

Moynihan never once refers to the necessity for such a program, but talks only about the necessity to lower our voices. Mr. Nixon also talks about "bringing us together," but he has done nothing to further that goal. On the contrary, his policies have deepened divisions and broadened the base for extremism. But of this Mr. Moynihan has nothing to say.

Several years ago, at a national board meeting of the Americans for Democratic Action, held soon after the violence in Newark and Detroit, Moynihan urged that liberals form a coalition with conservatives in the interests of social order. He himself, with the courage of his convictions, has entered into such a coalition. As a result he has in effect become an important ally of the conservative cause.

Writing in *Commentary* some months back, Andrew Hacker pointed out that if Nixon is to build a Republican majority out of what is essentially a right-center coalition, he will have to undertake two approaches simultaneously—a reactionary strategy, led by such men as John Mitchell and Spiro Agnew, which would appeal to the right, and a more progressive strategy, directed by such house liberals as Robert Finch and Moynihan, which would appeal to the center.

From this point of view Moynihan's role in the Nixon administration becomes tragically clear. As the liberal cover for a conservative administration, he is not advancing liberalism so much as helping to entrench conservatism. If President Nixon is successful in building his majority, Moynihan's memo will take on a significance that was perhaps not intended by its author.

Historical periods are often defined by single phrases which seem to capture the mood or the political climate of a nation at a particular point in time. In America today we are dangerously on the verge of entering a period when social problems are ignored and allowed to fester until they emerge at some future time in such a diseased condition that the social order is threatened with a general breakdown.

We have been through a period of difficult change, and people are tired. They do not want to be reminded that there are still problems, most grievously that problem which Gunnar Myrdal called "the American dilemma." Whites are retreating, becoming hostile and fearful, blacks are becoming enraged, and liberals are confused and discontented. And the federal government, the principal agency through which we can find a way out of our racial agony, is in the hands of men who lack progressive intention. "Benign neglect," a phrase borrowed from the past, seems to define the present. Neglect of problems that are difficult to solve, avoidance of realities that are unpleasant to confront—Mr. Moynihan's phrase speaks to our society's weaknesses, its capacity for self-delusion and apathy.

We have not entirely reached this point yet. There is still time to reverse our direction, to move forward. To fail to seize this opportunity today may make it impossible for us to do so in the future. Perhaps the lack of vision evinced by Mr. Moynihan can shock us into a recognition of how far we must still go to achieve the evasive yet splendid goal of racial justice.

VIOLENCE AND THE
SOUTHERN STRATEGY

Much of the social turmoil which our society experienced in the 1960's can be attributed to what sociologists and political scientists have called the revolution of rising expectations. This means that for an upwardly mobile group the achievement of social progress is far more likely to stimulate demands for change than to satisfy them. This is certainly one important factor that added momentum to the Negro protest movement.

The sword, however, cuts both ways. In a conservative period we are likely to see a counterrevolution of rising expectations. The moment it becomes clear that a reaction has set in against further change, the progressive forces are put on the defensive, while the reactionaries, who were held at bay during the liberal years, sense that their time has come. They now come out from hiding, flex their muscles, and boldly prepare to attack the agents of progress as well as progress itself. At this point the floodgates of hatred and racism are opened, and society enters a very dismal and dangerous period.

Something like this counterrevolution is occurring in the South today. During the past fifteen years, the South has undergone a tremendous social transformation as a result of the civil rights movement. The period was traumatic for many Southerners, but there have been indications that the region as a whole has been adjusting to the new situation. School integration was proceeding slowly, but it *was* proceeding, and it was becoming an accepted fact of life for a growing number of white Southerners.

But now this positive trend has been reversed. Segregationism is regaining its respectability. Even more ominous, the bombings, the burnings, and the physical attacks upon blacks which some had thought to be relics of Southern history are taking place with greater and greater frequency.

If we are to find the cause of these developments, we need look no further than the President's Southern strategy. More than any single factor, it has been a signal to Southern reactionaries that the tide has turned in their favor. It has both stimulated and sanctioned opposition to court orders and

From the *New York Amsterdam News*, April 23, 1970.

federal laws that require integration. As such, it is responsible for transforming reluctant acceptance of change into violent resistance.

For example, when Governor Claude Kirk of Florida dramatically refused to comply with a school integration plan imposed by a federal district court, the Justice Department did not oppose him and even went so far as to join with him in trying to have the plan changed in an appeals court. This outrageous defiance of the law by both a governor *and* the Justice Department was a clear message to other Southern governors that they are under no pressure from the Nixon administration to comply with any court integration orders.

The new mood of resistance to integration by federal and state officials has encouraged violent acts by local Southerners. In a report in the *Wall Street Journal* (April 17, 1970), Neil Maxwell gives a detailed account of the numerous bombings and burnings of black churches, schools, and community centers which have resulted from Nixon's Southern strategy. As Paul Anthony, director of the Southern Regional Council, told Maxwell, "All the things coming out of Washington these days and the new defiance by leaders just can't help but encourage a greater degree of white resistance—and the only way some people know how to respond is with violence."

Mr. Nixon talks of law and order and points an accusing finger at black America. But he would do better to examine his own policies which have caused a revival of violence and lawlessness in the South. By placing politics above law, the Nixon administration has set in motion a series of events which might well end with a racial war that would be a tragedy for the South and for the entire nation.

DEATH IN BLACK AND WHITE

No recent event has more clearly underlined the persisting racial division in American society than the killing of four Kent State students by the Ohio National Guard. The deaths of these students represent a tragedy which must be mourned by all decent Americans. But what concerns me here is not the deaths themselves but how we as a nation have reacted to them. We reacted not as *one* nation, but as two—one white and the other black.

The predominant reaction among white Americans was shock and disbelief. The picture of the young girl kneeling beside the body of a dead student with a look of fear, grief, and helplessness on her face became a symbol of the national mood. No doubt the mass media encouraged this mood as much as they responded to it, and for more than a week the killings rivaled the American intervention in Cambodia as the major news story. No doubt also there were many white Americans who did not share in this mood and even felt that the students deserved their terrible fate. But though there were conflicting reactions, it seems clear that the killings assumed a central place in the nation's consciousness to a degree that few events have in recent memory.

The reaction of black America was considerably different. Though blacks also grieved over the students' deaths, they could not help feeling that far more attention was being paid to the Kent killings than had ever been paid to young Negroes who died under similar circumstances. To explain this discrepancy, most blacks could only conclude that the Kent students were mourned with such tremendous emotion *because they were white*.

Most white Americans probably do not recall that only two years ago three black students from Orangeburg's South Carolina State College who were demonstrating to integrate a bowling alley were killed by highway patrolmen. These students were entirely innocent; one was even shot in the back. Moreover, the demonstration was largely peaceful, while the Kent killings had been preceded by the burning of an ROTC center, looting and window-breaking, and rock-throwing at the National Guard. Yet somehow

---

From the *New York Amsterdam News*, May 21, 1970.

the horrible injustice of the Orangeburg killings has never penetrated our national consciousness.

I am reminded of the brutal killing of three civil rights workers in 1964. Two of them were white, and for that reason alone most Americans were outraged. The hundreds of black deaths in Mississippi which preceded those killings never received more than a tiny news story.

In the last few weeks we have been provided with fresh examples of American hypocrisy. In Augusta, Georgia, six blacks were killed in racial violence that followed a protest against the inhuman conditions in the local jail. All of them were shot in the back, some as many as nine times, and possibly four were bystanders. At Jackson State College in Mississippi, highway police fired into a crowd of students, killing two and wounding nine. There is no evidence to prove the police claim that they were being fired on by snipers, but there is evidence which indicates that the police fired on the students *with automatic weapons*. And finally, there is the report from the Chicago grand jury that the killing of two Black Panthers last December did not result from a "shoot-out" between the Panthers and the police, as the police had claimed. All the available evidence points to a police ambush in which the Panthers were murdered.

What are black Americans to think when such events are forgotten almost as soon as they happen, while the death of young white students is made into a national tragedy? The answer is obvious, and, sadly, it is one that we have known all along: that in America the life of a white person is considered to be more valuable than the life of a black person; that the killing of a white student thrusts a lance of grief through the heart of white America, while the killing of a black is condoned or rationalized on the grounds that blacks are violent and thus deserve to be killed, or that they have been persecuted for so long that somehow they have become "used to" death. My own feeling is that the word "racism" is thrown about too loosely these days, but considering what has happened in the last few weeks, I think it accurately describes much of what goes on "in white America."

A WEST SIDE STORY

The 1968 Housing Act calls for the annual construction of 2.6 million homes, more than twice the present rate. Since its passage, the housing situation in the United States has steadily deteriorated. High interest rates, the rising cost of land, materials, and labor, and, most critically, the failure of the Nixon administration to commit itself to the goal of securing a decent home for every American have produced one of the worst housing shortages in our nation's history. Nowhere is that shortage more evident than in New York City. In one neighborhood in particular, the lack of adequate housing has led to a series of unfortunate events which are probably not uncharacteristic of what has taken place elsewhere in the city and in other cities as well.

For over a decade now, a section of the upper west side of Manhattan, consisting of twenty square blocks, has been undergoing urban renewal and rehabilitation. The goal of the renewal project is to create a stable community with a population that is mixed both economically and racially. About one-third of the homes have been set aside for poor families whose rent would be subsidized with public funds. That project could become the prototype for a solution to our urban crisis, since it tries to avoid the disastrous consequences of racial and economic ghettos. We are too familiar with such consequences: crime, inferior schools, terrible housing, and a tax base too depleted to provide funds for adequate social services.

Two stages of the project have now been completed, but the third stage has been held up because of bureaucratic delays, insufficient funds, and the need to relocate displaced families. A community group has been formed called CONTINUE, which has pledged itself to the fulfillment of the renewal project. Represented in the group are churches, block clubs, businesses, and other organizations in the community.

Some other people, however, have concluded that the renewal project is dead. Chief among these are Father Henry J. Brown, the head of the Stryckers Bay Neighborhood Council, and William Price, the director of Community Action, Inc., which operates in the neighborhood. These men have spearheaded what has become known as "Operation Move In," a program

From the *New York Amsterdam News*, July 2, 1970.

that "liberates" boarded-up dwellings in the rehabilitation area by illegally moving poor families into them. The "move in" began in May and there are now about 135 "squatter" families living in the renewal area.

The families already living in the neighborhood have reacted with alarm and concern to the "move in" for two reasons. First, if it continues, the renewal project will never be finished; and second, because the boarded-up apartments have no plumbing, heating, or fire escapes, they represent a health hazard to their inhabitants and a fire hazard to the community.

In order to find out whether the city is planning to go through with the renewal project, the block association held a meeting two weeks ago to which they invited several city officials. The meeting was held at the home of Dr. and Mrs. Arthur Logan, two outstanding fighters for justice in the black community who had been close friends of Dr. Martin Luther King, Jr., and raised substantial funds for him. Dr. Logan is the former director of HARYOU and president of the city's anti-poverty program. Mrs. Logan has worked endlessly to improve the neighborhood; for example, she was primarily responsible for the construction of a beautiful park used by hundreds of neighborhood children.

When people arrived at the meeting, however, their way was blocked by a group of demonstrators who claimed that the purpose of the meeting was to remove the squatters. They also claimed to represent the people of the community even though they arrived in cars and the majority were white and middle class. After shouting insults at the Logans, Borough President Percy Sutton, and others, three of the demonstrators—Father Brown and two women—agreed to participate in the meeting and the demonstration was called off.

The following day Mrs. Logan was visited by one of the women, who said she had come to apologize. She said that at the meeting she realized the Logans and the other neighborhood people were not "enemies," as she had been told they were by some of the leaders of "Operation Move In," but were really interested in the welfare of the entire community, including the poor. She added that at the demonstration she had been handed a mimeographed sheet of paper on which were written the insults she was to shout at the Logans. Feeling that she had been "used" by the leaders of "Move In," she now wished to prepare and circulate a document, written in both English and Spanish, explaining to all the poor in the area what the real situation was. She and Mrs. Logan agreed upon the need to form a coalition of community people and squatters to fight the real enemy.

Who is this enemy? In the immediate sense it is those people who call themselves the champions of the poor but who actually exploit the poor for whatever reasons they may have. Certainly the poor people who were "moved in" to the community were misinformed about the situation and cannot hope to benefit from the whole misguided operation. But in a larger sense the enemies are the city officials who have not fulfilled their promises and the Nixon administration, which has been so irresponsible in the area of housing construction, not to speak of employment, education, and health care. It is they who have created the context in which the poor can be "used" and in which communities can be destroyed. And it is this larger social crisis which must be solved if we are ever to live in peace with one another.

THE STORY OF A BLACK YOUTH

If we are to believe what we read in most newspapers and magazines, poor black youths who grow up in the ghetto end up as social outcasts of one sort or another. They become, or so we are often told, either criminals or violent revolutionaries, wanting only to destroy the society which has inflicted so much hardship upon them. No doubt in many cases these stories are true, in addition to being newsworthy. The difficulty is that the stories of other youths who have also been brutalized by society but whose lives have taken a different course have been left untold.

Victor Rivera is one such youth. He was born twenty-six years ago in New York City and attended the city's schools until, like so many other youths, he dropped out before completing high school. He took a job so that he could have money to buy fancy clothes and other things that would give him status in the ghetto. Eventually he began selling dope and stealing, even though he felt guilty about violating principles his parents had taught him.

Victor embraced the ghetto ideology which was then developing in order, as he said, to justify his own wrongdoing. By using the assertion of black pride to "rationalize" his rebellion and to justify his apathy, he was "misusing a truth." He continued to be troubled by vague feelings of guilt and uncertainty. Sensing in the back of his mind that he deserved punishment for what he was doing, he began committing irrational acts which ultimately led to his arrest for armed robbery.

He decided not even to fight his case. He willingly accepted his four-and-a-half-year prison sentence as a period during which he could pull himself together. "The hardship of the bust forced me to mature, to face reality," he said. "I had no more facades. I had to deal with myself, my raw self."

He learned many things in prison. He joined the Black Muslims, who stressed the need for blacks to better themselves. "In order for a black man to really come into his own, to understand himself as a person and as part of an ethnic group, he may have to go through the Muslim stage. It's a vehicle, a means toward an end." The most profound influence on him was

From the *New York Amsterdam News*, July 30, 1970.

Collins Hinton, a teacher who was crippled by the loss of his hands. "I have my blackness and my books," Hinton told him, "and I made it. You've got your health, so I know you'll make it too." Every free moment Victor had, he studied economics, math, science, and literature. He began to develop a new conception of what society is—an evolving organism which in many ways is wrong and unjust but which is subject to change through peaceful means. He came to see that in order to change the institutions of the society, one must be part of those institutions, that repudiation of the society is only an escape from its problems, not a solution to them.

On his release from prison Victor got a job as a tutor with the Joint Apprenticeship Program, which finds work for young blacks in the building trades. The hardships he had lived through, especially his prison experience, were an asset to him in his new job, since he could communicate with the ghetto youths recruited by the JAP. Though he has not yet completed his first year, Victor has already become one of the JAP's best tutors. Normally about 40 per cent of the "tutees," black and white, will pass an entrance examination for the building trades. Recently Victor tutored ninety-five carpenters, and eighty-six of them passed the test. Many were among the highest scorers.

Victor's range of activities has expanded in the last year. He speaks frequently at high schools, representing the JAP. He recently returned from a three-week stay in Washington, where he studied economics and labor history at the AFL-CIO's Labor Studies Center. He is a member of the board of directors of the East Harlem Environmental Extension Service, which is designed to improve living conditions in poor neighborhoods. And he is now enrolled at Pratt Institute, from which he hopes to get a B.S. degree in science and engineering.

What enabled Victor to pull himself together? It was probably a combination of strong character, inner resources imparted to him by his parents, and a certain degree of good fortune. Whatever it was, Victor is now part of the institutions of this society and is struggling every day to change them. It is doubtful that these institutions, being what they are, will change quickly, but certainly there would be no hope at all were it not for young people like Victor Rivera, who are capable of rising above the brutal conditions of their lives and contributing toward the advancement of society.

FEMINISM AND EQUALITY

The women's liberation movement, which has created much controversy in recent months, is not a new phenomenon but part of a long struggle for women's equality. The fact that a major feminist demonstration was held on August 26, 1970, indicates the historical character of this movement, since the date was the fiftieth anniversary of the passage of the Nineteenth Amendment, granting female suffrage.

The modern feminist movement differs from the suffragette movement of a half-century ago in that its demands have to do more with economic equality than with political rights. To a considerable degree, this is a reflection of technological changes that have taken place in the society—changes which have freed the more affluent women from household chores and enabled them to gain a high degree of education. These women are now demanding that jobs and other opportunities be opened to them on a nondiscriminatory basis. The force of their argument is reflected in economic statistics showing that the income differential between men and women is greater than it is between whites and blacks.

If the women's liberation movement should be criticized, it is not because its demands are unjust but because they do not go far enough. The three demands put forth at the August 26 demonstrations were for free abortions, twenty-four-hour day-care centers for children of working mothers, and equal educational and employment opportunities.

I would personally take issue with none of these demands, but they are inadequate in that they are proposed in isolation from the broad social and economic context of American life. The feminists are making the same mistake that many other social protesters have made: they do not relate their demands to the larger issues which ultimately will determine whether the demands are met.

For example, I am entirely for free abortions on demand, since I think women should be able to choose whether they want to have children. But I think that the feminists would be wiser to make this specific demand part of a larger demand for socialized medicine. Our current health system does

From the *New York Amsterdam News*, August 27, 1970.

not permit all women, or all Americans, to obtain adequate medical care, and good health is a prerequisite for "liberation," however one cares to define that word. Similarly, it is not enough to have day-care centers that will free mothers from constant supervision of their children. There should also be a demand for the expansion of preschool education and for high-quality integrated schools that will liberate the minds of the children and enable them to develop their potential to the fullest. Finally, the demand for equal employment opportunities cannot be met in the absence of full employment. As long as a sizable portion of the population is unemployed, workers, regardless of their sex or race, will have to compete for jobs and employers will be able to hire those willing to work for the least pay. Here it should be added that the demand for female equality is too often stated in terms of giving women the same rights as men. What happens then is that women consider their own special rights—such as the legal protection of women workers—to be expendable. Rather than give up these rights, they should be demanding that such provisions be extended to all workers.

Thus far the women's liberation movement has failed to make its demands within this larger social context. That failure is not accidental; it is, in fact, a commentary on the affluent background of many of the feminists. They are, for the most part, women who already have access to adequate health care, whose children (if they have them) probably attend excellent schools, and who don't need jobs, just *better* jobs. This is one reason why so few black women have participated in the feminist movement. If the feminists do not make the larger demands I have suggested, their movement will become just another middle-class foray into limited social reform, the main result of which will be to divert valuable social energies away from the problem of fundamentally transforming our society's institutions. Without such a transformation, leading to full social equality for all Americans—female and male, black and white, poor and rich—our people will not be free.

A WORD TO BLACK STUDENTS

Your generation has lived through a period of unprecedented upheaval. Most of you were only five years old when the Supreme Court declared school segregation unconstitutional. You were seven when a young black preacher named Martin Luther King emerged as the leader of the Montgomery bus protest. At eleven you witnessed the beginning of the sit-in movement in Greensboro, North Carolina, and for the next ten years—your adolescent years that were to shape the perspective with which you now look out on the world—you lived through a period in black American history more eventful than any other decade, including the decade of the Civil War. The March on Washington, the outbreak of large-scale violence in hundreds of Negro communities, and the rise of the black power movement—these events no doubt had their precedents in the March on Washington movement of 1941, the race riots of 1919 and 1943, and the black nationalist Garvey movement in the 1920's. But in the 1960's they occurred with a driving momentum that made the race problem the central issue in our national politics.

It is difficult to judge precisely what the effect of this experience with uninterrupted social protest has been on your generation (I am referring here to young whites as well as to young blacks). But I would not doubt that it has made the political consciousness of this generation sensitive primarily to what we may call *the upward arc of historical movement*. The problem is that such a consciousness finds it hard to come to grips with the reality that history consists of alternating periods of movement and stagnation, of action and reaction, of tremendous hope and enthusiasm, which can be followed by cynicism and exhaustion. I am not suggesting that this process is inevitable, though to a certain extent it does seem to contain an internal dynamic that operates independently of human will. What I am suggesting is that we must understand this process if we are to be in a position to influence it.

This commencement address delivered by Bayard Rustin to graduating students at Tuskegee Institute on May 31, 1970, was published in *Dissent*, November–December 1970.

What we must first understand is that the pendulum of history has *already* begun to swing downward. It is impossible now to gauge the extent of this reaction. My own feeling is that the drift to the right in American politics can be reversed if we do the correct thing. But we cannot escape the conclusion that, for the present at least, the conservatives have made important and ominous gains. They control the White House and, through the power of presidential appointment, have gained a majority on the Supreme Court.

What is happening today is not very different from what happened in the 1870's. At that time, the country had been through a period as turbulent as the one we have just experienced. The Civil War and its aftermath left the North with a moral burden it simply could not bear. It was far more interested in pursuing its own commercial interests than in advancing the welfare of Negroes in the South, and of course the North also suffered from the disease of racism. All hope for black equality collapsed when Northern Republicans worked out a compromise with Southern Democrats in the disputed election of 1876. The Southern Whigs agreed to let the Republicans retain control of the White House, in return for which federal troops were withdrawn from the South and large subsidies were provided for the construction of the Southern railroad system. The Compromise of 1876 initiated the darkest period in the history of American Negroes. The system of Jim Crow was established and lynchings and terrorism became commonplace as poor Southern whites, embittered by poverty, were encouraged to unleash their wrath upon Negroes.

Things have not yet reached that stage today, but the parallels are frightening. The Southern strategy of the Nixon administration is based upon the same principle as the Compromise of 1876: namely, that Northern Republicans and Southern conservatives share common interests and together can rule this nation. I do not think it is possible to condemn too harshly what the President has done in the South in order to form this alliance. Indeed, I can think of no recent President who has more blatantly sacrificed the ideals of equality and racial justice for his own political ends. Nor is Nixon simply riding the wave of reaction. He is encouraging that reaction, for he knows that he became President because of divisions in the society, and that it is in his interest that these divisions grow wider. More specifically, he wants to see another anti-black Wallace vote in 1972, only this time he wants it cast for himself. This is the prime motivation behind the President's opposition to the extension of the 1965 Voting Rights Act, his nominations of Haynsworth and Carswell to the Supreme Court, and his clear message to Southern segregationists that the federal government will not oppose any efforts to roll back whatever advances had been made in school integration. By means of such acts he has helped foster a mood of confrontationism and racial hostility. He has profoundly and perhaps permanently alienated blacks, he has put the white moderates of the South on the defensive, and he has given a go-ahead signal to the reactionaries.

What worries me most about the present situation is that there has been a decline in the effectiveness of some of the forces that have traditionally held reaction at bay. In the case of the South, we have already seen how the federal government, formerly an ally in our struggle, has contributed to the resurgence of conservatism. Nationally, the progressive coalition of blacks, liberals, and the trade union movement, which has been responsible for the major social advances since the New Deal, is now weakened by internal divisions. In part this is due to conflict between blacks and lower middle-class whites. This conflict has probably been exaggerated in the press, but a disturbing amount of it *does* exist, primarily because of economic competition between the two groups. Such competition can be reduced to a minimum if an expanding economy provides enough opportunities for everybody. But today, as a result of the Nixon administration's disastrous economic policies, we are in a recession. Consequently, the likelihood is that there will be an increase in racial tension, which will further eat away at the unity of the progressive coalition.

Finally, the dramatic events of the last few years seem to have totally disoriented a sizable portion of the liberal community. Many liberals have lost a sense of purpose and direction. The traditional goals of integration and the expansion of the welfare state are no longer thought to be feasible or even desirable. But they have found no goals to replace the ones they have cast aside, with the result that they have become politically immobile. A number of theories have been created to give this mood a forward-looking image, but it is really little more than an accommodation to the new conservatism.

By no means do I want to give the impression that the situation is hopeless. There is a tendency today to anticipate the apocalypse. Such ideas are sheer indulgence, because even if there were any truth to them—and I do not believe there is—it would be our duty to act so as to prevent the worst from happening rather than to enable the fulfillment of our prophecies. Such moods can be harmful, for, as George Orwell has pointed out, "an effect can become a cause, reinforcing the original cause and producing the same effect in an intensified form, and so on indefinitely. A man may take to drink because he feels himself to be a failure, and then fail all the more completely because he drinks." Our struggle is too important, there is still so much that remains unaccomplished, that it would be a grave error were we to indulge in this "end-of-the-world" chatter.

The situation is not hopeless. There are progressive forces at work in American society that did not exist in 1876. There is, first of all, the militant desire for racial justice, which is shared by countless numbers of young blacks like yourselves. In the words of the civil rights song, I don't think that anybody is going to turn you 'round—not now, not after we have come so far. Then there is the black vote, which in both the North and the South has become a major new factor in American politics. This vote has increased not only in numbers but also in sophistication, and in addition to the gains it has already won for blacks, it exercises a restraining influence on the scope and effectiveness of anti-Negro forces. The problems George Wallace had in the Alabama primaries should make this point eminently clear.

Last, there is the trade union movement which, though much maligned from both right and left, remains the strongest bulwark against reaction. Let us be very clear that the civil rights forces alone could not have defeated Haynsworth and Carswell. They succeeded only because they were allied with the trade union movement, and it is this alliance, based upon mutual interest between blacks and labor, which offers the greatest hope for future progress.

Thus there are factors working both for and against the achievement of full racial equality. In a very real sense, we are at a crossroads. If Mr. Nixon succeeds in carrying out his Southern strategy, then the commitment to equality, on which America defaulted almost one hundred years ago, will again be deferred to some future time. And if he fails, then we will be provided with an opportunity to resolve once and for all a central dilemma of American life—the relationship of blacks to American society and, in an even more profound sense, their relationship with themselves. Our task is to see to it that he fails.

If we are to have any hope of accomplishing this task, it is essential that we make an important distinction between issues of politics and problems in psychology. We should see this as a distinction between what we do in order to influence the political and economic relations in the society and what, in a more personal way, we do to achieve self-knowledge and identity. Now I do not think that these are hard and fast categories that totally exclude one another. A just society certainly encourages a healthy psychology, and individuals can find personal fulfillment through political involvement. But I think we must make this distinction, because in periods of great social upheaval—and we are living through such a period—there is a tendency to politicize all things, including scholarship, art, friendship, and love. The most extreme form of this total politicization is totalitarianism, a stage we have not yet reached. But even a moderate form of it can be dangerous since it can lead to a politics so preoccupied with psychological issues that the goals of political action are obscured and even rendered unobtainable.

As you well know, a great cultural revolt is taking place among many young black Americans. Young blacks are striking down the traditional symbols of racism. They are taking new pride in their cultural heritage and are demanding to be accepted as full and equal human beings. I think this is an exciting and creative social phenomenon, but it raises three political problems, which we must analyze carefully.

The first is that in some instances the cultural revolt includes a demand for racial separatism, which is entirely self-defeating from a political standpoint. Translated into political terms, the cultural revolt too often expresses itself as a desire for self-determination. Now this is a very complex issue, . . . [but behind it is] a political principle that we must never forget. As long as blacks constitute only 11 per cent of the population, any go-it-alone strategy is bound to fail. Separatism can only aid Nixon's Southern strategy, which is designed to build a conservative majority on the basis of hostility to blacks. In this sense separatism is the opposite of self-determination, because it can lead to the continued subjection of blacks. Real self-determination can be achieved only by a unified black movement joining with other progressive social forces to form a coalition that represents a majority of the population. We must keep this in mind if we are to prevent the black cultural revolt from playing into the hands of white conservatives and segregationists who are the very worst enemies we have.

The second problem is that the cultural revolt has been accompanied by a growing tendency to justify, and sometimes engage in, violence as a form of political struggle. A clear distinction must, of course, be drawn between the violence of the oppressor and the reactive violence of the oppressed. Morally, the former is more reprehensible than the latter. But we must also judge the use of violence by the oppressed from a *political* standpoint. The question here is whether violence is an effective form of political struggle.

I think it can be demonstrated that for a racial minority the use of violence is not only politically ineffective but counterproductive and even suicidal. Who benefits when blacks engage in violence? Do blacks benefit, or do George Wallace, Spiro Agnew, John Mitchell, and Richard Nixon? I ask this question rhetorically, since it should be clear that violence can do nothing more than produce a reaction against blacks that will strengthen our enemies and thereby make it impossible to achieve the things we so badly need. In the end, it is not the black community that stands to gain from some of the more extreme activities of the Black Panthers and similar groups; it is the people who call for more police and less social spending. The problem is not only that violence obstructs the achievement of social change by strengthening the right; it also obscures the very meaning of social change by offering the desperate adventures of a few "revolutionaries" as an alternative to the mobilization of political majorities, and by making it appear that killing a cop is a serious alternative to full employment. I am not here discussing the motives of young blacks who preach violence. But I do call into question the effects of their actions. If we are to think strategically about eliminating racial injustice, then we should not be satisfied with an approach that results in aggravating our problems.

Finally, the third problem raised by the cultural revolt is that it has been exclusively preoccupied with racial issues and has thus tended to ignore other issues that are also vitally important. Ralph Ellison has written of his "struggle to stare down the deadly and hypnotic temptation to interpret the world and all its devices in terms of race." He wrote this as an artist who has devoted his life to portraying human reality in all its complexity. I would like, if I may, to apply Ellison's idea to the economic situation of black Americans today.

It goes without saying that Negroes are brutalized by racial prejudice and discrimination. What is not often remembered, however, is that were we to eliminate racism today we would have solved only part of the problem, and perhaps not even the major part. The fact is that we live in a society that not only tolerates a relatively high level of unemployment, but is willing to increase that rate in order to combat inflation. Automation is eliminating thousands of jobs that were held by both whites and blacks. This problem does not spring from blackness but from a technological revolution that has affected all poor people, regardless of their race. We might psychoanalyze racism out of all the prejudiced white people in the country, but until we are willing to accept the principle that every able-bodied man or woman has the right to a decent and well-paying job, we shall not have begun to attack the economic roots of racial injustice. We need a social and economic program that will wipe out poverty, and we need that far more than we need pure white hearts. I do not mean to disparage the attack on racism, but if we do only that, we shall provide an out for those whites who are far more interested in "giving a damn" about impoverished blacks

than in doing the economically more uncomfortable things that could eliminate hunger and deprivation.

I emphasize these economic problems for a special reason. You are part
of an intellectual elite among blacks. As such, it is extraordinarily important
that you do not lose touch with the problems and aspirations of the great
mass of blacks who are not part of this elite. In order to do this you must
guard against the possibility of becoming concerned only with intellectual,
cultural, and racial issues while the problems of lower- and working-class
blacks remain economic. These millions of black people do not have the
choice of withdrawing into the kind of concerns, sometimes mere fantasies,
which are now prevalent among certain elements of the black intelligentsia,
and until they do have that choice, it is your responsibility to fight for programs that will enable them to achieve full economic justice.

I think it is also your responsibility, especially those of you who will go
on to graduate work and university teaching, to protect the intellectual integrity of the university. In *The Souls of Black Folks*, W. E. B. Du Bois
wrote that the function of the university is above all "to be the organ of
that fine adjustment between real life and the growing knowledge of life,
an adjustment which forms the secret of civilization." You must help it perform that function, particularly in the controversial field of black studies.
The study of the black experience in America is so vital to an understanding of our country and our people that it must attract scholars of the very
highest intellectual eminence. We must not permit this promising area of
study to become a refuge for charlatans more skilled at intellectual intimidation than at investigation. For this reason it is essential that those students and faculty members who are committed to upholding the scholarly
standards of black studies firmly refuse to accommodate anyone who would
debase them.

We are living in a time of such rapid change that we must continuously
redefine our terms and reassert those principles which seem to hold some
truth. I do not regard as radical or progressive any black person who does
anything that strengthens the forces of conservatism. I therefore do not
regard as radical those who talk of separatism, however loud may be their
words and however militant and controversial their actions. For all practical purposes, they stand with the opponents of our struggle. I do not regard as radical those who advocate violence only to bring about repression.
I do not regard as radical those who moralize about the evils of white society, if at the same time they do not present a program that can solve the

problems of black society. Nor are they radical who assume a revolutionary posture, but who then propose nothing more than an escape from American political reality and from the grinding social struggles that we must participate in. The real radical is that person who has a vision of equality and is willing to do those things that will bring reality closer to that vision. And by equality I do not mean "separate but equal," a phrase created by segregationists in order to prevent the attainment of equality. I mean equality based upon an integrated social order in which black people, proud of their race and their heritage, shall have no door closed to them.

In such a social order there will no longer be walls, representing fear and insecurity, to separate people from one another. Such walls, whether constructed by whites or by blacks, are built to oppress and repress, but never to liberate. I admit that most likely we will not achieve such equality next month, or next year, or even in this decade. But it is a goal that we must hold ever before us, even in the darkest of times; for it not only confers dignity upon our struggle, but it should indicate to us how we must act toward one another today if we are to preserve for tomorrow the possibility of a just society.

THE BLACKS AND THE UNIONS

One of the main articles of faith in liberal dogma these days is that the interests and objectives of the American trade union movement are in fundamental conflict with the interests and objectives of black America. One can hardly pick up any of the major journals of liberal opinion without reading some form of the statement that the white worker has become affluent and conservative and feels his security to be threatened by the demand for racial equality. A corollary of this statement is that it is a primary function of the labor movement to protect the white worker from the encroaching black. Furthermore, the argument runs, since there are no signs that the blacks may be letting up in their struggle for economic betterment, a hostile confrontation between blacks and unions is not only inevitable but necessary.

It may well be that historians of the future, recording the events of the past five years, will conclude that the major effect of the civic turbulence in this period has been in fact to distract us from the real and pressing social needs of the nation. And perhaps nothing illustrates the point more vividly than the whole question of the relations between blacks and the unions.

This question itself, however, cannot be properly understood except in the larger context of the history of the civil rights movement. Negro protest in the sixties, if the movement is in its turn to be properly understood, must be divided into two distinct phases. The first phase, which covered something like the first half of the decade, was one in which the movement's clear objective was to destroy the legal foundations of racism in America. Thus the locale of the struggle was the South, the evil to be eliminated was Jim Crow, and the enemy, who had a special talent for arousing moral outrage among even the most reluctant sympathizers with the cause, was the rock-willed segregationist.

Now, one thing about the South more than any other has been obscured in the romantic vision of the region—of ancient evil, of defeat, of enduring rural charm—that has been so much of our literary and intellectual tradition: for the Negro, Southern life had precisely a quality of clarity, a clarity which while oppressive was also supportive. The Southern caste system and folk

From *Harper's Magazine*, May 1971. Reprinted by permission.

culture rested upon a clear, albeit unjust, set of legal and institutional relationships which prescribed roles for individuals and established a modicum of social order. The struggle that was finally mounted against that system was actually fed and strengthened by the social environment from which it emerged. No profound analysis, no overriding social theory was needed in order both to locate and understand the injustices that were to be combated. All that was demanded of one was sufficient courage to demonstrate against them. One looks back upon this period in the civil rights movement with nostalgia.

During the second half of the sixties, the center of the crisis shifted to the sprawling ghettos of the North. Here black experience was radically different from that in the South. The stability of institutional relationships was largely absent in Northern ghettos, especially among the poor. Over twenty years ago, the black sociologist E. Franklin Frazier was able to see the brutalizing effect of urbanization upon lower class blacks: ". . . The bonds of sympathy and community of interests that held their parents together in the rural environment have been unable to withstand the disintegrating forces in the city." Southern blacks migrated North in search of work, seeking to become transformed from a peasantry into a working class. But instead of jobs they found only misery, and far from becoming a proletariat, they came to constitute a *lumpenproletariat,* an underclass of rejected people. Frazier's prophetic words resound today with terrifying precision: ". . . As long as the bankrupt system of Southern agriculture exists, Negro families will continue to seek a living in the towns and cities of the country. They will crowd the slum areas of Southern cities or make their way to Northern cities, where their family life will become disrupted and their poverty will force them to depend upon charity."

Out of such conditions, social protest was to emerge in a form peculiar to the ghetto, a form which could never have taken root in the South except in such large cities as Atlanta or Houston. The evils in the North are not easy to understand and fight against, or at least not as easy as Jim Crow, and this has given the protest from the ghetto a special edge of frustration. There are few specific injustices, such as a segregated lunch counter, that offer both a clear object of protest and a good chance of victory. Indeed, the problem in the North is not one of social injustice so much as the results of institutional pathology. Each of the various institutions touching the lives of urban blacks—those relating to education, health, employment, housing, and crime—is in need of drastic reform. One might say that the Northern race problem has in good part become simply the problem of the American city

—which is gradually becoming a reservation for the unwanted, most of whom are black.

In such a situation, even progress has proven to be a mixed blessing. During the sixties, for example, Northern blacks as a group made great economic gains, the result of which being that hundreds of thousands of them were able to move out of the hard-core poverty areas. Meanwhile, however, their departure, while a great boon to those departing, only contributed further to the deterioration of the slums, now being drained of their stable middle and working class. Combined with the large influx of Southern blacks during the same period, this process was leaving the ghetto more and more the precinct of a depressed underclass. To the segregation by race was now added segregation by class, and all of the problems created by segregation and poverty—inadequate schooling, substandard and overcrowded housing, lack of access to jobs or to job training, narcotics and crime—were greatly aggravated. And again because of segregation, the violence of the black underclass was turned in upon itself.

If the problems of the ghetto do not lend themselves to simple analyses or solutions, then, this is because they cannot be solved without mounting a total attack on the inadequacies endemic to, and injustices embedded in, all of our institutions. It is perhaps understandable that young Northern blacks, confronting these problems, have so often provided answers which are really non-answers, which are really dramatic statements satisfying some sense of the need for militancy without even beginning to deal with the basic economic and political problems of the ghetto. Primary among these non-answers is the idea that black progress depends upon a politics of race and revolution. I am referring here not to the recent assertions of black pride—assertions that will be made as long as that pride continues to be undermined by white society—but about the kind of black nationalism which consists in a bitter rejection of American society and vindicates a withdrawal from social struggle into a kind of hermetic racial world where blacks can "do their thing." Nationalists have been dubbed "militants" by the press because they have made their point with such fervent hostility to white society, but the implication of their position actually amounts to little more than the age-old conservative message that blacks should help themselves—a thing that, by the very definition of the situation, they have not the resources to do.

The same is true of black proposals for revolution. For to engage in revolutionary acts in a contemporary America—where, despite a lot of inflammatory rhetoric, there is not even a whisper of a revolutionary situation—not only diverts precious energies away from the political arena where the real battles for change must be fought, but might also precipitate a vicious counterrevolution, the chief victims of which will be blacks.

The truth about the situation of the Negro today is that there are powerful forces, composed largely of the corporate elite and Southern conservatives, which will resist any change in the economic or racial structure of this country that might cut into their resources or challenge their status; and such is precisely what any program genuinely geared to improve his lot must do. Moreover, these forces today are not merely resisting change. With their representative Richard Nixon in the White House, they are engaged in an assault on the advances made during the past decade. It has been Nixon's tragic and irresponsible choice to play at the politics of race—not, to be sure, with the primitive demagoguery of a "Pitchfork Ben" Tillman, say, but nevertheless with the same intent of building a political majority on the basis of white hostility to blacks. So far he has been unsuccessful, but the potential for the emergence of such a reactionary majority does exist, especially if the turbulence and racial polarization which we have recently experienced persist.

What is needed, therefore, is not only a program that would effect some fundamental change in the distribution of America's resources for those in the greatest need of them but a political majority that will support such a program as well. In other words, nothing less than a program truly, not merely verbally, radical in scope would be adequate to meet the present crisis; and nothing less than a politically constituted majority, outnumbering the conservative forces, would be adequate to carry it through. Now, it so happens that there is one social force which, by virtue both of its size and its very nature, is essential to the creation of such a majority—and so in relation to which the success or failure of the black struggle must finally turn. And that is the American trade union movement.

Addressing the AFL-CIO convention in 1961, Martin Luther King observed: "Negroes are almost entirely a working people. There are pitifully few Negro millionaires and few Negro employers. Our needs are identical with labor's needs—decent wages, fair working conditions, livable housing, old age security, health and welfare measures, conditions in which families can grow, have education for their children and respect in the community."

Despite the widely held belief that the blacks and the unions have not the same, but rather irreconcilable, interests—and despite the fact that certain identifiable unions do practice racial discrimination—King's words remain as valid today. Blacks *are* mostly a working people; they continue to need what labor needs; and they must fight side by side with unions to achieve these things.

Of all the misconceptions about the labor movement that have been so lovingly dwelt on in the liberal press, perhaps none is put forth more often and is further from the truth than that the unions are of and for white people. For one thing, there are, according to labor historian Thomas R. Brooks, between 2,500,000 and 2,750,000 black trade unionists in America.* If his figures are correct, and other estimates seem to bear them out, the percentage of blacks in the unions is a good deal higher than the percentage of blacks in the total population—15 per cent as compared with 11 per cent, to be precise. And since the vast majority of black trade unionists are members of integrated unions, one can conclude that the labor movement is the most integrated major institution in American society, certainly more integrated than the corporations, the churches, or the universities.

Moreover, blacks are joining unions in increasing numbers. According to a 1968 report by *Business Week*, one out of every three new union members is black. The sector of the economy which is currently being most rapidly unionized is that of the service industries, and most particularly among government employees, such as hospital workers, sanitation workers, farm workers, and paraprofessionals in educational and social-welfare institutions. This category of worker is, of course, both largely nonwhite and shamefully underpaid.

Like other workers, blacks have gained from the achievements of their unions in the way of higher wages, improved working conditions, and better fringe benefits. To be sure, in some unions whites still possess a disproportionate number of the higher paying jobs and there is not yet adequate black representation at the staff level and in policy-making positions. But the question of what continues to account for the perpetuation of such inequities cannot properly be answered by the fashionable and easy reference to racial discrimination in the unions. Statistical surveys have shown that the participation of blacks in the work force is no higher in nonunionized occupations than in unionized ones. Indeed, as Derek C. Bok and John T. Dunlop have pointed out in their remarkably informed and comprehensive study, *Labor and the American Community*, even in the automotive and aerospace industries, where the unions have been known for dedication to racial justice, the percentage of blacks, particularly in the skilled jobs, is not appreciably higher than in other industries.

* "Black Upsurge in the Unions," *Dissent*, March–April 1970.

There have, therefore, to be far more fundamental social and economic reasons for present inequalities in employment. Primary among these reasons are certain underlying changes within the entire society which are being reflected in the evolving character and composition of the work force itself. The upsurge of union organization of minority-group workers in the fields of education, sanitation, and health care, for instance, is the result of the rapid expansion of the service sector of the economy.

Another crucial factor here is government economic policy. The tremendous growth in the economy from 1960 to 1968 increased nonwhite employment by 19 per cent, 4 per cent higher than the increase for whites, and during the same period the unemployment rate for nonwhite adult men dropped from 9.6 to 3.9 per cent. A large number of these new black workers entered unions for the simple reason that they had jobs. And now many of them are out of jobs, not because of union discrimination but because the Nixon administration's economic policies have so far caused a sharp increase in unemployment.

All of which is not to exonerate the entire labor movement of any possible charge of wrongdoing. It is rather to put the problem of economic inequality into some useful perspective. The inequalities which persist within the unions must of course be corrected. They are in fact being corrected through the work of the labor movement itself—the role of the civil rights department of the AFL-CIO is particularly noteworthy here—the civil rights activities of the federal government, and the efforts of black trade unionists who are taking over leadership positions in their locals and are playing more of a role in determining union policy. The union drive against discrimination was exemplified by the fight made by the AFL-CIO to have a Fair Employment Practices section written into the 1964 Civil Rights Act. Both President Kennedy and Robert Kennedy were opposed to including an FEPC section because they thought it would kill the bill, but George Meany pressed for it. He did so for a simple reason. The AFL-CIO is a federation of affiliates which retain a relatively high degree of autonomy. The parent body can urge compliance with its policies, but the decision to act is left up to the affiliates. Meany felt that the only way the AFL-CIO could deal effectively with unions practicing discrimination would be to demand compliance with the law of the land. He testified before the House Judiciary Committee that the labor movement was calling for "legislation for the correction of shortcomings in its own ranks." And the passage of the 1964 Civil Rights Act greatly speeded the process of this correction.

Most labor leaders, I believe, are opposed to discrimination against the blacks on moral grounds. But they also have highly practical grounds for their position. They understand that discrimination hurts the entire labor movement as much as it hurts blacks. They know from long experience as unionists that anything which divides the workers makes it more difficult for them to struggle together for the achievement of common goals. Racial antagonisms have undermined solidarity during strikes and have been exploited by management as a means of weakening unions. The following passage from the classic study *The Black Worker*, written in 1931 by Sterling D. Spero and Abram L. Harris, may not be typical of every company's approach to its work force, yet it describes a practice commonly in use till this very day:

> The Negro is now recognized as a permanent factor in industry and large employers use him as one of the racial and national elements which help to break the homogeneity of their labor force. This, incidentally, fits into the program of big concerns for maintaining what they call "a cosmopolitan force," which frees the employer from dependence upon any one group for his labor supply and also thwarts unity of purpose and labor organization.

People no longer lend much credence to the idea that management continues to think and operate in such convoluted terms. But it does, and so does labor. Indeed, such terms as "labor solidarity" or "labor disunity" are standard tools of the trade in labor-management relations. A further error is to imagine that unions might, from such reasoning, increase unity within their ranks by excluding blacks. On the contrary, given the character of the American working class, the *only* possibility for genuine labor solidarity is for the blacks to be fully integrated into every level of the trade union movement. If they are not, then they will continue to exist outside the unions as a constant source of cheap labor exploitable by management to depress wages or to break strikes.

Another notion which has passed into vogue among some blacks as well as some whites is that the whole problem of integration can be finessed by organizing the workers into dual unions. This is not a new idea, nor is its feasibility any greater today than was evidenced by a record of impossibility in the past. For were there to be racially separate unions, it would naturally follow that the interests of blacks would be diametrically opposed to those of whites, with whom they would be in competition. And once again, no matter how innocently or unintentionally, the blacks would remain in the role of a reserve army that could be called into action whenever companies felt the white workers needed a good kick in the pants.

Of course the blacks would also be victims in this situation, since they would be at the beck and call of management only if they were chronically unemployed. Thus, exploitation is as much the effect of poverty as its cause. It is only the poor, those who are needy and weak, who can be manipulated at the whim of the wealthy. This introduces another notion concerning the welfare of black and white workers about which there has grown up a misplaced skepticism—namely, the function of the supply of labor. Put very simply, it is in the interests of employers for the supply of labor to be greater than the demand for it. This situation obtains when there is high unemployment or what is often called a "loose" labor market. Under these conditions, the bargaining position of the unions is weakened since labor, which is after all the product unions are selling, is not in high demand and also because there are a lot of unemployed workers whom the companies can turn to if the unions should in any way prove recalcitrant. Generally speaking, an excess of supply over demand for labor exerts a downward pressure on wages, and, vice versa, there is an upward pressure on wages when the demand for labor outpaces the supply.

In addition, this dynamic of supply and demand affects the level of racial antagonism within the work force. If supply exceeds demand, i.e., if there is a high level of unemployment, there will be tremendous competition for jobs between white and black workers and racial tensions will increase. Under conditions of relative full employment, there will be little job competition and greater racial harmony. As George Lichtheim recently pointed out, "If economic conflict as a source of political antagonism is ruled out . . . the residual cultural tensions . . . need not and doubtless will not fall to zero; but they can be held down to a tolerable level."*

These ideas shape the conceptual universe as well as the behavior of many of the principal actors in our country's economic conflicts. The fact that they tend to be ignored in so much current discussion of blacks and unions is as much a testimony to the naïveté of liberal journalists as it is to the public relations skills of corporations. A good example of what I mean is the press treatment accorded the terrible racial conflict in the building trades and the administration's policies in this area.

Racial discrimination exists in the building trades. It is unjustifiable by any moral standard, and as to the objective of rooting it out there can be no disagreement among people of good will. How truly to achieve this objective is another matter. An important distinction here is often overlooked. One cannot set varying moral standards in judging the performance of institutions; the same standard must be applied equally to all—to the unions, the corporations, the churches, etc. But beyond the realm of moral judgment

* "What Socialism Is and Is Not," *The New York Review of Books,* April 9, 1970.

is the crucial question of social utility. Blacks could attack Jim Crow in the South without regard to the welfare of the lunch counters, the hotels, or whatever, because they had little or no stake in them. This is not the case with the trade union movement, a social force in which blacks *do* have a stake. If blacks attack the unions in such a way as to damage them irreparably, they will ultimately harm themselves. At it happens, certain presently self-styled friends of the Negro are in fact not at all averse to such a possible development.

Writing in the *New York Times*, Tom Wicker reflected the views of many liberals when he described the Nixon administration's strong and forthright position on the building-trades issue as "remarkable." Wicker's analysis, however, never advances beyond this point. He never asks why the Nixon administration, particularly Attorney General Mitchell and most particularly given other administration policies, would suddenly take such an interest in the welfare of blacks. The question is neither gratuitous nor idle. Why, in fact, would a President who has developed a "Southern strategy," who has cut back on school integration efforts, tried to undermine the black franchise by watering down the 1965 Voting Rights Act, nominated to the Supreme Court men like Haynsworth and Carswell, cut back on funds for vital social programs, and proposed a noxious crime bill for Washington, D.C., which is nothing less than a blatant appeal to white fear—why indeed would such a President take up the cause of integration in the building trades?

To begin with, Mr. Nixon's Philadelphia Plan—which requires contractors to make a commitment to hire a certain quota of black workers on a job where over $500,000 of federal funds are involved—actually does nothing for integration. In order to meet this commitment, a contractor could shift the required number of black workers in an area onto a particular job, a procedure known in the trade as checkerboarding. He would thus satisfy federal requirements *for that job*, but no new jobs would be created for blacks and no Negroes would be brought into the building trades. In fact, the contractor can even achieve compliance simply by making an effort of good faith, such as contacting certain people in the area who are concerned about black participation in the building trades. If those people do not produce any workers, the contractor has done his job and can get the federal money. The Philadelphia Plan makes no provision for training, nor does it provide a means for blacks to attain the security of journeyman status within the unions. It is geared only to temporary jobs, and even in this area it is deficient. It is designed primarily to embarrass the unions and to organize public pressure against them.

In simple truth, the plan is part and parcel of a general Republican attack on labor. The same administration which designed it (as well as the Southern strategy) has also sent to Congress a measure that would increase federal control over internal union political affairs. Republican Senators and Representatives have introduced dozens of anti-labor bills—one of which, for example, would create a right-to-work law for federal employees; another would restrict labor's involvement in political activities. Moreover, the administration has turned the heat on labor at the same time that it has cooled pressure against discrimination by the corporations.

The advantages to the Republicans from this kind of strategy should be obvious. Nixon supports his friends among the corporate elite and hurts his enemies in the unions. He also gains a convenient cover for his anti-Negro policies in the South, and, above all, he weakens his political opposition by aggravating the differences between its two strongest and most progressive forces—the labor movement and the civil rights movement.

The Philadelphia Plan and related actions are also part of the administration's attempt to pin onto labor the blame for inflation in construction costs. The *Wall Street Journal* has suggested that contractors welcome the thrust for integration in the building trades, since this "might slow inflation in construction by increasing the supply of workers." There is reason to believe that Mr. Nixon thinks in these same terms. It will be remembered that on almost the very day he proposed the Philadelphia Plan, he also ordered a 75 per cent reduction in federal construction—thereby reducing the number of jobs available in the industry and producing the twofold effect of exerting a deflationary pressure on wages and increasing competition among workers over scarce jobs. When Nixon finally freed some of the construction funds some months later (a move no doubt designed to improve the economic picture for the 1970 elections), he warned that "a shortage of skilled labor runs up the cost of that labor." He said he would issue directives to the Secretaries of Defense, Labor, and Health, Education and Welfare to train veterans and others toward the goal of "enlarging the pool of skilled manpower."

It should be pointed out in passing that the President's approach to the problem of inflation in construction costs cannot succeed since he has made the typical businessman's error of identifying wages as the major inflationary factor. According to the Bureau of Labor Statistics, on-site labor costs as a percentage of total construction costs decreased between 1949 and 1969 from 33 per cent to 18 per cent. During the same period, the combined cost of land and financing rose from 16 per cent to 31 per cent of the total cost. Thus land and financing, not labor, have been the major causes of inflation in construction. Nevertheless, the President continues his crusade against "wage inflation."

The concern with increasing the supply while reducing the cost of labor is what motivated the Nixon administration's most recent act in the construction field—the suspension of the 1931 Davis-Bacon Act. Here the "deflationary" intention is more evident than in the case of the Philadelphia Plan, but the similarity between the two moves is striking, particularly with regard to the anti-union role envisioned for the unorganized Negro worker.

The Davis-Bacon Act requires contractors on federal or federally assisted projects to pay all workers, union or nonunion, the prevailing union wage rates. The suspension of the Act will not directly affect the wages of unionized workers who are protected by their contract. It will, however, enable contractors to cut the wages of nonunion workers, and this, in turn, should encourage the employment of these workers instead of the higher paid unionists. Thus, there will be fewer jobs for organized workers (there is already an 11 per cent unemployment rate in the construction industry), and the bargaining power of the unions will be weakened. Since many of the unorganized workers are nonwhite, it might be argued that this is a boon to their fortunes since they will be more likely to find work. Aside from the fact that they will be working for lower wages, the question is again raised whether it is in the interests of blacks to let themselves be used by employers to hurt unions. I do not think that it is. Their interests lie in becoming part of the trade union movement. Ironically, the current attack on labor may speed the process of their entrance into the labor movement, for in situations where union standards have been threatened by open shops, unions have been spurred on to fully organize their industry.

It should be emphasized that this would only encourage changes that have already been taking place for a number of years as a result of pressure from civil rights groups and union leaders.

Seventy-nine Outreach programs now operate in as many cities and have placed over 8,000 minority-group youngsters in building-trades apprenticeship training programs. Sixty per cent have been placed in the highest paying trades—the plumbers, electricians, sheet-metal workers, carpenters, pipe fitters, and iron workers. This is far from sufficient, of course, but within the past two years, these programs have expanded by over 400 per cent, and they are continuing to grow. The role of civil rights activists should be to continue to see that they grow.

The blacks have a choice. They can fight to strengthen the trade union movement by wiping out the vestiges of segregation that remain in it, or

345

they can, knowingly or unknowingly, offer themselves as pawns in the conservatives' game of bust-the-unions.

The choice must be made on the basis of a critical assessment of the current economic plight of blacks. More than any single factor, the Nixon administration's policies of high interest rates, "fiscal responsibility," and economic slowdown are undermining the gains which blacks have made during the past decade. Dr. Charles C. Killingsworth, a leading manpower economist, predicted some months ago that within a year the unemployment rate is likely to go up to 8 per cent. We could expect the rate for blacks to be twice as high. Nixon's managed recession may calm the fears of businessmen, but it will do so at terrible cost to blacks and to all other working people. There are, no doubt, many well-meaning people who are concerned about the plight of unemployed workers under Nixon, but it is only the labor movement that is fighting every day for policies that will get these workers back on the job.

Thus, it is clear why unions are important to black workers. What may perhaps seem less obvious and must also be sharply emphasized is that the legislative program of the trade union movement can go a long way toward satisfying the economic needs of the larger black community. The racial crisis, as we have seen, is not an isolated problem that lends itself to redress by a protesting minority. Being rooted in the very social and economic structure of the society, it can be solved only by a comprehensive program that gets to the heart of why we can't build adequate housing for everybody, why we must always have a "tolerable" level of unemployment, or why we lack enough funds for education. In this sense the racial crisis challenges the entire society's capacity to redirect its resources on the basis of human need rather than profit. Blacks can pose this challenge, but only the federal government has the power and the money to meet it. And it is here that the trade union movement can play such an important role.

The problems of the most aggrieved sector of the black ghetto cannot and will never be solved without full employment, and full employment, with the government as employer of last resort, is the keystone of labor's program. One searches in vain among the many so-called friends of the black struggle for a seconding voice to this simple yet far-reaching proposition. Some call it inflationary, while to others, who are caught up in the excitement of the black cultural revolution, it is pedestrian and irrelevant. But in terms of the economic condition of the black community, nothing more radical has yet been proposed. There is simply no other way for the black *lumpenproletariat* to become a proletariat. And full employment is only one part of labor's program. The movement's proposals in the areas of health, housing, education, and environment would, if enacted, achieve nothing less than the transformation of the quality of our urban life. How ironic that in this period, when the trade union movement is thought to be conservative, its social and economic policies are far and away more progressive than those of any other major American institution. Nor—again in contrast to most of the other groups officially concerned with these things—is labor's program merely in the nature of a grand proposal; there is also an actual record of performance, particularly in the area of civil rights. Clarence Mitchell, the director of the Washington Bureau of the NAACP and legislative chairman of the Leadership Conference on Civil Rights, a man more deeply involved in Congressional civil rights battles than any other black in America, has said: "None of the legislative fights we have made in the field of civil rights could have been won without the trade union movement. We couldn't have beaten Haynsworth without labor, and the struggle against Carswell would not have been a contest."

Labor's interest in progressive social legislation naturally leads it into the political arena. The committee on political education of the AFL-CIO, the political action committee of the UAW, and the political arm of the Teamsters were active in every state in the last election, registering and educating voters and getting out the vote. This year trade unionists were more politically active than they have ever been during an off-year election. The reason for this is clear. With so many liberal Senators up for reelection, and with political alignments in great flux, 1970 presented itself as a year that would initiate a new period in American politics—a period which would see the regrouping of liberal forces or the consolidation of a conservative majority.

One of the important factors determining the kind of political alignments that will emerge from this period of instability will be the relationship between the trade union movement and the liberal community, and today this relationship is severely strained. Differences over the war in Vietnam are frequently cited as a major cause of this division, but there has been a great deal of misunderstanding on this issue. The house of labor itself is divided over the war, and even those labor leaders who support it have enthusiastically backed dove Congressional candidates who have liberal domestic records, among them such firm opponents of the war as Mike Mansfield, Edward Kennedy, Vance Hartke, Philip Hart, Howard Metzenbaum, and Edmund Muskie.

A better understanding of the trade union movement by liberals may be developing, but for the present the antagonistic attitudes that exist cast an ideological pall over the chances for uniting the Democratic left coalition.

347

It must be said that the vehement contempt with which the liberals have come to attack the unions bespeaks something more than a mere political critique of "conservatism." When A. H. Raskin writes that "the typical worker—from construction craftsman to shoe clerk—has become probably the most reactionary political force in the country"; or when Anthony Lewis lumps under the same category the rich oilmen and "the members of powerful, monopolistic labor unions"; or when Murray Kempton writes that "the AFL-CIO has lived happily in a society which, more lavishly than any in history, has managed the care and feeding of incompetent white people," and adds, "Who better represents that ideal than George Wallace"; or when many other liberals casually toss around the phrase "labor fascists"— one cannot but inevitably conclude that one is in the presence not of political opposition but of a certain class hatred. This hatred is not necessarily one based on conflicting class interests—though they may play a role here— but rather the hatred of the elite for the "mass." And this hatred is multiplied a thousandfold by the fact that we live in a democratic society in which the coarse multitude can outvote the elite and make decisions which may be contrary to the wishes and values, perhaps even the interests and the prejudices, of those who are better off.

It is difficult not to conclude that many liberals and radicals use subjective, rather than objective, criteria in judging the character of a social force. A progressive force, in their view, is one that is alienated from the dominant values of the culture, not one which contributes to greater social equality and distributive justice. Thus today the trade union movement has been relegated to reactionary status, even though it is actually more progressive than at any time in its history—if by progressive we mean a commitment to broad, long-term social reform in addition to the immediate objectives of improving wages and working conditions. At the same time, the most impoverished social group, that substratum which Herbert Marcuse longingly calls "the outcasts and the outsiders," has been made the new vanguard of social progress. And it is here that liberals and new leftists come together in their proposal for a new coalition "of the rich, educated and dedicated with the poor," as Eric F. Goldman has admiringly described it, or in Walter Laqueur's more caustic phraseology, "between the *lumpenproletariat* and the *lumpenintelligentsia*."

This political approach, known among liberals as New Politics and among radicals as New Leftism, denotes a certain convergence of the left and the right—if not in philosophy and intent, then at least in practical effect. I am not referring simply to the elitism which the intellectual left shares with the economic right, but also to their symbiotic political relationship. Many of the sophisticated right-wing attacks on labor are frequently couched in left-wing rhetoric. Conservative claims that unions are anti-black, are responsible for inflation, and constitute minorities which threaten and intimidate the majority reverberate in the liberal community and are shaping public opinion to accept a crackdown on the trade union movement.

While many adherents of the New Politics are outraged by Nixon's Southern strategy, their own strategy is simply the obverse of his. The potential for a Republican majority depends upon Nixon's success in attracting into the conservative fold lower-middle-class whites, the same group that the New Politics has written off. The question is not whether this group is conservative or liberal; for it is both, and how it acts will depend upon the way the issues are defined. If they are defined as race and dissent, then Nixon will win. But if, on the other hand, they are defined so as to appeal to the progressive economic interests of the lower middle class, then it becomes possible to build an alliance on the basis of common interest between this group and the black community. The importance of the trade union movement is that it embodies this common interest. This was proved most clearly in 1968 when labor mounted a massive educational campaign which reduced the Wallace supporters among its membership to a tiny minority. And the trade union movement remains today the greatest obstacle to the success of Nixon's strategy.

The prominent racial and ethnic loyalties that divide American society have, together with our democratic creed, obscured a fundamental reality—that we are a class society and, though we do not often talk about such things, that we are engaged in a class struggle. This reality may not provide some people with their wished-for quotient of drama, though I would think that the GE strike or the UAW strike against GM were sufficiently dramatic, and it may now have become an institutionalized struggle between the trade union movement and the owners and managers of corporate wealth. Yet it is a struggle nonetheless, and its outcome will determine whether we will have a greater or lesser degree of economic and social equality in this country. As long as blacks are poor, our own struggle will be part of this broader class reality. To the degree that it is not, black liberation will remain a dream in the souls of an oppressed people.

Abernathy, Ralph, 55, 61
AFL-CIO, 229, 340
Africans, 255–258
Agriculture, mechanization of, 94, 180;
  Negroes' vulnerability to, 112, 180, 293.
  See also Revolution, technological.
Alabama Interracial Council, 58
American Friends Service Committee, 76
Anthony, Paul, 317
Antipoverty programs, 159–160
Anti-Semitism, black, 171–173, 232–233,
  237
Arnold, Matthew, 214–215
Asheville, N.C., 22
Atlanta, 248; conference of Negro leaders
  in (1956), 100–103
Automation. *See* Revolution, technological.

Bakke, Edward Wight, 148
Baldwin, James, 173
Bankhead, Senator John, 9
Bariol, Claude, 77–79
Bassett, W. T., 150
Bedford-Stuyvesant, 209–210
Bilbo, Rep. Theodore G., 123
Billings, Thomas A., 280–283
Birmingham, Ala., 9; civil rights struggles
  in, 107–108, 111–112
Black capitalism, xiii, 251, 259–260, 295–
  297
Black community control, xiv, 297–298
Black Manifesto, 302–303
Black Muslims, 115, 136, 176, 323
Black nationalism, xiv, 124–125, 255–258,
  260, 265, 293, 337
Black Panther party, 155, 294, 303n, 313,
  319
Black power, xiv, 154–157, 160–165 *pas-
  sim*, 185, 226, 256, 275, 294
Black studies, xiv–xv, 253–254, 281–285,
  300–302, 333
Black Worker, The, 341
Black Workers Alliance, 299
Bloom, Benjamin, 278
Bolivar Co., Miss., 67–68
Bombings, 60, 100, 101, 317
Bond, Julian, 242
Brimmer, Andrew, 292, 310

Brotherhood of Sleeping Car Porters, 262
Brown, Edward P., 140
Buckley, William F., 185
Burns, James MacGregor, 198
Bus drivers, responsibility of, 23
"Buy Black" campaigns, 159

Cairo, Ill., 183
Campaigns, presidential, cost of, 250
Carmichael, Stokely, 154, 155, 160, 161,
  207–208, 232
Caste system, Southern, 22, 23
Chain gang, 26–49; authoritarian system,
  39–40; captain, 28–29, 30, 31–32, 33,
  44–47; punishments on, 31, 41–42;
  theft, 48–49; working conditions, 42–44
Chalmers, Alan Knight, 65
Chapel Hill, N.C., 21–22, 24
Charleston, Miss., 66–67
Chicago, 155, 210; Democratic convention
  in (1968), 245, 246–247
Children, Negro: effects of segregation on,
  88–91
Church, Negro, 11
CIO, 159
Civil Rights Act of 1964, 129, 130, 141,
  161, 193, 264; fair employment section,
  129, 340
Civil Rights Act of 1965, 141, 161
Civil Rights Bill of 1966, 158, 161
Civil rights movement, 107, 227, 293, 335;
  antagonizes moderates, 116, 117; coalition with labor movement, 227–228;
  evolution into social movement, 115,
  193–199; expansion of base within
  Negro community, 111; the left in, 126;
  nationalist trends in, 124–125; "no-win"
  policy, 116–117, 161, 293–294; political
  action, 112; political cutting edge, 122;
  programs for, 129–131; responsibility to
  peace movement, 166–168, 170; revolutionary quality, 117–118; rightist threat
  to, 123–124; shift in focus, 111–112;
  spreads to North, 111
Clark, Kenneth, 90, 148, 268
Class struggle, 349
Cleaver, Eldridge, xiv, 244–245, 247, 303n
Columbia University, 230

Communist party, 125–126; attack on fair employment practice legislation, 125; attack on March on Washington movement (1941), 125

Community, Negro: divisions within, 195, 224, 271, 294–295; economic reforms needed by, 118, 130; expansion of civil rights movement in, 111; family in, 310; fight for freedom, 107; identification with, 11; self-help in, 114–115, 126; support for Martin Luther King, Jr., 224–225

CORE, 13, 156, 159, 161, 162, 294, 299

Cornell University, 267–268, 300

Council of Economic Advisers, 292

Courier (Pittsburgh), 9

Crowds, danger of, 24

Daley, Richard J., 156, 195–196

Danzig, David, 111

Dawson, William, 155, 156

Demagogues, right-wing, 269–270

Democratic party, 244, 246, 250, 307; 1968 convention, 245, 246–247, 250

Detroit, 179, 181, 183, 184, 192

Dewey, John, 213, 215, 221

Dirksen, Sen. Everett, 185

Dixiecrats, 156, 185, 242; coalition with Republicans, 186

Dollard, John, 90

Douglass, Frederick, 273

Du Bois, W. E. B., 158, 262, 273, 333

Eastland, Sen. James, 59, 62, 68, 69

Economic Opportunity Act, 131

Education: needs in, 188, 209; for Negroes, 114, 149–150. *See also* Schools; Black studies.

Eisenhower, Dwight D., 93, 103

Elections: of 1964, 120, 123, 247; of 1968, 244–251

Electoral College, 249

Elijah Muhammad, 135, 136, 137

Employment: full, 190–191, 192, 346; job and training programs, 151; of Negroes, 130, 150–152, 163, 168, 305–306; in public facility construction, 189, 191

Fair Employment Practices Commission, 9, 10, 152, 263

Farm Home Administration, 63, 72, 73

Federal Bureau of Investigation, 126

Fellowship of Reconciliation, 13

Ford, Gerald, 185

Forman, James, xiv, 302, 303

Frazier, E. Franklin, xiii, 148, 274, 295–296, 336

Freedom Budget, 152, 163, 185, 186, 232, 264

Frustration, philosophy of, 232–235

Full Employment Act (1945–1946), 163

Gandhi, Mahatma, 11, 103

Garvey, Marcus, xii, xiv, 159, 258, 262, 298, 299

Gass, Oscar, 191

Ghettos, 113, 180, 187, 190, 212, 236, 311–312, 336, 377; businessmen in, 233–234, 235; isolation of, 226–227; Moynihan's view of, 311; psychology of, 208–209, 234; teachers in, 234–235; violence in, 209–210, 225, 230; welfare worker in, 235

Goldfinger, Nathaniel, 188–189

Goldwater, Barry, 121–122, 123, 185, 198

Gray, Duncan, 65

Greenville (Miss.) Army Air Base, 79–80

Gregory, Dick, 247

Hamer, Fannie Lou, 194

Harlem, 172, 231; renaissance, x; riots in (1964), 126–127, 141, 231

Harrington, Michael, 116, 189

Hayes, Roland, 8–9

Health, national plan, 131

Health care: needs in, 188; for Negroes, 181, 190

Health, Education and Welfare, Department of, 161

Hillsboro, N.C., 26

History, Negro, 218–219, 328

Hoffer, Eric, 114

Housing, 158, 236; fair, 144, 150; needs, 188, 292, 320; in New York, 320–322; public, 118

Hughes, Langston, 142, 174–175

Humphrey, Hubert H., 187, 243, 244, 247, 248, 249, 250

Immigrants, 164, 272

Income, of Negroes, 112, 163, 181

Indianola, Miss., 63

Innis, Roy, xiii, xiv, 296, 305

Jackson, Justice Robert H., 51–52

Jackson State College, 319

Jensen, Arthur, 277–279

Jews, 113, 231, 232, 237, 271–272

Jim Crow, 96, 111; against interstate travelers, 13–25; in armed forces, 50–52, 263; on public transportation, 5–7, 8, 99

Job Corps, 152, 159

Johnson, Lyndon B., 120, 121, 122, 123, 162–163, 229
Journey of Reconciliation, 13–25, 26n, 50
Justice Department, 161
Juvenile delinquency, 114–115

Keenan, Theodore, 71–74
Kennedy, John F., 120
Kennedy, Robert, 240–241, 244
Kent State University, 318
Kentucky, 25
Kenyatta, Jomo, 124
Kerner Commission. *See* National Advisory Commission on Civil Disorders, Report of.
King, Martin Luther, Jr., x, 57, 58, 60, 99, 100, 103, 137, 146, 154, 156, 161, 169–170, 184, 210, 222–229 *passim*, 231, 232, 240–241, 244, 272, 338
Kirk, Claude, 317
Ku Klux Klan, 96, 159

Labor movement, 251, 347; allied with black Americans, 262, 298–300, 306–307, 330, 335, 338–346; in elections of 1968, 248; force for progressive social legislation, 120, 216; segregation in, 96–97, 98; supported by civil rights movement, 227–228; teachers' unions, 216, 218
Laws, enforcement of existing, 197–198
Leadership, Negro, 107
Leadership Conference on Civil Rights, 229
Left, the, 125–129; in civil rights movement, 126; ultra, 126; unaffiliated, 127–129
Lenor, Nellie, 85–87
Lewis, Rufus, 57
Logan, Dr. and Mrs. Arthur, 321
Los Angeles, 143, 269; police department, 146–147
Lynchings, 158

Malcolm X, 117, 132–139, 157
March on Washington (1963), x, 109, 120, 264; movement in 1941, 10, 125, 159, 263
Market, imperfect functioning of, 113–114
Marshall, Thurgood, 239
Mboya, Tom, 256–257
McCarthy, Eugene, 250
McCone, John A., 140
McCone Report, 140–153
McKissick, Floyd, 154, 155, 160
Meany, George, 340

Middle class: Negro, 271–276; white, 10, 273–274
Militancy, 116, 117, 128, 179, 209, 210, 211, 212, 225
Minimum wage, 130, 191–192, 236
Minneapolis, 183, 269
Mississippi: civil rights activity in, 112; Delta, 62–87; killing of civil rights workers in, 319; Negro population of, 62; school system, 63
Mississippi Freedom Democratic party, 122, 194
Mitchell, Clarence, 347
Moderates, 116, 117, 137, 139
Money, Miss., 83
Montgomery, Ala., bus boycott of 1956, 55–61, 93, 94, 99, 100, 101, 262, 263–264
Montgomery Improvement Association, 55, 58
Moore, Amzie, 74–77, 81–85
Morgan, Irene. *See Morgan* v. *Commonwealth of Virginia.*
Morgan v. *Commonwealth of Virginia*, 13, 22, 23
Morse, Sen. Wayne, 50
Moses, Bob, 112
Moynihan, Daniel P., 180, 192–193, 286–287; "benign neglect" memo, 309–315
Moynihan Report, 140, 141
Muhammad Ali, 176–177
Myrdal, Gunnar, 115, 207

NAACP, 62–70 *passim*, 74, 159, 194, 229, 239, 272
National Advisory Commission on Civil Disorders, Report of, 228, 235, 238
National Sharecroppers Fund, 76–77
National Urban League, 194
Negro Leaders Conference on Nonviolent Integration, 100–103
Newark, 192
New Deal, 159, 247
New Left, xiv, 269, 348–349
Nixon, E. D., 55, 56, 262
Nixon, Richard M., 103, 242, 243, 244, 248, 249, 250, 307; policies of, 250–251, 252, 291–292, 305, 311, 313, 314, 316–317, 322, 328–329, 338, 343–345, 346, 349
Nonviolence, 7, 10–12, 25, 94–95, 108, 144, 156, 157, 159, 160, 166, 196–197, 203
North: Negroes in, 108, 209, 336–337; schools in, 113. *See also* Ghettos.
North Carolina, 25
Nuremberg trials, 51–52

Index

Oakland, 182
Orangeburg State College, 318–319

Parker, William, 140, 145, 146, 147
Patterson Plan, 68–71
Peace movement, 166–168; Negroes in, 167, 168, 170
Peace Walk, San Francisco to Moscow, 110
People's Voice, 9
Petersburg, Va., 21
Philadelphia, 182
Philadelphia Plan, 343, 344
Phillips, Channing, 247
Police, 5–7, 23–24, 63, 68, 129–130, 146–147, 183, 209–210, 233
Political equality, Negro, 62–63
Political power, Negro, 118–119, 154, 159; through coalition, 119–120, 156, 164–165, 193, 199, 200–201, 207, 229, 247, 264, 270, 276, 307–308. *See also* Voter registration; Voting behavior.
Poor People's Campaign (1968), 202–205
Poverty, 163, 211–212; among Negroes, 275–276; cost of, 237; war on, 189–190
Powell, Adam Clayton, 155
Proletariat, black slum, 180, 183, 251, 336, 346
Public works programs, 118, 130, 235, 236–237

Racism, 223, 224, 238, 319; America polarized by, 223, 224, 237; bond between Africans and Afro-Americans, 255; in intelligence studies, 277–279; in social institutions, vs. individual attitudes, 238–239
Randolph, A. Philip, 50, 152, 159, 163, 184, 204, 209, 231, 232, 248, 261–266, 273, 299
Reconstruction, 95
Redding, J. Saunders, 90
Reece, Jeanette, 56
Religious groups, 120, 156
Republican party, 242; coalition with Dixiecrats, 186; 1968 convention, 245–246, 250
Revolution, social, 179–180, 184–186, 207, 291, 308; black, 291, 292–293, 331–334, 337–338
Revolution, technological, 209; effect on Negroes, 114, 181, 264, 293. *See also* Agriculture, mechanization of.
Reynolds, Grant, 50
Riots, 113, 162–163, 185, 231; after World War I, 158–159; attitudes following, 193; Detroit (1943), 179; Harlem (1964), 126–127, 141, 231; in summer

of 1967, 178–180, 183–184, 187, 206; Watts (1965), 140–147 *passim*. *See also* Ghettos, violence in; Violence, mass.
Roosevelt, Franklin D., 263
Rowan, Carl T., 137–138
Roxboro, N.C., chain gang, 26–49
Ruleville, Miss., 68
Rumford (fair housing) Act, 144
Rustin, Bayard; in civil rights movement, x; on class differences, xiii; conscientious objector in World War II, 109; editor of *Liberation*, 110; member of War Resisters' League, 110; member of YCL, 109–110; pacifist, 109; participates in Montgomery bus boycott, 55–61; personal qualities, xi, 110; political experience, xiii; Quaker, 109; remembers best teacher, 213–214; sentenced to chain gang, 26–49; social objectives, ix–x, xv; theory of black history, xi–xii; on treatment of criminals, 47–48; youth, ix

Salinger, Pierre, 123
Scholarship Defense Fund, 194
Schools, 206, 216–217; decentralization of, 221, 264; integration of, 221, 264; militant demands for, 211; in Mississippi, 63; Northern, 113, 211; parent-teacher coalitions in, 217, 218; role in society, 215; segregated, 112–113, 158, 219
SCLC, 204
Seale, Bobby, xiv
Segregation: history of, 95–96; in labor movement, 96–97, 98; psychological effects of, 88–91; of schools, 112. *See also* Jim Crow.
Self-defense, Negro, 156–157
Self-help, 114; in Negro community, 114–115, 138–139
Senate Subcommittee on Manpower and Employment, 130
Shannon, William V., 193
Sheetmetal Workers Union, 151
Shuttlesworth, F. L., 100
Smith, J. Holmes, 11
SNCC, 155, 161, 162, 272, 294
Soul, xi, 223–224
South, 335–336; choice between integration and chaos, 103, 108; economic pressures against Negroes in, 71–80, 85–87; migration of industry to, 92; national parties in, 92–93, 112, 121, 198; Negro behavior in, 93–94, 97–98, 121; out-migration of Negroes from, 92, 94, 168, 236, 336; programs to benefit Negroes in, 209; social changes in, 316–317; upper, 25

Southern Negro Leaders Conference on Nonviolent Integration, 101–103
Southern Regional Council, 194
Southerners, attitudes of, 25, 123
Soviet Union, 110
Spanish-Americans, 200–201
Steele, C. K., 100
Stereotype, of Negroes and Jews, 171–173, 223–224
Sumner, Miss., 83–84
Sunflower Co., Miss., 68

Taft-Hartley Act, 130
Tallahatchie River, 82
Tennessee, 25
Thurman, Howard, 103
Trade union movement. *See* Labor movement.
Trailways Bus Co., 25
Transportation, needs in, 188
Truman, Harry S., 186, 263

Unemployment, 311, 342; of Negroes, 112, 148–149, 157–158, 181–182
U.S. Congress, 186, 187, 189, 198, 204, 229, 249, 292; Joint Economic Committee, 187, 191
U.S. Supreme Court, 13, 63, 99, 111, 239, 291–292

Vietnam war, 243; cost of, 192; effect on civil rights movement, 196, 210; Negroes in, 159–160, 168, 210; statements by Martin Luther King, Jr., 169–170
Violence, mass, 10, 59, 60, 99–100, 178, 267–268, 270, 317. *See also* Riots.
Virginia, 25
Voter registration: of Negroes, 63, 97, 129, 194, 198; national law for, 249–250
Voting behavior, Negro, 119–121, 123–124, 242, 247–248; in South, 93–94, 97–98, 121, 154–155, 156, 198, 248. *See also* Political power; Voter registration.
Voting Rights Act of 1965, 193, 194, 291

Wallace, George, 244–245, 248, 250, 268
Washington, Booker T., xii, xiii–xiv, 158, 257, 299
Washington, Walter, 203
Watson, Charles, 79–80
Watts, 144; conditions of Negro life in, 147–152, 210, 231; riot in (1965), 140–147 *passim*
White Citizens Council, 59–67 *passim*, 68–80, 95, 96
White-Negro tension during World War II, 8–12
Whites: allied with Negroes, 131; counter-reaction among, 184, 229, 293, 338; liberals, 58–59, 113, 125, 137, 161–162, 165, 185, 247–249, 265, 284–285, 303–305; middle class, 10, 273–274; more hostility against, in interracial groups, 25; reluctance to change social structure, 195
Wilkins, Roy, 154, 160, 161, 184, 232
Wilkinson, Horace C., 9
Williams, Hosea, 298
Wirtz, Willard, 114
Women, liberality of, 25
Women's liberation, 325–326
Workers Defense League, 151
Working class, Negro, 107. *See also* Labor.
World War I: Negroes in, 158, 168
World War II: Negroes in, 159, 168, 181, 236

Yorty, Samuel, 146, 147
Young, Whitney, 154, 184, 232
Youth, Negro, 160, 182–183, 184, 323–324; desires of, 230, 331; historical consciousness of, 327